'*Smart Mothering* translates research, clinical psychology, theory and experience into practical advice and simple strategies. It is a great resource that people can look to during the early years of parenting. Natalie presents a view that supports the emotional well-being of the mother, simultaneously with that of her infant and their relationship.'

—Dr Tanya Wright, child and adolescent psychiatrist

SMART MOTHERING

What science says about caring for your baby and yourself

DR NATALIE FLYNN
of wowMama

ALLEN&UNWIN
SYDNEY•MELBOURNE•AUCKLAND•LONDON

For Elijah, Maya and Leon

First published in 2019

Allen & Unwin
Level 3, 228 Queen Street
Auckland 1010, New Zealand
Phone: (64 9) 377 3800
Email: info@allenandunwin.com
Web: www.allenandunwin.co.nz

83 Alexander Street
Crows Nest NSW 2065, Australia
Phone: (61 2) 8425 0100

A catalogue record for this book is available from the National Library of New Zealand.

ISBN 978 1 98854 708 4

Design by Cat Taylor
Cover image by Ohhlanla/Shutterstock.com
Illustrations by Megan van Staden
Set in 11/16 pt Sabon LT Pro
Printed and bound in Australia by Griffin Press
10 9 8 7 6 5 4 3 2 1

CONTENTS

INTRODUCTION

So, what set me off on this adventure to discover what is *really* known about caring for babies? It's hard to pin it to any one event. Of course, my own experience of mothering has given me a passion for the area, but my drive to examine the advice that today's mothers are bombarded with has more to do with my work as a clinical psychologist than with my personal life. My interest in providing mothers with fact-based parenting choices has only grown during my years specialising in maternal health.

It is only fair that I tell you right at the outset that things were relatively easy for me as a mother of young babies. I was and am in a stable relationship with a partner who takes parenting seriously. We had enough financial security that I was able to take time off from paid work when I had young babies. I had little trouble breastfeeding, and I found it rewarding. I knew how to watch out for signs of depression or anxiety, and I knew what to do if I was feeling exhausted or overwhelmed.

I was by no means a perfect new mother—even by my own standards. I do not think screen time is good for very young children; when a parent looks at screens while actively caring for their baby, I believe it is poor modelling. So did I ever watch TV while feeding my baby late at night? You bet I did—and I ate chocolate at the same time. But did I beat myself up over it? No, I didn't. I told myself the same thing that I tell my clients: be loving, be calm and look after yourself.

Some of the women I see professionally are having just a little trouble adjusting to new motherhood. Others need more help, especially if they have had some hardships in life or are experiencing emotional health difficulties, such as depression or anxiety. Some women simply need reassurance, or to find clarity in the face of an overload of parenting advice. Most of these women worry about making the right choices for themselves and for their babies, and they often look to me for answers to the following questions (and many more). Can I work and meet my baby's emotional needs? Do I have to breastfeed? What about immunisations—are they safe? Will my baby be harmed by a rise in cortisol levels if I introduce controlled crying? Did I damage my baby by having a Caesarean section?

For years I have thought that, much of the time, these mothers are being made to worry unnecessarily. And then, when their worries are perfectly understandable, there are so many conflicting answers.

What I have discovered is very reassuring. When I checked peer-reviewed research and pieced it together for reliable conclusions, I found that a loving, responsive mother has lots of choices about the way she parents. I found there are answers for working mothers, there are answers to screen time, there are answers about babies and crying. There is also tested advice about helping your baby to sleep longer at night without distress—and more.

Of course, I was only able to do this research long after those exhausting first few years of a baby's life were behind me; my children are now thirteen, eleven and eight years of age. The paradox of 'informed' parenting is that the very years during which you need confirmed information are also the very years you have no time to look for it, even if you do know how to examine the research. You will no doubt look to Google for help—and you are only likely to find more confusion there. You will be bombarded with conflicting advice that claims to be supported by science.

I want this book to cut through all of that for you. I want you to have what all mothers deserve: informed choice.

What you need to do first with a new baby is look after yourself. If you are worn down, if you have anxiety or depression, how can you do your best for your child? That is why you'll find that the section on looking after yourself comes ahead of the section on looking after your baby in this book. Your family is in this together. Be calm and caring to your baby. Be kind to yourself. Be armed with fact-based parenting information.

Getting to the bottom of what the research says was time-consuming. It isn't possible to simply rely on any one study—or even on a *lot* of studies. It's important to read what all of the well carried-out studies have to say, then to read what the key researchers in each area have to say about one another's work. In each area, I found there were one or two 'masterminds' who were well respected and immersed in the field. It is necessary to understand their criticisms. It is also necessary to go deep into the discussion and method sections of the research papers, which often reveal outcomes that don't quite match what is said in the nutshell summary given at the start of each study.

This book was a labour of love, and it surprised me over and over again. I hope you will share my enthusiasm for getting to the bottom of things, and enjoy hearing the outcomes of my endeavour.

PART I

THE MODERN
PARENTING
CLIMATE

CHAPTER 1
BOMBARDMENT STRESS: SORTING FACT FROM FICTION

We live in an age of information. The answer to any question that pops into our heads is, quite literally, at our fingertips—but, more often than not, there's more than one answer proffered, and it can be quite impossible to discern which is the 'correct' answer. Rather than making things simpler and clearer, our instant access to information often does the opposite. We find ourselves overwhelmed and misinformed. As the adage goes, you can have too much of a good thing, and information is no exception.

Worry about 'information overload' is certainly not a new thing. It has plagued people since long before there were computers and smartphones, and even before there was a printing press. For those who enjoy biblical references, in Ecclesiastes 12:12 Solomon warned that 'of making many books there is no end, and much study wearies the body'. Aeons later, in the year 2000, psychologists Sheena Iyengar and Mark Lepper published a paper titled 'When choice is demotivating: Can one desire too much of a good thing?'. Their work took a closer look at what happens when we are offered an abundance of choices.[1] As part of their research, Iyengar and

Lepper conducted a field study in which they set up a tasting stall in a gourmet supermarket. During alternating hours they put either 24 varieties of jam on a table, or 6 varieties of jam. The study found that while far more customers were attracted to the stall when it had 24 varieties, they were ten times more likely to buy a jar of jam when the table had fewer choices. Only 3 per cent of those exposed to 24 choices actually made a purchase. It appears that those encountering more choices had suffered from decision-making paralysis.

The researchers then looked at a similar situation involving a choice of chocolates. This time they had three scenarios: no choice, a large choice set, and a limited choice set. They found a similarly low level of satisfaction when comparing no choice with the large choice set. However, those offered a limited choice showed significantly more satisfaction and less regret.

Finally, they tested whether choice overload had an impact beyond the commercial world. First-year university students were offered extra credit if they chose to write a two-page essay. One group was given a choice of 30 essay topics and the other a choice of six. Seventy-five per cent of the group who were offered a limited choice opted to do the essay. Only 60 per cent of those who were given a choice of 30 topics took up the offer.

Parenting involves choices that are far more profound than decisions about which type of jam or chocolate to buy. Furthermore, those choices are continuous rather than episodic—they are relentless. They rain down on parents from numerous sources: the internet, other parents, friends, experts and fanatics. If deciding which type of jam to purchase can bring on momentary mental paralysis, deciding on parenting styles and techniques can cause decision-making stress which can continue for months or even years.

Bombardment stress (or BS) is the term I have coined to describe the negative psychological impact that information overload can have in the context of lifestyle choices. Simply put, parents can be overwhelmed by a mass of contradictory opinions, information or advice that comes from multiple sources and is commonly expressed as reliable or even absolute fact. Mothers can experience feelings of confusion and self-doubt, resulting in inertia, paralysis or flip-flopping from one course of action to another. The initialism 'BS' is meant to be irreverent. The double entendre is deliberate. It accurately describes the quality of most of the information these mothers are being bombarded with.

Over the past decade, and in particular over the last five years, I have noticed that excessive and conflicting information is having an increasingly negative impact upon many of my clients. I believe the predominance of social media in people's lives has played a role in this. The advice forums that have sprung up on various social media sites have quickly become platforms where anyone who can type can put their ideas forward as fact, places where experience, knowledge and training are no longer necessary prerequisites. In this online arena, dispassionate objectivity has ceased to be the standard and has been replaced with emotive half-truths and guilt-laden half-threats.

This kind of misinformation isn't confined to new mothers, either; it extends to everyone else around them. Everyone seems to have an opinion about what constitutes 'good parenting' or about what will cause irreversible damage to a baby—and they're all too willing to share those opinions. What's worse, new mothers are not just passively exposed to an excess of conflicting information; they are being actively *bombarded* with it. The various opinions go in all directions, and some of the mothers I see are beside themselves with worry about what they've read online. There is no escape.

Mothers overwhelmed with conflicting advice can lose touch with their capacity to make decisions in line with their values, emotions, needs and logic. Instead, some rely on the ever-changing and often-unreliable torrent of information provided by others, including advice from well-meaning but ill-informed friends along with the anachronistic suggestions of relatives. Bombardment stress is, perhaps, an unsurprising product of the frenetically paced, digitally driven, time-poor era we live in.

SOME EXAMPLES OF BS

If you are a new mother, here are some typical BS ruminations you might experience.

'I just can't decide which parenting approach to take: routine-led or baby-led? If I go with the first I might not be meeting his needs; if I go with the second he might develop sleep problems later in life.'

'I'm losing sleep over what to do, and whether it's OK to try controlled crying. I Googled what could happen if I don't get enough sleep and I don't want to become more irritable or depressed, but I also read that if I leave my baby to self-settle he might get stressed and his cortisol levels could result in permanent damage. But then a friend told me that she read online that cortisol levels can't be accurately measured.'

'Sometimes I feel bored when I'm at home with my baby, and I want to go on social media so that I feel more connected. Will she know what I'm doing and feel neglected? I read somewhere that being on my phone could affect her attachment, but a new study says it's no different to me reading the paper in front of her.'

'I want to go back to work, but I read that it's better for my relationship with my baby if I stay at home. Some people say children do worse at school if they are in daycare. But my mother says she read that it makes kids more resilient and they do better. If I do go back to work, should I use a daycare with trained teachers, which I read was important, or should I get someone to come to the house so that there will be less cortisol, which I also read was important? I would like my daughter to see me out there in the world, so I can be a role model for her.'

BATTLING THE BS

If a new mother comes to me with concerns about dealing with conflicting information, the first thing I do is check whether her worries have deeper contexts, such as depression or anxiety. If none of these difficulties are present, I use a two-step approach in dealing with BS, the aim being for the new mother to learn to trust herself to make the right decisions for her and her family.

First, I'll give some advice about separating opinion from science. Second, I'll discuss ways to make decisions based on a combination of fact and personal values. Facts are important, but when it comes to parenting they're not everything. What a new mother and her family value, need and want are equally important.

Let's take a look at those two steps in some more detail.

SEPARATING OPINION FROM SCIENCE

When it comes to distinguishing between BS advice and scientific opinion, look for the following red flags. If you maintain a healthy scepticism about advice that falls into any of the these categories, it will help you to eliminate the bulk of unhelpful information.

+ Opposing views and studies are not provided.

+ The advice requires extreme lifestyle changes.

+ Sweeping claims are made that cover a wide variety of outcomes.

This book is all about cutting through the unhelpful information and leading you to a more scientific perspective. By considering these three points, you will be able to begin sorting fact from fiction, and will be a bit more discerning about what advice you take—and what advice you simply leave by the wayside. Just because something claims to be 'true' doesn't mean it necessarily is, and just because something worked for someone else doesn't mean it will (or even has to) work for you. You don't have to believe everything that you read or that you are told, no matter how well meant the information is. Having the confidence to be critical about the advice you receive will in turn give you confidence as a parent.

In this book, I'm going to help you put some common parenting ideas to the test. Together, we are going to examine some of the information you may have been given against what good research has to say. Some experts are more reliable than others, and in order to tell the difference it's important to understand precisely what constitutes 'good' research and why. It is not possible in a few pages to fully explain why one type of study is better than another. Fortunately, I am not preparing you for an examination, and I can simply focus on the main types of studies carried out in relation to childcare—at least the ones you will encounter in this book. The categories listed here start with the least convincing and move up the ladder to the most convincing.

+ **Retrospective observational studies.** These are really the first step on the ladder. Here we often encounter large data sets. Such studies can boast massive numbers, and if well designed can potentially provide good-quality data about whatever they were set up to test. However, too often these large data sets are used for quite a different purpose than the one initially intended (i.e. a secondary study). Information necessary to make a valid conclusion for the secondary study is missing and must be guessed at. Also, because retrospective studies look backwards for information, memory biases are inevitable—for example, a parent's recollection of how old her baby was when he first slept through the night.

+ **Case-control studies.** These come next up the ladder. When an event (problem) occurs rarely, such as cot death (SIDS), researchers may have no option but to examine as many cases as they can and do their best to account for biases or variables (such as income or family genes) by matching each 'case' with a 'control' (a non-affected person) of similar background. Too often, case-control studies make little effort to match for important traits. They simply choose a group of non-affected subjects and call them controls. Sometimes, even with the best intentions, it is not possible to match traits because little is known about the background of cases. Case-control studies can only show an association, not a cause.

+ **Sibling-pair studies.** These are particularly good examples of case-control studies and are therefore considered to be another rung up the ladder. Comparisons between one sibling and another can provide very compelling evidence because they are typically free from the most important confounding factors: the siblings share the same parents and, in most cases, the same or similar socioeconomic background. However, there are still confounding factors to account for. For example, a mother may be at home in the early years for one sibling but in paid work for the other sibling's early years.

+ **Identical twin studies.** Because identical twins share the same genes, studying them provides a unique opportunity to work out how important genes are compared to environmental factors. For example, a German study discussed in the appendix (see page 463) shows that if one identical twin has Crohn's disease (a bowel disease), there is a 35 per cent chance the other twin will also have Crohn's disease. This suggests that the factors that contribute to the disease are 35 per cent genetic and 65 per cent environmental. Twins are also useful when trying to work out which environmental factors are significant. For example, the same study showed that the identical twin who was exposed to more meat product associated with E. coli (thought to be a precursor of bowel disease) was more likely to have Crohn's than the other twin. This result is more convincing than had they been merely siblings. However, as identical twin studies are a type of case-control study, only an association can be claimed (not a cause). The cause of Crohn's *could* be E. coli infection, but it might also be the antibiotics used to treat E. coli infection—or some other unknown cause.

+ **Prospective observational studies.** (For example, cohort studies.) At this rung of the ladder there is a shift from retrospective (looking into the past) to prospective (collecting data as it occurs). High-quality cohort studies follow participants for years or even decades, which eliminates many memory biases and other confounding variables found in retrospective studies. Prospective studies can provide more valuable information than retrospective studies, but they are not without their own difficulties. First, they are very expensive. Second, they are prone to attrition: the loss of participants over time. Because attrition isn't random, it can result in the study group becoming more and more uniform—for example, families in poverty tend to move around more frequently than other socioeconomic groups, thereby dropping out of studies and making the cohort increasingly middle class.

+ **Randomised, controlled studies.** If done properly, these studies are the pinnacle for attaining reliable results because the researchers do not need to worry about controlling for variables. The non-randomised studies we have considered so far need to purposefully control for any variables that might have an impact on results (parental education, etc.), but the problem is that it's impossible to control for the variables you don't know about yet. Consider, for example, the historical studies which have looked at child obesity—many of them controlled for factors that were obvious at the time: socioeconomic background, parental education, and so on. However, recently we have come to understand that parental weight (and probably parental weight at the time of weighing the child) is a key confounder that was often not controlled for in existing, non-random studies of child obesity. The great thing about a well-designed, truly random study is that confounders are not an issue. Randomisation itself assures that all confounders are evenly distributed between the experimental and control groups. It has been proven over and over again that, if a population of sufficient size is randomly split into two groups, the differences (education, family finances, maternal weight and so on) between those two groups will be too small to interfere with the reliability of the study's results.

So, randomised controlled studies are the gold standard. The difficulty is that in most circumstances you cannot ethically carry out randomised experiments on humans. You cannot, for example, tell one group of mothers to let their children 'cry it out' and tell another group to comfort their babies to sleep, just so that you can establish which method leads to better sleepers.

Because all researchers know that a random study is the highest quality possible, the 'random' label is too often undeservedly claimed. Just because a study calls itself random does not necessarily mean that it is. It's important to examine how the study was set up to see if it deserves that status.

TRUSTING YOUR OWN DECISIONS

Sorting fact from fiction in all of the information you're bombarded with is just one step on the way to overcoming the BS. Just as important is learning to understand your own values and to trust your own choices. This takes time. It can be a slow process involving self-reflection, discernment, self-compassion and patience. In order to take care of your baby, you also need to be able to take care of yourself, and I'll address that in more detail in Part II of this book.

In terms of starting to trust your own decisions, it's worth reminding yourself that parenting has just a few simple requirements.

+ As new parents, we need to look after our own physical and emotional health.

+ We need to take pleasure in our babies and give them stimulation.

+ We need to develop healthy relationships with our babies. Above all, we need to be bigger, stronger, wiser and kinder.

+ We need to be calm.

+ We only need to be good enough—not perfect.

As the famous paediatrician Dr Benjamin Spock once said, 'Trust yourself. You know more than you think you do.'

THE ROAD TO BS-FREE PARENTING

Given that people have been parenting for as long as there have been human families on earth, it's fair to wonder at this point why there hasn't already been a piece of scientific research to conclude once and for all what the single best way is to raise children. Instead, there are over 230 million internet results telling you how to parent, thousands (possibly even millions) of books and a cacophony of opinion to wade through. No wonder it can be so overwhelming for new parents trying to figure out how to look after their precious baby in the best way possible.

There are actually some very good reasons why we don't have the findings of just one master parenting study to rely on. For a start, it would take at least eighteen years of research to find out whether one parenting style or another results in the best adults. Then, in addition, researchers would need to randomly assign babies to different parenting styles to be sure other factors weren't causing the differences. As a research project, it just isn't possible. Even the best longitudinal studies (which involve information about an individual or a group gathered over a long period of time) do not have the advantage of being an experiment where babies are randomly assigned to different parenting styles.

So, what we are left with instead are lesser studies about smaller parts of parenting. By putting these together in an objective way, it may be possible to connect the dots and make at least some rational decisions about parenting. Fortunately, we can agree on a few fundamentals which no longer need to be researched: we can all accept that a child needs food, warmth, love and stimulation to thrive. However, beyond that, the experts rage between themselves as to how much, how often, and who needs to provide it—just the information that new parents are wild to know.

There is no shortage of true-believers from every parenting style ready to inform, preach and bully you into their way of thinking, but I hope that after hearing me out you'll feel empowered to make your own decisions. There might be an awful lot of information and BS out there, but it's not insurmountable. With the right tools in your belt, you can choose the parenting style or styles that suit you. You don't have to grab at the first option that floats past in order to save yourself from drowning in choice.

CHAPTER 1: THE MAIN POINTS

+ Mothers are often overwhelmed by a mass of contradictory parenting opinions from various sources—some more reliable, some less so.

+ Battling the BS requires a two-pronged attack: first you separate fact from fiction, and second you need to trust your own decisions.

CHAPTER 2
THE CHANGING FACE
OF THE PARENTING
RELATIONSHIP

Since the 1940s, approaches to parenting have diverged to fall under two broad umbrellas: the more structured 'parent knows best' approaches, and the more permissive 'baby knows best' approaches. Within each category exists a plethora of parenting styles, each claiming to be the best way to raise a child, and making sense of the advice can be overwhelming.

In particular, as more permissive baby-led styles of parenting have gained support in recent decades, 'extreme parenting' styles have emerged—styles which make extraordinary demands on parents, but in reality mainly on mothers.

In this chapter, I'll examine how parenting styles have evolved since the forties, the increasing emphasis placed on attachment theory (which has been used to justify some extreme parenting styles) and whether the science behind it all stands up to scrutiny. Following this, I will give you techniques to build a positive relationship with your baby and conclude the chapter with a close look at routine and on-demand feeding.

Despite the fact I'm about to go into a lot of detail, you'll see by the time you reach the end of this chapter that all the skills and information you're about to learn boil down to a pretty uncomplicated message: take the time to tune in to your baby's cues, and respond to them with warmth and maturity. Also tune in to your own needs so you can get help early if necessary.

When it comes to parenting, you do not have to be perfect. None of us are. All you have to be is enough—good enough, loving enough, consistent enough—so that your baby knows he can depend on you.

PARENT KNOWS BEST VS BABY KNOWS BEST

Generally speaking, a 'parent knows best' approach to parenting is more traditional and structured, and sits at the authoritarian end of the spectrum. Parents might be advised by advocates of this kind of approach to start with a strict routine from the earliest age. Infants, parents are told, should have regular feeding times, regular sleep times, and be put in a dark room to let them know it is time to sleep. This, the theory goes, helps a baby feel secure and learn to self-regulate, which is not only good for the baby but for the whole family. When a baby is old enough to sleep through the night, parents are advised to put up with a few tears as the price of more sleep for everyone, including the baby.

The more permissive 'baby knows best' approaches sit at the polar opposite end of the spectrum. Advocates of this kind of approach let a baby set the routine: the baby decides when she will eat, sleep and so on. This sort of baby-led style first became popular as a response to harsher authoritarian parenting styles, but has since taken on a life of its own. Nowadays, it is often advocated through various forms of extreme parenting.

WHAT IS EXTREME PARENTING?

Extreme parenting approaches are baby-led, and take a few accepted principles from attachment theory—for example, the need infants have for a nurturing parent—and push those principles to extreme conclusions.

Advocates of extreme parenting approaches might advise parents that their baby should have physical skin contact with them around the clock, and that they must earn their child's trust by feeding on demand and sharing a bed through the night. In short, parents should always put their baby's needs ahead of their own.

Extreme parenting proponents will warn parents that providing anything less than this (or that) level of care will damage a child's brain, decrease their IQ and lead to delinquent behaviour. These advocates are quick to claim they have good science on their side, and their often-contradictory theories flood the internet, creating moral panic among many new parents.

WHAT IS FEEDING ON DEMAND?

When you feed on demand, you keep your baby close enough to be able to hear her. When she cries, you feed her. This is in contrast to routine or scheduled feeding, which sets particular times or intervals for feeding.

You cannot spoil or overfeed your baby by feeding her on demand when she is newborn. After that, it's up to you whether you continue to demand-feed or shift to a routine. If you are working or planning to go back to work, there is a lot to be said for routines. If you are going to be home and are not in a hurry to get more sleep at night, then demand-feeding may be your choice.

Turn to pages 76–83 for more discussion on scheduled feeding and feeding on demand.

The most dominant and well known of these extreme-parenting schools of thought is what is referred to as attachment parenting, which we'll look at in more detail in due course. Other lesser-known examples include intensive parenting, proximate parenting, evolutionary parenting and natural parenting. One baby-led theory gaining ground recently is RIE (Resources for Infant Educarers) parenting. In her book *Your Self-confident Baby*, the founder of RIE, Magda Gerber, emphasises constant verbal and emotional communication, rather than physical contact. The baby is to be respected at all times. When parents are with their baby, they must be 100 per cent there: no distracting cellphones, TV or music. Gerber advises parents to fight the urge to use motherese (or baby talk) or to compliment their baby's efforts, and to instead speak to their baby in the first person, in a regular voice and without praising them. While there is no harm in RIE, it can put a great deal of stress on caregivers if followed to the letter. Most RIE parents I see are flexible in the way they use RIE principles.

Personally, I love some elements of extreme parenting because these approaches are often grounded in the intention to be sensitive and responsive to a baby's needs. Some common aspects include parents being encouraged to tune in to a baby's cues, acknowledging the baby as an individual and reducing technology to better respond to the child's needs.

THE RISE OF EXTREME PARENTING

In order to understand where extreme-parenting styles have come from, it's necessary to take a moment to look back over the recent history of parenting theory in the West. Before the Second World War, the tendency was for parents to view their children as potentially good creatures who required guidance—and, if necessary, coercion—in order to develop into morally independent adults. The idea that a newborn infant held equal footing to a parent would have seemed utterly absurd.

However, the 1940s heralded a new way of looking at children and at child-rearing, starting with Sigmund Freud's teachings as advanced by psychoanalyst Melanie Klein. Freud famously theorised that physical illness could have a purely psychological origin and, observing his patients through this lens, made connections between mind and body that to this day greatly influence the way we think about ourselves. The most relevant of Freud's ideas to child-rearing was that of an infant and child needing to gratify such basic drives as sucking and sexual exploration. Freud believed that, far from being deviant, a young child's curiosity and drive for exploration is a necessary part of development. Punishing or restricting this would only force a 'neurosis' to pop up in its place; if psychic energy is repressed in one place, the theory went, it must be used up (or bottled up) somewhere else.

In the early forties, Klein applied Freud's theories to young children and these ideas trickled down to a small number of educated parents. By projecting Freud's general theories regarding adults back to the earliest days of infancy, Klein posited that a newborn's central interest was survival, and in particular being fed. The source of the feeding itself was of no consequence until much later in the child's development. According to Klein's theory, children had to go through a sequence of developmental stages before their mother could be seen as a single entity to be loved (for providing sustenance) or hated (for not providing sustenance). A mother could not be missed or grieved over until that stage was reached. The immediate and practical impact of this theory on new parents related to a child's desire to gratify the sucking instinct and called for increased and less-scheduled feeds. It also meant delaying weaning, which in turn had direct consequences for the baby's sleep schedule. Those parents convinced by Freud's theories worried they might stifle their children, deny them their core needs, and cause them later harm both mentally and physically.

Thus, as early as the 1940s, two sharply contrasting parenting styles were emerging: a permissive style (followers of the Freudian view), and the more traditional authoritarian style. The beginnings of baby-led parenting had arrived.

For some time, permissiveness remained the minority approach—until a young paediatrician by the name of Benjamin Spock came along. Spock was immensely taken with Freudian views, and in the first edition of his ground-breaking 1946 book *The Common Sense Book of Baby and Child Care* promoted permissiveness and child-centred parenting, including feeding on demand. This was a more punitive era, and Spock's alternative views struck a chord with a great many parents who had felt it was their duty to be harsh but had never liked it. Spock gave these parents licence to be kinder. They did not even need to know that Freud existed. Dr Spock was so universally admired for his sensible medical approach that parents felt safe following his more liberal parenting advice. Permissiveness took the United States—and soon other Western countries too—by storm.

As it grew in popularity, however, this new wave of permissive-style parenting began to take on a disturbing life of its own. Eventually, Dr Spock felt that other experts were taking permissiveness too far, expressing concern that parents had lost control. In one newspaper article, he was quoted as saying, '[the] inability to be firm is, to my mind, the commonest problem of parents in America today'. He added that parents had become afraid of alienating their children to the point of not even demanding their children come in for lunch.[1] Around the same time, other child experts were similarly alarmed and began to look for a third option: a more palatable way to regain some control without resorting to authoritarian parenting. An important figure at this time was clinical and developmental psychologist Diana Baumrind, who in a 1966 paper advocated for 'authoritative parenting', which combined the best elements of authoritarian and permissive parenting.[2] This parenting style centred on directing the child in a supportive, rational manner; helping, consulting with and listening to the child, but keeping the parent in place as the ultimate decision-maker. Authoritative parenting had its followers then, and still does now.

The next wave of thinking in regards to parenting came to be known as 'behaviourism', which promised a way to shape children with them barely realising it. Psychologist Burrhus Frederic (B. F.) Skinner was interested in the work of the Russian scientist Ivan Pavlov who, in the late nineteenth century, had famously found that dogs could be 'conditioned' to salivate when a bell was rung, even when no food was produced. It was Skinner, however, who saw the potential for shaping human behaviour in the 'stimulus-response' mechanism represented by the bell, and turned the idea into a powerful tool for moulding behaviour. Studies by Skinner and, later, his followers expanded and refined the application of the stimulus-response theory. These studies showed, for instance, that the most powerful way to condition a pigeon or a rat is to reward it with food only intermittently. When the animal learns that a certain action will eventually be rewarded, but doesn't know precisely when, it will repeat the action again and again in the hope of a reward. According to Skinner, behaviour learned this way is hardest to 'extinguish'. Parents and teachers were told that lack of consistency would create problems most difficult to correct.

Behaviourism offered a more benign way than punishment to improve the behaviour of children. Reward a child with praise, the theory went, and the behaviour you want will increase. Ignore the behaviour you don't want, and it disappears; it will be 'extinguished'. This view eliminated harsh punishment (including smacking, yelling and debasing a child), but if things got tough, parents could resort to 'negative rewards', such as putting the child in time-out or in a room devoid of entertainment. Of course, some questioned whether such strategies were not, in fact, punishment.

Informed by behaviourism, a type of modified permissiveness started to become the parenting path generally accepted in the 1970s and early 1980s. Dispute persisted on the fringes over aspects such as what did or did not constitute punishment, but Freudian psychoanalytic theory might have been submerged entirely beneath the influences of behaviourism had it not been for John Bowlby.

THE BOWLBY INFLUENCE

Psychoanalyst John Bowlby's theories emerged onto the parenting scene in the early fifties—and, if you scratch the surface of any modern parenting style, you will find it still must justify itself in light of his theories or fail. In a nutshell, Bowlby theorised that a baby has a biologically determined drive to seek and maintain proximity to a caregiver. Certain behaviours such as sucking and smiling, Bowlby believed, are instinctual responses that bind the infant and mother to form an attachment. Bowlby disagreed with Klein's Freudian-based theory that children must go through a sequence of stages before forming an attachment (or otherwise) with their mother. Rather, he believed attachment-seeking behaviours begin at birth.

The child of an upper-middle class British family, Bowlby had experienced both long periods of separation from his mother and the permanent loss of his beloved nursemaid, Minnie. As a consequence, he believed he suffered psychologically all his life. It was perhaps his own acute sense of loss that caused him to question the psychoanalytic view at the time that very young children cannot genuinely grieve for such losses.

Bowlby used animal studies to support his position, most notably those of Austrian ethologist Konrad Lorenz and of American psychologist Harry Harlow. In 1935, Lorenz had published research which showed that the goslings of greylag geese form an unshakeable bond with something they see moving within a short time (approximately twelve hours) of hatching.[3] After that, the goslings are imprinted on that 'something' (usually their mother) and will follow it everywhere. Furthermore, Lorenz found that if the goslings do not have the opportunity to imprint within a certain time (approximately 32 hours), they will never imprint. Bowlby used these observations to support his view that children have an instinct to attach to a protective figure, that this instinct appears early, and that it has a deadline.

The other major influence on Bowlby's theory was Harlow's experiments with baby monkeys, the findings of which were published in 1958.[4] In these experiments, baby monkeys were completely deprived of contact with other monkeys, and were instead offered the choice of two surrogate 'mothers': one made of wire that simply supplied milk, the other made of cuddly cloth with the roughly stitched outline of a face. Harlow found that the baby monkeys clung to the cuddly mother in preference to the wire one, especially when alarmed. In other words, comfort was more important than food. This was not in line with contemporary Freudian thought, which would have predicted that human babies, and therefore baby monkeys, would cling to the surrogate 'mother' that provided milk, and Bowlby used these findings to give weight to his belief that feeding in and of itself was not equated with a secure mother–baby relationship.[5]

Harlow's study had also shown that duration of separation from other monkeys was critical: while the effects of a separation less than three months were completely reversible, beyond one year they became completely irreversible. The monkeys that had experienced extended separation (of more than one year) could never be socialised, and their behaviour was permanently aggressive and withdrawn.

All this put Bowlby's own surmises from his 1944 paper 'Forty-four juvenile thieves: Their characters and home-life' into context.[6] There, he had found that seventeen of the very young thieves he studied reported an early and prolonged separation of at least six months from their primary caregiver before the age of five. In 1951, Bowlby published an influential report for the World Health Organization (WHO) called *Maternal Care and Mental Health* in which he said, 'the infant and young child should experience a warm, intimate, and continuous relationship with his mother (or permanent mother substitute) in which both find satisfaction and enjoyment'.[7]

Nowadays, Bowlby's theory of attachment is widely accepted. It influences most parenting styles, either by name or by implication, but is variably interpreted. It is important to remember that, when Bowlby spoke of maternal deprivation and its negative consequences, he was thinking of something quite substantial: being rarely in the presence of the caregiver, being rarely responded to by the caregiver, or being separated for prolonged periods from the caregiver. (Remember also that Bowlby defined the caregiver as the person who responds to the child's emotional and physical needs, not necessarily the person providing nourishment.) Some modern parenting approaches use Bowlby's theory that serious maternal deprivation leads to negative outcomes as proof that extreme mothering is required in order to prevent negative outcomes. They use results from research on homeless children, orphaned children and children who have experienced trauma, then apply those results to children who are not in physical or verbal contact with a caregiver at all times.

ENTER ATTACHMENT PARENTING

At the root of many extreme-parenting styles lies one name: Jean Liedloff. Born and raised in New York, Liedloff dropped out of university in the mid-fifties and travelled to Venezuela, where she became fascinated with the peaceful Ye'kuana tribe. Years later she resumed her studies as a social anthropologist, and eventually published her unsubmitted doctoral dissertation as a book called *The Continuum Concept: In search of happiness lost* in 1975.

The Continuum Concept was hugely influential, and appeared at a time when anthropologists such as Margaret Mead were revered for providing insight into the true state of man once civilisation was stripped away. In *The Continuum Concept*, Liedloff warned of the ill effects for both mother and child if a baby was not immediately in its mother's arms from the moment of birth. These ill effects, specifically, included colic for the baby, post-partum depression for the mother, then later in the child's life criminality, addiction and promiscuity. Liedloff's work showed an acceptance of psychoanalytic thought not uncommon among anthropologists of the time—that is to say the belief that thwarting a child's urges will later result in a variety of neuroses.

According to the Liedloff Continuum Network, a website advocating the principles described in *The Continuum Concept*, a baby's basic needs include: constant physical contact with a caregiver from birth; sleeping in a caregiver's bed (bed-sharing), in constant physical contact, until the child leaves of her own volition; being constantly carried by an active person; and having caregivers respond immediately to her signals without judgement.[8] In a 1998 interview in which she described her theory of the natural instinct of mother and child to bond and be with each other, Liedloff explained that crying was a child's way of saying, 'Pick me up. Don't put me down. Don't leave me!', adding that a baby who isn't picked up thinks, 'I haven't done the right thing. I'm not worth responding to.'[9] What is more, she went on to explain that the person who carries a baby must also be physically active in order to discharge the baby's energy for her.

ATTACHMENT PARENTING IS NOT ATTACHMENT THEORY

Attachment parenting borrows its name from Bowlby's theory of attachment, but some advocates go beyond the reach of researched evidence to make unsubstantiated claims about the importance of bed-sharing, baby-wearing, breastfeeding, feeding on demand, prevention of crying, instant post-birth skin-contact and non-medicated labour. They incorrectly promote these practices as necessary for a baby to have a secure attachment with his caregiver.

Misinterpretation of attachment theory isn't new. In the fifties, Bowlby himself noted that, even though his theory was based on prolonged maternal separation, it was causing some mothers to be frightened to leave their baby's side. Bowlby reassured them that these fears weren't warranted.[10] Bowlby didn't say anything about bed-sharing, medication-free births, feeding on demand, baby-wearing or preventing crying, and of breastfeeding he said, 'it seemed to me that the feeding variable was totally irrelevant, or almost totally irrelevant'.[11]

My only concern about extreme parenting is when it has a negative psychological effect on mothers and, in turn, an impact on true attachment needs. Ultra-demanding parenting styles such as attachment parenting are just fine so long as those styles don't stress you to the point of unhappiness. Around-the-clock physical contact is not a prerequisite for your child to form a secure attachment with you. If it brings you pleasure, by all means do it—but not for any other reason. I hope if you do choose to adopt an extreme-

> parenting style such as attachment parenting it's simply because
> you personally find it enjoyable.

When Liedloff died in 2011, *The Guardian* published an obituary saying that she had 'longed to be on *Oprah*'.[12] Well, she might not have made it there in life, but in a way she did posthumously, through the man who picked up her theories and ran with them like no one else: Dr William Sears. American couple Martha and William Sears first entered the parenting-theory fray in the mid eighties, and have since become the celebrity face of the new era of extreme parenting. Between them, the Sears have published at least 40 books translated into eighteen languages, and William Sears regularly appears on television, including *Oprah*, and has graced the cover of *Time* magazine.

In 1993, William Sears published the runaway bestseller *The Baby Book* as a follow-on from his less-successful 1982 book, *Creative Parenting: How to use the new continuum concept to raise children successfully from birth to adolescence*. It was Sears who coined the phrase 'attachment parenting' and, as a consequence, gave his brand of parenting the credibility associated with Bowlby's theories. This has caused confusion among parents who are not in a position to distinguish between the two. Sears' essentials were much the same as Liedloff's—breastfeeding on demand, bed-sharing, constant baby-wearing (by carrying the baby in a sling), and avoiding the baby crying at all—but his warnings were more in tune with modern anxieties.[13] If parents failed to follow the rules (for example, by allowing a baby to cry), their children would face difficulties including ADHD, a lower IQ and inadequate social development.

William Sears is a paediatrician and therefore carries the prestige of a medical title, so unlike Liedloff, who lacked those credentials, he could make claims about the scientific validity of his views. This gave him a position of trustworthiness in the eyes of parents eager to get things right. However, in 2012, *Times* journalist and science writer Jeffrey Kluger examined the research upon which Sears rested his theory that ordinary crying can cause serious harm.[14] Kluger found that, of the four studies Sears put forward as his strongest support, two involved rats and one was a primate study. The fourth, titled 'Transition to child care', showed temporary elevations of the stress hormone cortisol among toddlers starting daycare.[15] However, while there is indirect evidence associating extreme amounts of cortisol (the sort produced from experiencing violence and ongoing neglect) with permanent brain damage, Kluger found that the researchers did not share Sears' concerns. 'There is no evidence that small increases in cortisol had any adverse consequences,' they told Kluger.

Kluger also approached psychologist Alicia F. Lieberman regarding a 1995 study of hers that Sears also used to support his position.[16] She told Kluger that her study 'is not relevant to the argument [Sears] makes because my work involves babies and young children whose parents are in the pathological range of neglect and maltreatment . . . not children with normative, "good-enough" parenting'. Yet another author Kluger contacted was psychiatrist and researcher Joan Kaufman, who told Kluger that the paper of hers that Sears had cited referred to abuse and neglect, not to routine or brief stressful experiences. 'It is a mis-citation of our work to support a non-scientifically justified idea,' she said.

WHO, EXACTLY, ARE THE SEARS?
Martha is a registered nurse and certified La Leche League health coach, while William is a paediatrician. Both are committed Catholics.

Neither William nor Martha enjoyed an ideal childhood—something they are happy to talk about. William's father abandoned his family when William was one month old, and his mother worked long hours. He has said he appreciates the work ethic his mother instilled in him, and that she did her best to make up for his father's absence by ensuring he had good male role models. Martha fared rather worse on the childhood front. Her mother, a teacher, suffered from a severe mental health disorder, and Martha recalls a great deal of anger and unhappiness at home. Her mother wasn't there much for her, and her father drowned when she was only four years old. [17]

The two married while William was still a student, and their children arrived in quick succession. Since William was still studying when they had their first three children, Martha had to be the bread-winner, working three days a week while the kids were looked after by a caregiver. When their fourth child—and first daughter—arrived, things changed drastically. She had colic. The Sears were desperate to find a solution, and it was around this time that Martha became aware of Jean Liedloff's theories. The Sears committed to around-the-clock proximity to their daughter, with Martha carrying her in a sling during the day and keeping her in bed with them at night. William started writing on the subject, and Martha helped him with his books.

Four more children soon came along, as well as an adopted daughter. You might wonder if there was a notable difference between the Sears' first three children and the others. Did putting the elder three children in childcare, making them sleep alone, not carrying them around and letting them cry sometimes impair their intellectual development and cause antisocial behaviour? Did being with the younger children 24/7 in their early years result in better adults?

Well, of the eight children raised by the Sears, seven have gone on to tertiary education ranging from medicine to vocal performance. A number of them, from the firstborn to those born later, have also made contributions aimed at helping others. They remain a close-knit family, and often work together on projects. The youngest son was born with Down's syndrome, and from what Dr Sears says on his website (askdrsears.com) they have all learned a lot from him.

So, although the Sears employed two very different parenting styles, it apparently all resulted in much the same outcome. How is that possible? Here's my suggestion: the one thing that remained the same with all of the Sears' children was that William and Martha were good enough, loving enough parents—and it probably didn't hurt that they passed down great genes for intelligence.

PUTTING BOWLBY'S ATTACHMENT THEORY TO THE TEST

When Bowlby, the father of attachment theory, and other psychologists and psychoanalysts used animal studies to support their theories, many thought they had all the proof they needed. Bowlby, for example, used studies on goslings and baby monkeys to support his theory that human babies are born with an intrinsic need for an emotional connection with a primary caregiver, and that the quality of early care is important for healthy development—but this left massive gaps. First off, how was it possible to know for certain that humans are like other animals in their need to form an attachment with a particular caregiver? How was it possible for researchers to measure whether a human child was attached to a caregiver or not? Is a child either attached or not attached? Are some attachments better than others? Bowlby didn't answer any of these practical questions, until Canadian psychologist Mary Ainsworth came on to the scene.

Now there are some well-researched basic dos and don'ts for caregivers during a baby's first year—and we have Ainsworth to thank for most of them. Ainsworth came from an academic family, and gained her PhD in psychology from the University of Toronto. Both before and after the Second World War she taught at university, and in 1950 accompanied her husband to London in the UK, where he pursued his PhD—a move that proved fortuitous for Ainsworth and for our understanding of caregiver–child relationships. Ainsworth got a research job at Tavistock Clinic in London, where none other than John Bowlby was testing the impact of maternal separation on long-term development.

Ainsworth brought her own academic interest in infant security to the job, and when she went through Bowlby's papers she identified a variety of patterns that he had overlooked. Bowlby and Ainsworth collaborated for many years and published together, but it was Ainsworth who uncovered three different types of attachment, what they mean for a child, and how different maternal behaviours are connected to different attachment styles. It was, in other words, Ainsworth who gave scientific proof to Bowlby's attachment theory.

After spending time studying infant–mother attachment behaviour in Uganda, Ainsworth moved to America and continued with this line of research. Along with her colleague Sylvia Bell, Ainsworth studied mother–baby pairs in Baltimore, spending 72 hours over the space of a year with each pair, in their own homes, gathering detailed information about how the pairs interacted. Once the babies were one year old, the individual mother–baby pairs were then observed through a one-way glass in an experimental setting that Ainsworth called the Strange Situation Procedure. The babies were tested as to how they behaved on four fronts: when their mother was absent, when a stranger was there as well as their mother, when a stranger was there instead of their mother, and when their mother returned. The babies were rated on such behaviours as exploring, stranger anxiety and reunion behaviour. From these ratings an attachment pattern was determined for each baby.

Since Ainsworth's team had observed each of these mother–baby pairs for the year prior to the Strange Situation Procedure, the researchers were able to make specific associations between a baby's attachment pattern at twelve months and the mother's way of interacting with her baby. Ainsworth concluded that a baby's attachment pattern was the result of early maternal interactions. Both Ainsworth and Bowlby's work has enabled other researchers to link early attachment styles to much later child development and, importantly, to draw conclusions about important aspects of caregiver–infant interaction that lead to the best outcomes for a child.

'ATTACHMENT THERAPY': A WORD OF WARNING

Be careful not to confuse attachment-based parenting approaches with a dangerous intervention called 'attachment therapy', also known as 'holding therapy'. Attachment therapy does not lead to a secure attachment. Quite the opposite. This intervention was reasonably popular in the 1970s, and focuses on extinguishing behaviours in traumatised children by forcibly restraining them until they are reduced to an 'infantile state' and can be 're-parented'. It flies in the face of what Bowlby and Ainsworth recommended.

It was used to treat vulnerable children, including distressed foster children and children with autism, which was wrongly believed to be caused by maternal failure (resulting in the use of the untrue and insensitive term 'refrigerator mothers'). Professionals who advised attachment therapy thought they were doing good, but they weren't. There have even been a couple of child deaths.

I am currently working with a warm-hearted couple who were advised by therapists in the seventies to use attachment therapy and hold their traumatised adopted four-year-old down while she screamed. Her biological father was in jail, and she had been orphaned when she found her mother dead. This child has not done well in life, most likely because of her significant early trauma; however being held down by her adoptive parents can't have helped. Her parents are haunted by their actions, with her father describing how removed he felt from his little girl, how he emotionally distanced himself as a way of containing his anger as he held her down for hours while she screamed. They both have bitter regrets, but they were following professional advice.

I also work with an adult who was a victim of attachment therapy. She was wrapped in a blanket many times during childhood and held down by family members. She remembers fearing death from suffocation. Unsurprisingly, we are still working through this trauma in therapy.

This is certainly not what Ainsworth meant by caregiver sensitivity and responsiveness (see pages 42–43). Not by a long stretch.

ATTACHMENT PATTERNS AND THEIR OUTCOMES

Ainsworth observed that babies show three main patterns of attachment to their mother, reflecting different caregiving behaviours. Her work is almost universally accepted, and has since been advanced by other researchers, with her original findings (which focused on mothers) extended to fathers and other caregivers. In 1986, her colleague Mary Main described a fourth attachment pattern, called disorganised attachment.[18]

The main attachment patterns are as follows.

+ **Secure attachment.** These babies see their caregiver as a secure base from which to explore and to seek out when they need care and comfort. This is the ideal attachment scenario.

+ **Insecure avoidant.** These babies seek little physical contact with their caregiver and are less responsive to being held. They often appear very independent.

+ **Insecure ambivalent.** These babies are often clingy, demanding, angry, upset by small separations, and limited in exploration.

+ **Disorganised attachment.** These babies may show incongruent care-seeking behaviour: freezing and approach–avoidance conflict.

So, I imagine you are wondering, what was it that the mothers of securely attached babies did differently from the mothers of insecurely attached babies? Well, a secure attachment was linked to a mother's ability to be sensitive to her baby's cues such as crying, smiling, hunger or tiredness, and to respond to them promptly and appropriately. Ainsworth called this 'maternal sensitive responsiveness': a mother's ability to understand her baby's behaviour and respond to it. These mothers were quick to return their baby's smiles. Mothers of insecurely attached babies, on the other hand, were either insensitive and unresponsive to their baby's cues, or inconsistent in their responses, or rejecting of their babies.

When Ainsworth published her findings in 1967, they caused an immediate stir.[19] At that time, the prevailing view of many parents and professionals was that mothers should not respond too quickly to their baby's cries for fear of turning them into 'cry-babies'. Ainsworth's findings went against the grain, showing that at the end of their first year securely attached babies cried and 'clung' less than insecure babies did. Ainsworth concluded that consistent maternal responses to a baby's signals give babies less reason to cue their mothers by crying and clinging.

Importantly, Ainsworth found that it wasn't the quantity of maternal attention that dictated attachment styles but the quality. For example, the secure babies weren't necessarily held for longer than the insecure ones; rather, the secure babies were more likely to be held when they wanted to be held. As for feeding, in contrast to the rigid four-hourly schedules popular at the time, Ainsworth noticed that mothers of secure babies either fed them on demand or gently coaxed them away from feeding if they didn't think it was time. Also, the secure babies who were bottle-fed were more likely to be fed at their own pace, while the insecurely attached bottle-fed babies were more often fed with faster-flowing teats. When it came to face-to-face interaction, the mothers of secure babies smiled and talked to their babies more and adjusted their pace of emotion with their baby's emotions.

Since the 1970s, further research has been conducted to see whether or not a secure or insecure attachment style in early childhood predicts a child's future. The evidence is clear: by preschool, securely attached babies are more likely to be popular with their peers, to be flexible and to have good self-esteem. By the age of six, they are more likely to be warm, more cuddly and open with parents. By mid-childhood, they have closer and more long-lasting friendships. In adulthood, they are more likely to be able to access a range of emotions, and more often go on to have babies with secure attachments themselves.

It needs to be said here that although an insecure (anxious and ambivalent) attachment is not the ideal, these attachment patterns are common and 'normal'. It is disorganised attachment that is associated with the least favourable outcomes (for a description of attachment patterns see pages 44–45).

Other research has backed up the importance of early caregiving by showing that the impact of a child's earliest (or pre-verbal) experiences are more difficult to change than later experiences. This is thought to be because pre-verbal information is hardest to access in later years. Therapists are aware of this and understand that negative self-beliefs stemming from early abuse and neglect are often the hardest to shift.

TAKING INFANT TEMPERAMENT INTO ACCOUNT

You might have a baby who regularly takes a long time to settle, doesn't smile at you as often as you would like, isn't particularly cuddly or who cries much of the time, but it is important to remember that this does not mean that your baby can't form a healthy attachment with you. You might just have to work a bit harder to meet your baby's needs. Equally important, know that even easy-to-read, smiley babies need a secure attachment. Attachment matters for all babies. However, maternal sensitivity and early caregiving isn't the only important factor in terms of outcomes for a child; a child's temperament and other inborn characteristics will also influence who that baby becomes (as will many other factors such as family harmony and socioeconomic well-being). An attachment style is the result of the dynamic way your baby seeks your care and how you respond to her. Maternal care and a child's temperament both have a role to play.

Some psychologists, such as Jerome Kagan, believe that inborn characteristics are more enduring than the effects of early maternal care. Kagan suggests that attachment theorists are confusing what they see as 'secure' and 'insecure' attachment to a caregiver with a baby's inborn temperament which simply springs from a baby's genes.[20] Twin studies consistently find that twins raised apart have very similar personalities and ways of relating to others. These studies also confirm that pathologies such as obsessive compulsive disorder, bipolar disorder, anorexia, psychosis and even psychopathy are highly genetic. So is Kagan right to say that genes have more of an impact on development than early mother-love does?

An answer to this question seems to lie in the research of child psychiatrist Stella Chess. Along with her husband Alexander Thomas, Chess was a lead researcher in the New York Longitudinal Study, which began in 1956 and spanned two decades. A total of 231 infants were studied, and classified into different temperament groups based on characteristics such as activity level, approach or withdrawal, and adaptability. From this, Chess created four broad temperament categories that can be ascertained within a few months of birth:

+ **Difficult.** (Now referred to as 'high needs') Characterised by negative mood with intense reactions, more frequent crying, and irregular feeding and sleeping patterns.

+ **Slow to warm up.** Characterised by neutral mood, low activity level, and a tendency to withdraw from new situations and people.

+ **Easy.** Characterised by positive mood, ready adaptability to new experiences, and having regular feeding and sleeping patterns.

+ A group of babies with a mix of temperament characteristics.

Chess found that, while inborn temperament did have an impact on long-term outcomes, for each of the temperament categories above the outcomes were better when caregivers responded sensitively to a baby's needs. The reverse was true as well: babies born within the same temperament category had very different outcomes depending on how their caregivers responded to them from infancy.

The good news is that, while some characteristics such as temperament are hard-wired from birth, any baby can form a secure attachment. As a caregiver, you need to be able to respond appropriately to what your infant brings to the table. There is no need to be dismayed if you have what Chess categorised as a 'high-needs' or 'slow to warm' baby. These children can turn out to be the most interesting, complex and rewarding of them all—trust me on this—but this can depend on having received warm and consistent caregiver responses from infancy. An easy maternal fit for a high-needs baby, for instance, will be a mother who finds it easy to stay calm and available—and if she has lots of energy, all the better! An easy fit for a baby who is slow to warm up might be a mother who was a cautious child herself and understands it can take time to get used to new situations and people.

It is within your power to figure out what your child needs, and to adjust your responses to do the best for your baby. If a cautious child is pushed into singing in public it could put her off singing altogether; alternatively, if the same child is encouraged to watch with a caregiver, then join in at her own speed, she may happily sing in the school choir in her own time—and later become the one to compose sensitive and beautiful music for others.

We can't change the inborn traits of our children, or the fortunes and misfortunes that befall them. All we can do is scaffold their environment the best we can, by getting to know them, being sensitive to their needs, responding with warmth and by celebrating diversity. Science tells us that the way we are with our babies in their first year has a profound impact on their personality, their beliefs about themselves and the world. As a psychologist, I can tell you that any baby can be made to feel loved and secure in that love.

BONDING VS ATTACHMENT

People often use the words 'bonding' and 'attachment' synonymously, but there's a subtle (yet important) difference.

Strictly speaking, bonding goes one way—it's the connection a parent feels towards their child. Attachment is shared and it is one aspect of the parent–child relationship.

Attachment depends on a relationship. There is never just a baby; there is always a baby *and* another person. That is one reason why I use the term 'secure relationship' as well as 'secure attachment'.

Bonding begins before a baby is born, perhaps even earlier. It develops rapidly after birth as a carer comes to know the child. Attachment interactions begin at birth, becoming recognisable patterns by 10–18 months, and form the basis of how we relate to others.

BUILDING A POSITIVE RELATIONSHIP

If more new parents realised how simple the information they need on attachment really is, a lot of scaremongering parenting philosophies would wither on the vine. It all boils down to tuning into your baby's needs, meeting those needs in a warm and consistent way, and taking charge when necessary. Babies are not judgemental aliens who land in your house and can't wait for you to put a foot wrong. Quite the opposite. Your baby is programmed to love you, and uses prewired biological cues (signals) such as crying, sucking and smiling to prompt you to care for him. What's more, babies are quite resilient. You don't need to understand *exactly* what they want *every* single time; you just need to work it out enough of the time to make you dependable. You will almost certainly have days when you aren't feeling the love, but even on these days you can still tune into your baby's needs and respond in ways that make him feel secure. Your relationship with your baby is what enhances his curiosity, social and emotional abilities.

Current understanding of infant and child psychology today remains deeply obligated to the work of Bowlby and Ainsworth, and attachment theory is now supported by an enormous body of empirical evidence. Parent-education and therapy models have moved in this direction so that, when caregivers turn to professionals for help, the focus is rarely on changing the behaviour of the caregiver or the child in isolation, but on strengthening the early relationship between the two. When a secure attachment is built, more positive childhood behaviours tend to naturally follow. Caregivers are encouraged to perceive their baby's or child's behaviours not as 'bad' or 'good', but as the way their child communicates his needs. This perspective leads to higher caregiver empathy and warmth.

You can employ a parenting approach with a relationship focus no matter what parenting style (or styles) you choose to go with. Focusing on building a secure relationship can become a compass to guide you through so many of the confusing debates—bottle vs breast, to sleep-train or not, and so on. Tuning into your baby's needs and responding with consistency and warmth goes straight to the heart of what is important in mother-love.

In order to build your relationship with your baby (and to develop her social and emotional world), there are six main techniques at your disposal, which I'll describe in greater detail over the following page. These techniques are: mutual gaze, 'serve and return', a loving touch, taking delight in your baby, riding the wave of emotions, and being a 'good fit'.

THE CIRCLE OF SECURITY

When a baby or child shows early difficulties, there are a number of well-researched and effective interventions that provide wonderful guidance. They are easy to follow and provide a wealth of information that would benefit any parent.

One example is the Circle of Security, which was developed by Glen Cooper, Kent Hoffman and Bert Powell in 1998. Circle of Security International describes itself as an 'early intervention program for parents and children', and carries out research and provides training to professionals around the world.

The Circle of Security emphasises that the caregiver needs to provide both a 'secure base' (from which a baby or child feels confident to leave and explore, with the caregiver watching) and a 'safe haven' available for comfort. The phrase 'Always be bigger, stronger, wiser and kind' is the backbone of the Circle of Security's balanced parenting approach. The idea is for a caregiver to follow their child's needs when possible, while also remembering that their child needs them to be the adult, taking charge when necessary.

For more information, visit circleofsecurityinternational.com.

YOU CAN'T BE PERFECT, BUT YOU CAN BE KIND

Earlier in my career as a clinical psychologist, I took part in training through the Circle of Security International and it was there I learned the phrase 'Be bigger, stronger, wiser and kind'. These words resonated strongly with me, and have guided many of my clients since. Psychologist Mark Cary has elaborated on this idea as follows:

> At the heart of secure attachment is a child's recognition that she/he has a parent who can be counted on to lovingly provide tenderness, comfort, firm guidance and protection during the

inevitable difficulties of life. If the truth be told, all of us have this need some of the time, no matter what our age.[21]

Many mothers I have worked with (myself, as well!) have found the phrase 'Be bigger, stronger, wiser and kind' useful when feeling anxious, bored or angry. Before responding to their baby's needs, they take a deep breath and ask, 'What does my baby need from me?' With another deep breath, they remind themselves, 'He needs me to be bigger, stronger, wiser and kind.'

Doing this gives a mother space to respond to her baby in a skilful and calm way. I did this a *lot* in the middle of the night when my children were babies, and I continue to do it most mornings now when the bus is waiting and my pre-teens can't find their school shoes or books.

MUTUAL GAZE

Mutual gaze is when two people make eye contact with one another. Right from the moment each of us is born, eye contact helps us to connect with others at an emotional level—with friends, colleagues and, of course, when we fall in love. Mutual gaze is one way we tune in with each other.

Within hours of birth, babies show an interest in looking at their caregiver's face. Some babies even imitate facial expressions within a few days, and if this is done in response to something it appears it is intentional. You can support your baby's head and body from day one to see if she is ready to gaze at your face. Do this when she is calm, alert and still, and hold her head about 30 centimetres from your face. Connections will start to form in her brain just from looking at you and listening to you talk to her directly. You are enough for her. From day one, she will start holding your gaze for a

few seconds and she will start following your movements with her eyes. Shortly after she'll be able to follow your gaze.

There are a number of reasons why mutual gaze is beneficial for both you and your baby.

+ **It promotes 'sensitive responsiveness'** by helping you learn about your baby, her cues, her likes and her dislikes. Babies have emotions right from birth, so as you watch your baby, consider how she might be feeling. Ask yourself what she is telling you with her eyes, movements and sounds. Trying to read her cues in this manner helps develop what Ainsworth called 'maternal sensitive responsiveness', which is the foundation for promoting a secure attachment.

+ **It can have cognitive and social benefits.** Mutual gaze helps your baby learn about human emotions. However, mutual gazing usually takes place at the same time as both physical contact and verbalisation, so there's some question about whether mutual gaze is beneficial in and of itself. In 2016, Amanda Dettmer, Stefano Kaburu and Elizabeth Simpson, ethologists from the Eunice Kennedy Shriver National Institute of Child Health and Human Development, published research that suggested that face-to-face interactions from birth promoted social interest and competency in young primates.[22] They specifically conducted a controlled experiment which showed that this effect wasn't due to physical contact alone, and found that infant monkeys who engaged in more neonatal face-to-face interactions with their mothers had increased social interactions at two and five months.

+ **It promotes mutual respect.** As adults, most of us naturally maintain respectful eye contact with others. We make eye contact, but we also let others look away when they need to. You can't force mutual gaze; it requires both parties to be respectful of the other's need to have a break sometimes. The same applies with babies. Don't push eye contact with your baby if he is not receptive. He is telling you he needs a break. In the early weeks especially, it's common for your baby to briefly look away after a bit of eye contact, and he might blink before looking at you again. Let him. Looking at you takes a lot of energy—you are pretty exciting to your baby! It might be tempting to encourage your baby to look back at you, but resist the urge. Babies become stressed if we ignore their need to pause or end mutual gaze. As your baby gets older, he will look at you for longer periods, but he'll still need to look away from you to calm down and gather energy.

STILL-FACE STUDIES

When you gaze at your baby, remember that she is looking at you for information about emotions, so use a welcoming facial expression to show her that you like watching her. This doesn't mean you have to smile constantly; simply convey that you find satisfaction in looking at her. Be conscious of what are you feeling and thinking as you look at her.

You never want to present your baby with a blank, still face. No one likes to receive a still face, and babies are distressed by it. In 1978, American developmental psychologist Edward Tronik conducted a series of studies illustrating how tuned in babies are to their caregiver's facial responses. As part of his research, he observed and filmed what happened when a mother faced her baby and held her face still (that is to say, expressionless and unresponsive to her baby's behaviours). Tronick found that a mother's still face caused her baby to become agitated and stressed.

You can find videos of this disturbing experiment online—but please be warned that they can trigger some strong emotions, so pick the right time. I do, however, think it is worth caregivers watching them at some stage, as recent research has shown a mother's face staring at a screen (such as a phone screen) has much the same effect on children. I'll discuss this study in greater depth in Chapter 16.

Case Study: Zach

When her first baby, Zach, was just a few weeks old Janine started to worry that he was too unsettled. As the months passed, she grew convinced that she was doing something wrong and wasn't 'cut out for mothering'. When she came to see me, Zach was five months old. While he was lying peacefully on the ground, I asked Janine to interact with him. She got down to his level and initiated play with a bright smile, getting very close to his face and clapping his hands together. Zach flickered a smile and made momentary eye contact—then grizzled and looked away. Janine moved her face to follow his and force eye contact, while Zach cried and looked in the other direction. 'See,' she said tearfully. 'He doesn't like me being near him.' As we talked, I learned that Janine had a difficult relationship with her own mother and was worried that history would repeat. Together, we discussed reasons other than 'dislike' that might be causing Zach to become upset and look away, and soon established that the reason was quite simple: he just needed a break. When Janine tried to force him to look at or interact with her, he experienced too much stimulation too quickly, and needed a little space to regulate his emotions. Zach loved being with his mother. All that Janine needed to do was let her son take the lead, and to learn that he found too much animation intrusive.

TIPS FOR MUTUAL GAZE

+ Mutual gaze can happen any time your baby is ready, but a good time to try is when she is fed and settled. You can't force mutual gaze.

+ Don't expect too much from young babies, as they can't focus or sustain gaze for very long. If your baby looks away from you, just wait and let her show you when she is ready for more by facing you again on her own.

+ Beware of drawing faulty conclusions when your baby looks away. It doesn't mean she is bored with you or that she isn't social. She simply needs to look away to regulate her emotions and calm down.

+ When you see your baby gazing at an object, you can follow her gaze and say the name of the object. This helps language development.

+ Remember that every baby is different. Some will enjoy more animated eye contact and facial expressions than others, and some will look away more often than others.

+ Don't angst over mutual gaze. Most likely you are already doing this naturally, but you just didn't have a name for it. Simply focus on responding sensitively when your baby looks at you. If you can, set aside some special uninterrupted time for mutual gazing with your baby.

SERVE AND RETURN

You can start conversing with your baby from the moment he is born. When you talk back to a baby who has made a sound, when you stick out your tongue to a baby who has just stuck out his tongue, you are affirming the baby's worth. He feels important to the most important person in the universe: you! He might even squirm with pleasure.

Babies understand tone of voice long before they understand

individual words, and telling him in a loving tone how much he means to you will never get stale. Babies are flattered and nourished by your responsiveness to them.

When you and your baby 'talk' in this way, using your eyes, voice, touch and tone, it can be described as 'serve and return'. When your baby serves you a smile, eye contact, noises, babbles, body movements or cries, you return with eye contact, a smile, a warm tone of voice, or touch. Just like mutual gaze, you are probably already having these sorts of conversations with your baby throughout the day, but it's also nice to make some special time to talk.

Harvard University's Center on the Developing Child provides excellent further information about 'serve and return' on their website. To read it, visit: developingchild.harvard.edu/science/key-concepts/serve-and-return.

When you are conversing with your baby, tune into his emotions and adjust your actions to suit. Think about it—if you smile quietly at the beginning of a conversation with a friend, it would be unusual for them to suddenly whoop and clap their hands or roar with laughter. Conversations work their way up to frivolity. It's just the same when you talk with your baby: match his emotion and build up and down gently, watching him for clues about how he is feeling.

Some parents worry that too much responsiveness will spoil a baby. Others worry that anything less than 100 per cent responsiveness will harm a baby. Neither is true. You cannot spoil a baby in the first nine or ten months. While researchers are finding that responsive parents tend to have children who are less demanding and more self-reliant as they get older, your baby will not go into a decline if you are not constantly on tap for these exchanges. The point is to be with your baby *enough*; to tune in and respond to your baby enough to be dependable.

AN EXAMPLE OF 'SERVE AND RETURN'

A conversation with your baby in the first weeks might go something like this.

Baby: looks at your face

You: smile and widen your eyes

Baby: keeps looking, then turns his eyes away for a break and blinks

You: let your baby take a break by waiting patiently

Baby: turns his eyes back to your face and coos

You: smile again and coo back.

And so on.

As the weeks go by, your baby will copy you more and more as well as initiating his own way of talking. He might initiate a smile, to which you smile and coo in response. If he coos, you might respond in a more animated way, for example by widening your eyes. Your baby might then move his limbs about in excitement—then turn his eyes or head away from you to rest. If this happens, you wind down your animation and wait for him to turn back to you.

As your infant gets older, his cues will become more extensive and more subtle. Instead of crying for attention, he might hold out his arms. He might simply check to see if you are watching his little triumphs over gravity. Your willingness to answer these subtle requests for attention, comfort, holding, exploration and discovery will provide an increased sense of security for your child.

A LOVING TOUCH

Babies love to be touched. Stroking your baby softly while talking to her in a soft voice is relaxing for both of you. As Harlow's experiments with monkeys showed, touch is essential for a baby's well-being. Hold your baby during feeding whether she's breastfed or bottle-fed and, where possible, hold her next to your skin. Since breastfeeding takes longer than bottle-feeding, there is more time for skin-to-skin and eye contact. That is a good reason to breastfeed if it works for you, but if you prefer to bottle-feed simply make sure she doesn't miss out on lots of holding, touch and mutual gaze. Some advocates of extreme parenting styles such as attachment parenting will suggest that breastfeeding is necessary for a good mother–baby relationship, but that simply isn't true. Here is what you need: to be tuned into and responsive to both your baby's needs and your own, no matter what parenting style you choose.

DELIGHT IN YOUR BABY

Let your baby know he is a good person to spend time with. Have fun together. Take delight in time with your baby, and encourage her to take delight in time with you. Just like adults, babies have different ways of expressing delight. Not all babies give a jolly laugh or smile; sometimes they will show delight simply by maintaining a quiet interest.

Of course, it's unrealistic for any caregiver to delight in their baby all the time. I certainly didn't. However, we need to delight in them at least some of the time. If you are not finding any pleasure in caring for your baby, it's a sign that something is amiss, so consider getting checked out by a professional such as your midwife, family doctor, maternal nurse or a perinatal psychologist.

TIPS FOR HAVING FUN TOGETHER

There are many ways to foster special moments with your baby. Here are some suggestions.

+ **Talk to your baby.** It's important that you talk directly to your baby, not just to others around her or out loud to yourself. Parents often say, 'She will learn by osmosis' but, in fact, language development is boosted by talking directly to your baby. Give your baby a running commentary of even the most pedestrian daily events, for example, 'It's time for your bath! Let's start running it. You need to get undressed first. Oh, does that warm water feel nice?' She will love hearing your voice and will learn by associating meaning with the events and objects that you describe.

+ **Read to your baby.** You can start reading to your baby from day dot. Just like when you give her a running commentary, she will love hearing your voice and will start to associate sounds with meanings.

+ **Massage your baby.** Massage is an extension of touching. Remember, touch should always be gentle and your baby should be in the right mood before you start. Wait until she is calm and receptive. Don't massage her if she has a flu or virus. You can find good videos on massaging a baby on the internet, with the International Association of Infant Massage (IAIM) providing some useful ones.

+ **Play with your baby.** By about three months, your baby will enjoy repetitive games, such as rhyming games like 'Round and Round the Garden' and 'This Little Piggy'. As well as strengthening your relationship, these games stimulate your baby's senses. Naming games, such as 'Head, Shoulders, Knees and Toes' are also fun, and 'Peekaboo' is a great way of letting your baby know that your face is gone for a second but will come back (object permanence). You will be able to tell if your baby enjoys a game by her response. Try to notice which games excite your baby, which calm her and which she doesn't like.

+ **Bathe your baby.** Bath-time can be a lovely opportunity for play, progressing from a soothing experience to a fun game of splashing as the months go by! You can even bathe with your baby.

+ **Listen to music.** Babies love music! You might even notice your baby respond to music you played while you were pregnant.

+ **Feed your baby.** Breastfeeding or bottle-feeding can be a great way to build a secure attachment, so long as it is mutually enjoyable. Try to have some feeds where you stay focused on your baby and avoid multitasking. When possible, have skin-to-skin contact while you feed, and be available for eye contact. Feeding time is also a good time to sing or talk to your baby. If you are bottle-feeding, pace the feeds to your baby's hunger, gently tipping the bottle down from time to time to give her the opportunity to pause or stop feeding.

> **+ Smile at your baby.** Get in the habit of greeting your baby with a smile. Make it a lifelong habit—no matter how busy you are, you can always look up for a moment and smile at your child when you greet her.

RIDE THE WAVE

Start humming the opening strains of Ben E King's 'Stand by Me' and it's almost a certainty that anyone who is nearby will be able to join in and sing the chorus with you. The same is true of Simon & Garfunkel's 'Bridge Over Troubled Water'. Both songs have an important idea in common: that we'll be OK, even in the darkest moments, so long as there's someone standing alongside us. The fact that these songs, released in 1961 and 1970 respectively, remain so familiar that most of us know the words is testament to the fact that this idea resonates strongly with all of us.

It's not just adults who need to know there's someone there for them; babies and children need exactly the same thing. Parents sometimes worry that comforting a baby who's grizzling or placating a toddler who's in a grump is the 'wrong' thing to do, because it rewards 'bad' behaviour. However, these are the moments when your child needs your calm presence the most. More than anything, your baby needs to have his emotions acknowledged and accepted (or, in other words, validated) by you. Most of the time he will be as confused as you are about why he feels sad or angry—and, actually, it doesn't matter *what* your baby is upset about, or whether from an outside perspective it seems trivial. You don't need to be a detective; you just need to let your baby know you understand he is upset, then calmly be with him while he rides the wave of emotion. It can be useful to consider how you would want someone to respond to you if you were hurt, sad or angry before you respond to your child.

If your baby is upset or crying, gently hold him and reassure him by saying comforting things to him in a soft voice (see my list of Comforting Dos and Don'ts for suggestions). Trying to remain relaxed and keeping your voice gentle might be the last thing you feel like doing, especially when all you'd like is a moment of peace, but guess what? That moment of peace will come, and sooner if you acknowledge and accept your baby's emotions. Making negative comments, grimacing, sighing or withdrawing your presence will only prolong your baby's feelings of sorrow, frustration and anger. He will try more intense and inventive ways to encourage you to acknowledge his pain or give up seeking comfort.[23]

You can continue to validate your baby's emotions as he gets older by continuing to stay calm and present as he 'rides the wave' of emotion. Over time, he will learn that emotions are not something to be afraid or ashamed of, and that every emotion passes eventually. Children experience the same wide range of emotions as we do, and with your help your child can learn to express and tolerate them.

COMFORTING DOS AND DON'TS

When your baby or child cries or grizzles, either hold her gently or sit nearby and make it clear you want to stay. Do say:

+ 'Mama's here.'

+ 'What's happened?'

+ 'Does that hurt?'

+ 'Do you want a cuddle?'

+ 'I'd feel the same.'

+ 'I love you.'

+ 'You look upset/worried/angry.'

+ 'We can just sit here together.'

Try to avoid saying:

+ 'Stop crying.'

+ 'No grizzling.'

+ 'That doesn't hurt.'

+ 'It doesn't matter.'

+ 'You're fine.'

+ 'I'll come back when you feel better.'

+ 'That's life.'

+ 'For God's sake!'

BE A 'GOOD FIT'

There was a time when people believed babies were born a blank slate, and who they became depended on how they were nurtured. Now we know for sure that nurture is only part of what makes a person who they are; a large chunk of it is already there at birth. Inherited genes have a huge influence on things like intelligence, artistic talent, athletic prowess and even temperament.

When it comes to getting an idea of where your own child's temperament has sprung from, it is a help to first look at yourself and your extended family. As a general rule children tend to be like their parents in temperament, but parents often carry genes that aren't expressed and may come out in surprising ways in their child. It's your job as a parent to figure out what temperament your child has, then let that guide how you respond to her. This will take time, but you can start looking for clues from weeks old.

TIPS FOR GETTING TO KNOW YOUR CHILD'S TEMPERAMENT

+ **Notice.** Just like adults, babies vary in the way they respond emotionally to their world. Notice how your baby responds when you play with him, soothe him and when he is in a new situation. What calms him? What excites him? How much stimulation is too much for him? Do this for a week, then move on to the next tip.

+ **Describe your baby to yourself**, as though you are introducing him to a friend. Researchers use categories such as 'easy', 'difficult (or high needs)', 'distractibility' and 'mood' when studying temperament, but they need to do this in order to make sense of their data. This isn't the right language for parents; try to describe your baby's behaviour and personality in your own words. For example, instead of 'easy' you might say 'smiles a lot and is quick to settle'. Instead of 'shy', you might say 'likes to watch a while before joining in' or 'takes time to get used to new people'—no child should hear themselves described as 'shy', lest their confidence is stifled. Likewise, it is more constructive to say 'takes lots of cuddling to settle at night' than 'difficult'.

+ **Be a good fit.** View your baby's temperament in a child-centred way. See things from his perspective, and adjust your parenting along with your expectations to match his emotional needs. We might want our children to be a certain way, but we can't change their temperament. The only wise choice we have is to help them feel good about who they are.

You cannot change your child's temperament, but you can help her to flourish within that temperament. Stella Chess found that the best outcomes for children occur when there is what she referred to as a 'goodness of fit', which is to say a good match between a baby's temperament and the parent's expectations. If you understand and accept your child's temperament, you will be able to respond to her in a sensitive way, in a way that enables her to learn without feeling overwhelmed. If your baby is often cautious, for instance, you don't need to entirely eliminate any activity that's outside of her comfort zone; instead, go slowly, and introduce her to a new activity step by step. If she doesn't like it, you can shelve it and try again later when she is ready.

Again, it's good to remember that not all babies are overly smiley and cheerful. Some are quite the opposite, and seem to take the world very seriously—and that's OK. As psychologist Martin

Seligman explains, people often confuse happiness with cheerfulness. Seligman's findings have shown that cheerfulness doesn't play much of a role in an individual's sense of well-being, and actually half of us can be classified as not being very cheerful (or having 'low-positive affect'). In his 2011 book *Flourish*, Seligman points out that, 'Even though they lack cheerfulness, this low-mood half may have more engagement and meaning in life than merry people.'[24]

Likewise, some babies are more sensitive than others, in the sense that they respond strongly to stimuli (rather than in the artistic sense). As a young child, I was super-sensitive to disapproval and, possibly for this reason, I didn't like the word 'no'. When my mother taught me the parts of the face, she had to say 'nostril' instead of nose, or I would cry. Fortunately for me, my mother thought this was just another charming aspect of who I was and she went with the flow. She was, in other words, a good fit.

ACCEPT YOUR BABY FOR WHO SHE IS

If your baby has a temperament that falls short of your ideal, let it go. Your baby is who she is, and there's no use in worrying about what this or that trait means for her future because you simply don't know.

What is important, however, is that you work out what your child needs from you in order to feel good about herself and to reach her goals. The less you try to change your baby's temperament and instead focus on her needs, the more resilient she will become.

For example, suppose your baby has a fear of balloons, which is linked to a fear of sudden loud noises. If you are at a birthday party where there are balloons and you force your child to stay in the room, she will feel ashamed about her fear. As time goes on, that shame can lead to your child avoiding parties and social events altogether. You can't talk your baby out of feeling afraid; adults often can't even talk themselves out of feeling afraid. A better solution is to instead move away with your baby so you can both watch from a safe distance. With time, and as she gets older, your child will learn that sudden noises, such as the sound of a balloon popping, are nothing to fear.

Case Study: Dave

At six years old, Dave wore his heart on his sleeve. Some days, he was all smiles and full of excitement about some new discovery he'd made. Other times, he would be distraught, head flung back, tears flowing.

On one occasion in particular, he was upset because he wanted a friend to come over after school, but his mother needed to go to the supermarket. Instead of changing her plans to stop him having a meltdown, Dave's mother responded to him kindly, validating his emotions without compromising her role as his parent. 'I can see why you're upset,' she said to him. 'It's a shame Jenny can't come over, but I have to go to the supermarket because we need some food. Let's call Jenny's mother later and see if she can come over tomorrow.'

As well as recognising Dave's grievances, his mother made sure to tune into his mood when he was full of joy by sharing in his delight. 'How exciting!' she'd exclaim when he told her about a new game he'd played at school.

Since Dave's mother responded to his emotions by validating them, she was ultimately rewarded with a swift resolution when he was upset, and a child who came to have better control over his emotions.

Case Study: Mark

At the end of Mark's first day of school, his mother was waiting for him when the bell rang and he came outside.

'How was it?' she asked.

'I hate school,' Mark said, stamping his foot on the concrete path. 'I don't want to come here ever again.'

'Of course you do. School's great!' she said, at the same time shaking her head with a look of disapproval on her face.

Mark started to cry. 'I hate it. It's stupid.'

'Oh, just stop it.' His mother sighed and rolled her eyes. 'Here, give me your bag and we'll go home.'

The next day, the same thing happened, only Mark was even more agitated, his nose running while his eyes streamed. Each day, he became increasingly distressed and his mother became increasingly impatient. By the end of the week, however, Mark came out of class looking sad and tearful but said nothing. He didn't seek any comfort. Mother and son walked away together in miserable silence.

Mark's mother was there for him physically, but she didn't meet him emotionally. If she had validated his emotions, instead of trying to ignore them, it might not have made him want to be at school but at least he wouldn't have felt alone. Instead of tolerating Mark's emotions, she dismissed them, shaming him for feeling sad, angry and most likely afraid. Eventually, since he wasn't receiving her comfort, he stopped seeking it.

There are many possible reasons for why Mark's mother was unable to validate his emotions. Perhaps she had been discouraged from expressing her own emotions as a child, and Mark's emotions triggered her own unresolved hurts. Maybe she'd had postnatal depression, and hadn't responded to Mark consistently during his infancy, which had lead Mark to express high emotion to try to get her attention. This pattern of communication doesn't happen overnight, but builds over many years. Whatever the reason, one thing is almost certain: Mark's mother loved him, but she lacked the skills and insight necessary to strengthen their interaction.

YOUR OWN EMOTIONAL HEALTH: THE OTHER HALF OF THE EQUATION

In order to take care of your baby, you also need to take care of yourself. Your emotional health has a huge part to play in building a secure attachment with your baby. I'll discuss looking after yourself as a mother in greater detail in Part II of this book, but for now there are some important points to bear in mind with regard to keeping well for your part in the mother–baby relationship.

SEEK HELP EARLY

First up, stress, depression, anxiety and other emotional-health difficulties all affect the way you tune into and respond to your baby. The impact of postnatal depression and anxiety in particular on mother–baby relationships is an area of keen interest to researchers. Caregivers with depression tend to have reduced sensitivity and responsiveness to their infant's cues, and sadly about 70 per cent of women with postnatal depression have relationship difficulties with their infants.[25] Postnatal depression can also contribute to a cycle of mother–baby relationship patterns that continue even when maternal mood improves.[26]

Australian psychologist Jeannette Milgrom has studied the effects of postnatal depression on mother–baby relationships, and believes that existing treatments for postnatal depression should include a brief intervention to protect mother–infant relationships.[27]

I am not trying to frighten you if you are experiencing mood difficulties, but it is important to know the risks of leaving mood disorders untreated. About 50 per cent of women diagnosed with postnatal depression refuse help for various reasons, including denial, shame or negative beliefs about the help available. If your mood is affecting your relationship with your baby, please don't delay seeking help. The sooner, the better. It's hard to form a healthy new relationship with anyone, including your baby, when you are feeling depressed or anxious.

LEARN TO SKILFULLY INTERRUPT RUMINATIONS

When we ruminate, we repetitively think about distressing or difficult emotions or situations. This can have a profound effect on our mood, making us feel low and anxious, which in turn leads to more rumination. It's a vicious cycle. Rumination is a key feature of depression and anxiety, and can stop you from focusing on building a secure relationship with your baby.[28] It takes you away from the present moment, preventing you from being completely 'there' with your baby.

TIPS FOR FOCUSING ON THE PRESENT MOMENT

Some of us tend to ruminate more than others, but thankfully it's possible to interrupt these ruminations. To do so, you first need to be able to notice when your mind is going over and over the same ground without actually problem-solving. If you are worrying about a problem and can solve it, then please go ahead. If you are worrying without finding a solution, however, you're ruminating. It's time to try to bring your mind back to the present moment.

Every now and then, check in with your thoughts. If you notice that you are ruminating, gently move your thoughts away from the ruminations and back to the present moment. You can do this by looking at your baby, reading or noticing a tree—whatever works. You might have to do this repeatedly, but that's OK.

DON'T LET YOUR PAST INTERFERE WITH YOUR PRESENT

Sometimes, without realising it, our past meddles with our present. The way that we ourselves were parented can interfere with our own parenting, and having a baby can trigger memories about our own childhood experiences. Sometimes our memories are positive, and strengthen our bonds with our parents and our children. Other memories can trigger sadness, shame or anger. As mothers often tell me, 'Now that I have a baby, I feel so grateful for everything my parents did.' Other mothers say, 'I didn't really think about it until now that I have someone precious to care for, but I feel so angry and sad about the way my parents treated me.'

Sometimes having your own baby evokes what is known as 'ghosts from the nursery'. These ghosts refer to your negative past experiences, which 'haunt you' when interacting with your own baby. If any ghosts are impacting on your enjoyment or quality of mothering, then they need to be acknowledged and addressed.

TIPS FOR EXORCISING 'GHOSTS FROM THE NURSERY'

The way that your caregivers responded to your childhood emotions can have an enormous impact on your own ability to accept and validate your baby's emotions. For example, if your parents showed irritation when you were afraid, you might find it hard to respond sensitively to your own child's fear. If your parent chastised you when you cried by telling you to 'stop whining!' you might find it hard to be sensitive and kind in the face of your baby's tears.

Be insightful and reflective. Ask yourself, 'Am I responding to my baby's emotions on autopilot? Am I reacting without taking time to think things through?'

How do you respond when your baby shows strong emotions such as excitement, anger, fear, sadness, curiosity or happiness? Do any of these emotions routinely cause you to feel more uncomfortable than his behaviour warrants?

If you find yourself feeling uncomfortable, pause. Look at things from your baby's perspective. Choose to push through your discomfort, and be alongside your baby.

YOU DON'T HAVE TO BE EVERYTHING TO EVERYONE

If you've got more than one child, you will inevitably find it impossible to be in tune with every one of your children at once. Sometimes when my children were little, I felt like I was playing singles tennis with three players on the other side of the net! What's important to remember is that all you need to do is be tuned in and responsive enough to be predictable and dependable. You can't meet everyone's needs all of the time. Furthermore, getting agitated because you're not achieving the impossible isn't helpful, either.

You can't do everything, and you don't need to. You *can* behave in a calm way—and you can do this even if you feel anything but calm. When you behave calmly, your children feel safe.

TO ROUTINE OR NOT TO ROUTINE?

Now that we have established that being sensitive to your baby's cues and responding with warmth and maturity is a necessary approach to mothering in order to build a secure attachment in your child, you may be thinking, *That's all well and fine . . . but it doesn't tell me whether I should be following a routine parenting style, or a baby-led style.* After reading the following pages, I hope you will agree that a sensitive and warm approach is possible regardless of whether you choose a routine or baby-led parenting style, and that both have merit.

The decision of whether to follow a routine or not is possibly the most misunderstood aspect of modern-day child-rearing. For exhausted parents, it's also a burning question. Once upon a time, 'schedule-feeding' was associated with disregarding a baby's hunger or need for comfort in slavish obedience to a routine, but that is no longer the case. You would be hard pressed to find any baby book today that recommends leaving a baby to cry for more than the briefest time. These days, schedule-feeding means being pre-emptive by giving babies what they need before they cry and demand it. As a result, today's version of routine parenting tends to put the mother on a schedule as much as her baby. Nonetheless, even this level of schedule is rejected by many as being unnatural, and extreme-parenting views certainly would not favour any manner of maternal control.

ROUTINE VS SCHEDULE

The terms 'routine' and 'schedule' can cause some confusion.

Outside of the arena of caring for babies, the two words mean something quite different from one another. A **routine** is used to describe a set of behaviours completed in a certain order. For

---

example, your daily routine might look something like this: wake up, have breakfast, go to work, go home, go for a run, have a shower, eat dinner, and so on. A **schedule** puts set times to a routine.

However, when it comes to caring for babies, the two terms are often used interchangeably. Many baby sleep and feeding experts prefer the term 'routine', in order to distance themselves from the negative connotations associated with old-fashioned and rigid 'schedules'.

If a routine appeals to you more than setting a strict schedule, the Pediatric Sleep Council website (babysleep.com) offers month-by-month advice on sleep routines.

If you decide to refer to a baby book for routine or schedule-feeding advice, be sure to get a recent edition. Don't be tempted to buy or borrow an earlier edition. Over the last decade, most experts have softened their views and don't recommend leaving young babies to cry. If you are breastfeeding, they also now recommend feeding on demand until you have established a good milk supply.

A BRIEF HISTORY OF ROUTINE PARENTING

Over two thousand years ago, the great physician Hippocrates said of babies: 'They that have scant [bowel] movement yet being gross feeders are not nourished in proportion . . .'[29] It was possibly the only thing he ever said about babies. Yet, from that moment right up until today, how babies are fed, how much they are fed and how often they feed has remained a major topic of debate.

An early baby book, *The Nursing of Children*, was written in the sixteenth century by a French physician by the name of Guillemeau, who advised mothers to feed an infant 'as often as he crieth'.[30] Two centuries later, French doctor N. Brouzet advised mothers in his *Medicinal Education of Children* to 'give the breast to the infant as often as he seems to desire it and wait until he leaves it himself. Thus, the quantity is varied according to the appetite of the infants, and I believe there can be no danger in suffering [allowing] them to satisfy their hunger.'[31]

Although Guillemeau's and Brouzet's words foreshadowed modern-day feeding-on-demand schools of thought, there was always an opposing school that stressed the need for parental control and the limiting of food. Children were seen to lack that control for themselves. Throughout the centuries, overfeeding was held accountable for hiccups, diarrhoea, vomiting, rickets and a number of other arcane maladies.

By the nineteenth century, the cure for overfeeding was seen to lie in strict schedules. In 1859, Thomas Bull in his *Hints to Mothers* advised four-hour intervals and warned that irregular feeding results in 'overloading of the stomach, dyspepsia, fever and often death'.[32] Towards the end of the nineteenth century, New Zealander Sir Frederic Truby King made a crusade of it: he advocated a strict schedule of four-hour feeds, an equally strict sleeping schedule, regular bowel motions (he believed constipation would lead to masturbation), and restricted cuddling to ten minutes a day at a fixed time. He travelled the world to speak about the 'dangers of overfeeding', and under his leadership an army of specially trained nurses weighed babies regularly and noted the outcome in pounds and ounces in a small book.

As we've seen, in the late forties, Dr Spock turned the King movement on its head by advocating a baby-led approach to feeding, but the impact of Dr King and his campaign against overfeeding lingered well into the fifties. In 1952, English paediatrician Ian Wickes wrote in the *British Medical Journal* that he was seeing a steady stream of babies brought into his clinic who had been diagnosed with 'overfeeding' but who were actually malnourished.[33] These babies were bottle-fed and breastfed alike, and had all manner of symptoms, including colic, diarrhoea, green stools and vomiting. He said babies were not being allowed enough food, and argued that it was difficult to overfeed a baby.

SOFTENING THE SCHEDULE

What is amazing is that, even though this subject—whether a parent or a baby should decide when, how and how much the baby should be fed—has been batted around by great minds across the centuries, there is very little in the way of research to support one view or another. Instead, advocates of both strict routines and of extreme baby-led practices have called on 'higher powers' and nature to support their views. In the case of strict routines, this can be an argument for following 'God's way', while advocates of extreme baby-led feeding practices rest their theories on 'nature' by citing the practices of traditional tribes or animals.

Some modern-day advocates of extreme-parenting approaches claim that the well-studied presence of the stress hormone cortisol in crying babies is evidence that parents should feed on demand. This assumes one or both of two things:

1. a normal amount of crying is damaging, and/or

2. routine or schedule-feeding involves a dangerous level of crying.

While studies show that cortisol levels rise in crying babies, they do not show it results in any harm. For example, in Chapter 9 you will see that cortisol levels rise during breastfeeding, but no one has suggested that breastfeeding therefore causes harm. What is thought to be true is that the level and duration of cortisol in abused children *does* cause harm. You cannot, however, take the result of extreme situations and apply them to normal situations.

As for routine leading to a lot of crying, modern baby books that advocate schedules and routines take crying very seriously and many have, in recent times, revised their advice in response to pressure from paediatricians and parents alike so that it can be considered safe by all but the most extreme parenting views. British mothers in particular tend to more openly embrace schedules, and seem to be far more interested in taking the advice of someone with a proven track record, such as a nanny, than from someone with academic or medical credentials. These mothers want someone who speaks their language and listens to their needs, and in the UK the reigning Queen of Routine is Gina Ford, the author of bestselling *The Contented Little Baby Book* and *The One-week Baby Sleep Solution*. Ford's fixed-times routines focus on teaching babies to settle themselves to sleep so that mothers don't end up exhausted, and mothers are grateful to her when her system works for them—and it often does. However, while Ford's methods can increase night-time sleep more quickly than if a mother continues feeding on demand, achieving it without causing stress to the baby comes at a cost to the mother. By this I mean that it's not just the baby who is put on a routine; the mother must also follow the same strict routine, and keep one step ahead of her baby at all times.

Parents tend to fall into one of two camps when it comes to Ford. There are those who try to follow the rules exactly, and invariably find themselves feeling exhausted, trapped, isolated and like a failure. These parents complain that Ford's approach binds them to the house, restricts their day, and keeps them from enjoying the company of friends. Then there are those who use Ford's advice as a guide, and ignore the prescriptive 'musts'. These parents appreciate the helpful hints about routines, but don't necessarily follow the strict sleep and feeding schedules to the letter. They adapt her advice so that it works for them, and they love it. As one writer for *The Independent* said, when he and his wife had their first baby, 'the installation of a routine was a huge help for us all . . . we took on a kind of Ford-lite regime and things improved markedly'.[34] Indeed, an article titled 'The routine of 15 contented little babies' on the official Contented Baby website (contentedbaby.com) insists that Ford's routines are not set in stone, and can be adapted to each individual child. The article offers fifteen examples of different routines, all of which share one advantage: longer sleep times at night. It seems there's a moral in all of this, and it's that the 'Ford-lite' approach is a popular way to go.

If you do think that modern-day scheduling or routines will help you (particularly with sleep), then go for it. There is no credible evidence suggesting it will adversely affect your child. However, a schedule or routine relies on the parent—and usually the mother—being one step ahead, and that may not suit you and your needs. It's about working out what's best for you: while a routine may pay off with longer night-time sleeps sooner, it may also require more effort than feeding on demand in the short term. It is your choice, and what you choose can depend entirely on your temperament, beliefs and practical needs.

FEEDING SCHEDULES AND IQ: DOES IT MATTER?

In 2013, the results of the first—and possibly only—study into the effects of scheduled feeding versus on-demand feeding made quite a splash.[35]

According to the researchers, the study showed that scheduled feeding lowered a child's IQ by four points, and this was reflected in school performance. In an article headlined 'Babies fed on demand "do better at school"', *The Observer* proclaimed, 'New study shows that babies who are fed when they are hungry achieve higher test scores'.[36] The piece featured interviews with various people,

---

including the lead researcher, but never questioned the study itself—and it should have.

This study was a perfect example of researchers trying to force data collected for an entirely different purpose to support their own ends. The researchers relied on information from the 1990 'Children of the nineties' longitudinal study concerning the well-being of mothers and babies in Bristol, England.[37] The only question in that study relevant to feeding asked mothers, when their babies were four weeks old: 'Is your baby fed (either by breast or bottle) on a regular schedule (e.g. every four hours)?' Only 7 per cent answered 'yes', but nothing further was established about the remaining 93 per cent—whether, for instance, they schedule-fed in a less rigorous way, or whether they began schedule-feeding after four weeks, or indeed whether they'd correctly understood the question.

When the researchers compared the small group of schedule-fed children to those of the other mothers in the study, they found that these children were more than twice as likely to have been admitted to a special care birth unit. The babies in the schedule-fed group tended to be born prematurely, be smaller and to have mothers who smoked during pregnancy. The mothers themselves were, the researchers said, 'younger, more likely to be single, more likely to be social tenants [i.e. on a benefit], and less well educated'.

Some very important data was missing from the Avon study. In order to make any claim about the IQ advantages for a baby from feeding on demand, measures for a mother's intelligence are necessary. However, not even the mother's level of education was listed as a variable by the researchers in the 2013 paper; it would appear that they used the mother's home address as a substitute for her IQ. What's more, the two groups were so very different in so many ways that the researchers could not legitimately compare them. The researchers tried to make up for this by using a statistical technique called propensity score matching, which would estimate the missing data. However, their raw data did not reach the standard for using this technique. As Stanford professor Kristin Sainani has pointed out, 'If the groups have little overlap . . . they are inherently incomparable, and no statistical tricks can overcome this problem.'[38]

Since the two groups of mothers were 'inherently incompatible', the results of the study had no validity—at least not in the areas of intelligence or cognition. The only thing that could be said is that children born at risk through prematurity, with mothers who smoked during pregnancy, and who lived on a benefit in poor neighbourhoods, did worse in school and on standardised IQ tests than children whose mothers suffered fewer of those deficits. That's quite a different conclusion, don't you think?

CHAPTER 2: THE MAIN POINTS

+ Keep it simple. Tune into your baby's needs and meet those needs in a warm and consistent way. Tune into your own needs and get help early if necessary.

+ You don't have to be perfect. You just need to be 'bigger, stronger, wiser and kind'.

+ A secure attachment is the ideal attachment pattern (but note that anxious and ambivalent patterns are also common and 'normal').

+ Both parent and baby contribute to the parent–baby relationship.

+ To build a positive relationship with your baby and to support your baby's social and emotional development, you can use the following techniques: mutual gaze, 'serve and return', a loving touch, showing delight in your baby, riding her wave of emotions, and being a 'good fit'.

+ Whether you follow a routine or schedule or neither is entirely up to you. It is your choice, and depends on the needs of you and your family.

+ Any parenting style can work.

PART II

LOOKING
AFTER
YOURSELF

CHAPTER 3
HAPPINESS AND
WELL-BEING

Mothering myth: When you have a new baby, meeting your own physical and emotional needs can wait.

Truth: You need a good sense of well-being in order to look after your baby effectively.

In order to look after your baby, you also need to look after yourself. It might sound obvious, but sometimes looking after yourself can be quite difficult—it may involve asking for help, or acknowledging that things aren't quite the way that you imagined they might be. This is especially relevant when you become a mother. There are an awful lot of ideas out there about what a mother 'should' be, and there's no shortage of people who share and spread these 'mothering myths'. The reality for most mothers is that settling into this new role will be filled with wonderful, joyous moments and also some really challenging moments. That's normal. In Part II of this book, I'm going to cover some of the main areas where looking after yourself as a mother is important, but we're going to start with the most obvious one: your happiness and well-being.

All of us desire happiness, and we'll often say, 'I just want you to be happy,' or ask, 'How can I make myself happier?' In actual fact happiness is rather subjective; when we talk this way, we assume that 'happiness' is the same for everyone. The truth, however, is that you could have a room full of people saying those words, and every one of them could be talking about something completely different. For some, happiness might mean having a good time at a party. For others, it's having a sense of satisfaction and contentment. For yet others, it could be a certain achievement.

HAPPINESS AND WELL-BEING

What, exactly, happiness *is* has long been a source of debate. Back in Ancient Greece, Plato concluded that happiness or well-being came from virtuous thought and conduct, rather than pleasure. In more recent times, we can turn to the work of Martin Seligman, a leading psychologist in the area of happiness.

Seligman is a pioneer in 'positive psychology', or the scientific study of what makes life most worth living. In 2002, he published the bestseller *Authentic Happiness*, in which he described his theory that happiness can be divided into three elements: positive emotion, engagement and meaning.[1] A combination of these three elements of happiness leads, Seligman said, to the measurement of one's 'life satisfaction'.

Since writing *Authentic Happiness*, however, Seligman has considered the limitations of this original analysis of happiness. For example, it did not explain why parents, who claim that their children are the source of their greatest happiness, score lower than non-parents on traditional scales measuring happiness. In his new book, *Flourish: A visionary new understanding of happiness and well-being*, Seligman revised his original theory. First, he has added two new elements: positive relationships and accomplishments. This brings the total number of elements to five, all of which account for well-being and allow us to 'flourish'. Then, importantly, he claims that behaving virtuously (specifically in the Ancient Greek sense—with virtues and strengths such as social intelligence, kindness, humour, courage and integrity) is essential for each of these five elements.[2]

For Seligman, a great advantage of his new approach is that measures of well-being don't rely heavily on how someone feels in any given moment. Instead, it is a more objective measure that takes into account a wider and longer-term view. This provides a more scientifically testable construct. For example, it could be said that parenting calls on more virtues and strengths than almost any other activity, and success in parenting will therefore lead to a great sense of well-being—but not necessarily pleasure.

CIRCUITRIES FOR HAPPINESS

Psychiatrist Tony Fernando is another researcher in the field of positive psychology, and he believes you can bring happiness into your day by calling on three 'circuitries for happiness'.[3] These brain circuitries are: the excitement pleasure circuit, the calm and contentment circuit, and the connection compassion circuit.

I like exploring these circuitries of happiness with mothers, because they can each be utilised no matter how busy you are. Let's take a closer look at them now.

EXCITEMENT PLEASURE CIRCUIT

The main neurotransmitter involved in the excitement pleasure circuit is dopamine. Neurotransmitters are chemical substances that transfer information from one nerve cell to the next, and dopamine is one of these chemical substances. It plays a particular role in attention, movement, addiction, reward, pleasure and motivation. Behaviours that stimulate the excitement pleasure circuit can include eating sweets, spending money, having sex and surfing the internet. There is nothing wrong with doing any of these things some of the time, as we all need some excitement and pleasure. Problems occur, however, if we depend on this circuit for our happiness. Why? Because this type of happiness is short-lived. We are always after our next hit.

CALM AND CONTENTMENT CIRCUIT

At the times when you are unable to be calm and content, it is not possible to have a sense of happiness and well-being, so this circuit is fundamental to bringing happiness and well-being into your day. Anxiety and happiness, for example, are incompatible. It is important to notice what induces calm and contentment for you. Prescription medication is targeted to relieve stress and anxiety, and helps many people, as does practising mindfulness, a skilful and portable way to induce calm. Some people find a bath calming, while others complain of being hot and bothered. Some like a brisk walk, while others find it a hassle. Alcohol or other non-prescription drugs can induce calm and contentment in the short term, but can lead to longer-term difficulties.

WHAT IS MINDFULNESS?

According to Jon Kabat-Zinn, professor emeritus of medicine and mindfulness expert, mindfulness is 'paying attention in a particular way: on purpose, in the present moment, and non-judgmentally'.[4]

Practising mindfulness can be an extremely effective way to induce an internal sense of calm and contentment. Paying attention to the present moment allows you to notice your thoughts and feelings without getting 'caught up' in them. Noticing gives you the opportunity to make a choice: to continue thinking about the past or future, or instead to gently move your attention to the present moment. This doesn't mean you push away uncomfortable thoughts and feelings (as the saying goes, 'what we resist persists'); rather, you are fully aware of them so that you can choose where to place your attention. For example, you might notice yourself thinking about an event that made you sad or angry—this is just fine, and being aware that you are doing so puts your mind in the driver's seat.

Another way to describe mindfulness is to consider the opposite— mindlessness, or autopilot. Everyone experiences this. Ever read a page of a book only to realise you haven't taken any of it in? Ever driven home without really noticing the journey? If the answer is yes, then you have been on autopilot. You are not, as Shauna Shapiro and Linda Carlson write in their book *The Art and Science of Mindfulness*, 'fully awake to the reality of the present moment'.[5]

Needless to say, being mindful when you are with your baby gives you more opportunity for moments of delight, getting to know her, and letting her know that you are fully present with her.

Paying attention non-judgmentally is an integral part of mindfulness. No thoughts or feelings are 'good' or 'bad'; they just *are*. Be kind to yourself. You can't control the automatic thoughts that pop into your mind; you can only control the way you relate to them, and how you decide to behave. Your behaviour might be as simple as gently moving your focus away from unhelpful thoughts and on to other thoughts or to what is right in front of you.

Remember, mindfulness isn't about getting rid of life's stresses, but it is a conscious way of relating to your experiences. Stresses will always come your way, but if you can learn to be mindful you will have a better chance of experiencing calmness and contentment.

Mindfulness is an experiential process. You need to practise it to fully understand. Tuning in to your emotions by noticing and describing your feelings, thoughts, physical sensations and action urges in any given moment is a way of being mindful (see Chapter 4). You can also simply remind yourself throughout the day to fully notice your thoughts in any given moment.

There's a heap of information out there—in books, online, apps— that can support your practice of mindfulness. Some specifically focus on mindfulness while mothering. One app that many mothers I work with love is called Headspace.

Before deciding to practise mindfulness, be clear about your intention. Why is it that you want to be mindful? It might be that you want to better regulate your emotions, lift your mood, remain calm with your baby or explore your values and motivations. Setting your intention—which is to say, being aware of your goals—reminds you why you are practising mindfulness.

CONNECTION COMPASSION CIRCUIT

For most people, this circuit provides the most sustainable form of happiness. Importantly, unlike the other two circuits, it is 'internally reignited'. Just thinking about loved ones or times of laughter can make us feel connected; we cannot, however, get much pleasure from just thinking about eating chocolate or induce much calm by imagining mindfulness without engaging in it. A fantastic way of being connected with other people is through compassion.

English psychologist Paul Gilbert, the founder of 'compassion-focused therapy', is to compassion what Seligman is to positive psychology and happiness. In his book *Mindful Compassion*, Gilbert describes compassion as a motive rather than an emotion. Although compassion requires feeling empathy (an awareness that someone is suffering), compassion is about *acting* on that empathy—it's the motivation to relieve that suffering (and, if necessary, acquire the skills to do so).[6]

Gilbert applies an evolutionary perspective to suffering and compassion, citing, for instance, fossils which show evidence that around a million years ago our ancestors evolved into a species that looked after their old and diseased as well as their young.

Many of us understand Gilbert's point about compassion being a motive, as we have experienced how good it feels to actively relieve the suffering of others. So what can get in the way of us being compassionate? Fear, says Gilbert. Fear of others taking advantage of us, fear of others depending on us, fear that we will not be able to tolerate the distress of others. Sadly, according to Gilbert, those who are afraid of *giving* compassion are also more likely to fear *receiving* it from others, and less likely to show it towards themselves. Fear of compassion makes us more vulnerable to depression, stress, anxiety and self-criticism.

We need to practise compassion, Gilbert says, or it won't be there when we need it. When you have young children, alleviating the suffering of others can sometimes be the last thing on your mind, but it's important to know that practising compassion doesn't need to take much time. For example, when you see a mother having trouble fitting her pram through a door and you help, you have shown compassion. When a mother at school pick-up appears socially nervous and you take time out from your friends to make small talk with her, you have shown compassion.

Of course, compassion isn't the only way to connect with others. When you smile and sincerely thank the person at the check-out who has gone out of their way to carefully pack your shopping, you are connecting with them. When you give a mother you haven't seen before a compliment about her baby, you are connecting with her. When you connect with people in any of these ways, notice you are doing so and take the time to pay attention to how it feels.

One modern block that gets in the way of real connection is social media. Yes, you can get a lot out of chatting with like-minded parents in online groups—however, if you spend too much time on social media, you lose out on the stronger and more enduring feelings you have when you are present and connected with your baby and others around you. (For more on technology and your baby's brain, see Chapter 16.)

Case study: Karen

Sometimes when Karen was at home with her ten-month-old baby, Harry, she felt cut off from the outside world. Her smartphone—and the instant access it provided to all of her social media platforms—was a convenient way to remedy her feelings of isolation.

Karen felt torn. She knew the amount of time she was spending on her phone was interfering with her connecting with Harry as much as she wanted to, but it was just so compelling. She also wondered about her role-modelling for Harry, who was beginning to take an eager interest in her phone.

So, she decided to do something about it.

First, Karen armed herself with information. She realised that the Silicon Valley businesses that create all the apps she was using are extremely motivated to keep her glued to her phone's screen as much as possible, by manipulating her excitement pleasure brain circuit.

She made the decision to be more discerning about how she used social media, and made a point of noticing what feelings were driving her to turn to her phone. Usually, these feelings were boredom, loneliness and curiosity. She asked herself whether looking at social media made her feel any better. Sure, sometimes it did—and sometimes it didn't.

Karen came up with a strategy using the three circuitries of happiness. When she was with Harry, she put away her phone; instead, she connected with him by being available to make eye contact and verbalise with him, and saved social media time for when Harry was napping. Karen made sure to plan something that would give her pleasure, such as having a hot chocolate while she checked her phone once Harry was asleep. In the meantime, she induced calm by accepting that she was spending time with Harry. She noticed when she felt driven to look at her phone and gently shifted her attention to Harry instead. Karen reminded herself that choosing to be present with Harry, instead of scrolling through her social media feeds, would pay off for their relationship.

Karen began to really understand that using social media will always come second best to connecting with people face-to-face. So, as well as focusing on being present with Harry, she also made sure to regularly catch up with other mothers for coffee. When out and about, she made an effort to connect with strangers by saying hi or smiling at them, instead of staring at her phone. Additionally, Karen made sure to spend a few hours a week away from Harry, in order to feel fully connected with other adults.

Reducing the amount of time she spent on her phone was hard to do at first, but it soon paid off. And, the less time she spent on her phone, the easier it was to stay off it.

REMEMBER THE POTENTIAL

To avoid a sense of despondency, remember the word 'potential'.

Complimenting a mother won't bring connection if she is aloof, eating sweets won't bring you pleasure if you crack a tooth, and having a hot shower won't bring you calm if someone rings the doorbell while you're in it. These are all events with the potential to meet your needs, but they don't always work out.

But here's the thing: if you don't try at all, there is zero potential.

NOTICE THE POSITIVE

Unfortunately, our brains are adapted to pay more attention to the negative aspects in our lives than the positive. According to evolutionary psychology, this would have once helped us to survive, since paying attention to a movement in the leaves (that could be a predator) was more useful than noticing how pleasant the sunshine was. Think about it—when you talk about your drive home, do you mention the person who waved you through ahead of them, or are you more likely to complain about the car that cut in front of you?

Your brain might not always notice the positive straight away, but, importantly, it *can*. Make a point to notice and remember when you feel pleasure, connection and calm. When you are with your baby, really notice how you feel when you touch his skin, when he gives you a gummy smile, when you easily soothe him.

Positive psychologists have been studying the impact of virtuous actions on various groups for some time, and gratitude is generally considered a fundamental virtue. In 2008, a group of researchers divided early adolescents into three groups: one group was asked to write down what they were grateful for, another group was asked to write what they found to be a hassle, and a third group did neither (this was the control group).[7] The researchers found that the students who acknowledged the things they were grateful for had increased optimism and life-satisfaction, and decreased negative mood; the most significant finding was increased satisfaction with their school experience.

Then, in 2014, a group of North American psychiatrists and psychologists found that, when patients with suicidal thoughts were given nine different positive psychology interventions, those related to expressing gratitude came out on top in terms of improved mood.[8] In 2015, another study (modelled after the 2008 study mentioned above) found that gratitude intervention was effective in reducing depressive symptoms in a stressful workplace.[9]

It appears that in a surprising number of situations, placing focused attention on what you are grateful for has the effect of improving a sense of optimism and life satisfaction, and decreasing negative emotions.

GRATITUDE JOURNALS

More recently, the practice of writing down what you are grateful for has grown popular in the form of 'gratitude journals'. A great many people find this practice enhances their well-being.

If you like the idea of starting your own gratitude journal, it's easy. Simply make the time each evening to record three things that you are grateful for from the day—that the car started on time, a friend made you laugh, that your baby smiled at you. Anything at all that you have to be grateful for. Look back over your diary from time to time.

It is a good idea to make sure that at least some of your journal entries have the theme of connecting with other people. For example, that another parent smiled at you in the playground, or that a friend phoned you for advice.

As you go about your day, set your intention to notice what you are grateful for. This needs to be done purposefully, or you will miss opportunities to notice gratitude. Congratulate yourself when you do notice something to be grateful for. Eventually, noticing gratitude will become a habit, and as time goes on you will notice more and more experiences for which you can be grateful. Keeping a journal will ensure that you keep your intention alive.

It is never too early to model gratitude to your baby. Do this by pointing out things to be grateful for, such as saying, 'Look! The sun has come out. Aren't we lucky?'

PRACTISE SELF-COMPASSION

Self-compassion benefits your emotional health and well-being, and therefore helps you look after your baby effectively. Sometimes self-compassion can be a bit of a hard sell to the mothers I work with. Some wonder if it is really a researched tool or just pseudoscience. Others worry that self-compassion is self-indulgent, and stops them taking responsibility for their actions.

In fact, there is solid research showing that self-compassion is more likely to contribute to personal responsibility than detract from it. When we make a mistake or act inappropriately, the fear of self-criticism can lead us into denial. Researcher and author Kristin Neff is an expert in self-compassion, and sees self-compassion as simply compassion turned inward. She believes that when we gently tune in to how we are feeling, accept our mistakes or flaws, and talk to ourselves kindly, we are less likely to blame others.[10] Rather than being self-indulgent, practising self-compassion as parents moves us on from ruminating and provides us with more opportunity to meet our baby's needs.

DO YOU SHOW YOURSELF COMPASSION?
Take a moment to consider how well you show self-compassion. Imagine, for instance, that you are at your friend's house and you spill a glass of red wine on the carpet. What would you do? Be honest. Would you apologise, accept responsibility, pay for the cleaning and then consider some ways to be more careful in future? Or would you ruminate and chastise yourself? Or would you try to shift the blame on to your friend?

If you'd normally respond in one of the latter ways, take a different approach towards your mistakes or flaws. Notice when you are suffering or make a misstep, and be gentle with yourself. Avoid name-calling. Would you call someone who was having a hard time 'stupid' or 'an idiot'? No? Then don't call yourself names either.

Now, think about how you would respond to a friend who tells you that she feels guilty about being bored when she's with her baby, or guilty for being disappointed with her baby's development. I'm sure you wouldn't chastise her and tell her she isn't a good mother, and that you would instead show her compassion by reminding her that she's not alone and that you care. Show yourself the same compassion.

In order to show yourself compassion, you need to first tune in to your pain and suffering. Physical and emotional pain is an inevitable part of life, and can be the result of a range of stimuli, such as rejection or disappointment. Suffering is our response to a painful stimulus, and many clinicians believe, as I do, that by accepting your pain you can alleviate your suffering. Accepting is very different from liking, or from refusing to problem-solve. Accepting simply means that you stop struggling against the reality of your situation in the moment.

It is easy to recognise major events (such as significant illness or death) as paths to pain and suffering, but what about the more mundane events? When your friend moves cities and you feel sad or anxious and miss them, it is a point of pain and suffering. When you are stressed because your baby doesn't smile and you're worried there's a developmental delay, it is a point of pain and suffering. Watching the clock and feeling bored while you are at home with your baby is a point of pain and suffering, and so is being left out of a coffee group and wondering why. Usually the source of the suffering lies in your interpretation of the event—thinking, for example, that you can't cope, are unkind, trapped or unworthy.

Take a moment to think about the times as a parent when you

might have made a mistake or had unpleasant feelings towards your baby. Did you give yourself a hard time? Did you ignore your pain? Try practising self-compassion instead. Following are the three steps to self-compassion that Neff suggests.[11]

1. **Notice without judgement that you are suffering.** Next time you are caught up in unpleasant feelings, such as boredom, anxiety, jealousy or inadequacy, and/or thoughts such as *I can't do this right,* name this as suffering.

2. **Remember you are not alone.** Pain and suffering are universal. Neff calls this 'humanity vs isolation'. Many other mothers are experiencing the same thoughts and feelings too—and many of them right at the same time you are. That's what unites us.

3. **Treat yourself with kindness.** Tell yourself exactly what you would tell a friend in the same situation. For example, 'This is really hard and you are doing your best. No one is perfect.' Humans respond to physical touch, so Neff suggests pressing your hand gently above your chest as a way of comforting yourself.

Being kind to yourself takes practice, but it is worth it. It is an important part of taking care of yourself, which in turn will help you better take care of your baby.

CHAPTER 3: THE MAIN POINTS

+ The five elements of Seligman's theory of well-being are: positive emotion, engagement, meaning, positive relationships and accomplishment. These elements, he says, enable individuals to flourish.

+ The three 'brain circuitries for happiness' are: the excitement pleasure circuit, the calm and contentment circuit, and the connection compassion circuit. We need experiences that trigger each of these circuits to balance out the unpleasant and mundane parts of everyday life.

+ Practising mindfulness can be an effective way to induce an internal sense of calm and contentment.

+ Remember to notice the positive. Keeping a gratitude journal can help with this, and can enhance your sense of well-being.

+ Practise self-compassion. Be kind to yourself.

CHAPTER 4
TUNING IN AND
KEEPING CALM

Mothering myth: A good mother always enjoys being with her baby.

Truth: It is completely normal for good mothers to experience a range of pleasant and unpleasant emotions.

Babies are hardwired to experience a range of feelings, and their feelings are strongly affected by how they perceive their caregivers' emotions. For this reason, it is important for parents to be in control of their own emotions. Psychologists call this 'emotional regulation', which means having the ability to respond to experiences with a range of emotions and to behave in an effective way. Good emotional regulation allows you to delay your behavioural responses to difficult emotions in order to meet the needs of you and your baby. When you respond to your baby in a calm way, she feels safe, secure and positive about her environment.

Remember that every single parent experiences a combination of pleasant feelings (such as pride, delight and contentment) and unpleasant feelings (such as anger, loneliness and boredom). A key to good parenting is noticing unpleasant feelings, but choosing to be calm and positive with your baby anyway. You might feel anxious or resentful, but you can still choose to soothe your baby in a regulated way. You might feel bored, but you can choose to focus on and play with your baby. You might feel angry, but you can choose to control your temper and smile down at your baby when she looks up.

The first step to staying emotionally regulated is becoming aware of your emotions. Mothers often ask what I mean by this. 'Surely I know when I am stressed or sad or frustrated,' they tell me. In fact, unless we purposefully tune in to our emotions, we are often unaware of them until it's too late. By the time they become intense enough for us to notice them, we are already behaving in unhelpful ways. It is much easier to use skills to calm yourself down or be positive when you are only 30 per cent stressed, sad or angry than it is when you're at 80 per cent.

THE FOUR PARTS OF AN EMOTION

We have an emotional response to everything around us, be it a joke, a baby smiling, an offhand comment or walking in the sunshine. Observing our emotions is not a new idea; it has long been an integral part of therapeutic models, from Freudian psychoanalysis to modern positive psychology. Theorists and writers vary in the way they define an emotion, but I draw on the description given in an excellent therapy workbook called *Mind and Emotions*.[1] In this book, the authors describe an emotional response as having four parts: affect (which I simplify to feelings), thoughts, physical sensations and action urges.

Before I explain in more detail how to tune in to your emotions, let's take a moment to examine each of the four parts of an emotion.

FEELINGS

Feelings are often the part of an emotional response we notice first. Feelings can usually be summed up in one word, such as 'happy', 'sad' or 'irritable'. Of course, we can experience more than one feeling in any situation. We may feel overwhelmed *and* excited when we first see our new baby.

Stop and ask yourself: 'What am I feeling right now?'

If you come up with words like 'content', 'enriched', 'overwhelmed' or 'curious', you are describing your feelings. If you come up with a whole sentence, you have identified a thought rather than a feeling.

THOUGHTS

A feeling almost always has a thought connected to it. Thoughts can both trigger and intensify feelings. Often, the kinds of thoughts you have are determined by how you interpret an event—as good, bad, annoying or whatever. These interpretations are influenced by many different things, including past experiences, values or even something you just read or watched.

One way of illustrating the connection between your thoughts and your feelings is by looking at two different interpretations of the same event. In each of the following case studies, notice how the different interpretations are linked to different feelings.

Case study: Rose

Rose's father has just arrived at her house after a long journey. He has come to visit and help her with the baby, but he has gone to have a lie-down. Just as Rose sits down for a cup of tea, she hears her baby cry out.

She might think, *Dad isn't really here to help. He's just here to have a holiday and get a change of scene.* This interpretation might cause her to feel irritated.

Alternatively, she might think, *Oh, Dad needs a nap after coming such a long way on the train to see me. He really is getting old.* If she does, this interpretation might cause her to feel sad but grateful.

Case study: Aroha

Aroha is putting her baby down for a nap, and has asked her seven-year-old to be quiet. Just as her baby is starting to drift off to sleep, she hears a loud crashing noise coming from the kitchen.

She might think, *What's wrong with him? I told him to be quiet! Doesn't he know how hard it is for me to settle the baby?* If she does, this interpretation might cause her to feel angry.

Alternatively, she might think, *Oh, he's hungry and trying to get some food for himself without bothering me.* If she does, this interpretation might cause her to feel proud.

PHYSICAL SENSATIONS

Every feeling is accompanied by changes in the body. When we feel angry, our muscles tense. When we feel anxious, we might experience light-headedness. When we feel excited, our heart beats faster. Just like thoughts, these physical sensations both trigger and strengthen our feelings. For example, if you experience a physical sensation such as shortness of breath, you might interpret it as evidence that you really *do* have something to be afraid of—even if the cause is only a mountain of laundry, which can be annoying but not life-threatening! In turn, the feeling of fear might lead to other physical sensations such as tightness in your chest, and so on.

ACTION URGES

Every feeling is connected to an 'action urge', or a hardwired drive to behave in a certain way. When we feel angry, our action urge is to fight. When we feel anxious, our action urge is to avoid whatever is causing our anxiety. When we feel sad, our action urge is to withdraw. When we feel fear, our action urge is to flee.

Although an urge is an instinctive response to a feeling, you can still choose whether to act on it or not. It's not uncommon (and completely understandable) for a new mother to give in to her action urges by responding to her baby in a clipped, intrusive or distracted way. However, even though it might not seem like it, she does have a choice: she can either go with her action urge, or she can respond skilfully by tuning in to her emotions before she decides how to behave.

The key to choosing is identifying the space—or, the time and opportunity—between tuning in to an emotion and the behaviour you respond with. If your action urge when your baby cries is to pace, to sigh, to watch the clock or to ruminate, you can use the space between noticing the urge and responding to it to make the choice to speak with a soft voice, stay focused, problem-solve or interrupt your ruminations (for more on interrupting ruminations see page 73).

Some mothers don't believe that they have space between an action urge and the behaviour they choose. They say they 'can't help' shouting at their partner in front of their baby, or tensing up while they soothe their baby to sleep, or furrowing their brow when their toddler interrupts them. Granted, some people with emotional difficulties might have developed a fast or dysregulated behavioural response to their emotions—which is to say they have less space between their action urge and behaviour—but *everyone* can learn to use space to decide whether or not to act on their urges.

There is only one time when using space is not adaptive—or

safe—and that is when we are in real physical danger. When a sabertooth tiger or a car is coming towards us, our action urge is to run; it isn't safe to thoughtfully consider whether to go with the urge to flee or not. However, unless you are facing a prehistoric predator, an oncoming vehicle, a natural disaster or some other life-threating situation, you do have space to choose how you behave.

SKILLS FOR TUNING IN

Now that we've covered the four parts of an emotion—feelings, thoughts, physical sensations, and action urges—we can turn to how you can practise tuning in to your emotions skilfully. You might be wondering why you should bother tuning in at all. Well, in addition to enabling you to stay emotionally regulated so you can respond to your baby in a calm way, there are a couple of other very good reasons to develop the skill of tuning in.

For starters, emotions—both pleasant and unpleasant—are there whether we tune in to them or not. Tuning in gives us the freedom to choose how we respond to our emotions, rather than just acting without thinking.

Not noticing, suppressing or avoiding unpleasant emotions can cause a whole raft of difficulties. If we try to avoid social anxiety by not going out, for example, we can become even more isolated and depressed. Imagine a three-year-old trying to show you a painting while you are engrossed in conversation with another adult. The more you ignore the toddler, the harder she will try to connect with you; alternatively, if you just acknowledge her and her efforts, then she will be satisfied and more likely to go off and play. Emotions are the same as the toddler. If you ignore them, they will just keep building up and hang around for longer.

Just as importantly, if we don't tune in to our pleasant emotions, we don't get our money's worth out of the day. For example, a new mother pushing a pram in the sunshine might not notice the feeling of contentment she has when the sun warms her face. By not noticing her contentment, she misses out on getting the most from the moment. It's especially important to notice pleasant emotions throughout the day when you are a new mother, so that you can collect them and reflect on them later, especially when you are exhausted from the demands of mothering.

GENTLY DOES IT

When you are tuning in to your emotions, try to notice your emotional responses in a gentle, non-judgemental and compassionate way—not in a harsh, critical way. There is no need to judge your feelings, thoughts, physical sensations and action urges as either 'right' or 'wrong'. If you take a judgemental approach to your emotional responses, you can quickly find yourself in a downward spiral of negative feelings about yourself and your baby.

Remember that it's not your thoughts, feelings, body sensations and urges that measure who you are; it's your behaviour that counts. You can gently notice an unhelpful thought, then move away from it, instead turning your attention to a balanced thought or something in your environment.

For example, if a friend tells you she has become pregnant quickly and you're in the middle of your third round of fertility treatment, it is completely natural to have envy-driven thoughts. However, you can still treat your friend with warmth and respect. Your initial thoughts don't reflect your character; it is how you behave towards your friend that counts.

A tutor at a workshop I attended some years back described tuning in to emotions as something to be done by candlelight—with warmth and curiosity—not with a surgeon's laser beam. It's an analogy that has stuck with me, and resonates with many of my clients.

A THOUGHT IS JUST A THOUGHT

You might sometimes find yourself surprised—or even horrified—by your thoughts or feelings, but you don't need to take them so seriously. A thought is just a thought. It is not a fact. It is not an intention or a goal. And it is certainly not a behaviour.

ALL THINGS COME TO AN END

It's vital to remember that emotions cannot hurt you in any way. It is your response to emotions that can be unhelpful or damaging. Even though it might seem as though an unpleasant emotion is going to last forever, remember that all emotions have a limited time span. They all come and go in waves. We simply cannot sustain one emotion for very long.

Trying to ignore your emotions is futile. They're there whether you want them to be or not. Remember, 'What we resist persists'. If you acknowledge your emotions without judging your thoughts or feelings, you will start to accept your internal experiences. You will stop struggling against them and ultimately getting completely caught up in them. In Part I, I talked about 'riding the wave' of an emotion with your child (see pages 64–65). It's important to do the same with yourself. If you ride the wave of your emotions, you won't get thrashed in the surf.

PRACTICE IS KEY

Practice is key. Although tuning in to your emotions takes practice, it will soon start to feel natural. At first, you might feel overwhelmed and think that tuning in just takes too much time—but remember that it will soon *save* you time, by enabling you to notice and interrupt meaningless and unhelpful thought patterns and behaviours. Think of it like learning to ride a bike: to begin with it's a bit clumsy, and you have to think through each part of the process, but before long you just do it automatically. The same is true with tuning in and responding skilfully.

TIPS FOR SETTING YOUR INTENTION TO TUNE IN

One way to set your intention to tune in is to notice your emotional response as soon as you wake up in the morning. Identify your first feelings, thoughts, physical sensations and action urges.

Then, set your intention to continue tuning in to the four parts of your emotions throughout the day. Here are some ideas.

+ You can use stickers or post-it notes to remind you to practise tuning in. Stick them up around the house, on your baby's pram and in your car, and tune in each time you look at them.

+ You can also simply make a point of tuning in when you perform a specific action—for example, every time you go through to a different room, or every time you get into your car.

+ You could set some 'tune in' reminders on your phone!

At first, tuning in might seem clumsy but after a while it will come naturally. You will soon notice the benefits.

TUNING IN TO YOUR EMOTIONS

When I am working with mothers who are learning to tune in to their emotions, we work together on identifying the four parts of emotions—feelings, thoughts, physical sensations and action urges—

that they experience in response to different events or scenarios. The following three case studies show how to break emotions down in this way.

Case study: Angela

When Angela's six-week-old daughter smiles at her for the first time, she feels excited and proud.

She thinks, *He looks happy. I can't believe I have such a beautiful baby. I hope he smiles again soon.*

Physically, she notices that her breathing has grown faster (from excitement).

Her action urge is to smile back at him and coo.

Case study: Maia

At four in the morning, when Maia's three-month-old baby wakes up for the fifth time in the same night, she feels overwhelmed and helpless.

She thinks, *I am so tired. I'm not going to manage during the day if I don't get any sleep.*

Physically, she notices that her stomach is tight and her heart is beating fast.

Her action urge is to pull the duvet cover over her head and cry.

Case study: Rachel

When Rachel looks at a photo of her toddler cuddling her newborn baby, she feels contented.

She thinks, *They are so adorable. I love them.*

Physically, she notices her face is soft and her shoulders are loose and relaxed.

Her action urge is to keep looking at the photo.

Now it's your turn. Look at the picture of the triplets below and ask yourself:

+ What are my feelings?

+ What are my thoughts?

+ What are my physical sensations?

+ What are my action urges?

Look at the picture of the pregnant woman below and ask yourself the same questions:

+ What are my feelings?

+ What are my thoughts?

+ What are my physical sensations?

+ What are my action urges?

Your responses to these pictures will be different from another person's. For example, when you look at the triplets you might think, *How do the parents cope?* and that might trigger a feeling of worry—or relief that it's not you who's feeding them! Meanwhile, another person might think, *Adorable. I bet they will have fun together*, and that might trigger a feeling of happiness or of envy.

Remember, at first it might feel strange or forced to do this, but it will start to come naturally the more you do it. The benefits of tuning in to pleasant emotions and controlling unhelpful behaviours will be worth it.

DIFFUSION

Often, just tuning in to your emotions will be enough to calm you down or remind you to behave in a helpful way. Simply recognising anger, sadness or stress early on can encourage you to take a moment to readjust your thoughts and actions. On other occasions, however, tuning in isn't enough, and we need further skills to help us to behave calmly and make wise choices.

There are two skills in particular that can help you to keep calm: diffusion and space therapy. First, let's take a closer look at diffusion.

Diffusion is a way of noticing your thoughts and detaching from them, so that they will be less potent—that is, less likely to trigger or exacerbate unhelpful feelings. When you diffuse, you separate yourself as a person from the experience you are having, which allows you to fully experience your emotions without getting caught up in them.

Research has found that people who are more troubled by their thoughts tend to 'fuse' more tightly to them, believing that their thoughts are *who* they are. This is very different from realising that, actually, the person they are just happens to be *having* thoughts.

A good way to understand diffusion is to imagine you are watching another mother in the supermarket, and she is having a challenging time with her toddler—perhaps the toddler is demanding a bar of chocolate. Think about how you would describe the emotions of that mother. Since this imaginary mother is a stranger to you, you'll most likely describe her emotional experience in a calm, detached way. The trick is to replace the imaginary mother with yourself, and to describe your own emotional responses in the same distanced way as you would hers.

An effective way to diffuse—or to separate yourself from your thoughts—is to change the way you phrase them. Instead of saying, 'I'm angry', try saying, 'I am experiencing the feeling of anger.' After all, you are not anger. Likewise, instead of saying, 'I can't stand this', try saying, 'I am experiencing the thought that I can't stand this.' Making this subtle change in language is a reminder to yourself that your mind produces your thoughts, but *you* have control over your behaviours. The following case study shows this slight difference in language.

Case study: Georgia

It's the end of the day, and Georgia has just put her newborn baby to bed. Just as she is about to sit down to have a rest, she remembers that no one has done the laundry. When she sees the enormous pile of dirty clothes waiting for her beside the washing machine, she feels irritable and stressed, her shoulders tense and she wants to slam the laundry door and forget about it.

Instead, she reminds herself to tune in to the four parts of her emotions and preface her thoughts with, *I'm experiencing...*

Her train of thought goes like this:

I'm experiencing feelings of irritability and stress. I'm experiencing the thought 'This house is so chaotic! How did it get so messy so quickly?' I'm experiencing the physical sensation that my stomach is tight and my shoulders are tense. I am experiencing the urge to slam the door.

It sounds longwinded, but by doing this Georgia is reminding herself that her thoughts are not who she is. She is diffusing.

Now, you get to have a go! Look at the following picture of a baby crying, then tune in using diffusion by asking the following questions. Remember to start your answers with 'I am experiencing . . .'

+ What feelings am I experiencing?

+ What thoughts am I experiencing?

+ What physical sensations am I experiencing?

+ What action urges am I experiencing?

SPACE THERAPY

We've already discussed that all-important space between tuning in to your emotions and acting on them, but when it comes to particularly strong or difficult emotions it helps to have some extra tools to make the best use of that space. I call this 'space therapy', and it includes two basic techniques: 1-2-3 and C-A-L-M. 1-2-3 is a technique that uses a small number of questions with 'yes' or 'no' answers, while C-A-L-M is a short list of reminders to calm yourself.

You can use either of these on their own, or you can use both. To help ensure that space therapy is successful, it's important to recognise and use the skills that work for you. Sometimes it will be enough to simply tune in to your emotions and notice how you are feeling, then remind yourself to relax and take some deep breaths. Other times, when experiences are more challenging, you may need to put these space-therapy skills to use to get you through.

Since these two skills are applied to your emotions, it's necessary to identify the nature of your emotions. When mothers report particularly difficult emotions, their thoughts generally fall into two categories: negative predictions and self-criticism.

NEGATIVE PREDICTIONS AND 1-2-3

When we are feeling distressed, we often make negative predictions. For example, if your baby is having trouble sleeping, you might think, *My baby is so unsettled. I bet he will have a difficult personality*, or, *I'm not going to sleep well for years and then I will be an irritable, terrible mother*, or, *The sleep strategies I'm using will harm my baby's development*. These are all examples of negative predictions, which are our mind's way of trying to eliminate uncertainty about the future. We believe that, if we can predict the worst, then there will be fewer surprises waiting for us. However, instead of reassuring us, making negative predictions really just sends us into a downward spiral of anxiety and uncertainty.

While no thoughts are 'right' or 'wrong', some thoughts are more helpful than others. Sad thoughts make us sadder. Anxious thoughts increase our anxiety. Actively noticing when you make negative predictions is important, otherwise they can hum around in your mind, triggering and increasing your worry.

Once you have tuned in to negative predictions, there are a few questions that you can calmly ask yourself.

1. Is there hard evidence that this prediction is true, or is it driven by emotion?

2. Can this negative prediction be problem-solved?

3. Is making this prediction helping me?

The following case study shows how Nicola puts these questions—or the skill of 1-2-3—to use when she tunes in to negative predictions.

Case study: Nicola

Nicola's son is nearly one and is still waking up in the middle of the night for a feed. In the wee hours of the morning, while she feeds her son, she starts making negative predictions, thinking, *My baby will never give up his night feed. I'm going to be doing this forever!*

She then tunes in to her emotions, using diffusion. *I am experiencing the feeling of being angry,* she thinks. *I have an action urge to rock him in an abrasive way.*

In the space between tuning in to her emotion and responding to it, she asks herself the 1-2-3 questions, and comes up with the following answers.

1. *There is no hard evidence that this prediction is true. All babies eventually give up their night feeds. I'm just tired right now.*
2. *Maybe the night feeding can be solved eventually . . . but not right now.*
3. *Making this prediction isn't helping me right now. It is spiralling me down.*

Nicola's goal is to calmly get through this feed, and asking the 1-2-3 questions helps her to do that by giving her perspective on emotion-driven predictions.

WHEN TO LET IT GO

If you can problem-solve a negative prediction immediately, then go ahead.

If you need to wait until later to problem-solve it, then make a time to do so and stick to it.

However, if the thought has no solution, then simply acknowledge it—*Thanks for the thought, mind*—and let it slide away, like butter off a hot pan. Then change your focus to whatever it is that you are doing in that moment—cuddling your baby, reading a book, making dinner, looking at a leaf, listening to the radio. You might have to do this over and over until your mind tires of the cycle of negative predictions.

SELF-CRITICISM AND 1-2-3

Feeling stressed or unhappy makes us prone to self-criticism, and thoughts such as *I'm not a good mother* or *I'm hopeless at settling my baby*. Often self-critical thoughts have a 'should' in them, for example, *I should be able to settle my own baby*, *I should be able to keep up with the housework* or *I should be able to look after my baby on my own.*

Judging yourself negatively in this manner is your mind's way of trying to get you to improve yourself, to lift your game. However, just like negative predictions, these thoughts rarely do what they are supposed to, and instead send our mood into a downward spiral, which is counterproductive to good mothering.

When you notice self-critical thoughts, there are a few questions you can ask yourself.

1. Is there hard evidence that this thought is true or is it driven by emotion?

2. Is this thought helping me?

3. What would I tell a friend who was having this thought?

The following case study shows how Kate puts these questions—or the skill of 1-2-3—to use when she tunes in to self-critical thoughts.

Case study: Kate

Kate is a partner at a law firm, and in her professional life she is very used to handling complex situations and tricky clients. Now, when her eight-month-old son, Gus, cries for lengthy periods she feels helpless. She thinks she is an incompetent mother.

She tunes in to her emotions and thinks, *I am experiencing the thought that I am incompetent. I am experiencing a feeling of helplessness. I am experiencing an action urge to sit and dwell on my shortcomings.*

Then, in the space between tuning in to her emotions and acting on them, she asks herself the 1-2-3 questions and comes up with the following answers.

1. *There's no evidence that this thought is true. After all, who says I should be able to settle Gus easily? I have fed him, changed him and now I am holding him. I am doing exactly what a competent mother does.*

2. *This thought is not constructive. Since there's no hard evidence that I'm an incompetent mother, it's not constructive to brood about this thought. The best thing to do is to let it slide off me and away.*

3. *I'd tell a friend, 'Your baby is fed and warm. You are a competent and good mother. All babies cry—it's frustrating, but it's normal.'*

Kate's goal is to continue to sit calmly with Gus and remind herself that she is doing the best that can be done. Asking the 1-2-3 questions helps her to remember that it is normal for babies to cry, and that she is doing a good job.

WHO SAYS?

Self-criticism often arises from the idea that you *should* be doing something more or something different. It also arises from the misguided notion that, if things are not perfect, it is because you haven't done something you *should* have done. And, to add to it all, there are many people only too willing to heap guilt on a mother for not doing what they think she *should* do.

So, if you tune in to self-critical thoughts that include the word 'should', ask yourself 'Who says?'

For example, where is it written that you should be able to care for a baby *plus* have visitors *and* keep on top of the house? Who says you should be able to make your own baby food instead of buying it?

That pesky word 'should' too often gets in the way of mothers asking for help, as they think, *I should be able to do this on my own.*

A good trick is to replace 'I should' with 'I prefer'. You might *prefer* to be doing things a certain way, but a preference is different from a 'should'.

C-A-L-M

Many of the mothers I work with love this skill! C-A-L-M stands for: Child-centred, Accept the situation, Lose the tension, and Make mindful choices. Like 1-2-3, you can use C-A-L-M in the space between your emotion and your behaviour, and you can use all of C-A-L-M or just the parts that work for you at any given time. C-A-L-M can be used when you have difficult emotions but need to behave effectively instead of following unhelpful action urges.

Here's some more detail on each of those parts.

+ **Child-centred.** Ask yourself, 'What does my baby need right now?' Ask yourself this frequently throughout your day. The Circle of Security (see pages 51–52) offers a great example answer: 'My baby needs me to be bigger, stronger, wiser and kind.'

+ **Accept the situation.** Ask yourself, 'Can I change this situation?' If you can't change it, then simply accepting the situation can help to keep you calm. Remember, accepting is not the same as liking.

+ **Lose the tension.** Take a moment to notice where you are tense, then focus on relaxing that part (or parts) of your body. Notice your breathing, too. Noticing may help to soften shallow or fast breathing.

+ **Make mindful choices.** You can't choose your emotions, but you can be aware of them—and then choose to behave calmly in response.

Case study: Kim

Kim has a doctor's appointment to get to, and is trying to get everyone out of the house so she can make it in time. Just as she is bundling everyone out of the house, her toddler takes her shoes off—and refuses to put them back on. Meanwhile, the baby has soiled his nappy and needs a change *right now*. Kim is poised to feel angry, so she tunes in to her emotions.

I am feeling angry, she tells herself. *I'm thinking, 'Why am I always late? Why is this happening to me? I can't stand this! Why won't she put her shoes on?*

Kim notices that her shoulders are tense, and that she's tearful and breathing hard. Her action urge is to shout, but in the space between her emotion and her behaviour she uses C-A-L-M as follows.

Child-centred: *My children need me to be bigger, stronger, wiser and kind. I am going to talk in a calm voice and remember that my daughter is only three and that babies have no control over when they need a nappy change. If we are a bit late it is not the end of the world.*

Accept the situation: *I can't change that we are running late and that my baby needs a new nappy. I don't like it, but that's the way it is. Losing my cool will only make things worse.*

Lose the tension: *I'll soften my shoulders and pay attention to my breathing.*

Make mindful choices: *I know I have an action urge to shout, but this is my choice. I can choose to do something different.*

Kim's goal is to calmly change her baby's nappy and leave the house without shouting at her toddler. C-A-L-M helps Kim do that by allowing her to use the space between her emotion and behaviour to reflect on what is important.

CHAPTER 4: THE MAIN POINTS

+ Good 'emotional regulation' means having the ability to respond to experiences with a range of emotions and to behave in an effective way. When you respond to your baby in a calm way, she feels safe, secure and positive about her environment.

+ Tune in to your emotions by identifying the four parts of emotions: feelings, thoughts, physical sensations and action urges.

+ When you are tuning in to your emotions, try to notice them gently, without judgement. Remember that all feelings come to an end and a thought is just a thought.

+ The more you practise tuning in, the easier it will become. Use the space between tuning in to your emotion and acting on it to choose how you will behave.

+ When you tune in to difficult emotions, you can use diffusion or space therapy. Space therapy includes the skills 1-2-3 and C-A-L-M.

CHAPTER 5
REFLECTING ON YOUR
BIRTH EXPERIENCE

Mothering myth: A good mother gives birth vaginally, without any pain relief or medical interventions.

Truth: The way you give birth has absolutely nothing to do with whether you are a good mother.

Giving birth is a big deal. It doesn't matter who you are or how you do it, it is a truly pivotal life event for every single mother who experiences it. No two births are the same, and every mother is an individual. Even for the same woman, one birth experience can be completely different from another. Every woman comes to the birth process with her own expectations, wishes, pain thresholds, philosophies and professional advice. Some births go smoothly and meet those expectations and wishes; some births have moments of triumph; some births are better than the mother could ever have dreamed. However, some births are disappointing and some are traumatic.

Elsewhere in life when we experience a momentous event—for instance, travelling to a foreign country or embarking on a new career—we spend time reflecting on it and talking about it with friends and family. We discuss the parts we loved, and we share the parts we found difficult. However, when it comes to reflecting on the experience of labour and birth, sometimes the chance to do so is eclipsed by the other important events that quickly rack up: feeding, bonding, soothing and so on. Many women have told me that the first time they talked about their birth experiences was with women they barely knew at a mothers' coffee morning.

It's a good idea to ensure that you get some time to reflect on your birth experience, ideally in the days after labour. Reflecting means you examine your thoughts and feelings, alone or with others. In the case of birth, the thoughts and feelings you experienced during labour can influence your mood in your early days as a mother. Sometimes mothers recognise this well after the birth is behind them, and wish they had taken the time to process their experience earlier. Indeed, it's a pity to not relish feelings of pride and satisfaction, or to share disappointing birth experiences with people you trust.

TRIGGER WARNING FOR READERS

Sometimes, mothers feel confused about what happened during parts of their labour. For example, they might wonder why their birth plan wasn't followed, or whether there were periods of risk during the birth. If this is the case for you, know that you can ask to go over your medical notes with your maternity provider.

A word of warning: if you experienced a particularly difficult or traumatic birth, you might not want to start reflecting deeply until you are with someone you trust. Therefore, I suggest you skip over the questions which follow in the box on page 127.

If your birth experience is impacting on your mood or your mothering, then it is best to contact a health professional.

REFLECTING ON YOUR LABOUR AND BIRTH EXPERIENCE

To guide you in your reflections, ask yourself the following questions.

+ What wishes, plans and expectations did you have for your labour? Did you have a birth plan, and was it followed?

+ What influenced any plans you had? Was it your values? Societal expectations? Information you had seen online, or heard from relatives, friends or lobby groups?

+ Think about the intensity and length of your labour. What was the best part? What do you wish was different?

+ What positive and negative feelings did you experience? What thoughts and specific events during labour were these feelings linked to?

+ What professionals were with you? Did they listen to your wishes and point of view? Were they compassionate?

+ What feelings did you have when you first saw your baby? What thoughts did you have?

BIRTH TRAUMA

Birth trauma is common and can arise from different experiences, some dramatic and life-threatening and others related to feelings of helplessness. It may resolve with time and reflection, but sometimes women need professional support to recover.

There is no standard definition for birth trauma; a woman's

interpretation of events is what dictates whether a birth is traumatic. For example, in the UK 1 per cent of births are considered life-threatening yet about 25 per cent of women report feeling traumatised.[1] A woman certainly doesn't have to perceive her labour as life-threatening or dangerous to feel traumatised. Trauma can be a result of the mother not feeling listened to, cared for or respected. It can also be a result of her feeling a lack of control during labour.

Traumatic memories trigger difficult feelings such as distress, anger or fear. Memories that trigger intense emotions are sometimes referred to as 'hot memories'. Hot memories are overwhelming. We want them to eventually become 'unpleasant memories', which is to say memories that are unpleasant to think about but don't overwhelm you. Often these memories naturally fade from 'hot' to 'unpleasant' simply by talking with people who care about you, but sometimes professional support is necessary. How helpful talking is will partly depend on who you are talking with and how they respond to what you tell them. Some people will be more skilful at giving you the support you need. There are also online forums and support groups that you might find helpful.

For some mothers, without professional help, the distress from birth trauma can persist for years, and can even put them off having future pregnancies. What's more, sometimes the impact of trauma is delayed and doesn't rear its head until a subsequent pregnancy. I have worked with women who experienced birth trauma but left it unexplored, only to find themselves frightened about the prospect of labour when they became pregnant again.

CHILDBIRTH-RELATED POST-TRAUMATIC STRESS DISORDER (PTSD)

Up to 6 per cent of women who experience birth trauma will go on to develop postpartum PTSD (post-traumatic stress disorder). PTSD differs from birth trauma in that certain criteria need to be met in order for a diagnosis of PTSD to be made. Mothers who develop childbirth-related PTSD commonly report:

+ avoiding situations that remind them of the birth (this can be particularly distressing if the sight of her baby triggers a mother's distress)

+ intrusive thoughts or images about the birth

+ nightmares

+ a changeable or low mood

+ flashbacks

+ difficulty bonding

+ fear of medical interventions or future births.

Some of the factors that contribute to the emergence of PTSD include:

+ a difference between the amount of care a mother expects from health professionals during labour and the amount she actually receives (for example, if she encounters a lack of compassion or respect during labour and birth)

+ having a baby who spends time in a neonatal intensive care unit (NICU)

+ having a baby who is stillborn.

+ experiencing unexpected medical interventions, such as an emergency Caesarean section

+ a personal history of trauma or abuse.

Not everyone responds to the same events in the same way. Whether or not you are traumatised by an event depends on how you interpret it. For example, if you interpret a heart-monitor reading as dangerous, this might traumatise you regardless of whether or not there was actually any real danger. For similar reasons, partners or others who were part of the birthing process can also be traumatised—and sometimes partners are traumatised even when the birth mother is not.

Post-traumatic symptoms are a normal response to a traumatic experience; your mind is trying to make sense of the trauma through re-experiencing it. Symptoms will often resolve over a month or so, but if they don't or if they are interfering with your day-to-day life, then you need to deal with this quickly. If at any time you think you or your baby is at risk because of your mood, please get help straight away. Helpful interventions include debriefing with a professional and therapeutic interventions such as cognitive behavioural therapy, specifically exposure and response prevention (ERP). ERP involves being guided through controlled exposure to traumatic memories with the goal of diminishing distress. If you see a professional, make sure they are qualified and use evidence-based models of therapy.

GUILT

Many mothers feel guilt about their labour and birth experience. For some women, this guilt arises from being unable to give birth vaginally; for others it's because they used pain relief; and for yet others it's attached to the IVF process. All of these forms of guilt have little to do with fact, and a lot to do with expectations. Let's take a closer look at each, starting with the most common: guilt about having a Caesarean section.

CAESAREAN GUILT

Sadly, many women feel guilty or ashamed about having a Caesarean section (C-section). Unbelievably, they are sometimes even shamed by other mothers or by special-interest lobby groups who promote generalisations and misinformation as fact. The phrase 'too posh to push' is often bandied about in the West, and illustrates how some people view mothers who have a C-section. It is understandable that a woman who has been traumatised by the circumstances that lead to her C-section would find this judgement particularly stinging. It is important to realise that emergency and most elective (planned) C-sections are necessary for health reasons.

In New Zealand approximately one in four births are by C-section. Over half of these are emergency C-sections.[2] The remaining C-sections are classified as 'elective', but that term is misleading. People generally think elective surgery is a matter of personal choice and does not involve a genuine medical justification. However, in the case of elective C-sections, there are often serious medical considerations behind the decision. Perhaps a better terminology would be 'planned'. The rate of C-sections in the UK[3] and in the USA[4] are similar.

Let's make one thing clear: if you give birth by C-section you should be every bit as proud of yourself as if you'd given birth vaginally. Many women are relieved that they had a C-section, and felt in control and fortunate that their baby was helped by modern medicine. However, there are also many mothers who feel a sense of failure because they needed a Caesarean delivery. Unfortunately, this sense of failure can lead to depression. When I see mothers who are experiencing Caesarean guilt, they often tell me that they replay their birth experience in their mind, wondering if they could have done anything differently—eaten differently, been more assertive, walked differently, breathed differently. Many wonder if they weren't 'strong' enough to avoid having a C-section.

That is a shame, because there are many valid reasons for having a C-section: a medical emergency, health risks to mother or baby, and also psychological reasons. Regarding psychological reasons, if a woman has a history of sexual abuse she might fear that giving birth vaginally will re-traumatise her. Indeed, the routine check-ups performed by professionals during pregnancy can be re-traumatising all on their own. Another reason might be that a woman has a deep sense of fear (or a phobia) about vaginal birth, possibly as a result of either her own experiences, such as a previous traumatic birth, or observing and hearing about the difficult birth experiences of others. With professional support, birth phobias can often be worked through, but unfortunately specifically targeted research-based interventions are hard to come by without a large price tag attached. From what I've experienced working in New Zealand and in the UK, and heard about from people in the USA, I am unaware of any public services in any of those places that offer a good number of free or low-cost sessions for birth phobia, unless a woman is in severe distress.

It is important to recognise that, for some women and their babies, vaginal birth can be very dangerous indeed. There are small risks associated with C-section births, but 'natural' birth advocates often exaggerate the safety and benefits of vaginal birth over Caesarean. The most cited evidence for a link between the type of delivery and health outcomes is the difference in the intestinal bacteria (the microbiome) of infants born by C-section compared with those born vaginally; the suggestion is that vaginally delivered babies benefit from picking up their mother's bacteria as they pass through the vagina, and many unsubstantiated claims about the long-term effect of this are made.

VAGINAL SEEDING

Those who hold the belief that exposure to bacteria through vaginal birth is beneficial are understandably very concerned about C-section births. Many mothers who must have C-section deliveries are also worried. In 2016 a 'study' of four (yes, four) infants delivered by C-section and swabbed with their mother's vaginal fluid was published.[5] The researchers claimed this 'partially' restored the newborn's microbiome and called the procedure 'vaginal seeding'. Following this publication, there was an explosion of mothers demanding that their baby be swabbed immediately after birth. If the doctors refused, some mothers were doing it themselves.

The amount of serious infection, sometimes life-threatening, which resulted from this practice caused alarm in the medical community. Babies were exposed to diseases that mothers were unaware they were carrying. Consequently, in 2018 a thorough review of all the research in that area was carried out by the Division of Obstetrics and Gynaecology at the University of Western Australia.[6] It found the research was seriously flawed by extremely small numbers (between five and 20 C-section mothers) and a failure to control for variables. They found that newborns acquired all their maternal microbiomes inside the placenta, and that they did not pick up any detectable microbiomes in the course of a vaginal delivery. They did find a 'transient' (very short-term) difference between the microbiome of babies born by C-section and vaginally born babies, but demonstrated that this was almost entirely due to antibiotics used in the course of C-section delivery.

The message the researchers were keen to give was this: you will not change your baby's microbiome through applying vaginal swabs. The researchers said that, should future research show there is indeed a benefit from 'vaginal seeding', parents should use safer probiotic formulations of vaginal bacteria, which are already on the commercial market. The guidelines of both the American College of Obstetricians and Gynecologists and the Danish Society of Obstetrics and Gynaecology support this advice.[7] As it happens, a serious study in this area will take place in New Zealand. Researchers in Auckland are preparing to carry out a double-blind twin study of 40 twin pairs in which one baby in each pair will be seeded following C-section and the other will not. It will be some time before this study is complete, and many years before anything can be said about more than transient differences.

Researchers have identified a number of risk factors for vaginal delivery, including:

+ diabetes mellitus

+ having had a previous C-section

+ having narrow hips or being short (implying narrow hips)

+ depression

+ being obese

+ the mother's age (a first-time mother at age 40 has twice the chance of irreversible faecal incontinence following a vaginal birth than a 20-year-old first-time mother).

C-section does, of course, come with its own risks. It certainly increases the risk of both infant and maternal infection, and it may also involve more pain and discomfort following birth. However, since C-section rates are increasing at the same time as such health concerns as asthma and diabetes, the procedure may have been unfairly blamed for these disorders and more. There is a great deal of speculation connecting C-sections with negative outcomes. Some studies point to an association between Caesarean section and obesity and asthma. However, the number of studies is small, and many have not included important confounders such as parental obesity and atopy.

One study linking C-section delivery with obesity had an odd result showing that for most children there was no significant difference in obesity associated with how they were born, but for a small group of children, not only was there a difference in weight but the difference was massive. Such a peculiar result raises questions about the sample selection.[8] However, because you might well expect consequences from early exposure to antibiotics (which is inextricable with C-section delivery), longer-term consequences of C-sections are worthy of further study. As you will see in the appendices, researchers in a number of areas have been calling out for studies into the long-term effects of antibiotics.

DOCTORS TOLD TO DISCLOSE RISKS OF VAGINAL BIRTH

In 2015, the Supreme Court of the United Kingdom ruled that women who face any risks if they give birth vaginally must be told of those risks.[9] The particular case in point was that of Nadine Montgomery, whose son was born in 1999 with serious disabilities as a result of suffering oxygen deprivation during his birth. Despite the fact that Montgomery had type 1 diabetes, and was therefore at risk of a number of significant birth complications, her obstetrician decided not to warn her of those risks, in case it would influence her to have a C-section. Women with type 1 diabetes are more likely to have larger than average babies, and also have a 10 per cent chance of a serious condition called 'shoulder dystocia' during birth. When shoulder dystocia occurs, the baby becomes trapped. It is an obstetric emergency, and poses a danger to both the mother and the child—and it's exactly what happened to Montgomery. As a result, complications arose during delivery, and her son was deprived of oxygen and ultimately born with serious disabilities. Montgomery later indicated that if she had been aware of the risks she would have opted for a C-section.[10]

The Court held that medical staff should have warned Montgomery about these risks, and awarded her a landmark sum of £5.25 million in compensation. In her judgment, Supreme Court Justice Lady Hale described the obstetrician's behaviour as 'paternalistic' and her views on Caesarean delivery as no more than a personal value judgement. Wherever a mother or a child is at risk from vaginal delivery, Lady Hale determined, doctors *must* volunteer both the pros and cons of Caesarean delivery. Furthermore, the other judges hearing the case clarified that whether or not this information was provided was not to be 'reduced to percentages' of risk. If there is any risk at all, mothers must be told.

SOME TIPS FOR PREVENTING CAESAREAN GUILT
If you know you are having a C-section, here are some suggestions.

+ Beware of the mothering myths you might hear about the importance of vaginal, non-medical, no-medication births.

Both vaginal and Caesarean births carry their own small risks.

+ Be flexible. By all means have your ideal birth plan, but also imagine and talk about various scenarios with a health professional before you give birth. Be sure to discuss any concerns you might have about birth interventions with a health professional you trust and your birth partner or support person.

+ Remember that you are far from alone. One in four women in New Zealand, the UK and the USA have C-sections.

SOME TIPS FOR OVERCOMING CAESAREAN GUILT

If you have had a C-section and are feeling a sense of guilt attached to the experience, the following might help.

+ Remember you were supported by a medical professional who had both your interests and your baby's at heart.

+ No matter what, you did what you thought was best at the time. That is exactly what good mothering is all about.

+ Every birth is different, but the desired outcome is the same: a healthy baby.

PAIN-RELIEF GUILT

Many mothers worry that pain relief during delivery might affect their baby. There are still those out there who argue that a mother shouldn't interfere with the pain of childbirth, because it is an important part of mother–infant bonding. Let me assure you, this is not true.

But, what of other potential effects of pain relief during childbirth? Some have claimed that pain-relief medications (analgesics), including epidural, affect the baby's respiration and cause neurological impairment. However, a 2014 meta-analysis of research in that area found no differences between infants born with the help of epidural drugs and those who were not.[11] The review included a massive total sample size of 2,859 newborns, and considered only studies which were randomised and controlled for confounding variables. It looked at side effects using the Apgar score (the measure of the physical condition of a newborn infant), which includes respiratory depression and neurobehavioural changes in newborns.

Although there have been a lot of claims about adverse effects of pain relief during childbirth, the limited research in the area does not confirm adverse outcomes. There is no reason to feel guilty if you have chosen to have pain relief.

IVF GUILT

Successful in-vitro fertilisation is frequently accompanied with a surprising guilt tax, and a number of women I see suffer from IVF guilt. 'I ought to be happy. What's wrong with me?' these mothers often ask themselves. 'How dare I complain about a tough childbirth or start to mothering? I should be grateful, especially when we paid such a massive amount of money for it.'

These mothers have what some psychologists call 'the double bad': they feel bad about feeling bad, and this can cause a downward spiral. As it stands, women who have undergone IVF are already at an increased risk of perinatal (pregnancy and post-birth) emotional health difficulties, but they can also feel guilty about having these difficulties. As a result, these mothers are more likely to hide their distress and less likely to ask for support.

Anyone who has had IVF knows why they are more vulnerable to perinatal emotional health problems. Here are just some of the distressing thoughts mothers I've worked with have voiced.

+ 'After so many miscarriages, dashed hopes and hormone injections, I was running on empty before the pregnancy even took hold.'

+ 'By the time I was four months pregnant, I was recovering from the trauma of repeatedly not being pregnant. I was a nervous wreck, just waiting to miscarry.'

+ 'I didn't dare to bond with my baby while I was pregnant. I was frightened to in case I lost her. It didn't ever seem real. When she came, I was not mentally prepared for motherhood because I had blocked out thinking about what being a mother would be like, to avoid disappointment.'

+ 'There was no way I could tell my family that I felt sad during my pregnancy. They had been through so many ups and downs with me while I was trying to get pregnant, and finally they were happy for me. I didn't want to wear them out any more.'

+ 'God, it was so exhausting, pretending not to be anxious and depressed throughout my pregnancy. Everyone was so happy for me, and I had to play along. When I had my baby, I couldn't fake it any more, but I didn't know who to turn to.'

+ 'No way was I going to tell anyone that I didn't enjoy being a new mother. The humiliation! Especially after crying on their shoulder when I couldn't get pregnant.'

+ 'I was frightened to tell my husband I was depressed, in case he didn't want to try for another baby. I really want two. Also, we had remortgaged the house. How could I tell him I wasn't coping?'

SOME TIPS FOR OVERCOMING IVF GUILT

+ Remember the only difference between you and mothers who didn't need IVF is how you conceived. In every other way, you and your baby are exactly like any other mother–baby pair. You have exactly the same reasons and rights as anyone to feel whatever you feel when you are pregnant, during childbirth and after.

+ Perinatal emotional difficulties can happen to anyone and, guess what? You had a harder road getting here than many other mothers. If you are depressed or anxious, it is more than likely that your painful fertility journey contributed to the way you feel.

+ Don't bottle up your emotions. Ask your friends and family for help. Chances are, nobody expects you to be immune to the emotional difficulties that all mothers share.

+ Get professional help if you need it sooner rather than later. Feeling bad about feeling bad is not helpful for anyone.

CHAPTER 5: THE MAIN POINTS

+ It can be helpful to take some quiet time to reflect on your labour and birth experience in the days after having your baby. Relish feelings of pride and satisfaction, or share disappointment with people you trust.

+ Birth trauma is common and can result from different experiences. While it may resolve with time and reflection, many women also need professional support to recover.

+ If you have a C-section, remember this: there is no reason that you shouldn't feel the same sense of satisfaction and pride as if you give birth vaginally.

+ If you use pain relief during labour, know that it will not interfere with you bonding with your baby.

+ If you have had IVF, you have every right to experience all the same feelings as any other new mother—including difficulties and distress.

CHAPTER 6
BABY BLUES AND BEYOND

Mothering myth: Motherhood brings nothing but joy.

Truth: Motherhood brings joy *and* stress. Many mothers experience the baby blues, and up to 10 per cent experience perinatal depression. It's a mark of good mothering to ask for help if you need it.

Since you will experience a whole range of emotions post-birth, it's completely normal to have some emotional turbulence. Many women wonder how they *should* feel post-birth, asking themselves, 'Should I feel content? Should I feel blissful and happy?' They might also worry if they don't feel the way they think they should.

Well, there's no *one* way you should feel about any new experience—let alone childbirth and becoming a mother. Fluctuating emotions after childbirth are extremely common, but it can be tricky to figure out whether you're experiencing the baby blues, which can appear in the first few days after your baby is born, or a more serious perinatal mental health condition. If it's the latter, it's time to ask for help. Even if you're not sure, ask for help—it never hurts to ask, but it might hurt if you don't.

Let's take a closer look at the conditions a new mother might experience, starting with the most common: the baby blues.

THE BABY BLUES

The baby blues affect many mothers, and are not considered a mental health difficulty. Most mothers find that the blues resolve with time and with self-care. It is important to clarify that the baby blues are *not* the same thing as postnatal depression. The blues usually appear from day two following birth and last from a few hours to about two weeks. If your mood is particularly low or is not stabilising after a couple of weeks, do not shrug this off as the blues; you should see a professional.

Some mothers describe the baby blues as being like exaggerated premenstrual tension, and some notice a more dramatic change in mood for a short period of time (less than two weeks). Symptoms might include the following.

+ You might feel more vulnerable and sensitive than usual.

+ You might have spells of crying or irritability.

+ You might have periods of low mood, sadness or anxiety.

Given the hormonal changes in your body immediately post-childbirth combined with the complexities of mothering a newborn, it is little wonder so many women experience the baby blues. During pregnancy, your levels of the hormones oestrogen and progesterone are higher than at any other time in your life, but they plummet after childbirth and this can trigger the baby blues. Hormones are not the only factor, either. Giving birth can be profound but also exhausting, and parts of your labour might have left you feeling out of control or even distressed. To add to this, mothering your newborn can present all manner of challenges; for instance, parts of your body might be sore, it is likely you are sleep-deprived, and if you breastfeed you might have trouble or pain.

TREATING THE BABY BLUES

Even though most new mothers get the blues, it's still important to address them and take care of yourself.

First, remind yourself that most mothers go through the same thing. You are not alone. It is not your fault.

Next, make self-care a priority. See the tips box below.

TIPS FOR SELF-CARE

+ **Sleep when your baby sleeps.** This adage is a popular one, and there's actually a good reason for that. I cannot overstate the importance of sleep when it comes to preventing depression and other mental health difficulties. I know it can be hard to do, but try to get some sleep as soon as your baby sleeps, since you don't know when he will next wake up. Make sleep a priority, especially in the early days. Prioritise sleep before the housework, social media or visitors.

+ **Get practical support.** Ask friends and family for help. There is always something others can do for you and your baby, such as washing the dishes, cooking a meal or soothing your baby.

+ **Get emotional support.** Ask others to encourage you to rest, to make sure you eat well, to notice and tell you when you are being a good mother. Importantly, when they do this, *allow* them to do it. Ask them to be calm and supportive if you cry, to reassure you if you are worried, and to help you keep visitors to a minimum when you are tired.

+ **Heal.** Gentle exercise helps heal your body and keep your mood up—*gentle* being the key word here. A walk is great, but this is no time to train for a marathon.

+ **Self-compassion.** Mothering is complex, and perfection is impossible. Perfection simply doesn't exist. Be kind to yourself. (For more on practising self-compassion, see pages 97–99.)

Case study: Maree

Maree came to see me when her second child, Ben, was one month old. She told me she'd felt fine during her pregnancy and was happy to be a second-time mother, however she did have a previous history of depression—one episode in her early twenties after a relationship breakup, and a second after the birth of her first child, who was now three years old. On both occasions the depression had resolved within months with the help of therapy and medication.

Since Maree had realistic expectations, she wasn't surprised when the baby blues surfaced a few days after Ben was born. By the time she came to me, her mood had generally improved, but she wasn't getting much sleep and felt overwhelmed and tearful.

I soon learned that Maree wasn't taking the opportunity to sleep when she got it during the day or in the early evening, because she was prioritising her to-do list. When her baby slept and her toddler was at day-care, she was doing the chores. Like so many mothers, Maree found it hard to get used to the slow pace of being at home with a newborn again. She struggled to limit herself to two main goals: attending to her children, and looking after herself.

Maree and I worked on her gaining a sense of accomplishment from mothering well, while also keeping her sense of identity as a professional and an art-lover. She learned the importance of prioritising sleep over *everything* except the absolute must-dos—for example, the family *needed* clean clothes (a must-do), but the laundry didn't *need* to be folded.

When I saw Maree just before she went back to work, Ben was nine months old. She was able to look back over her time at home with him and feel a sense of satisfaction and accomplishment—she had raised a contented little nine-month-old *and* a three-year-old *and* staved off depression and anxiety!

WHEN IT'S MORE THAN JUST 'THE BLUES'

Although the blues and postnatal depression share some symptoms, they are not the same. Symptoms in common can include low mood, poor concentration, feeling dependant on others, crying and irritability. However, depression (unlike the blues) is sustained over time and, in addition to low mood, sufferers often find that little provides them with pleasure. Depression can also be accompanied by persistent feelings of low self-worth, thoughts about not being a good enough mother, and feeling despondent about the future.

Whereas the baby blues usually appears between two and five days post-birth, postnatal depression can emerge any time in the first year with a spike in prevalence at two or three months post-birth. Some women describe depression as building up slowly, while others notice a sudden drop in mood or pleasure.

We expect the blues to resolve within two weeks, usually with self-care alone. Postnatal depression, on the other hand, can last much longer and even persist for years if left untreated.

If you notice depression any time during the first year post-birth, approach a maternal-care specialist.

TAKE IT SERIOUSLY

Thoughts or plans to harm yourself or your baby require immediate professional help. Suicide is the highest contributor to maternal death in the first year following birth, and family and friends *must* take any disclosures of this kind seriously.

Some mothers and families fear that professionals will judge them as 'unfit' if they report thoughts about self-harm or harming others. Let me assure you, I have never come across a professional who takes this view. Quite the reverse, in fact. When mothers come forward for help, professionals see this as a positive sign.

In the absence of 'risk' thoughts (of harming or self-harm), it can be difficult to tease out when you need professional support—but you don't need to figure this out alone. A good rule of thumb is: if you are wondering, always approach a professional.

PERINATAL MENTAL HEALTH

Until recently, postnatal depression was the main focus of research and intervention within the arena of perinatal mental health. However, we now know that mental health difficulties are just as likely to arise during pregnancy as in the year following birth. Half of all depressive episodes occur before the birth, so the focus has expanded to include both periods—what's referred to as the perinatal period.

The perinatal period extends from conception to one year after birth, and the umbrella term 'perinatal distress' is now used to describe all the different mental health difficulties which occur within that timeframe. The proportion of mothers reaching a diagnosable level of perinatal distress is about 10–15 per cent,[1] although some studies say up to 20 per cent.[2] Perinatal mental health difficulties include anxiety and depression, as well as conditions such as post-traumatic stress disorder (PTSD), obsessive compulsive disorder (OCD) and bipolar disorder. The tendency of perinatal mental health difficulties to co-occur is the rule rather than the exception—so, where one perinatal mental health difficulty is identified, it is likely that another will also be present. For example, depression often co-occurs with general anxiety or panic attacks. When two or more mental health diagnoses are present at the same time, professionals use the term 'comorbidity', and comorbidity is associated with worse mother and baby outcomes.

Perinatal distress can strike anyone. It strikes lawyers, teachers, accountants, stay-at-home mothers and artists. It strikes those who you might think have special skills to give them immunity, such as nurses, kindergarten teachers, psychologists and obstetricians. It even strikes celebrities—and women such as Courteney Cox and Brooke Shields have done a great service by revealing their own struggles.

With the right intervention, it is possible to recover from perinatal distress. Getting on to it quickly is a key to success. Read on to familiarise yourself with the signs and symptoms of both the common perinatal concerns (depression, anxiety and OCD) and the less common but very serious (bipolar disorder and psychosis).

PERINATAL DEPRESSION AND ANXIETY

Clinicians recognise that perinatal depression can happen any time during pregnancy, or at any time during the first year following birth. The symptoms are the same, regardless of whether depression occurs before or after birth. Anxiety can occur alongside depression or on its own, and at least as many women suffer from perinatal anxiety as from depression. It is completely normal for new parents to experience a little worry during and following pregnancy. However, too much anxiety and worry can interfere with your enjoyment of life and your ability to cope with the daily activities associated with parenting. Persistent feelings of anxiety or panic that last longer than two weeks indicate that you should contact a professional.

First, let's look at the symptoms of perinatal depression. In order to diagnose perinatal depression, many clinicians use the *Diagnostic and Statistical Manual of Mental Disorders, Fifth Edition* (DSM-5) criteria. It is the same criteria for depression that is used at any other time of life, but needs to take the impact of having a new baby into account. Five or more of the following symptoms need to be present during the same two-week period, and need to represent a change from your usual level of coping. Additionally, at least one of the symptoms must be either of the first two points—depressed mood, or loss of interest or pleasure.

+ Depressed mood most of the day and nearly every day, as noticed by you (for example, you feel sad, empty or hopeless) or as observed by others (for example, you appear tearful)

+ Markedly diminished interest or pleasure in all (or almost all) activities most of the day and nearly every day (as noticed by you or by others)

+ Significant weight loss or gain, or a decrease or increase in appetite [taking into account breastfeeding]

+ Difficulty sleeping [even when you are tired and your baby is sleeping] or oversleeping

+ Others observe you being restless or slowed down in your movements

+ Fatigue or loss of energy [even if you have had a good sleep]

+ Feelings of worthlessness or excessive guilt

+ Difficulty concentrating, poor memory or difficulty making decisions

+ Thoughts of death, self-harm or suicide.[3]

There is a very useful and well-validated screening tool (see opposite) which is specific for postnatal depression but has also been validated for use during pregnancy. The Edinburgh Postnatal Depression Scale (EPDS) is a screening tool because it cannot be used to make a clinical diagnosis—it does not replace a professional assessment. Some professionals advise that you contact your health provider if your score is 10 or higher. A score of 13 or more for English-speaking women indicates that depression is very likely. (Note that the cut-off for fathers is two points lower than for mothers—this is because men often score lower on items such as crying, but carry the same level of distress nonetheless.) If you have a positive score on Question 10 you should reach out for help immediately.

The EPDS has been translated into many different languages (with the cut-off score differing between cultures). If you are in doubt about your score you might find it useful to repeat the EPDS in two weeks' time. Answer the questions yourself, without consulting others, unless your English is limited. Remember, this is a screening tool and does not replace an assessment; if in doubt always reach out for help.

EDINBURGH POSTNATAL DEPRESSION
SCALE (EPDS)[4]

Tick the answer that comes closest to how you have felt in the past 7 days–not just how you feel today. Find your score by adding each number beside your ticked answer. [See previous page for advice regarding interpretation of your score.]

1. I have been able to laugh and see the funny side of things:

    As much as I always could   ___ (0)

    Not quite so much now   ___ (1)

    Definitely not so much now   ___ (2)

    Not at all   ___ (3)

2. I have looked forward with enjoyment to things:

    As much as I ever did   ___ (0)

    Rather less than I used to   ___ (1)

    Definitely less than I used to   ___ (2)

    Hardly at all   ___ (3)

3. I have blamed myself unnecessarily when things went wrong:

    Yes, most of the time   ___ (3)

    Yes, some of the time   ___ (2)

    No, not much   ___ (1)

    No, not at all   ___ (0)

4. I have been anxious or worried for no good reason:

    No, not at all   ___ (0)

    Hardly ever   ___ (1)

    Yes, sometimes   ___ (2)

    Yes, very often   ___ (3)

5. I have felt scared or panicky for no very good reason:

   Yes, quite a lot   ___ (3)

   Yes, sometimes   ___ (2)

   No, not much   ___ (1)

   No, not at all   ___ (0)

6. Things have been getting on top of me:

   Yes, most of the time I haven't been coping at all   ___ (3)

   Yes, sometimes I haven't been coping as well
      as usual   ___ (2)

   No, most of the time I have coped quite well   ___ (1)

   No, I have been coping as well as ever   ___ (0)

7. I have been so unhappy that I have had difficulty sleeping:

   Yes, most of the time   ___ (3)

   Yes, sometimes   ___ (2)

   Not very often   ___ (1)

   No, not at all   ___ (0)

8. I have felt sad or miserable:

   Yes, most of the time   ___ (3)

   Yes, quite often   ___ (2)

   Not very often   ___ (1)

   No, not at all   ___ (0)

9. I have been so unhappy that I have been crying:

   Yes, most of the time   ___ (3)

   Yes, quite often   ___ (2)

   Only occasionally   ___ (1)

   No, never   ___ (0)

10. The thought of harming myself has occurred to me:

Yes, quite often _____ (3)

Sometimes _____ (2)

Hardly ever _____ (1)

Never _____ (0)

Now let's look at some of the symptoms of perinatal anxiety. The experience can vary from person to person, but can include feeling:

+ anxious, scared, overwhelmed or panicked

+ irritable or on edge

+ a sense of dread.

In terms of behaviours and physical sensations, it can also include:

+ avoidance

+ restlessness, pacing or rapid speech

+ difficulty sleeping (for example, worries keep you awake)

+ compulsive behaviours

+ physical sensations, such as a racing heart, dizziness, trembling, sweating, or feeling immobilized or frozen.

And, in terms of thoughts, you might worry that harm might come to others, be preoccupied with a need for control or perfection, have obsessive, repetitive or intrusive thoughts, or have thoughts of worst-case scenarios.

Like depression, anxiety can either appear suddenly or build up over a period of time. Importantly, often mothers will have symptoms of both anxiety *and* depression, without reaching full diagnostic criteria for either. This combination of symptoms can be debilitating and requires treatment.

So, what predicts a vulnerability to perinatal depression and anxiety? Well, just like the blues, hormones can trigger both conditions, but they are not the whole story—after all, men and same-sex partners can also develop postnatal depression and anxiety, but they don't experience the hormonal drop. There are many contributing factors. A personal history of depression or anxiety is the best predictor, but some other predictors are as follows (in no particular order).

+ Relationship difficulties with a partner, for example an unsupportive spouse

+ A lack of practical support, for example tight finances or little social support

+ Life stresses and adverse life events, such as stopping or starting work, illness, an unexpectedly difficult pregnancy or birth, IVF, having a baby born with a disability or having a high-risk pregnancy

+ A family history of depression or other mental health difficulties

+ Severe baby blues

+ A difficult relationship with own mother

+ A history of physical or sexual abuse

+ Personality styles, for example perfectionism, a tendency to self-blame, a drive to be organised or a tendency towards worry

+ A mother's own history of childhood neglect or abuse can trigger an onset of perinatal depression and anxiety. Some mothers compare the love and protection they feel for their baby with the abuse they endured at the hands of their parents, and this can impact on their mood. Negative past experiences that impact on your parenting are sometimes referred to as 'ghosts from the nursery' (see pages 74–75).

TREATING PERINATAL DEPRESSION OR ANXIETY

Treatment for perinatal depression or anxiety often depends on the depth of distress and whether or not there are safety issues. It is difficult to determine a person's level of depression or anxiety without an assessment. Generally speaking, mild depression or anxiety is treated with self-care (for self-care tips, see pages 144–145) and perhaps some therapy. Moderate depression or anxiety is treated with therapy or medication, and sometimes both. Severe depression or anxiety is treated with medication, therapy and sometimes requires time in hospital (hopefully in a mother-and-baby unit if it's during the postnatal period).

If you do have depression or anxiety, it's a mark of good mothering to ask for help. Many mothers with depression or anxiety don't seek treatment, or refuse help when they are given a diagnosis. Feelings of guilt and shame, which are often part of depression and anxiety, influence help-seeking. Some people think that depression is part of the transition to motherhood, and perhaps a lack of value placed by society on providing care contributes to this. Shame, and stigma, make it harder to ask for help. Others worry that their baby will be taken away from them if they get professional help. Yet others believe that there is no real help available, and ask, 'What's the point?'

Sadly, it can be hard to get good free mental health support in many countries, but be persistent. If you make it clear to your health provider that you need help, some level of support should be made available to you. Seeking help can be tiring, so you can ask someone you trust to advocate for you. If you are in a remote area, you might consider accessing an assessment through Skype (or some other teleconferencing software). Make sure that you are talking to a health professional who has expertise in perinatal mental health and is qualified to carry out a diagnostic assessment. If cost is an issue, a good strategy is to seek an initial diagnostic assessment at a one-off cost. That assessment may direct you to your GP for medication, websites for self-care or to a counsellor who can use the assessment for effective therapy. The assessor can also write a letter to appropriate health professionals. If you are given a diagnosis of depression or anxiety, take it seriously. Both are treatable.

TIPS FOR PREVENTING PERINATAL DEPRESSION AND ANXIETY

Following are some steps you can take to help prevent perinatal depression and anxiety.

+ Know the signs and symptoms of perinatal depression and anxiety so that you can identify them early if they rear their head.

+ Have a support team that you trust for the birth.

+ Have realistic expectations for childbirth and motherhood.

+ Be flexible about mothering. Aim for good enough—not for perfection. Perfection doesn't exist.

+ Know where to go for support if you need it.

+ Sleep! At any time of life, simply getting enough sleep can either prevent the onset of or ameliorate the intensity of mental health difficulties.

A NOTE ON SUNLIGHT

Sunlight (or lack thereof) has been linked to seasonal depressive disorders, and 'bright light therapy'—when a person exposes themselves to an artificial light that mimics sunlight—is often used in treating such disorders.

A few studies have considered the implications of sunlight for perinatal depression in particular, and there has been some discussion over whether bright light therapy might be useful in treating perinatal depression. A 2012 review examined the rationales and evidence behind the use of bright light therapy in treating perinatal depression, and suggested that it's premature to draw any concrete conclusion about its efficacy from the existing body of research.[5] There have been very few studies, all with very few participants, and they did not all reach the same conclusion.

A common refrain from the perinatal studies is that larger studies are needed to determine whether hours of sunlight might be linked to perinatal depression.

LIVING WITH SOMEONE WHO HAS DEPRESSION OR ANXIETY

Cheerleading someone who has depression and anxiety is often exhausting, and can become isolating. Sometimes a mother will ask her partner not to confide in friends and family about her mental health, because she's worried about being judged—however, this can mean the mother is getting professional help while her partner has nowhere to turn.

To be good supporters, the partners of women who have perinatal distress need support too, and this is something that needs to be negotiated.

Following are some experiences that partners of women with perinatal distress have described to me.

+ 'Me, complain? No way. When I come home, she cries and tells me how hard it is for her, how lucky I am to go to work. Never mind that I'm exhausted all the time and just about asleep at the desk. I feel so lonely. I don't have anyone to talk with about how I feel.'

+ 'I miss our friends. I don't dare go out or invite people home because she tells me she feels anxious about something happening when I'm out late and she doesn't like visitors any more. Our baby is six months old, but it is never the right time to socialise or for me to do anything on my own. Say something? Are you kidding? I just want to keep the peace.'

+ 'Some of the things she says to me are mean. She never used to talk to me like this. If I don't go to our baby fast enough when she cries, she tells me I don't love my daughter. If I forget to put on the clothes dryer, she calls me useless and swears at me. I know I have to roll with the punches because she feels bad, but it's hard.'

+ 'To be honest, when I put the key in the lock in the front door, I have a feeling of dread. What will it be like inside? Will she be crying, shouting at me, telling me that I am the bad guy for being stuck in traffic? Sometimes I feel abused.'

+ 'If I do help, I haven't done it the right way. If I don't intuit what needs to be done, then I am lazy. What's the point? I don't feel good enough and I'm losing my confidence in parenting.'

+ 'I have been too scared to talk with her about how she is feeling. I guess I bury my head in the sand. I read that relationship stress can cause postnatal depression, and I am worried it is all my fault. I worry that I'm not good enough for her or our baby.'

+ 'Sex? No. I get that she is tired and doesn't feel like sex, but she moves away from me like I'm contaminated. We never talk about it because then I'm "insensitive". I think she doesn't find me attractive now.'

If you find yourself having thoughts and feelings along these lines, don't beat yourself up. It's normal. Supporting someone through depression and anxiety is hard, and you need to take care of yourself too. Talk to a professional if you need to, so that you can continue to be the support your partner needs without spiralling down yourself. And remember that partners get postnatal depression too.

PARTNERS GET PERINATAL DEPRESSION AND ANXIETY TOO

Major life changes that come with parenting happen for both parents. Fathers have about half the rates of perinatal depression and anxiety as mothers. The prevalence is much higher among fathers who have partners with perinatal distress.[6] This might be for a couple of reasons. It can be very stressful living with someone who has mental health difficulties, and stress can trigger depression or anxiety. Another reason is something called 'assortative mating', which means we tend to choose partners who have the same traits as us—including vulnerabilities to mental health difficulties.

Men have the same symptoms for perinatal depression and anxiety as they do at any other time of life. In the perinatal period, fathers might also experience difficulties bonding, avoiding home life, increased amounts of work outside the home, increased alcohol and prescription drug use, conflict, anger and concerns over their own health.

It appears there is a similar trend in prevalence whether or not a birth parent is involved. One study showed the level of depressive symptoms between adoptive and birth mothers were not significantly different; however, adoptive mothers reported greater well-being and less anxiety then birth mothers.[7]

Some studies have considered the perinatal health of same-sex parents. One peer-reviewed study of 31 female parents who identify as lesbian or bisexual concluded that the rate of depressive symptoms for biological lesbian and bisexual mothers was higher than for heterosexual mothers, while the rate for non-biological lesbian and bisexual mothers was the same as for heterosexual mothers. Lesbian mothers did not claim to receive any less social support than heterosexual mothers, but the researchers suggested one reason for elevated rates of depression could be having less support from family.[8]

If both parents have perinatal depression or anxiety, who is the buffer for the baby? A baby needs at least one primary caregiver who is sensitive, responsive and can take delight in them. Although health services are gradually starting to identify the need to assess and treat fathers, there are not nearly enough services and resources targeted at partners. Fathers are often left with informal support groups, but no specialised perinatal support. There isn't much support around for same-sex partners, either. Partners are not routinely screened in the same way that birth mothers are. We need to expand funding to develop perinatal teams that include partners, rather than having only a maternal focus. In the meantime, just as with a birth mother, partners can get an assessment in the private sector face to face or via Skype (or similar) from a psychiatrist or a psychologist who is qualified to make an assessment, and ask to be directed to services available in their area.

Case study: Ted

When Ted came to me, his baby, Ruby, was nine months old. Ruby was sleeping well, but Ted was often unable to sleep past 4 a.m. because he was thinking about work and about his own father, who had died from bowel cancer at the age of 39—just four years older than Ted was. During the day, Ted was feeling stressed and getting tension headaches. He was irritable with his staff at work. He had begun to find himself pushing Ruby's pram around the park, feeling miserable and fantasising about dropping Ruby home, then leaving his family. He was drinking more in the evenings and he knew this was unfair on his wife, Jenny, who was becoming increasingly angry with him.

Ted told me that he was in love with Jenny, and described how he had looked forward to having a baby. When Ruby arrived, however, he realised that he hadn't anticipated just how hard it would be, or how much he would miss his time alone with Jenny. He felt burdened with juggling a demanding job alongside doing his share with Ruby. He didn't dare complain to anyone, though. 'I feel like an idiot,' he said to me. 'I didn't give birth, but I'm the miserable one in the equation. All my friends enjoy their kids.'

As a father, as a husband and as a boss at work, Ted felt like a failure. He started to wonder if everyone would be better off without him.

Ted was suffering from postnatal depression. Once he understood this, he was able to start making sense of his thoughts and feelings. He began taking antidepressants, came to see me for regular sessions, and joined a male-only support group.

The cloud lifted. He was able to sleep again and he reduced his drinking. He found joy in his baby, in Jenny and in life again.

ASK FRIENDS AND FAMILY FOR HELP

Good social support is important for both mothers and fathers post-birth.

It might feel uncomfortable to ask your friends and family for help, or you may think that doing so compromises your independence, but do it for your baby as well as for yourself. It isn't fair on either of you if you become exhausted.

If you find it hard to ask for support, tell yourself that you will pay the favour forward in the years to come when you are less busy.

When you do get help, be positive. Thank the person helping you—even if they don't do things 'your way'. Remember that no baby ever came to any harm because their nappy wasn't put on well enough, or because a grandparent gently rocked them to sleep instead of encouraging them to self-settle in their cot.

Beware of the 'my mother did it on her own, so I should be able to' talk. Yes, over previous generations, mothers were expected to look after their babies and complete domestic chores on their own—and plenty of them were addicted to tranquilisers and shouted at their children.

So give yourself a break. If friends or family visit, ask them to pick up a broom or fold the laundry. Most people love to be able to help.

OUT-OF-CONTROL EMOTIONS

Some people are less in control of their emotions than others. They experience more intense and prolonged emotions than most people. When we are tired, depressed or anxious, we all experience unpleasant emotions more intensely than at other times, but I am talking about something different here. An out-of-control emotion can happen regardless of depression, anxiety or exhaustion—although, as noted, these difficulties certainly exacerbate out-of-control emotions.

Out-of-control emotions can cause particular stress when you have a new baby, because intense feelings of anger, anxiety and irritation affect your relationships with the very people who might otherwise offer you support.

Following are some warning signs that your emotions are out of control.

+ You behave in ways that others find extreme given the situation, such as shouting when someone hasn't cleared the table or when your baby isn't settling.

+ You feel guilty about behaving badly with friends, family, your partner or your baby.

+ You experience many intense feelings in close succession. For example, you quickly go from anger to sadness to happiness, and your moods and your thoughts feel 'all over the place'.

+ Your feelings, especially of anger and anxiety, have a specifically out-of-control quality to them. For example, you throw an object in response to feeling angry.

+ You experience chronic feelings of 'emptiness'.

+ You feel a lack of identity or sense of self.

+ You experience slight paranoia about or suspicion of others' motives. For example, you worry that people are talking about you, or don't like you, or will abandon you.

+ You express high emotion to get people to stay near you.

+ You wonder why you feel different from other parents.

+ You find past memories intruding on your mind, leaving little room for anything else.

+ You worry and feel guilty because you think, *I hate my baby sometimes.*

There are many different reasons for out-of-control emotions. Often people with this difficulty have a sensitive temperament coupled with having grown up in an invalidating environment. This could be a result of a childhood trauma, feelings of having been ignored, or exposure to heightened emotions from parents who themselves had limited emotional control. The most invalidating childhood environment of all is an abusive one.

If you are experiencing out-of-control emotions, you need to seek professional help. Out-of-control emotions can affect your experience of parenting, and can have a long-term impact on your baby.

The good news is that you can learn tools to control your emotions that will help you to lead a more satisfying life. (For more information on tuning in to your emotions, see Chapter 4.)

PERINATAL OBSESSIVE COMPULSIVE DISORDER (OCD)

Perinatal obsessive compulsive disorder (OCD) is much more common than many people are aware. The lifetime prevalence for OCD is about 2.3 per cent, with the perinatal period being an at-risk time for it to develop or resurface. For example, a woman who has recently given birth has twice (or more) the chance of experiencing OCD than at any other time in her life.[9]

An obsession is a thought (an idea or memory), an urge or an impulse that is intrusive, unwanted and causes you distress. A compulsion is a behaviour that, in the short term, brings you relief from the distress or discomfort triggered by the obsession. The great majority of new parents (both mothers and fathers) will have unpleasant urges, impulses or thoughts pop into their heads at some stage, but these experiences are termed a 'disorder' when either the obsessions, compulsions or both get in the way of usual functioning or cause significant distress. OCD also needs to be distinguished from personality traits that are not causing you distress, such as being tidier than most.

OCD can form over just about anything, but for therapeutic purposes there are some broad categories. One that many are aware of is contamination OCD, where people have obsessions about being contaminated by people or objects that most others see as benign. People with contamination OCD are compelled to repeatedly clean themselves (for example by washing their hands or taking long showers), to clean surfaces, or sometimes to clean their babies.

Another example is responsibility/checking OCD, where people have obsessions about being overly responsible for certain events and actions. People with responsibility/checking OCD are compelled to repeatedly check that they have performed the 'correct' action, for example that an email contains the correct information, that the door has been locked, or that the baby is strapped in the pram.

A third example is harm OCD, which includes obsessions—or unwanted thoughts, images or urges—that are focused on harming yourself or harming others. Harm OCD can be very distressing for mothers, particularly if they are not aware they have OCD—but remember that harm OCD is very different from having a *real* desire to hurt yourself or others. In a way, it is quite the opposite, because harm OCD is actually a *fear* of causing harm. People suffering from harm OCD are often compelled to avoid information or items that trigger their obsessions, or to complete mental tasks that 'neutralise' their obsessive thoughts and images.

Symptoms of perinatal OCD vary from mother to mother. Some of the common obsessions that a mother might experience during the perinatal period include:

+ intrusive thoughts or images of either intentionally or unintentionally damaging her body while pregnant, for example, by drinking cleaning products or by contamination or from eating the wrong food

+ intrusive thoughts or images of intentionally hurting her baby through throwing, dropping, stabbing, suffocating or sexual abuse

+ obsessive worry about accidentally harming her baby through carelessness, such as exposure to toxins like bleach

+ a recurring fear of making the wrong decisions regarding care during pregnancy or post-birth, which will lead to serious outcomes such as a fatality—for example, whether to exercise during pregnancy, whether to have her child immunised, or how to strap her baby in the car seat correctly.

Some of the common compulsions that a mother might experience during the perinatal period include:

+ avoiding, hiding or throwing out sharp objects

+ avoiding changing or bathing her baby alone for fear of being sexually abusive

+ repeatedly asking for reassurance from friends and family that her thoughts are 'normal' and that no harm has come to her baby

+ avoiding using cleaning products while pregnant or post-birth, in case her baby is harmed

+ over-cleaning in case her baby is 'contaminated' by dirt

+ monitoring herself for perceived inappropriate aggressive or sexual feelings towards her baby

+ repeatedly checking on her sleeping baby or repeatedly checking for illness.

TREATING PERINATAL OCD

Many mothers who present with perinatal OCD report signs going back to their childhood. OCD most often surfaces during childhood as worry about contamination (for example, a child complaining of feeling unclean or unwell because of something they have had contact with) or responsibility (for example, a child feeling compelled to perform rituals, such as 'checking', to keep people safe). Additionally, about one quarter of young people with OCD have sexual obsessions (unwanted sexual thoughts that are distressing), and many do not seek help from adults because they are ashamed.

Mothers experiencing perinatal OCD often don't confide in others about their symptoms or come forward for support, and many find the intrusive thoughts or impulses they have extremely shameful. It is estimated that only 10 per cent of people with OCD are in treatment. One of the hallmarks of OCD is that the intrusive thoughts or impulses are 'ego dystonic', which is to say in conflict with a person's goals, desires or self-image. This causes a significant amount of distress.

Many people mistakenly believe that these thoughts say something personal about them, such as whether they are 'good' or 'flawed', and this leads them to hide their OCD from others.

If you notice OCD, first check and see if the thoughts are ego dystonic (not in line with what you actually want to do). If you are having thoughts about harming yourself or your baby and have a genuine wish to do so, this is not a product of OCD; rather, it may signal depression or psychosis. You need to get help immediately.

If you are having thoughts that *are* ego dystonic, however, try acknowledging that the thoughts are just thoughts, not facts, and see what happens. Sometimes this is enough to relieve distress. Label intrusive thoughts or images as 'obsessions', and attempt to resist the urge to engage in compulsions. If this doesn't work, that's OK. The thoughts have no reflection on you as a person, and OCD is highly treatable through seeing a qualified professional. There are a number of evidence-based therapeutic interventions, and medication such as selective serotonin reuptake inhibitors (SSRIs) can also be very helpful.

BIPOLAR DISORDER

Bipolar disorder can emerge for the first time after childbirth. We know that at least 2 per cent of the population suffers from bipolar disorder, and a further 2.4 per cent from a spectrum of bipolar-type mood disorders. A diagnosis of bipolar disorder is made when a person suffers from an episode of mania or hypomania (a mild form of mania). Usually, people with bipolar disorder also suffer from depressive episodes, which is where the name bipolar (two poles) comes from.

The first episode can start with depression. There are a few clues that a depressive episode suggests the onset of bipolar disorder, including the following.

+ if the depressive episode is severe

+ if there are psychotic symptoms, for example delusions and/ or hallucinations

+ if the episode is preceded by over-exuberance

+ if there is significant slowing of thinking and movement

+ if there is significant oversleeping

+ if there is a family history of blood relatives with bipolar disorder.

Symptoms of mania, on the other hand, include:

+ being very energised, despite a marked decrease in the need for sleep

+ excessive confidence and planning

+ elevated or highly irritable mood

+ thoughts often feel 'sped up'

+ speech can be fast

+ actions the person later regrets, for example buying goods they can't afford, phoning people late at night

+ increased libido.

THE PINKS OR HYPOMANIA?

Many people have heard of the blues (see page 143), but not so many have heard of the pinks. The pinks are a consistent feeling of euphoria following childbirth.

Having the pinks is not a problem in itself. It could, however, be the onset of hypomania. While hypomania is a less marked form of mania—'hypo' means less of something—it can be very disruptive for a person, particularly with relationships and while looking after a new baby. See opposite page for symptoms of mania.

Both mania and hypomania can go on for weeks, or even months. Sometimes psychotic symptoms may develop (see pages 172–173 for more information on perinatal psychosis) so please take signs of hypomania seriously.

There is a very strong genetic component to bipolar disorder, so anyone who is pregnant and has a personal or family history of bipolar disorder or psychosis should make themselves known to a specialist team. However, a personal or family history is not a prerequisite for bipolar disorder to develop during the perinatal period. A number of factors may trigger bipolar disorder in a vulnerable person, including sleep deprivation or exposure to other stressors. In the case of mothers, the most important stressor is childbirth itself. Childbirth is more likely to trigger an episode of bipolar disorder than anything else.

TREATING BIPOLAR DISORDER

For the most part, bipolar disorder is treated with a combination of medication and therapy. Sometimes hospital admission is required.

PERINATAL PSYCHOSIS

The most rare and serious perinatal mental health condition is psychosis. Perinatal psychosis is considered a medical emergency, because a mother suffering from it can lose touch with reality very quickly—even within hours of her first symptom—and may become a threat to herself or to her baby. Postnatal psychosis occurs in about one in 500 to 1000 births. The onset is most often within two to three weeks of delivery, but is certainly not limited to this timeframe.

You are at increased risk of postnatal psychosis if you have a personal or family history of psychosis or bipolar disorder.

Symptoms of psychosis can include:

+ delusions or strange beliefs, for example that your baby is the next Messiah or, alternatively, the Devil

+ hallucinations (seeing or hearing things that aren't there)

+ feeling very irritated

+ hyperactivity

+ a decreased need for or inability to sleep

+ paranoia and suspiciousness

+ rapid mood swings

+ not making sense to others.

TREATING PERINATAL PSYCHOSIS

Perinatal psychosis is very treatable, but there is no time to waste. Immediate medical help is required if any mother or significant other notices any symptoms of psychosis, particularly post-birth. Don't wait for an appointment if your health provider is unavailable; get help straight away, even if this means going to an emergency medical centre.

CHAPTER 6: THE MAIN POINTS

+ The baby blues are extremely common, affecting many mothers. They are not considered a mental health difficulty, and most mothers find that the blues resolve with time and with self-care.

+ The baby blues are not the same as postnatal depression. If you notice symptoms of depression or anxiety any time during your pregnancy or the first year post-birth, approach a professional. If you are wondering whether you should seek professional help, then you should.

+ Don't be afraid to ask friends and family for help. Asking for help is a mark of good parenting; it is acknowledging your need to take care of yourself in order to take care of your baby.

+ Remember that fathers and partners get perinatal depression and anxiety, too.

+ Take thoughts or plans to harm yourself or your baby extremely seriously. Seek out professional help immediately.

CHAPTER 7

RELATIONSHIPS AND SEX

Mothering myth: Raising a baby brings parents closer together.

Truth: The birth of a baby can often cause disharmony, which needs to be worked through.

A recent study of over 84,000 Norwegian women showed that parents are never closer than when they are waiting for their first child to arrive.[1] The mother-to-be's self-esteem might take a bit of a nosedive due to body-image issues, but never mind that—pregnancy doesn't last forever. Hand in hand, the loving duo look forward to the future . . . and then, boom! The future arrives.

According to the same study, for the first six months of the new baby's life the mother's self-esteem lifts. However, a darker truth emerges on the parental relationship front. After the birth of the baby, the mother's satisfaction with the father declines almost immediately—and it doesn't rise again any time soon! It only takes a bit longer for the father's satisfaction with the mother to start declining, too.

Unfortunately, the current research into relationship satisfaction only makes it to three years post-birth, so it is unclear whether satisfaction ever returns to that high-water mark reached during the couple's first pregnancy.[2] Becoming parents, it would seem, isn't great for relationship satisfaction.

It's good news that the mother's self-esteem rises after birth, though—isn't it? Well, not so fast. I didn't mention that the same Norwegian study found that, after the first six months have passed, her self-esteem falls again—and in general stays that way for a good three years. After that, it seems to rise again. The aftermath of pregnancy and being the primary caregiver are simply not good for a mother's self-esteem.

'Surely,' I hear you ask, 'it's different for financially secure couples, couples who are living together, older and more mature parents, and those who carefully planned their pregnancy!' Apparently, it's not. Unlike smaller studies, which indicate different outcomes for self-esteem and romantic relationships depending on the age and social group of the parents and on whether or not the pregnancy was planned, this large Norwegian study found a similar pattern for all parents. What's more, things don't improve with the number of children.

Declining self-esteem during pregnancy is thought to be linked to a mother's changing body shape, worries about her baby's development, and fear of childbirth. After the birth of a first child, both declining self-esteem and declining romantic relationships have a lot to do with the new roles that each parent is expected to take on. All the research shows that, after the birth of a baby, parental roles generally become more traditional, with the mother expected to carry out the lion's share of childcare and domestic chores, while the father is expected to bring home an adequate income for everyone. Admittedly, this is changing, with some fathers staying at home while mothers go to work—but this is by far the exception.

The truth is that the transition to parenthood can be a breeding ground for resentment and misunderstanding. While this isn't the fairy tale you might like to hear, it is what you need to hear. As you become a parent, you will very likely experience some degree of conflict in your relationship with your partner. Sometimes just knowing that you and your situation is normal can be a big help. You might have couple friends who appear to never argue and to feel exactly the same about each other as the day they first met, but ask yourself how likely that really is. Things aren't always what they appear on the surface, and this is never truer than when it comes to relationships.

FROM A COUPLE TO PARENTS

Most couples anticipate the physical demands that a baby will bring (such as less sleep and leisure time), but many are taken completely by surprise by the challenges posed by making the transition from a couple to parents. When couples have unrealistic expectations about what being a new family will be like, disappointment is never far away.

The typical shift to traditional roles that I mentioned earlier—with mothers taking care of the domestic side of things, while the father earns the income—alters the power balance of a relationship in ways that modern women and stay-at-home dads are likely to find unfair. It can make the primary caregiver feel isolated, financially disenfranchised and completely dependent on the partner who is in paid work. At the same time, the earning parent may feel overwhelmed by the obligation to provide financial stability for a family.

This can all lead to resentment, with the first casualty being communication. Here are some suggestions that I have found useful, not only for the parents I see, but for my own family as well.

WATCH OUT FOR THE VICTIM-VILLAIN CYCLE

Often when disagreements or conflicts arise, both parties are so certain that they are the victim that it seems pointless to even discuss the matter. They each think it should be obvious to anyone with the slightest modicum of empathy just how poorly treated they are by the other.

If you're caught in the victim–villain cycle, you and your partner might find yourself in constant disagreement over who has the best end of the bargain. For instance, if you are a stay-at-home mother, there's nothing you'll be able to say that will convince your working partner that you do not spend the day sleeping and sitting by the fire, occasionally dandling your lovely baby on your knee. Conversely, there's nothing your partner will be able to say to convince you that he or she isn't having a lovely time at long work lunches, engaging in fascinating water-cooler discussions, and being able to go to the toilet uninterrupted. If this sounds like you, you and your partner will just have to agree that the hours you are apart are of equal value. Remember that you love each other. See one another as vulnerable, not as a villain, and try to figure out how you can both get more support.

When you are together, be fair to each other. When you are both at home, chores and baby-care need to be shared equally, as does leisure time. It is outrageous for either parent to sit doing their own leisure activity (such as reading, texting a friend or watching TV) while the other is busy looking after the baby or doing necessary domestic chores. In saying this, try to be generous with each other as well; if there really is some downtime that can be had, don't deny it of yourself or of your partner. For example, a stay-at-home mother might want to go for a run, while her partner looks after their baby. Similarly, the working parent might want to go to the gym during the weekend.

In order to recognise when resentment rather than practical reasons are getting in the way of you agreeing to a request, it can help to ask yourself: 'Is there a good reason why I can't agree?' Both of you should be asking yourself this question—and exhaustion and feeling frazzled is a perfectly good reason to say no. It's completely fine to respond with, 'I know you want to go to the gym, but I really need some help right now.'

TIPS FOR APPRECIATING ONE ANOTHER

Here's a golden tip: make sure you thank one another for the work you each do, both paid and unpaid. Get into the habit of doing this.

And another: if you know you are going to ask your partner to change a behaviour, make sure you also compliment his or her efforts. Think of this as putting money in the bank before you make a withdrawal.

ASSERTIVE COMMUNICATION

Sometimes, communication problems can arise from the style in which one parent (or both) communicates. An assertive communication style is the ideal—when you are calm and clear about your needs and wishes, and take responsibility for your feelings—but tiredness and low self-esteem can interfere with assertive communication.

A **passive communication** style is when you take care of your partner's wishes without regard to your own. For example, you agree to something unfair, then retreat, resenting the situation. For many mothers, pregnancy alone coincides with declining self-esteem, which can mean they tolerate what they perceive as unfair treatment and remain passive. Some bottle up any anger they might feel until they finally explode. This can go both ways, too—many fathers are very eager to please, and in the course of understanding how frustrating their partner finds it to be isolated and tired, become passive and resentful rather than talk about how they really feel.

Passive-aggressive behaviour is when, instead of directly addressing what is upsetting you, you behave in ways that are driven by your resentment. For example, you might agree to meet your partner's wish, but then be sarcastic to them or purposely keep them waiting when they are in a hurry. Passive aggression leaves the other person feeling confused and none the wiser about what you need.

THE DIFFERENCE BETWEEN ASSERTIVE AND AGGRESSIVE

Many parents mistake aggressive communication for assertive communication. Aggressive communication includes name-calling, shouting and put-downs. 'Oh, don't worry,' a parent using aggressive communication might say, 'I *am* assertive. If he comes home late, I really give it to him.'

I have worked with both mothers and fathers who allow themselves to communicate in an aggressive way.

The truth is that the two communication styles couldn't be more different. Assertive communication is the ideal, whereas aggression leaves others feeling fear, hurt or anger. Aggression is not the behaviour of choice if you are in the least bit interested in having a healthy, long-term relationship. It is certainly an ugly and damaging way to behave in front of babies and children.

The goal of **assertive communication** is a 'win–win' situation; the intention is for no one to feel oppressed and for everyone to get an outcome they can live with. It doesn't always work out that way, but assertive communication has a much better chance of success than being passive, passive-aggressive or aggressive does.

Assertive behaviour is characterised by a tendency to stand tall and make eye contact with others. Assertive communicators speak in a clear, confident and respectful tone of voice. They take responsibility for their feelings by using 'I' statements, rather than blaming others.

Being assertive is not just important in your romantic relationship but with friends and relatives (and strangers) who want to give unsolicited advice. The intention is to get your point across while leaving relationships intact.

You might not choose to be assertive all the time, but it is important to be aware of what communication style you are choosing in any given situation. The cost of choosing to be passive at the post office if someone cuts in front of you will not be as damaging as a cycle of passivity with significant others.

TIPS FOR COMMUNICATING ASSERTIVELY

+ When you are using an assertive communication style, it's important to use 'I' statements. For example, say, 'I feel sad when you do that.' Don't say, 'You make me feel sad.'

+ Making this subtle change in how you speak shows that you are taking responsibility for your own feelings. It also sends the message that you respect both yourself and the person you're talking with.

+ When requesting something, you need to be specific. It's too general to say, 'Help more with our baby.' You need to be specific about what, exactly, you want help with. For example, you could say, 'When you get home, please unload the dishwasher and take the baby to the park.'

The next time you want to make your point, you can use this template to communicate assertively.

I feel _____ *when [insert behaviour or situation]. I would prefer* _____.

Here's an example.

I feel frustrated when you come home from work and sit on the couch without helping me to cook dinner. I would prefer that you help with dinner, and ask if there's anything that you can do before you have a rest.

THE GIFT OF TIME

Martien Snellen, an expert on post-birth relationships, suggests that the formula for a happy family is for each parent to have time at least once a fortnight: on their own with their children (for example, one parent taking the children to the park); alone with their partner (for example, a date night); together with the whole family (for example, a family picnic); and apart from the family (doing anything of your choice alone or with friends).[3]

A partner who overdoes the 'apart from the family' time is being unreasonable, and in my experience I have found that there are two main reasons why one partner might go out more than they should. The first reason is a genuine sense of entitlement and a belief that their lives should not change just because there is a baby in the house. This is often the result of modelling by their own parents, and generally these feelings of entitlement are hard to budge without therapy. The second reason is somewhat easier to deal with, and is when a partner finds it difficult to be at home because they don't understand why their partner—who is the primary caregiver—is so angry. I can't tell you how many exhausted mothers I have worked with who do not express out loud what is running through their mind, and who end up feeling annoyed and injured because their partner doesn't help out without being asked.

It is so important to remember that your partner cannot read your mind. If the washing needs to be folded or the dishwasher emptied, just ask your partner to do it. Don't stew about it because they haven't seen what needs to be done. I regularly hear partners express fear of being at home in case they 'do things wrong'. These partners retreat to drinking with old buddies or going out where the world is more predictable. This is, of course, terribly unfair on the person who is left at home, and only leads to increased resentment. In these situations, it is often helpful to reach an understanding where, since the stay-at-home parent is the one who most often knows what needs to be done around the house, they will ask for help; when they do, they will do it directly and politely, without expecting everything to be done in a particular way.

Of course, despite a mother's best efforts, sometimes her partner doesn't play ball. This is incredibly frustrating. If you find yourself in this situation, I can recommend that you take a stand and suggest couples' therapy. It may be that your partner thinks *you* have it wrong, and you both need an independent person to confirm the fairness of your requests.

INTIMACY AND SEX

Having sex with someone who you love is one way of showing intimacy, but it's certainly not the only way. You might not be ready to resume your sex life in the weeks or months immediately after having your baby, but you can—and should—still be romantic.

HONEYMOON PHASE 2.0

In order to be romantic after their baby is born, some couples find it helpful to go back to doing some of the things they did when they first courted each other—revisiting the honeymoon phase, so to speak. Even if you don't have as much time to yourselves as you did back then, you can still leave chocolates under the pillow, send romantic messages and, importantly, compliment each other.

One way of being intimate is to set aside some time each day— say, 20 minutes after your baby is in bed—and use that time to tell one another about your day. Really listen to each other, without judgement, and ask what each of you needs from the other.

It's especially important to focus on being a couple, and not just parents. This isn't only for you as a couple, but also so your baby can see that you really matter to each other. There is no need to put your relationship on hold after your baby is born. Think about what made you a couple, what brought you together, and set aside time for these things. For example, if you used to like listening to music together, put away 'Baa Baa, Black Sheep' for the afternoon, and listen to music you both like. In the evenings, watch a TV show together that you both enjoy. Invite friends over for a pizza—but warn them in advance what time you need to get to bed!

Above all, know that it is OK to consider your own interests as a couple. A baby does not need to be stimulated at all times. Your baby might be the most important person in the world to you both, but your relationship is also important. Retaining your identity as a couple will make you stronger parents.

Your self-esteem goes hand-in-hand with the relationship you have with your partner. I'll look more closely at self-esteem in the next chapter, but part of your self-esteem comes from how you think you are regarded by society in general, by those you care about, and importantly, by your partner. Fathers as well as mothers are affected by the dynamic between relationships and self-esteem. Be kind to one other, both for your own sake and for the sake of your relationship, and also for your child's sake.

COMMON CONCERNS ABOUT SEX AFTER A BABY

Following are some of the concerns I have heard from parents I have worked with after their baby was born.

'It's been months since our baby was born, and neither of us want to have sex.'

Rest assured that this is an extremely common dynamic, and most couples with a new baby have little sexual contact. There are many reasons for this, including exhaustion, hormonal changes that can lead to vaginal dryness and reduced sexual urge and arousal, discomfort after childbirth, lack of time, and body-image worries. A low mood can also lead to lack of interest in most things, including sex (often referred to as low libido). If your libido remains low for a significant length of time you should talk with someone about this. You cannot put a deadline on this, as there are so many factors to take into account; if it is upsetting either one of you, it is time to take the first step and see your family doctor. Men often report feeling too exhausted to even contemplate sex; it's not just women.

'I love my partner, but I am all "touched out".'

'Cuddle fatigue' is very normal, and something that almost always comes up when I talk with new mothers. The intimacy of cuddling a new baby can be both fulfilling and exhausting, and many new mothers don't want any extra physical contact from their partner. This can have an adverse effect on a relationship if it's not brought out into the open. If you have cuddle fatigue tell your partner that being physically close with your baby is draining your reserves and that right now you are finding it hard to be touched. Make sure your partner knows that it is not anything to do with them.

However, other women tell me they would like to cuddle with

their partners, but not in a sexual way. At the same time, they fear that cuddling will lead to their partner expecting sex. They don't want to feel uncomfortable by repeatedly rejecting their partner's advances. If this sounds familiar, be honest. Tell your partner you want to be close and cuddle, but that you want some more time before anything more sexual. You may sense that your partner is eager to get sex back into your relationship, but if sexual contact is something you are not ready for yet you don't have to do it. No one should ever have sex unless they want to, but it is only fair to your partner to talk to them about it.

'We don't have sex or talk about it.'

This can cause real problems, especially if one partner worries that it's because the other doesn't find them attractive. It can also lead to a 'pursuer–chased' dynamic, where one person feels hassled for sex while the other feels like a pest. It's always better to lay your cards on the table and tell your partner where you are at in terms of sex, and what to expect. Reassure them that they are attractive, and if you are not ready for sex yet explain why.

'My partner loved my body before I got pregnant. I want to have sex, but I don't feel attractive anymore.'

Be mindful when you're physically intimate with your partner. Notice any negative thoughts and feelings about your body, let them slide away, and focus on being in the moment. (See pages 89–91 for more about practising mindfulness.) I am sure your partner loves you for exactly who you are, and for being the woman who gave birth to your unique and wonderful baby. If negative self-image persists, then you should check for low mood or depression.

CHAPTER 7: THE MAIN POINTS

+ Making the transition to parenthood can be a challenging time for relationships. As you become a new parent, you are very likely to experience some degree of conflict with your partner.

+ It's normal to be stressed, but negative communication cycles can damage your relationship. Focus on using assertive communication—use 'I' statements, and be calm and clear.

+ Watch out for the victim–villain cycle, and try to be fair to each other. Appreciate one another, and what each of you does.

+ Sex isn't the only way to be intimate; there are other ways you can show intimacy, including returning to some of the things you did for each other when you were first dating. Romantic gestures don't have to require a lot of time—they can be as simple as leaving chocolates under the pillow.

CHAPTER 8
MOTHERHOOD AND
IDENTITY

Mothering myth: Becoming a mother makes you feel complete.

Truth: Becoming a mother expands your identity, but is not your whole identity.

Who am I now? you might find yourself wondering after your baby is born. *Have I disappeared?* If you have ever asked yourself these questions, you are either joining the ranks of existentialists by wondering who you are in relation to the universe, or you are considering something a little more down-to-earth—namely *What makes me 'me'?*

As mentioned in the previous chapter, a woman's self-esteem can take a battering in early motherhood. Her identity can take a blow on two fronts: both her physical identity and her professional identity can be affected.

Unfortunately, many women are unhappy with the changes in their body after childbirth, with an average peak in body dissatisfaction at six months post-partum. Don't forget that a change in body shape is a natural part of pregnancy and motherhood. You can start working on getting back to old exercise routines and making sure to eat healthy food, but take care. This is a vulnerable time for eating disorders to start or resurface, and those who have previously experienced an eating disorder need to be particularly aware of what steps they are taking to lose weight.

TIPS FOR IMPROVING YOUR BODY IMAGE

If you are feeling dissatisfied with the way your body has changed post-birth, there are four things I suggest you do.

+ **Show yourself some compassion.** You have a lot to do at the moment, so go easy on yourself. When you look in the mirror and do not like what you see, it is a moment of suffering. Allow yourself to acknowledge this.

+ **Structure a healthy and safe fitness plan.** For example, you could begin by exercising your pelvic floor and abdominal muscles. Then, when your body feels ready, take brisk walks or try a gentle post-partum fitness class or online workout.

+ **Notice when you are ruminating about your body.** Then, choose to distance yourself from the recurring thoughts. You might interrupt ruminations by saying something to yourself such as 'just body image' to bring your awareness to the fact you are ruminating, then refocusing on whatever you are doing, e.g. reading or looking at your baby.

+ **Think about what you do like about your body and yourself.** If you cannot come up with much, this may well be an indication you are experiencing low mood or depression and you need to speak to someone about that.

When it comes to working, becoming a mother is often presented as a time to make a choice: do I continue working full-time, do I work part-time, or will I be a stay-at-home mother? In 2015, a qualitative study on new stay-at-home mothers who had valued their jobs found that these mothers did not see their decisions as being true choices; according to the researchers, a mother 'reconciling' herself to staying at home rather than working was not a 'choice'.[1]

It seems the change in workplace identity for a first-time mother begins with pregnancy, when she is often no longer seen as an integral part of the workplace. Even if she returns to work once her baby is born, she might be viewed as someone unlikely to stay late to get the job done or to mingle. She is someone who will put her family ahead of her work. She becomes an outsider even before she leaves, and remains an outsider even if she stays.

When a mother decides to stay home instead of returning to work, the pain of the transition depends on the degree to which the mother can 'cross boundaries' between her new identity and her previous one. For example, a woman who can carry on doing her work (even just a little bit) in her home finds the transition easier.

In the 2015 study mentioned above, the authors, Shireen Kanji and Emma Cahusac, suggest four stages for transitioning identity from paid work to motherhood.

+ In the first stage, a mother's feelings of guilt about not working as hard as others and letting her colleagues down is combined with her work becoming less important than her home life.

+ In the second stage, she experiences a sense of regret and loss, a sense that mothering is not valued. This is combined with increasing satisfaction from looking after her child.

+ The third stage is creating a new identity at home, actively defending the role, becoming involved in school or community, and bonding with other mothers.

+ The final stage is looking forward to the future and taking advantage of an opportunity to create a work–life balance.

Throughout each of these stages, mothers who have placed importance on paid work continue to do so and plan to return to paid employment. However, the parameters have changed and mothers talk about the need to put boundaries around work. What the study illustrates is that a mother's identity does not fundamentally change; rather it is modified and becomes more complex.

WHO AM I?

Self-identity is like composite rock, made up of different-sized stones and pebbles. The larger and more important 'stones', such as values and abilities, remain relatively stable over life. Other aspects, such as self-esteem, can change through loss of a job or financial independence. One important difference is that self-esteem is your present state of mind, whereas self-identity is all you have been, what you are now *and* what you plan for the future.

So, when new mothers say they are no longer who they used to be—that they have somehow 'disappeared' into motherhood—it is because they are too conscious of just one aspect of their self-identity, and that is their lowered self-esteem. That aspect of self-identity is transient. What new mothers need to consider are the core structures of who they understand themselves to be.

EXPLORE YOUR VALUES

Your values are a significant part of your self-identity. A value is something that you hold in high regard, and examples of values are love, competition, achievement, culture, luxury, appearance and creativity. You cannot hold, buy or sell a value—it is an abstract concept. We learn values from our parents, and we tend to adopt them as our own unless we consciously reject or add to the values our parents modelled. We also adopt values from society's expectations, many of which are driven by advertising. It is worthwhile to inspect your values, where they came from, and whether they are enhancing your life and who you want to be.

To explore yourself and inspect your values, consider the following points.

+ Think about what your parents valued as they raised you. One clue is what they spent their hard-earned money on. Was it education, or luxury? Another clue is which behaviours they praised, and which they corrected. Did they praise kindness, or effort, or achievement?

+ Now, think about which of those values you have kept, which you have rejected, and what values you have added. Adventure? Curiosity?

+ Finally, think about the values you had before you had your baby and the values you have now. Have any changed? Chances are not many have. You see? You are still the same person!

EXPANDING YOUR IDENTITY

Now that you have an appreciation of where your self-identity comes from and what your values are, you can consider your behaviours and goals with greater clarity. You are more likely to choose fulfilling goals and skilful behaviours if you align them with your values.

Values are not the same as goals. While values are abstract, goals are what you plan to achieve. So, for instance, if you value appearance, your goal might be to buy a dress. If you value creativity, your goal might be to own some art.

Similarly, values are different from behaviours. Behaviours are how you choose to act in order to meet your values. If you value kindness, your behaviour might be to look after a friend's toddler so she can go to the dentist. Behaving in ways that fit with our values gives us a better sense of self-identity and well-being.

Becoming a mother does not stop you from behaving in ways that line up with your values and self-identity. Some of the weight you gave to certain parts of your identity are likely to shift during motherhood. For instance, you might still identify yourself as a professional, but your value of caring puts boundaries around the amount of time you need to work in order to live up to this part of your identity.

Keep in mind that a value can remain stable even if your activities change. If you value intelligence, it doesn't matter that you no longer have time to read an academic paper; you can still learn something new, in keeping with that value. Maybe watch a short TED Talk, or start listening to a new podcast series.

Is culture one of your core values? Listen to music you enjoy, or visit exhibitions with your baby. If you value health, go for a walk and plan in small steps to get back to an exercise routine (see page 188).

When you are at home with your family or interacting with others in the community, you can live by your values by noticing 'choice points'.

+ When you are choosing how to respond to a situation, ask yourself, 'How will my behaviour line up with my value of [insert value]?'

Right now:

+ Pause for a moment. Choose two of your values.

+ Plan, even in a small way, how to meet these values every day this coming week.

Although you may worry that you have lost part of your identity by becoming a mother, being a parent is also an opportunity to make gains in other parts of your life. Perhaps you value intimacy, but have never had much time or opportunity to meet new friends. This can be a time to enhance that value. A great many women make new lifelong friends during this period. Take advantage of it. Mothers who can talk openly about their hopes and goals spur each other on. If you are going back to work quickly, look for women in the same situation. Keep in contact with these women by catching up over lunches or in message threads. Even if you find yourself very short on time, do your best to maintain friendships. We all have a desire to connect.

Becoming a mother doesn't detract from the person you were before you had a baby, but actually adds another facet to your identity. Above all else, know that you and your values and goals count. When you become a mother, you do not become a machine solely dedicated to the satisfaction of another human being. You have not stopped being you. Both you and your baby have separate identities to cherish and grow. I hope you love your baby and yourself unconditionally. It's good for both of you.

CHAPTER 8: THE MAIN POINTS

+ A woman's identity can take a blow on two fronts when she becomes a mother: her workplace identity, and her physical identity.

+ If you are feeling unhappy with the changes in your body after pregnancy and childbirth, be kind to yourself and practise self-compassion.

+ If you are concerned that you have somehow 'disappeared' into motherhood, you are focusing on just one part of your self-identity: your lowered self-esteem. This is transient, and is not the core of who you are.

+ To get a better grasp on your self-identity, explore your personal values.

+ Use your values to guide your goals and your behaviour. Becoming a mother does not stop you from behaving in ways that align with your values and self-identity.

+ You are a mother now, but you have not stopped being you.

PART III

LOOKING AFTER YOUR BABY

CHAPTER 9
CRYING

Mothering myth: Mothers should instinctively know how to settle their crying baby.

Truth: While mothers can often figure out why their baby is crying, there are also times when nothing can be done. During those times, you don't need to be able to stop your baby's tears; you just need to be with her—and keep calm.

Mothering myth: You can spoil your baby by responding to her every time she cries.

Truth: You can never spoil a newborn, or give too much attention. Being with your baby when she cries lets her know she is cared for.

Crying and sleeping are never far from the thoughts of new parents—and, especially in the early months of a baby's life, the two are never far from one another. If your baby isn't asleep, she may well be crying—and she won't care (or even know) whether it's 3 a.m. or 3 p.m. A baby's needs are very immediate, and when she's very little crying is one of the only tools she's got to communicate those needs.

Up to 25 per cent of babies under three months of age experience colic—which is to say they cry for hours every day for no apparent cause, and then mysteriously stop when they reach around four months of age. If your baby gets colic, there is nothing in the world you could have done differently to avoid it. There is possibly not much you can do to make it go away. The one thing you can know is that it will end, eventually. In the meantime, you can soothe your baby and be there with her.

Any parent knows what a challenge a crying baby who won't sleep is when you are exhausted from sleep deprivation yourself. It's important to remember that you are not alone. As you read this right now, there are parents all over the world soothing their inconsolable babies. Sometimes babies cry, and all you can do is be there with them and stay calm. Some babies take longer than others to learn how to sleep at night time, but they do all, eventually, sleep.

In this chapter, I'll introduce some skills for soothing crying babies during the early months of their lives, and also for soothing yourself. I'll also touch on sleep, as it relates to crying, during the first three months of your baby's life. And as for sleep after three months? Well, that's a whole chapter on its own!

WHEN YOUR BABY WON'T STOP CRYING: THE FIRST THREE MONTHS

When a newborn baby seems to be crying for too long, what most parents ask is, 'How can I soothe my baby to sleep?' Sleep, not soothing, becomes the goal. So, before we start, just how much sleep do babies need in their first three months?

All babies are born with common needs, namely lots of sleep, feeding, cuddles, soothing and attention. They are all born hardwired to form relationships with us. However, all babies are individuals from birth, with their own temperament (see page 48) and their own different sleep requirements. Much like adults, some babies fall asleep more easily than others, and have a relatively predictable, orderly sleep–wake–feed pattern from birth. Others are less predictable, and can take longer to fall asleep or not sleep as much. However, even the most intense, energetic, wide-eyed babies need more sleep than adults.

Following is my summary of the information that the Pediatric Sleep Council, a team of international paediatric sleep experts, offers regarding newborn babies up to three months old (on their website babysleep.com). Notice, in particular, the wide variation of sleep times.

+ Sleep, on average, ranges from about eleven to seventeen hours per 24-hour period. Expect your baby to sleep in periods from 30 minutes to three hours at a time during the day and night. General sleep–wake cycles and night-waking are typically driven by hunger.

+ As for naps, newborns are likely to be awake for about two hours at a time before napping. They might have their nights and days mixed up, but you can help them set their body clocks by keeping things dark and quiet at night, while exposing them to daylight and your usual noise during the day. You can wake them for feeding if you need to.

Some newborns might start to make the association between night-time and sleep-time early on during those first few months, and some might even naturally have that pattern from the start. Others, however, won't know anything about the difference between night-time and daytime. They'll need to learn the difference in order to sleep during the night—and, in the meantime, their parents will be up and down at all hours to soothe them when they cry.

Training your baby to sleep through the night isn't an option for at least three or four months, and experts recommend waiting until your baby is at least six months old if you want more reliable results.

So, in those early months, your primary focus will have to simply be on soothing your baby when she cries.

However, although there are a few common strategies for soothing your crying baby, each of those strategies comes with as many vocal detractors as it does ardent supporters—we are talking about babies here, after all! No matter what suggestion one person makes for how to soothe a baby, there will always be another who is militantly opposed to the intervention. Some people even oppose gently patting a baby, as they view it as a mild form of hitting. So my suggestion to you is this: use your own common sense, and choose the strategies you feel comfortable with and think are worth trying.

Keep in mind that it is normal for babies to increase the amount they cry before decreasing it again at around three or four months of age. However, if you notice a significant increase in how much your baby is crying, have this checked by a doctor as soon as you notice, if for no other reason than your own peace of mind. If you are not happy with your doctor's response, get a second opinion.

Let's take a close look at four main soothing strategies now—'the checklist', rocking, white noise and swaddling. Also, let me note that the studies I mention in relation to these strategies are all of a relatively low standard, usually because of small numbers (but for some other reasons as well). Also, if you try these strategies but your newborn continues to cry for long periods for no obvious reason, it's possible she is experiencing colic. I'll look at colic in more detail, along with specific soothing strategies, on pages 210–220.

STRATEGY ONE: 'THE CHECKLIST'
Your first soothing strategy is to go through the following checklist.

+ Offer your baby a feed.

+ Hold your baby.

+ *Calmly* check your baby's nappy.

+ Check to see if your baby is too cold or too hot.

+ Check if your baby needs to be burped (see page 346).

+ Allow your baby to suck something, for example a dummy.

+ Provide your baby with stimulation, for example by singing a song or walking into a different room.

+ Try to help your baby to get to sleep, after you have checked all of the needs above.

Part of this checklist comes from a 1984 clinical trial that was conducted on 40 babies with colic and found that parents who ran through a similar checklist (in no particular order) reported a significant reduction in crying compared with those parents who left their baby to self-soothe.[1] For more information about this clinical trial (and on soothing colicky babies) see pages 213–214. Now, let's take a close look at the items on this checklist.

Offering your baby a feed

Out of everything in the checklist, feeding is the most important. Whether you are breastfeeding or bottle-feeding, there is no risk in checking whether or not your baby is hungry. Many people will say that you should only nurse your baby when he is hungry and caution against letting him 'use you as a dummy'; however, in the early months it is really difficult—and, for many mothers, impossible—to tell one kind of a cry from another. There are a number of reasons why a baby may be hungry, even after a recent feed. For example, if you are breastfeeding and your milk supply is still maturing, you may need to frequently nurse to give your baby extra calories. This should also increase your milk supply.

That said, comforting your baby with a feed when he is hungry is not the same thing as allowing him to fall asleep at your breast or the bottle while feeding. It does seem that, if your baby falls asleep while feeding from birth, after a few months this can lead to an increase in the amount of times he wakes up during the night. Gina Ford, Britain's favourite nanny, warns against feeding your baby to sleep in her book *The One-Week Baby Sleep Solution*.[2] Her concern is that, after three to four months of age, a baby who is fed to sleep could go from sleeping long spells at night to frequently waking up without the ability to settle again without a feed. Ford recommends making sure that, between the second and third weeks post-birth, babies are put into their beds sleepy but awake.

If your baby is falling asleep while feeding, it is really up to you whether you choose to do something about it or not. Some mothers don't mind feeding their baby to sleep, and see it as natural and comforting. However, some mothers would rather their baby doesn't settle only while feeding; if this is you, and you'd like to wean your baby off feeding to sleep, you could check out *The One-Week Baby Sleep Solution*, which offers advice for gently breaking this habit.

Holding your baby, checking your baby's nappy, checking to see whether your baby is too hot or cold or needs to be burped are all self-explanatory. Let's have a look at offering your baby a chance to suck.

Allowing your baby to suck

We know that primate babies suck their fingers to self-soothe, and that human babies can start sucking their fingers just fifteen weeks from conception—it's not uncommon to see a baby doing this in the womb during an ultrasound scan. Sucking is a powerful reflex, and it remains powerful for about four months after birth. Beyond that time, it still gives a child pleasure so it's not unusual for thumb-sucking to continue for four years or more.

So, babies have a desire to suck—but there are big differences in how much each baby likes it. Some babies given a dummy (pacifier) will make a face and spit it out, showing no interest at all. Other babies will latch on to it for dear life; their need to suck is powerful. These babies will often feel settled by sucking on a dummy.

For all that has been written in favour of dummies in relation to reducing the risk of sudden infant death syndrome (SIDS), there is relatively little research into the benefits of sucking a dummy in relation to sleep. A 2016 paper titled 'Pacifier Use, Finger Sucking, and Infant Sleep' was only able to cite two other studies which had considered the relationship, and neither study showed any difference in sleep duration between babies who sucked on a dummy and those who did not.[3] The paper's researchers studied 104 infants aged zero to eleven months; 36 per cent used a dummy, 21 per cent sucked on their fingers, and the rest did neither. While the study found no significant differences in overall sleep time in a 24-hour period, finger suckers slept best at night while dummy suckers slept the least.

However, just because sucking a dummy doesn't increase sleep time, especially at night, this does not mean it won't soothe a distressed baby. A heel-prick study mentioned on page 204 actually considered dummies as well as rocking.[4] After the shock of a heel-prick, dummy use produced a sleep state, reducing the heart rate significantly more than rocking.

So, whether you embrace a dummy or not may depend on what your goal is. If your goal is to help a distressed baby, a dummy might be useful. If your baby is reasonably settled, on the other hand, you could be looking for night-time trouble down the track. If you are torn, there are two good reasons to go with a dummy. The first is that the AAP advises that sucking a dummy in the early months is associated with a lower risk of SIDS.[5] The second is that you have more control over a dummy than you do over your child's thumb, and it may be much easier to break a dummy habit than a thumb-sucking one. Generally speaking, sucking a dummy has served its purpose after six months, so you might consider getting rid of it about that time.

Providing your baby with stimulation
Infants can get bored. Sometimes they need extra stimulation. Simply going outside may be enough to distract a crying baby. Going into a different room in the house might help. Try singing a song. Even small babies are interested in patterns, and may stare at lines in the ceiling from the earliest weeks. Some may do the same with simple, bold drawings in books. You will be the best judge of whether the change of scene is calming your baby or further agitating her.

Trying to help your baby to get to sleep
This is the final instruction on the clinical trial's checklist. Your baby might be crying because he is tired. After the first trimester (especially after six months), there are a number of different ways to settle your baby to sleep, including sleep training—you can read all about them in Chapter 10. For a younger baby, you can try dimming the lights and using any of the soothing techniques discussed in this chapter. Remember, though, as much as we might like to, we cannot make a baby sleep; we can only provide a calm environment.

STRATEGY TWO: ROCKING
Another strategy you can use to soothe your baby is to gently rock him. The comforting effect of rocking is not confined to infants. A study on twelve male adults found that a slowly swinging hammock sent all of the men to sleep, but the same did not occur when the hammock was still.[6] The effect of the swinging could actually be

seen in their brainwaves. Another study found that rocking newborn babies after they'd been given a heel-prick test reduced both their crying and their heart rate.[7]

A third study compared the effect of swinging 70 crying babies in their mothers' arms with swinging them in a suspended blanket and found no difference between the two methods—both were equally successful.[8] This showed that the action of swinging actually has a beneficial effect separate from simply being held, and the researchers suggested this could be because repetitive and rhythmic movements stimulate endorphin secretions, which enable babies to feel 'more comfortable and relaxed'.

A fourth study measured the sleep time of 40 colicky one-month old babies for one full week before any intervention; then, after that, the babies were picked up and swung gently each time they cried.[9] This resulted in an average reduction of crying for each baby of about three-and-a-half hours a week (or 30 minutes a day).

However, although gentle rocking might be an effective soothing technique, the same issue applies here as with babies becoming reliant on being fed to sleep. Rocking your baby to sleep might be working now, but the day may come when you grow tired of it—as many do—and then you will have to break the habit. One advantage is that, unlike breastfeeding, at least a mother can share the load of rocking with someone else. Many babies cry so much in the first three months it may be better for your emotional health to just do what you can to ease the immediate burden, then deal with any resulting habits later.

When it comes to doing the rocking, besides your own arms of course, there is also a wide range of high-tech cots on the market. Some simulate car rides, and some rock gently and emit white noise when your baby cries. Some even alert you to the length and level of your baby's crying spell, so that you can get up and meet their needs if they don't settle quickly.

STRATEGY THREE: WHITE NOISE

White noise is a staticky, shushing sound which masks other noises, and also bears some resemblance to what a baby hears in the womb—which is apparently surprisingly noisy. Many parents use machines that produce white noise to help soothe their babies to sleep; other examples of 'white' noise include the sound of a vacuum cleaner, washer or dryer, a driving car, and the water filter in a fish tank.

White noise does appear to be effective when it comes to soothing babies. A small study carried out in 1990 compared two groups of 20 babies in their first week of life: one group was exposed to white noise, and the other not.[10] This study found that 80 per cent of the babies in the group exposed to white noise fell asleep within five minutes, compared with only 25 per cent in the other group. Likewise, the study mentioned above that found colicky babies cried less after being swung gently also considered white noise.[11] It found white noise was even more successful than rocking, reducing crying by a further one hour a week per baby.

Some vocal advocates recommend parents start using it at birth and keep the white-noise machine running all night for the first year of their baby's life. However, this trend came to the attention of Canadian ear surgeon Blake Papsin, who tested fourteen commercial noise machines and found some were capable of producing 85 decibels—a toxic, hazardous sound level for adult ears. All were capable of producing decibels considered unsafe for babies by American hospitals (greater than 50 decibels).[12] In 2014, Papsin co-authored an article in the journal *Pediatrics*, which concluded that commercial noise machines 'are capable of producing output sound pressure levels that may be damaging to infant hearing and auditory development.'[13] The article conceded that the researchers' main concern was the high-pitched sound levels, and that without further research they could not be certain what safe levels are. However, they outlined the following recommendations.

+ Place the noise machine as far away as possible from the infant, and never in the cot or on a cot rail.

+ Play the noise machine at a low volume.

+ Operate the noise machine for a short duration of time.

This brings us to Harvey Karp, a paediatrician and the author of the extremely popular book, *The Happiest Baby on the Block*.[14] For more on Karp's ideas turn to pages 218–220, but for now let's take a quick look at what he has to say about white-noise machines.

In short, Karp encourages the use of white-noise machines, but agrees they must be used safely. He has taken the concerns about decibel levels seriously, but claims there is no evidence that moderate sounds around 65 or 70 decibels (the sound of a soft shower) are harmful. Karp recommends using a strong, hissy white-noise sound that's as loud as your baby's crying at the start of a crying spell, but then advises turning it down to 65–70 decibels (as opposed to the hospital recommendation of 50 decibels).

He advises to keep the white noise going at this lowered volume (65–70 decibels) in the background, and to use it only at bedtime, night-time and during fussy periods. He also believes that high-pitched sounds promote calming, while deeper, rumbly, womb-like sounds promote sleeping.

The hospital position (50 decibels) and Karp's position (65–70 decibels) are further apart than you might think. You might at first wonder if the difference matters, because the two figures seem close. The problem is that sound intensity doubles with every 10 decibels, so 65 decibels is massively noisier than 50 decibels. What all this means is, if you do intend to use a white noise machine, be sure to buy one that displays the volume.

STRATEGY FOUR: SWADDLING

When you swaddle your baby, you wrap her snugly in a cloth to restrict her movements. Swaddling has a long tradition, and appears to work for many babies, and the theory behind this soothing strategy is that it prevents her from startling herself awake with sudden movements. Obviously, if your baby is restrained, it makes these movements less startling—but does it result in less crying or better sleeping? The results, it would appear, are less convincing than with rocking and white noise.

A 2006 study of 398 'excessively crying infants' up to three months of age showed a marginal advantage when swaddling was added to reducing stimulation, as compared with only reducing stimulation.[15] Infants between one and eight weeks of age reduced their crying by twelve minutes a day if they were swaddled as well as having stimulation reduced; after eight weeks, though, the benefit dropped to ten minutes a day. A much smaller study of 27 healthy infants, on the other hand, showed swaddling had no effect on sleep time.[16] Meanwhile, a German study of 85 infants all around seven-and-a-half weeks of age found that swaddling increased sleep time by 5 per cent.[17] If the average baby sleeps for twelve hours, this would mean approximately half an hour a day.

Swaddling is not without its detractors. If it is too tight around the chest, it can interfere with a baby's breathing. If it is too tight around the hips, it can result in hip dislocation. No one recommends swaddling once a baby can roll; if a baby rolls on to her stomach while swaddled, she's at increased risk of cot death.

There was a scare about swaddling and cot deaths a few years back, but all those deaths were the result of infants being swaddled and put to sleep on their tummies; as a result, the American Academy of Pediatrics (AAP) warns parents to stop swaddling at the first sign that your baby wants to roll. The AAP also advises that there is a risk of overheating with swaddling, so parents should check that their baby isn't sweaty or flushed. While the AAP does permit swaddling, they caution that swaddling works by reducing an infant's arousal. In the small number of remaining unexplained infant deaths, failure of arousal is one of many possible explanations being considered— but the AAP does not consider that possibility strong enough to override the benefits of swaddling.

In terms of technique, swaddling can be quite tricky to get the hang of. If you are considering swaddling, my advice would be to have a session with someone very familiar with the process so you can learn how to do it correctly; don't just rely on instructions in a book or a video on YouTube. If you do search for instructions online, be sure to start with Mayo Clinic's 'How to Swaddle a Baby' slideshow, which follows AAP guidelines (visit mayoclinic.org).

THE WONDER WEEKS

In 1975, ethologist Robert Horwich published an article saying that the infants of eleven species of primates and three non-primates all showed similar timing for periods of 'regressive' behaviour (that is, periods of more crying and clinging), indicating that the behaviour was genetically determined.[18] These periods preceded 'leaps' in development.

Then, in 1992, two Dutch researchers considered whether the same was true with human babies. Based largely on maternal reports, they found 'an impressive consensus' among fifteen mother–infant pairs and identified eight distinct points of regression in the first 60 weeks—or, as they referred to them, 'fussy' periods—where babies wanted more cuddling, cried more and slept less.[19] These researchers have gone on to publish the book *The Wonder Weeks*, and to create the popular Wonder Weeks app, which alerts parents when their baby hits a new leap and provides advice for how to deal with it.

A small body of subsequent research supports the idea that there are periods of regression (preceding leaps), but differs as to how many periods there are—and how predictable the timing is among human babies.

In 1998, a student of the Dutch researchers published a study that attempted to validate their initial findings through more direct observation of infants (rather than relying on parent reports). While this study did find regressions, it found fewer of them and variation between children as to when they occurred. A problem with this study is that there were only four children observed.[20]

In 2002, the original Dutch study was replicated in Spain with eighteen babies. The researchers found the same number of regression periods for the time period involved—specifically, eight regressions during the first 60 weeks of life. However, they found more individual differences in how babies displayed regression, and half of the babies reached those points either one week sooner or later compared to the original study.[21]

If you feel that a deeper understanding of your baby's stages of development can add to your mothering skills, *The Wonder Weeks* book or app might provide some interesting insights. However, given the very real possibility that your baby may not reach each leap at a precise time, having an app alert you to an event which has either passed or is still in the future could be frustrating. Remember that there are few studies of human babies in this specific area, and the numbers of children involved have been few. On the other hand, there does seem to be an agreed finding so far that periods of regression precede the onset of a new developmental stage in the first few years of life—and this knowledge alone might be enough to provide guidance for you.

COLIC

Too much crying and not enough sleeping are among the most common reasons why new parents take their baby to see their family doctor.[22] Up to 25 per cent of newborn babies experience colic—which is to say they cry inconsolably for hours every day. The stress this causes parents cannot be overstated. It can lead to depression, particularly in mothers, and in extreme cases results in babies being harmed. Despite what some baby theorists would have you believe, colic strikes babies everywhere on earth. It affects breastfed babies, formula-fed babies, babies with constant skin contact and babies in their own bedrooms equally.

The word 'colic' derives from 'colon' because people used to assume that the crying was the result of pain in the abdomen, and possibly gas. During bouts of colic, babies often cannot be settled and will eventually just stop crying; in the meantime, they draw their legs up and certainly look like they are in pain.

Investigations have failed to show what exactly causes colic. All we know is that between 20 and 25 per cent of babies under three months of age cry for hours every day with no apparent cause; then, for equally mysterious reasons, colic just disappears by about three or four months. It was previously thought that the amount of crying gradually increased to a peak at six weeks, then eventually disappeared by three months of age. However, a recent meta-analysis indicates a steadier amount of excessive crying in the first six weeks, with perhaps a small peak at six weeks, then a rapid and steady decline until it is uncommon in babies older than three months.[23]

The current 'rule' for colic crying is: three hours a day for three days a week. (The old requirement that it last for three weeks has been dropped.) The present consensus is that colic is an issue of development, with the first three months of a baby's life often referred to as the 'fourth trimester', since human babies are in many ways born three months 'early', evolutionarily speaking.

One possibility being considered is immature regulation, so that once the crying starts, the baby has poor control over stopping it—but there is no way to prevent colicky crying from starting in the first place.

THE FOURTH TRIMESTER

Since your baby makes a developmental leap at about three months of age, it is necessary to consider the first three months of life separately. This period is often referred to as the 'fourth trimester'.

This concept comes from the idea that human babies are born three months before their brain is really ready for the outside world. In order for a mother to survive childbirth, her baby must be born while his huge skull (a byproduct of a huge brain) is still small enough to pass through her narrow pelvis (a byproduct of walking upright). This does not mean you have to turn yourself into a walking womb for three months, but it does mean feeding your baby whenever he is hungry and holding him (as much as you can) while he is crying.

The hardest part of mothering in the first months (and often the first year) can be the combination of being sleep deprived and having to listen to your precious baby crying. It is no accident that a baby's cry is extremely compelling for a mother; it is designed to elicit caregiving. Human babies are not like kangaroo babies, who can crawl their way to food safely within a specially designed pouch. A human mother must stop whatever else she is doing and bring the food to her baby. Her reward is a calm, happy baby—or, it's meant to be. Alas, all too often, the crying simply continues.

COLIC HAPPENS TO BABIES EVERYWHERE

Colic is a universal phenomenon. Nonetheless, there is a popular myth that babies raised in Africa don't get colic, because they are worn in slings and have constant physical contact with their mothers.

In 1991, R. Graham Barr, an epidemiologist then at McGill University in Montreal, investigated crying in the !Kung San people of Botswana, whose culture is characterised by continuous holding and carrying a baby in a sling, and by immediate caregiver response to a baby's crying. The main purpose of Barr's study was to find out if the timeline of colic was the same everywhere.[24] Daytime observations of the !Kung showed the same pattern of excess crying during the first three months, followed by a sharp decline, as is seen in the West. However, Barr cautioned that he did not have evening or night-time information. Here, it's necessary to point out that 40 per cent of colic crying occurs in the evenings.

A few years later, in 1994, Ian St James-Roberts, a British professor of child psychology, released a study of a culture in the Himalayan town of Manali, India, with similar infant-rearing practices to the !Kung.[25] Mothers in Manali were asked how much their babies cried, and tape-recordings were made of their babies crying. These recordings were then compared to ones from London babies (the London babies studied were not carried in a sling or bed-shared at night). The results were twofold: first, the babies in Manali cried six times more than their mothers had reported; second, they cried as much as—if not more than—the London babies did.

Even though colic happens to babies everywhere, it defies treatment or explanation. It would be wonderful if one day a simple solution—like back sleeping, which knocked SIDS off its perch, for example—was discovered to relieve the symptoms of colic, even if not the cause. Until then, though, there's not much more parents can do if their baby has colic besides finding ways to get support and remain calm in the face of the crying.

Of course, some babies cry a lot and it's not because of colic, but for other reasons that can be attended to. In the 1984 clinical trial on 40 colicky babies that I mentioned on page 200, the babies and their parents were divided randomly into two groups.[26] (There was also a control group matched for a variety of characteristics.) Parents of the babies in one colic group were given a 'low-stimulation' set of instructions, which centred on babies being left to settle on their own. The parents of the other colic group were instructed to keep trying different tactics (in any order) from a list provided (see also the 'checklist' on pages 199–200), which included:

+   offering their baby a feed

+   allowing their baby to suck

+   holding their baby

+   providing their baby with stimulation

+   trying to help their baby sleep.

These parents systematically went through and checked for possible causes of their baby's crying, rather than leaving their baby alone in a cot. Significant improvement was reported by the parents in the group that used the checklist. In particular, the most severe cases of colic were seen to have the most dramatic results. Parents reported a 70 per cent reduction in crying when going through the list, in any order. Meanwhile, there was no reduction in crying when parents left their child to settle without help. The checklist in this study is included in the first strategy for any crying baby (see pages 199–200).

If, once you have gone through the checklist, your colicky baby is still crying, try any of the other three strategies suggested earlier for a crying baby: rocking, white noise and swaddling. If she is still crying, take a deep breath and remind yourself that it is a *normal part of development* for babies to have *increased* bouts of inconsolable crying during the first few months. Some babies cry more than others, whether they cry enough to have colic or not. It is normal for your baby to cry, and it is your response as her caregiver that is important.

IF YOU NEED TO, STEP AWAY

If at any time you are on your own with your crying baby and you worry that you are not safe with her, put her down in her cot on her back and take a break. Walk out to the letterbox, take some deep breaths, then go in to check on her when your distress has reduced. Phone someone and ask them to come and be with you, if you can.

Part of being a good mother is recognising and admitting your limits. Right now, as you read this, there are many other mothers taking a moment and walking away from their crying baby. No baby has ever died from crying.

While the colicky baby has been the subject of humour on sit-coms for years, it is no joking matter for a real-life family. The impact can be devastating. It is associated with maternal depression, and it can have a negative impact on parental relationships. Most horrifying, it can end in a baby being shaken and suffering brain damage as a consequence (see page 220).

Child psychologist Ian St James-Roberts is a pivotal figure in crying research—he has literally written the book on it.[27] However, it's not really a book designed for the general public, but for researchers and public officials interested in policy that will look after families dealing with colic. St James-Roberts has been responsible for turning the focus on to caregivers rather than the child, and says that crying is not the problem. Crying is normal. The problem is the way caregivers respond to a baby's cry.

You need to take care of yourself. Call on all the support you can get. If you can afford it, pay for extra help. If you feel you are reaching breaking point, you are not a bad mother for feeling that way. For more information on taking care of yourself, see Part II of this book.

COLIC OR HUNGER?

Some babies who seem to have colic may simply be hungry. If your baby isn't crying much, and seems to be thriving, you don't need to question your food supply. However, if you offer your baby a top-up of expressed milk or formula after he has had a feed and he feeds hungrily then stops crying, you need to make some decisions. You may, for instance, consider regular top-ups. If your baby doesn't stop crying after feeding hungrily on a top-up of breast milk and is not thriving, you may need to consider whether your breast milk supply is low; this happens, and often can be remedied.

A recent review of studies actually showed that formula-fed babies cry less—quite a lot less.[28] One particular study comparing 52 mothers who breastfed with 45 who did not showed that, at six weeks old, the breastfed infants cried an average of 40 minutes more per day than the formula-fed group.[29] Since this difference was on average, it could all come down to a small group of the breastfed babies not getting enough milk.

Despite what you might be told, the only way to be sure if your excessively crying baby is hungry is to offer him more milk—either expressed breast milk or formula. You might have been told that formula is harmful; this is simply untrue. You might also have been told that, if you mix breastfeeding and formula-feeding, your own milk supply will stop; this, too, is untrue. Just make sure to 'pace' your feeds whenever you use a bottle, tipping it down from time to time so that you can see when your baby is ready to stop the feed. (For more information on formula-feeding, see Chapter 12.)

If you are breastfeeding and it is important to you, but you are worried that you might have a low milk supply, you need to see a good lactation consultant right away. Your first priority is to make sure your baby is getting enough food. If your lactation consultant tells you that your baby isn't hungry, but he is feeding hungrily on expressed breast milk or formula after a breastfeed (not just tasting it), you may wish to discuss this further with your family doctor or another health professional instead. Be in the driver's seat.

For a discussion about comforting your baby at the breast and feeding to sleep see pages 200–201.

COLIC AND HOLDING

A 2006 study led by child psychologist Ian St James-Roberts compared crying between the following three groups.[30]

+ A 'proximal care' group, where there was physical contact 80 per cent of the time and bed-sharing at night.

+ 'London' parents, who had 50 per cent less physical contact with their baby than the proximal parents.

+ 'Copenhagen' parents, who fell in between the London and the proximal parents. For example, the Copenhagen parents took their babies into their bed to feed them, but put the baby back in their own bed to sleep.

This was a study of all infants, not just colicky babies, and it found that the babies of the London parents cried 33 per cent more than the other two groups during the first three months of life. There was no difference in the overall amount of crying between the proximal parents and the Copenhagen parents during those months. However, after three months, the babies of the proximal parents cried more than either the London or the Copenhagen babies.

In terms of overall crying, therefore, the Copenhagen style had advantages that persist. It is a style which could suit parents who have colicky babies—you can comfort your baby when she cries, but you don't have to feel pushed into bed-sharing or baby-wearing.

It seems most mothers find it hard *not* to try to soothe their colicky baby. Indeed, one study that tried to test the effects of less cuddling completely failed, because parents wouldn't comply.[31] A mother is hardwired to respond to her baby's cries. So, until there is a study showing it does any harm to soothe a colicky baby by holding him (and there is no such study), go ahead. Soothe your baby by holding him until it is too much for you, then pass him to someone else to hold for a while.

ARE THERE LONG-TERM CONSEQUENCES FROM COLIC?

No, not if it's really colic.

Many parents worry about crying and infant stress, especially since it has become popular for researchers to test children's cortisol levels, and the news media then connects one thing (or another) with heightened cortisol levels. (For more on cortisol, see pages 228–232.) It appears babies with colic do not have raised levels of cortisol. They do have a flatter level of cortisol (less range) to start with, but in the usual course of events this adjusts when the colic ends.[32]

In 2017, family sociologist Cynthia A. Stifter conducted a review of all the relevant studies and found that, although more mothers reported negative behaviour for a short period after colic ended, this was not seen by other observers.[33] (This may have been because mothers continued to misinterpret their babies' cues as an indication of colic.) No differences in behaviour or cognition at twelve months of age were found between babies who had colic and those who did not. Stifter also reported, reassuringly, that infants who developed colic were no more likely to be insecurely attached than infants who did not have colic. Citing two other studies, Stifter also commented that 'mothers of colic and non-colic infants were observed to be alike in maternal sensitivity shortly after the colic resolved'.

Understand that colic is not your fault. It happens everywhere in the world. Be responsive, and hold your colicky baby when she's crying for as long as you are able to. Your baby will be fine, with no long-term effects.

COLIC AND KARP'S 'CALMING REFLEX'

At this point, you might be wondering, *If one strategy helps a little, is it possible that putting them all together in a logical sequence could help a lot?* Well, Harvey Karp of *The Happiest Baby on the Block* fame thinks so. Karp's *Happiest Baby* DVD is the most-watched child-rearing DVD ever made.[34] His celebrity clients include Madonna and Pierce Brosnan.

Karp is convinced that babies are born with a previously unknown reflex—the 'calming reflex' (which he claims to have discovered)—that can be triggered by combining five interventions. Karp refers to this strategy as the 5 S's: swaddling, side/stomach position, shushing, swinging and sucking. You start with swaddling, then progress to one or more of the other four interventions until your baby's 'calming reflex' is triggered. The more your baby cries, the more of the 5 S's she may need. The 5 S's have to be done correctly, in accordance with your baby's requirements—which you have to figure out yourself.

Karp wants parents to know that, if they use his 5 S's, they will not have to listen to inconsolable crying. He's keen to get this message out, because he thinks it will solve a multitude of problems, including, in his own words, 'child abuse, failure of breastfeeding, marital stress, postpartum depression, excessive visits to an emergency room or doctor, excessive treatment for acid reflux, disturbed bonding, and perhaps sudden infant death syndrome/suffocation'.[35]

In 2010, a research team put Karp's 'calming' reflex theory to the test.[36] The researchers compared an experimental group of eighteen babies with a control group of seventeen babies. The mothers of the babies in the experimental group were shown a video with instructions about Karp's 5 S's. After viewing this video, mothers were allowed to take it home and watch it as often as they wanted. The control-group mothers, on the other hand, were shown another video about normal newborn care. Diaries were kept by the mothers during weeks one, four, six, eight and twelve after the baby's birth, and the baby's sleep duration and crying measured. The researchers found no statistically significant differences between the two groups at any week on either measure.

As with most of the studies we have looked at regarding soothing, this one had its problems. The numbers involved were small, and there was a high attrition rate (many participants dropped out). Karp was unhappy about the study and complained—quite legitimately—about the defects. He wrote to the journal that published the study to say 'other well-designed studies are being planned and conducted to evaluate the THB (5 S's) techniques'.[37]

There might have been serious defects in the 2010 study, but it was still one step better than no study at all—and we still have yet to see the other 'well-designed studies' that Karp promised.

In my opinion, there is nothing Karp recommends which is harmful, and much which could be helpful. The difficulty lies in his assertion that, if the 5 S's don't work, it is either because there is something wrong with your baby or because *you* are not doing it correctly.[38] This sets parents up for disappointment and self-recrimination when they're already at their wits' end. There is no scientific evidence that shows Karp's method works better than any other. Yet, if it doesn't work, parents are left with a sense that *they* have got it wrong. For some parents on the brink, this could be dangerous.

SOMETIMES BABIES JUST CRY

As I've noted, having a baby who cries for hours on end is immensely challenging—so challenging in fact, that vulnerable, exhausted parents can find themselves in a scary place if their frustration and sense of failure overwhelms them.

Developmental paediatrician and world expert in infant crying Ronald Barr has gained a high profile through the *Period of PURPLE Crying* programme, which he developed in association with the National Center on Shaken Baby Syndrome in the United States. It is now the most widely used prevention programme in the US and Canada, and is being rolled out elsewhere. The programme is evidence-based, relies on 50 years' worth of research into normal infant crying, and has two main aims:

+   to support parents and caregivers in their understanding of increased infant crying, and

+   to reduce the incidence of shaken baby syndrome/abusive head trauma (SBS/AHT).

Barr has rejected the idea that babies have a switch, such as Karp's 'calming reflex', which turns crying on or off.[39] What's more, Barr's colleague Ian St James-Roberts told *The New York Times* that Karp has a 'very interesting set of ideas but no evidence' and 'needs to run studies that collect data. Until he does, it's hard to know where the showman stops and the clinical science begins.'[40]

I recommend all parents check out the PURPLE programme website (purplecrying.info). Even babies who do not have colic often cry enough to distress their parents. It offers some wonderful information, including a video in which Barr explains that *all* babies increase their level of crying at about two weeks post-birth, that it gets worse and reaches a peak at different times during the first two months, then steadily gets better by three or four months.[41] Barr wants parents to know that this period of increased crying is part of a baby's *normal behavioural development*, and that a healthy baby can sometimes cry inconsolably for hours at a time and in spite of all of your best efforts to soothe him. His hope is that this knowledge will help parents to stop blaming themselves and reduce feelings of frustration and anger towards their baby.

TWO MORE IDEAS YOU MIGHT SEE ON THE INTERNET

+ **The Hold**. Robert Hamilton has been a paediatrician for 30 years and trained under Harvey Karp. His claim to fame is calming crying babies using a technique called 'the hold', which went viral on the internet. If you are going to try this, please find a video of Hamilton demonstrating it first so that you can see how to hold your baby safely.

+ **Extreme Respect**. A parenting style called Resources for Infant Educarers or RIE (see page 29) advises against soothing by patting and rocking to avoid babies getting used to calming down through parental intervention. Assuming your baby isn't in pain, RIE recommends you show her respect when she cries by sitting beside her, watching her and talking to her softly.[42]

SOOTHING THE SOOTHER

Some mothers quite naturally accept their baby crying, but for many mothers, acceptance is a learned skill. Accepting something is not the same as liking it; acceptance is about not struggling against what you cannot change right now. Pain comes from listening to your baby cry, but suffering comes from not accepting the fact that you cannot prevent it right at this moment. Acceptance doesn't just apply to your baby crying, either; it applies to all areas of your life. Have you ever had it happen that it starts to rain just as your guests arrive for a barbecue? Did you accept that you couldn't do anything about the rain and have fun anyway, or did you let the rain totally ruin the whole day for you? When life doesn't go according to plan—as inevitably happens sometimes—you can rail against it, asking 'Why me?' and complaining that it's not fair, or you can take some calming breaths, accept the moment, and problem-solve (if possible) for the future.

Settling your crying baby is just the same. You can't like the crying, but sometimes there is just nothing you can do to stop the tears. One skill the mothers I work with find useful when they have unpleasant thoughts and feelings while soothing their crying baby is taking a moment to tune in to their own emotions, before turning their mind to what their baby needs. For learning how to tune in to your emotions, turn to pages 109–113. This can help you approach soothing your baby in a calm and accepting way—and, if it does, wonderful!

However, if you need a bit more help, I've got another simple technique for you. I call it J-O-B, and it goes like this.

+ Just crying. Take a deep breath, and say 'just crying' to yourself, either in your mind or in a soft voice. This reminds you that it is normal for your baby to cry.

+ One thing at a time. While you are soothing your baby, focus on just one thing at a time—for example, his skin or his facial expression. If you find it too stressful to focus on your baby, turn your attention to the sound of music playing in the background, or to a tree outside of the window, or even to the wallpaper. Really focus on the music or the tree or the wallpaper, as though this is the first time you have ever noticed them. Turn back to your baby from time to time, and look at him for as long as you can tolerate.

+ Body. Notice what's going on in your body. Notice your breathing. Then look for any tension in your body, for example, your neck or shoulders. Consciously relax any tension you find in your body.

Go back to the beginning and repeat the whole process as many times as you need to in order to stay calm. You might have to do J-O-B over and over, but that's OK. Next time you feel as though you can't cope with your baby's crying, give it a try—hopefully you will be pleasantly surprised.

TIPS FOR SOOTHING YOUR CRYING NEWBORN

When it comes to the first few months of a baby's life, the best soothing advice I can give you is to tune in and to experiment, with realistic expectations.

+ **Tune in.** When your baby cries, be sensitive and responsive to her mood. Keep it low key. Don't try to jolly her—being jolly is for play time. Instead, be gentle and calm. If you were crying, you wouldn't want the person with you to immediately change the subject, let out a whoop and suggest that you party, would you? Being gentle with your baby will help you to feel calm, too.

+ **Experiment**—but have realistic expectations. As Barr and St James-Roberts have pointed out, it is completely normal for babies to be inconsolable at times. There is no scientific proof that any particular technique will soothe your baby every time. Sometimes your baby will just cry, and nothing you do will change that. It's important to truly accept this fact so that you don't become increasingly agitated if a particular intervention doesn't work—especially one you might have paid good money for. Who knows? You might find one of the soothing techniques out there works consistently for your baby. At the end of the day, the best technique for soothing your baby is the technique which allows you to feel the calmest.

+ **Keep calm.** To help you keep calm while soothing your baby, you can try the J-O-B technique on page 223.

YOU ARE NOT ALONE

Sadly, many mothers find themselves feeling guilty or remorseful because of negative thoughts that come into their minds when they are with their babies. These mothers are not acting on these thoughts, and they are being gentle with their babies, but they feel bad nonetheless.

I am here to tell you that you don't need to feel bad, and that you are not alone. To illustrate this, here are just some of the thoughts shared with me by mothers I have worked with.

I can't cope.

If you have this thought while you are soothing your baby, pause and ask yourself, 'What does "not coping" actually mean? Is my baby fed and warm and cuddled?' Remember that 'not coping' is different from feeling uncomfortable or stressed.

If you are actually coping, but you just feel worn out, it can help you to feel stronger by responding with a different thought: *I am not enjoying this, and I have a right to feel sorry for myself, but I am coping. Now, I am going to relax as much as possible and wait for my baby to stop crying.*

I can't do this. I'm a useless mother.

It is very normal to wonder about your competence when your baby isn't doing what you would like him to. But are you really a useless mother? Have a think about what you did right today. Did you provide your baby with nourishment? Did you smile at him? Talk to him? Sing a song? Delight in him? Most likely you did at least some of these things—and that is precisely what good mothering is all about.

I want to run away and leave. I wish you had never been born.
When you are feeling stressed, it is perfectly normal to sometimes wish you could turn the clock back to a time when you were free to do as you pleased or to wish you could run off and leave your baby in someone else's care. However, I doubt you *really* plan to run away. If you have a thought like this, simply notice it and let it float away. Then think about how, eventually, your baby will be big enough for you to resume doing many of the things you used to.

I can't stand this! I have so much to do. The house is a mess, and I want to tidy up.
It is so frustrating when we want to get jobs done and simply can't because our baby needs to be soothed. So, notice this thought and ask yourself, 'What is the *very worst* that will happen if I don't finish my chores?' Is the 'very worst' actually a disaster, or is it (more likely) a passing discomfort?

I hate you.
Some mothers feel very upset when this thought goes through their mind. Ask yourself whether this is really true or just a thought driven by exhaustion and frustration. Do you have this thought when your baby is calm or smiling? Again, notice the thought, let it float away and then re-focus on something external or a more positive thought.

If you have this thought repeatedly, not just when you are exhausted, you can turn to Chapter 6 for more information on maternal mental health.

Case study: Sophie

Sophie found her baby Lucca's crying very distressing. As soon as he cried, she would softly beg him, 'Please, don't cry.' By the time he was three-and-a-half months old, he was still crying for long periods and Sophie was feeling overwhelmed.

At the age of four, Sophie's own parents had taken her to see a psychiatrist because of her tantrums. Sophie took this to mean that showing difficult emotions was 'flawed' and learned to be bright and cheerful in order to get her parents' approval. She didn't allow herself to notice her feelings of anger or sadness, no matter what was thrown at her—but then along came Lucca.

Sophie had expected to love being a mother, and she was shocked by how hard she found it to listen to Lucca cry. His cries stirred up thoughts and feelings that she found hard to accept— thoughts like *Just shut up, Lucca!* and *I can't stand this.*

She worried that she was a bad person. *Imagine if my husband or the other mothers in my coffee group knew what I was thinking,* she fretted. In turn, she began to resent Lucca for triggering these feelings. She by no means wanted to hurt her baby, but she did believe that she wasn't cut out for mothering.

The more she pushed these thoughts and feelings down, the more strongly they appeared. She was on edge, often anticipating that Lucca might start crying, which spoiled her opportunity to enjoy him. Eventually, the negative thoughts became persistent, appearing even at times when Lucca was calm and peaceful.

Sophie decided to get some professional help, and she learned to accept that her thoughts were just thoughts. They were automatic, and not a reflection on her ability to mother or on her self-worth. Sophie learned to live more in the moment. She enjoyed

Lucca when he was settled, and calmly accepted her thoughts and feelings when he wasn't, knowing that she would always act kindly to him no matter what thoughts popped into her mind.

A PRIMER ON CORTISOL

No conversation about babies crying seems complete these days without mentioning cortisol, the stress hormone. In extreme circumstances, an excess of cortisol is linked to poor behavioural outcomes. This means many parents become concerned about possible increased cortisol levels from crying. However, research indicates that normal increases in cortisol under normal circumstances (such as colic) do not result in worse outcomes.

Cortisol's reputation has really taken a hit in recent times. It is often called the 'stress hormone', because people produce a lot of it when they are stressed, but it's pretty important in the body. Back in 1950, a team of scientists won a Nobel Prize 'for their discoveries relating to the hormones of the adrenal cortex, their structure and biological effects'—and one of those hormones was cortisol.[43] Using extracts taken from the adrenal glands of cows, these scientists had isolated 24 new steroids, including cortisol. Cortisol is a close relative of cortisone, which is what you'll find in creams we use to treat dermatitis and heal eczema rashes. It can save a person's life if they go into anaphylactic shock, and it can relieve the pain of gout. It is on the World Health Organization's list of essential medicines. Cortisol gives human beings the energy boost we need when we might have to use our muscles to chase food, defend ourselves or get out of the way. Cortisol goes through a cycle of peaks and troughs in our bodies during the day and night that help us to sleep and wake up.

Cortisol is essential for almost every aspect of foetal development, and under normal circumstances the placenta stands guard and makes sure a growing foetus gets just the right amount of cortisol from its mother. As the foetus grows, the mother's cortisol levels increase and the amount allowed through the placenta also increases—until, at the end of the pregnancy, the floodgates open in preparation for the impending birth.

Although cortisol has a number of helpful functions, there is also overwhelming evidence that massively too much of it—particularly before birth and during the early years of life—can have long-term damaging effects. We all produce cortisol when we are under stress. Research has started looking at the impact of unusually stressful events during pregnancy on baby outcomes. Some studies predicted that high levels of maternal stress during early pregnancy would result in worse outcomes for babies than later in the pregnancy, when high levels of cortisol are normal—and this prediction has since been repeatedly demonstrated to be correct. The effects of high cortisol levels have been observed in children who were in the early stages of foetal development following an earthquake,[44] following the 1998 ice storm in Quebec,[45] and other extreme events followed by observational study.[46]

As well as events that occur early on in pregnancy, there are also extreme stressors that may act for the entire duration of pregnancy (right from beginning to end) and cause the continuous release of cortisol from mother to baby. The most common of these stressors is poverty, with all its malevolent attendants: violence, abuse and want. High levels of cortisol have been found throughout pregnancy in the hair of women exposed to a lifetime of trauma linked with poverty.[47]

It is very important to keep in mind that studies which can link cortisol levels to poor outcomes are considering extremely traumatic situations. They are not looking at ordinary, everyday stressors, such as visits to the dentist, being overworked, minor disappointments or ordinary worries. It is unfortunate that the conclusions reached under these extreme situations have given rise to advice which makes mothers worry about minor fluctuations in their cortisol levels. While there are studies that show that cortisol levels of mother or child can rise during ordinary stress, there is no evidence that this level of change results in any poor outcomes.

It is important to note that historically this exposure to high levels of cortisol had a survival benefit. Before a baby is even born, it is being given some important clues about its future by the amount of cortisol it receives—namely, whether its life is going to be stressful or not. In the wild, this would have survival value for humans, as their babies would be born ready for the struggle to survive. However, in modern society, this translates to children who see the world as more hostile than it really is, and can therefore get into a lot of trouble at school and when they reach adolescence. Young people who are predisposed to find the world hostile as a result of their own personal history will be more easily triggered by stressors than young people who were gestated and born into calmer environments. In order to see how this works, it's important to understand the role cortisol plays in response to stress.

Physiological stress causes a pea-sized gland on the adrenal gland (which sits on one kidney) to produce cortisol. The cortisol then travels quickly to the pituitary gland in the brain, causing it to release an 'attack' hormone that gives rise to the 'fight or flight' response. If the sequence went in only one direction—from stress to 'fight or flight'—then, once the stress was gone, the fight or flight reaction would soon calm down.

However, an experiment on rats proved it isn't that simple, by showing that, when a rat's pituitary gland is stimulated with cortisol, it then sends the 'attack' hormone back to the adrenal gland at great speed.[48] This triggers another cortisol release, which in turn zooms quickly back to the pituitary gland. It is, in other words, a vicious cycle.

A young person who is already predisposed to a heightened stress response readily falls into this cycle. There is little time for rational thought between cycles of cortisol release and the 'attack' hormone release, and this keeps the person in a state of aggression. According to the authors of the study, the speed of this cycle sheds light on why young offenders can have difficulty controlling their behaviour once a trigger sets their stress response off.

Fortunately, though, a baby—whether rat or human—seems to get a second shot at fitting in soon after it's born. A brand-new dynamic takes over. The newborn baby now gets its cues from its mother or caregiver, and the mechanism for delivering these cues is no longer the placenta, but the mother's responsiveness to her baby (see page 45 for maternal responsiveness).

In 1988, Canadian researchers Alison Fleming and Carl Corter explored all the influences, including hormonal, on maternal responsiveness before and after birth.[49] After birth, they identified the significant factors as:

+ the mother's affective state—for example, if she is anxious, depressed, afraid or contented

+ her social relationships, and

+ her experience in caring for young.

Following birth, a good mother is positively and predictably responsive to her baby's emotional needs, and her baby being hungry or frightened comes first. Her baby's other needs (such as nappy-changing and so on) come next. If a mother is sensitive and responsive to her baby's needs, then her baby will most likely become attached in the best possible way—a 'secure attachment'. (For more information on secure attachment, see pages 44–45.)

What is encouraging about this study is that, even when a baby has been exposed to unusually high levels of cortisol before birth, the effects can be modified by parental behaviour after the birth.

MATERNAL CARE CAN UNDO HARM

After having coffee with a colleague who was working with rats, cancer geneticist Moshe Szyf found himself wondering, *Might early maternal care alter the way certain genes express themselves?*

Rats were the perfect candidate to test the theory. It is commonly agreed that among rats there are a variety of mothering styles with different outcomes—not unlike in humans. Indifferent mother rats lie flat, practically smothering their pups while feeding them, and engage in less grooming (licking). More engaged mother rats, meanwhile, arch their back while feeding and engage in more grooming.

In terms of outcomes for the pups, those with the more engaged mother do better in spatial and maze memory, and their response to stressful situations shows a lower production of the 'attack' hormone that's triggered by cortisol. What's more, they have a lowered startle response, and show an increased amount of exploring activity.

When the female offspring of each type of rat had pups, they behaved exactly the same way as their own mother had. Were the rats then genetically trapped by these differences?

To find out, Szyf switched the newborn pups from one type of mother to the other—and, just like that, the cycle was broken. The pups showed the characteristics of the new mother. When those female pups then went on to have their own pups, the changed behaviour was passed down to the new pups as well.

The story does not end there. The involved genes changed so clearly that it could be photographed—and you can see this change if you watch Szyf's TED talk online, 'How early life experience is written into DNA'.[50]

MOVING FROM SOOTHING TOWARDS A SLEEP ROUTINE

As I mentioned at the start of this chapter, some babies sleep well from day one, and have an early awareness of night and day. These babies are (both figuratively and literally!) dream babies. However, they're also pretty rare. As many parents will attest, most babies are born with only the very vaguest 'diurnal' rhythm—or, awareness of night and day.

With time (and sometimes a bit of encouragement from parents), babies learn to sleep for longer stretches each night. It's not generally advised to try any sort of sleep training or intervention before three or four months, but it is never too early to start helping your baby to make sleep associations (for sleep training options after three or four months see pages 248–252).

As mentioned earlier, the first three or four months of your baby's life might just as well be considered the 'fourth trimester'. Often a newborn baby, quite simply, is incapable of following any standard you set, no matter how modest. This was confirmed by a randomised study of 246 newborn babies, in which half the mothers were provided with sleep-intervention education and support; at the end of three months, there was no difference whatsoever in the babies' sleep between the two groups.[51] However, it needs to be noted that Gina Ford (the 'Queen of Routine') does not entirely agree. She recommends schedules with times attached from one week post birth.[52]

The best you can do at this early stage is to help build bedtime and sleep associations, which will later speed up night-time sleeping. Choose a few simple activities that you enjoy, such as bathing your baby and singing a lullaby, and be consistent. Do the same activities at the same times every night, so that your baby begins to associate these activities with sleep. When you respond to your baby during the night, keep the lights dim and avoid playing with her. If she cries, simply soothe her, using some of the suggestions at the start of this chapter. Remember that her sleep–wake cycle is predominantly driven by hunger at this age.

Following is my summary of sleep-routine advice for babies zero to three months old from the Pediatric Sleep Council website (babysleep.com).

+ You can start a bedtime routine as young as a few days old. For example, you could choose three calming activities and repeat them each night. Consistency is important.

+ At this age your baby is too young for formal sleep training. However, you can try putting him down when drowsy and see if he falls asleep on his own. Most newborn babies will need help to fall asleep.

+ At one to two months you can begin to separate feeding and sleeping by making feeding the first step of the routine. If he is falling asleep while being fed you can do a brief activity such as changing his nappy in between feeding and sleeping.

As the Sleep Council suggests, you might on occasion try putting her down in her cot when she is sleepy but still awake, to give her the chance to settle without you. Some people suggest putting a baby in her cot, leaving immediately, then coming back to comfort her as soon as she cries. If you do leave your baby to cry for a bit in the fourth trimester before going back to soothe her, do try not to leave her for more than a few minutes, because babies under three months usually need support to settle and the longer you leave her to cry, the harder it might be to settle her.

Whether you hold your baby and let her fall asleep in your arms or soothe her in her cot is up to you, but don't ever fall asleep holding your baby—especially if you are sitting on a sofa or a stuffed chair. It is just too risky. There are a couple of things you can do to avoid this. If you have a partner, you could feed your baby then pass her to your partner to settle. Alternatively, you might bottle-feed when you are exhausted during the night, using either milk you have expressed earlier in the day or formula. Bottle-feeding is faster than breastfeeding, plus you can get someone else to feed your baby if you need to. No baby ever died from a bottle, but sadly babies do die as a result of being accidentally lain on by exhausted parents.

DOES BED-SHARING DELAY LONGER SLEEPS?

Ian St James-Roberts thought that one of the most important findings to come out of his 'Copenhagen' study (see pages 216–217) was that bed-sharing and constant physical contact are not necessary to reduce crying. St James-Roberts was happy about this for two reasons: first, because of his concern about infant deaths associated with bed-sharing throughout the night; and second, because it meant parents could immediately start preparing their baby for better night-time sleeping.

It is very difficult to do this if your baby is sleeping in your bed, as babies wake frequently through the night. Before three months of age, it is thought that frequent waking is the result of a baby needing frequent feeds, and it has been noticed that higher-weight babies with larger stomachs sleep longer at night. By eight weeks most infants are showing a diurnal pattern, and by four months they are taking their largest feed at the end of the day. However, if their mother is right there in the bed, a baby will fully wake when they might otherwise resettle (without being fed or comforted). The mother will wake and respond, and this will reinforce your baby waking up rather than resettling.

Some parents use infant massage as part of their bedtime routine, or start doing a 'dream feed' a couple of hours after their baby has gone to bed. A 'dream feed' is when you give your baby a feed just before you go to bed, without waking her up—she feeds while she's dreaming, so to speak. The idea behind this is to try to stretch out your baby's night-time sleep, so she doesn't wake up because she's hungry. There is no specific research on this technique, but it appears to have the approval of public authorities in Western countries. One of my colleagues who is a midwife has noticed that dream feeds can suit babies who tend to fuss while they feed, as it's a chance to feed them while they are calm. Meanwhile, some people don't believe that dream feeds result in a longer sleep and just disturb a baby's natural sleep patterns. It's over to you. If you want to try it, then go ahead—you'll know best if it works for you or not.

Massage is not a way to settle an already agitated baby, as the baby must be calm before the massage begins. However, many parents who practise baby massage (and it is usual for Māori, Pacific and Indian caregivers) believe it helps a baby sleep. The practice has been widely adopted in the West. You can buy DVDs on infant massaging from trained experts, and there are also a number of demonstrations from the International Association of Infant Massage (IAIM) available to watch online. Although the AAP does not recommend massage specifically for enhancing sleep, they do approve of it generally for bonding and attachment.

Above all else, in these early months, do what feels natural and right for you and your baby. This is your baby, your breast milk or formula, your household and your mother–baby relationship. It is your choice.

Once your baby reaches three or four months of age, you can start with sleep interventions or sleep training, if you wish—and, for more on this, read the next chapter.

CHAPTER 9: THE MAIN POINTS

+ When your baby cries inconsolably, remember that you are not alone. All babies cry sometimes, and right now many other parents all over the world are in the same situation. The best thing for you to do is soothe your baby and keep calm.

+ Remember the four main soothing strategies: the checklist, gentle rocking, white noise and swaddling.

+ If at any time you are on your own with your crying baby and you worry that you are not safe with him, put him down where he is safe and take a break. Have a cup of tea or walk out to the letterbox.

+ Remember that accepting your baby's crying is not the same as liking it. Practise acceptance by not struggling against what you can't change right now: your baby crying.

+ If you need to, use J-O-B: remember it's *just crying*, focus on *one* thing at a time, and notice what's going on in your *body*.

+ You might not be able to start sleep training your baby in the first three or four months, but you can start to teach him positive sleep associations.

CHAPTER 10
SLEEPING

Mothering myth: A good mother doesn't feel sorry for herself, even when she is tired. She just focuses on what her baby wants.

Truth: All mothers feel sorry for themselves from time to time, and they have a right to—especially in the middle of the night, when they are sleep-deprived but their baby doesn't want to sleep.

By three to four months, most babies have reached their crying peak and are on their way down. At this point, the focus changes to getting a bearable night's sleep. Sleep deprivation can have an enormous impact on caregivers. If, when and how to sleep train babies has polarised professionals, parents, relatives, friends and pretty much any person who can type on social media. What experts do agree on is that the debate over sleep training and which method is best should be left until your baby is at least three or four months old. Some even say that sleep training will be more effective if you wait until your baby is six months old. Before three months of age, your baby is simply too young for controlled crying or other formal sleep-training methods.

Following is my summary of what the Pediatric Sleep Council website (babysleep.com) suggests you might expect in terms of sleep from three months to six months of age.

+ On average, at 3–6 months a baby sleeps between eleven and fifteen hours in a 24-hour period. There is wide variation.

+ Babies wake about two to six times during the night, with some returning to sleep on their own (self-settling) while others cry, alerting adults that they are needed. Some infants may need to be fed once or twice during the night, while many are able to sleep through without being fed.

+ Naps generally total about three to four hours of sleep during the day, with some babies taking fewer long naps and others taking more short naps. Try not to let your baby nap much past 4 p.m. as this might interfere with an early bedtime.

And here is my summary of what the Pediatric Sleep Council suggests you might expect in terms of sleep from six months to twelve months of age.

+ Babies continue to sleep eleven to fifteen hours on average in a 24-hour period, with great variability. They continue to wake two to six times during the night, with some babies self-settling and others needing help to settle. Most often, babies no longer have the physiological need to be fed during the night.

+ By nine months, your baby will probably have transitioned to taking two naps per day.

As you can see, there is wide variability in the amount of time that babies sleep during their first year of life.

WHEN YOUR BABY WON'T SLEEP: THREE MONTHS AND BEYOND

Most parents at this stage are less concerned about the total number of hours that their baby sleeps over a 24-hour period than they are about the number of consecutive hours their baby sleeps at night. While some parents are happy to continue getting up throughout the night to feed or tend to their baby, others might be starting to hit a wall of sleep deprivation and exhaustion.

After the first three or four months, many parents would like their baby to start sleeping for longer periods at night so that they themselves can get some sleep.

Even though parenting is a dynamic between the caregiver and the child, all too often well-meaning specialists provide advice without taking the caregiver into account. As I address in greater detail in Part II of this book, a healthy relationship requires two healthy players—and, when it comes to parenting, one of those players is most often the mother. When it comes to sleep, you are not doing you or your baby any favours by driving yourself to the point of exhaustion (at least not any more so than is inevitable with a new baby in the house).

So, before we look at getting your baby to sleep, I want to touch on how important it is that you sleep, too—specifically for your mental health and well-being. To take care of your baby, you need to take care of yourself. I cannot overstate how important sleep is when it comes to preventing and managing a mother's low mood and anxiety.

As well, sleep deprivation can lead to other serious consequences, such as affecting an enjoyable relationship with your baby. You need to be aware of the relationship between how much sleep you are (or aren't) getting and your mood—sleep deprivation can lead to low mood, and that can result in poor sleep, which in turn interferes with your mood, and so on. It's a vicious cycle.

Sometimes mild to moderate depression can be resolved simply by getting enough sleep. Bear this in mind if you are weighing up sleep-training strategies for your baby. Once you have mild to moderate depression, the trajectory is often towards more severe mood difficulties, so self-care from the outset—which includes adequate sleep—is very important.

There is no one right way to manage both your sleep and your baby's, and there are lots of strategies out there, both baby-led or parent-led (and we'll look at them more closely in due course). The important thing is that *your* mood isn't compromised.

Whatever you choose, make sure it works for you, then hold your head up high (or, even better, lie it down on a pillow) and know that you are the best judge of what is right for you and your family. For more information on taking care of yourself, see Part II of this book.

SHARE THE LOAD

If other adults are with you, there is no reason why they cannot help soothe your baby. A crying baby can be passed from person to person for soothing, just as is done in many traditional cultures.

Your baby's safety and your mental health come before anything else—before your values, parenting style or ideas about mothering. Notice any preoccupations you might have with helpers 'not getting it right'. Sure, they might not soothe your baby in the exact same way that you do—but that's OK, especially if you becoming exhausted or depressed is what's at stake.

If you are breastfeeding or bottle-feeding, you might like to feed your baby then hand her straight over to someone else, day or night, to be soothed.

There is no reason why someone else—your partner, your parent,

---

a friend—cannot provide your baby's night feed or last feed of the day in order for you to get an early night. What's more, if you are breastfeeding, you don't need to express milk for this if you don't want to (there is no harm in giving a bottle of formula).

In Chapter 13, I'll thoroughly examine the research into breastfeeding and breast milk. For now, suffice to say that, according to all the evidence, the only medical benefit a baby who is exclusively breastfed for six months gets is—at best—to suffer one or two fewer bouts of a low-level tummy bug. No other claim has stood up to scientific scrutiny.

If a mother comes to me as a client and reports distress in relation to her baby's failure to sleep, I usually ask her what is going through her mind while she attempts to soothe her baby. Sometimes, she'll be reluctant to tell me, because she doesn't want to hear herself say those thoughts out loud or she worries I will judge her as an 'unfit' mother. If this is the case, I'll reassure her that her thoughts are automatic, and connected to feelings; they are not a mark of her character or her ability to be a mother. Thoughts are just thoughts, not facts. (See page 108 for more on this.)

Invariably, mothers feel a sense of relief when they 'confess' their thoughts to me in my clinic, in broad daylight, where we can explore, normalise and decide how to respond to difficult thoughts. Negative or difficult thoughts are common—if you find yourself having them, you are not alone. As long as you feel safe with your baby and your mood is good, it is completely normal to have intermittent negative thoughts while you are soothing an unsettled baby. However, persistent negative thought patterns can be a feature of depression or other mental health difficulties, so if you find yourself having negative thoughts that are pervasive, that drive you to unhelpful behaviours or that happen when your baby is settled, it is a good idea to seek professional support. (For more information on maternal mental health, see Chapter 6.)

SOME COMMON CONCERNS

Here are some examples of worries expressed by many of the mothers I work with.

'If I feed my baby to sleep he will never sleep without my help, but I like it and it means I can get more rest—and I need it.'
Think about the word 'never'. Do you know anyone who has never stopped being fed to sleep?

'I feel depressed and exhausted, but leaving my baby to cry is inhumane. What about her cortisol levels?'
Is it inhumane? We know that untreated maternal depression can have a lasting impact on your baby, but there is no research to say that controlled crying in a loving environment will. The literature indicates that there is neither long-term nor short-term issues at stake. (For more on cortisol, see pages 228–232.)

'This schedule isn't working, but it's what our sleep consultant told us to do.'
Whatever you have been told is a recommendation, not a requirement. Even if you are feeling vulnerable, that doesn't mean you don't know when something isn't working for you. Try one method consistently for a while, and if it doesn't work try something else.

Case study: Mary

As a charge nurse on a busy A & E ward, Mary was used to being in control of all sorts of situations. Now on maternity leave, she enjoyed mothering her toddler, Ben, and was getting pleasure out of her eight-month-old baby, Kim, during the day.

Night-time, however, was a different story. Mary knew that Kim was perfectly capable of sleeping through the night without being fed, but Kim was still waking and crying out for a feed one or two times every night. It was frustrating. The baby was often happy to go back down to sleep straight afterwards, but Mary worried that Kim would never grow out of her night feeds. At the same time, Mary feared leaving her little girl to cry for even a short time.

So, her solution was to stop feeding Kim during the night. Instead, when Kim woke and cried, Mary would stand in the dark and swing Kim in her arms until she went to sleep (which could sometimes take an hour). Mary's theory was that this would stop Kim from associating waking at night with getting a feed. Her husband, Dan, refused to do this, because he didn't mind feeding Kim during the night.

Mary, though, was determined. She had to return to work in a few months, so the night feeds simply *had* to end. However, Mary's method failed to make any difference—and she could feel her mood dropping with each passing night.

Eventually, she realised that something had to give. She needed to be more flexible. Mary and Dan had to decide: either they fed Kim when she woke at night, or they did some sleep training. They decided to go with the sleep training, which involved some controlled crying at Kim's bedtime. They both found the crying stressful—but, after a week or so, Kim had learned to settle on her own and hardly ever woke in the night again.

   After that, everyone slept better, the house was a happier one and Mary enjoyed going back to work.

SLEEP-TRAINING? IT'S YOUR CHOICE

Mary's story is all too common. It is hard caring for a baby when you are exhausted, and when you are exhausted it is hard to make rational decisions. Until quite recently in the scheme of human history, we lived in groups of 20 to 30 people. These groups included relatives such as aunts, uncles, grandparents and cousins—all of them with an extra pair of hands to offer to help soothe and settle a crying baby. Soothing a baby wasn't just the mother's job; it was shared between the whole group.

   However, life isn't like that for most of us any more. Often, new parents are all on their own when caring for their baby, and commonly there is just one parent. When it comes to training a baby to sleep for longer at night, some people like to wag their finger and say that sleep training is 'only for the parents, and not the baby'. This irks me. The happiness between a baby and her parent is synergistic—the happiness of one contributes to and reinforces the happiness of the other. On the other side of the fence there are those who might suggest a parent is 'weak' if they just can't tolerate the crying that may come with sleep training. That is simply not true. Instead of criticising, let's be kind to each other. We are all doing the best that we can.

   Deciding whether or not to sleep train is entirely over to you. It is an individual decision, based on your baby's natural sleep patterns, whatever else you have going on in your life, the amount of sleep you need to stay emotionally and physically well, and your values. Furthermore, remember that what you need or want might change with time, so be careful not to back yourself into a corner by proclaiming that you will *never* try a certain sleep strategy. In my experience, sleep deprivation can turn even the most avid attachment parent to sleep training, and an unsettled baby can nudge an RIE parent to pick the baby up and rock him to sleep. This is a good thing. I feel heartened when a parent is able to change their mind. Flexible parenting is healthy.

Before I describe a few sleep-training strategies and how they work, let's look at when, exactly, it's appropriate to start sleep training after the three- or four-month mark. The Pediatric Sleep Council website (babysleep.com) offers some great free advice, and following is my summary of their helpful information for three- to six-month-olds.

+ Three months is a great time to start moving towards a consistent bedtime between about 7 p.m. and 8 p.m. It's harder to get a baby to sleep after 9 p.m. Make your night routine brief—about 20 to 30 minutes of bath, story and so on, and do these activities in the same order each night. Try not to let your baby nap much past 4 p.m., as this might interfere with falling asleep at bedtime.

+ Month three is a good time to start helping your baby to fall asleep at bedtime without having an adult in the room. If this isn't a goal of yours, don't worry. If you have trouble with night-wakings, though, self-soothing at bedtime will usually do the trick to help your baby sleep longer during the night.

+ Note that your baby should be weaned off her swaddle some time before the end of this period as it is unsafe to be swaddled if she can roll on to her stomach.

And following is my summary of the Pediatric Sleep Council's information for six- to twelve-month-olds.

+ Until your baby knows how to go to sleep on his own at bedtime, respond to night-wakings calmly and consistently. Try not to let your baby nap past 4 p.m.

+ Keep the same general bedtime routine with age-appropriate activities, such as bedtime books or a quiet, interactive song. You can end the routine by putting him in his crib, leaving the room and going in to check on him as frequently or infrequently as you like. When you go to check you can provide a brief and consistent verbal response. Alternatively, you can spend a few nights ending his routine by putting him down and patting him until he falls asleep. The next few nights, remain in the room or doorway until he falls asleep, again providing consistent verbal responses without patting. Finally, the next few nights, leave the room but consistently check on him.

+ If having your baby falling asleep on his own is not a goal for you, don't worry.

+ If your baby uses a dummy, you can teach him to get it himself by reaching out his hand to it in the crib and practising this at bedtime. If your baby stands up in his crib, guide him back down if he does not have the ability to do this on his own. Practise helping your baby to sit back down in the cot during the day.

+ By about six months, most babies no longer need to be fed overnight unless there is a feeding or growth issue.

+ Some babies experience a recurrence of night-wakings between nine and twelve months. Be sure to check with a health provider if you are concerned that your baby might be waking because of physical discomfort, such as teething or reflux.

(Note that, although the Pediatric Sleep Council remarks that most babies no longer need to be fed overnight after six months of age, they do not go so far as to recommend or provide any intervention involving ignoring a cue to feed in the night.)

The reason that sleep training will be more effective at six months and beyond is because your baby's sleep pressure (tiredness from sleepless nights) and circadian (day/night) rhythms develop by this age. Let's take a quick look at a few of the options available: graduated extinction, bedtime fading, scheduled awakenings, and a more baby-led approach.

GRADUATED EXTINCTION

Graduated extinction (controlled crying) is a more gentle form of 'crying it out', which you might have already heard of. The idea behind graduated extinction is that what isn't rewarded gradually diminishes—the same philosophy behind saying 'just ignore him and he'll stop doing it' when a child is misbehaving. Parents who use graduated extinction wait for progressively longer intervals before they respond to their baby's cries at night. For example, on the first night, waits might begin being two minutes long and end up being six minutes; by the seventh night, waits might begin at 25 minutes and end at 35 minutes.

Graduated extinction does usually work, but consistency is key with this approach. Also, some parents find it hard to ignore their baby crying. Unlike when a baby is crying with colic and the caregiver provides comfort, in graduated extinction the baby is left to cry on his own. This raises alarm bells with many mothers, who might worry about long-term effects, but (as you will see below) science does not support this worry.

BEDTIME FADING

The basis of bedtime fading is 'sleep reduction'—or, in other words, keeping your baby awake until she is ready to sleep. The baby's usual bedtime is pushed out by a certain amount of time each night (for example, 30 minutes) until the baby is falling asleep quickly after her bedtime routine; then her bedtime is moved gradually earlier each night until it returns to the original time. The hope is that she will fall asleep easily after her bedtime routine when she is less tired as well.

A 2016 study tested and compared graduated extinction with bedtime fading (two experimental groups) on babies under twelve months.[1] The researchers felt that bedtime fading would be easier on parents, since it didn't involve leaving a baby on her own. However, in terms of increasing night-time sleep, the researchers found that graduated extinction worked best.

Furthermore, for anyone concerned that these techniques go beyond normal stress, it is reassuring that no rise in cortisol levels were found in either of the experimental groups. At twelve months, the babies were assessed for behaviour and given the 'Strange Situation Procedure' to assess attachment (see pages 42–43). There were no differences in attachment security between the two experimental groups (sleep training) and the control group (no sleep training). However, both experimental groups did much better in terms of hours of sleep than the control group.

In 2007 a similar but much larger study of 173 children aged eight to ten months was conducted, and included both graduated extinction and bedtime fading.[2] This study was both random and blind (to the researchers), and therefore of the highest quality possible. It found that there was both a significant decrease in night waking and improved relationships between parent and child in both experimental groups (both graduated extinction and bedtime fading). As a consequence of this study, the American Academy of Sleep Medicine (AASM) classified behavioural techniques as standard practice. In 2012, a five-year follow-up of those children was published and found no difference between the experimental and control groups in emotional or conduct behaviour scores, psychosocial functioning (social interactions), attachment or anxiety.[3]

SCHEDULED AWAKENINGS

Scheduled awakenings are when you wake your baby up fifteen to 30 minutes before he would usually wake up on his own, and then settle him back to sleep. The scheduled awakenings are then phased out. The idea behind this technique is to disrupt spontaneous awakenings and teach your baby to settle himself to sleep. As a sleep-training technique, there doesn't appear to be much research on the efficacy of this approach. Scheduled awakenings are rarely used for babies under one year old—unless you count a 'dream feed' as a scheduled awakening. (See page 236 for more about dream feeds.)

A MORE BABY-LED METHOD

As child psychologist Ian St James-Roberts' 'Copenhagen' study (pages 216–217) showed, a baby's need for comfort is not the same as a baby's need to be fed. A baby's cry may need a response, but he is not necessarily asking to be fed. According to some researchers and experts, this logic can be applied to conclude something along the following lines: if you reliably respond to your baby's cry during the night, and reliably provide whatever comfort or feeding he requires, then increasingly your mere presence will be enough to settle him. This will lead to fewer feeds during the night, and longer intervals between your baby demanding a response.

The key to success is to not immediately jump in by picking your baby up or feeding her. Instead, start with a low level of support, and see if this is enough—for example, simply pat her. Then gradually build up to feeding her if that's necessary to settle her. At the beginning, going from low-level support to feeding can take place in as little as 30 seconds.

A 2017 study of 34 babies approximately six months old put delayed cuddling and feeding to the test.[4] The study's aim is apparent in its title: 'Response-based Sleep Intervention: Helping infants sleep without making them cry'. The researchers gave parents very clear instructions regarding settling their baby to sleep and tending to him at night. The instructions for bedtime included 'quiet time, direct physical contact, book reading, or massage', and instructions for when the baby woke between feeds were as follows.

> Low level of supportive care can include quiet verbal communication, comforting, stroking the infant, patting the mattress, or other low-level calming responses . . . During this short length of time, parents have the opportunity to watch or listen for cues, and the infant has the opportunity to self-regulate . . . if soothing without picking up does not calm the infant . . . provide increasing levels of response . . . which includes cuddling or feeding to comfort.

This was a three-day trial, and the results did show an increase in total sleep time, but there were a number of limitations for this study (which the researchers discuss). The sample size was small, and the results were biased because those reporting the results were not 'blind' (which is to say, observers knew which group the babies were in). Repeating this study on a larger group with blind testing would be worthwhile, especially if it was compared with a 'graduated extinction' or 'bedtime fading' group as above.

However, the logic behind following your baby's cues in a more subtle way makes good sense. Unlike either immediately feeding your baby or allowing him to cry, you are working out exactly what is enough for your baby. If all your baby wants is reassurance and she isn't hungry, what can you gain by being more energetic than is necessary to soothe her? No need to rush in with both barrels blazing.

SAFE SLEEP

From birth through childhood, the first year of life is the most tenuous. There are many reasons for this—prematurity, congenital abnormalities and injury account for the majority of deaths. The most recent statistics show that, in New Zealand, of the 61,000 babies born each year 330 die within their first year of life—and over half of those die in the first month. What's more, about 40 babies a year die unexpectedly and sometimes for no apparent reason—and 90 per cent of those deaths occur under the age of six months.[5]

Before 1992, things looked much worse for babies in the Western world. Up until that time, mothers had been following the advice of Dr Spock (see page 31) and put their babies to sleep on their stomachs. Spock's reasoning was that if a baby was to spit up while in his bed, sleeping on his tummy would prevent him from choking. Then two researchers on opposite sides of the globe made the connection between tummy sleeping and cot death at the same time—in the United Kingdom by Professor Peter Fleming, and in New Zealand by Professor Ed Mitchell.[6]

Within a few years of Fleming and Mitchell's discovery that tummy-sleeping was the mystery killer, the horror of cot death all but disappeared. In 1992, infant deaths started to plummet in New Zealand and in the UK—and continued to decrease so rapidly that within the space of just a few years sudden unexplained deaths had dropped by 75 per cent.[7]

SUDI OR SIDS?

Now that so many sudden deaths in infancy are understood to be the result of either sleep position or suffocation resulting from bed-sharing, unexpected deaths these days are referred to in two ways.

+ Sudden unexpected death in infancy (SUDI) is used for all sudden *unexpected* deaths in infants.

+ Sudden infant death syndrome (SIDS) is used specifically for *unexplained* deaths. (So, to clarify, SUDI includes SIDS.)

It's important to note that SUDI is a relatively new term, so when historic research is discussed SIDS is used to refer to all unexpected deaths.

Research medical biologists are beginning to converge in their views about what causes the remaining unexplained deaths (or SIDS). Notably, they pinpoint a cluster of developmentally delayed reflexes in the brain stem which are related to the regulation of breathing. While researchers have some evidence from human babies (for example, inadvertent recordings of breathing when a baby is dying, and other direct evidence from autopsies or brain scans of at-risk babies before death), a lot of the research is done with animal studies.[8]

THE 'BACK TO SLEEP' CAMPAIGN

It was almost by accident that Fleming and Mitchell stumbled upon the discovery that the major cause of cot death (SIDS) was tummy sleeping—a discovery that has ultimately saved thousands of lives. Fleming, a British physician and mathematician, had been looking at the association between infant death and infection, and in 1984 had set up the Avon infant mortality programme, which collected all the data possible at the death scenes of babies under one year in Bristol, England. Fleming only considered and recorded a baby's sleeping position in order to exclude it.[9] Gradually, however, he began to see the connection between a baby sleeping on her stomach and cot death (SIDS), but his findings were met with scepticism. When Fleming published a paper about his findings in the *British Medical Journal*, the paper was ignored.[10]

Meanwhile, at the same time on the other side of the world, researchers in New Zealand were following the same scent. Not long after Fleming published his findings, Mitchell published his own in *The New Zealand Medical Journal*.[11] By that time, Mitchell and his team had already begun to encourage New Zealand parents to put babies to sleep on their backs and this was showing a rapid decline in unexpected death.[12]

Combined, the efforts of Fleming and Mitchell presented powerful evidence. As a result, and under pressure from mothers, in 1991 the British Government launched the 'Back to Sleep' campaign. Proof of its effectiveness was immediate, and a year later in 1992 the American Academy of Pediatrics (AAP) considered the evidence and also recommended babies be put on their backs. The US took up the Back to Sleep campaign—and, soon after, so did the whole world. Typically, the decline in sudden infant deaths was at least 70 per cent. It is estimated that Fleming and Mitchell's discovery has, to date, saved 3,000 lives in New Zealand alone.

When the fog of tummy sleeping lifted—and, with it, the bulk of previously unexplained infant deaths was removed—an entirely new landscape revealed itself. A ground-breaking British study showed that, of the remaining babies who die suddenly, 50 per cent have parents who are unemployed, and 75 per cent have parents who are poor; meanwhile, a massive 87 per cent of mothers whose babies die of SIDS smoked throughout pregnancy. Researcher Peter

Blair uncovered these demographics while working on his PhD dissertation under Peter Fleming.[13] In New Zealand the infant death rate for the bottom socioeconomic 20 per cent is nearly three times greater than among the top 20 per cent.[14]

So unexplained infant deaths are, it seems, yet another affliction landed on the poor—a group also commonly associated with heavy smoking, drinking, drug use, and living in crowded, possibly unsanitary conditions. The occurrence of unexplained infant deaths continues to decline with each rung you climb up the social ladder. In New Zealand, if you are not poor, you did not smoke or drink during your pregnancy, and you do not bed-share, your baby's risk is only 13 per cent of the already small total of SIDS deaths.

Even if you are poor in New Zealand, your baby's risk is small, but if you are not poor it is significantly smaller. Claims that breastfeeding will reduce the incidence of SIDS do not stand up to scrutiny (see pages 266–269). Some claim that you can cut your baby's risk 'in half' by breastfeeding, but they are talking about an already negligible risk for the middle class and beyond, who have used up most of that breastfeeding gain anyway (if it exists) by looking after their baby before birth and by providing their baby with a safe environment after birth. To clarify, when we are talking about risk in the middle class and above, we are spreading eight deaths a year over 80 per cent of the population—if 61,000 babies are born in New Zealand each year, that works out to be an average risk of 0.0013 per cent. Risk declines as wealth increases.

SAFE SLEEP ADVICE FROM THE EXPERTS

In 2007, Mitchell reviewed the body of SIDS research and drew up a list of recommendations for infant safety while sleeping.[15] Following is a summary of what those were, with recommendations in bold and my commentary alongside.

+ **Put your baby to sleep on his back.** This applies for both daytime naps and at night-time, and is the most important piece of advice. You must do it.

+ **Do not smoke while you are pregnant.** Cigarette smoking is correlated with SIDS. The benefit to a baby is even greater if a low-smoking mother gives up smoking completely than if a heavy-smoking mother reduces smoking.

+ **Bed-sharing and smoking are a dangerous combination.** There is a definite and strong association between SIDS and mothers who both smoke and bed-share.

+ **Do not bed-share with siblings.** Having your baby bed-share with siblings is a risk factor for SIDS.

+ **Do not bed-share at all.** Now that we know about the dangers of tummy sleeping, bed-sharing is the greatest remaining risk for sudden death in infants. The more hours of bed-sharing, the greater the risk. (Note, however, that an opposing view to Mitchell's exists, which claims bed-sharing is safe if the parents neither smoke nor drink.[16] While there is some substance to this, abstaining from smoking and drinking still does not protect you completely.)

+ **Do not sleep on a sofa.** Infants sleeping on a sofa on their own are at a high risk of SIDS, and infants sleeping on a sofa with a parent (for example, if the parent falls asleep while feeding) are at an even higher risk than babies bed-sharing.

+ **Have your baby sleep in your bedroom.** An infant sleeping in the parental bedroom (co-sleeping) has been shown to be protective in two studies. (No one really knows why, and some question exists over whether research really does back this up.)

+ **Ensure your baby does not overheat.** Overheating was more of a consideration before the risks of tummy sleeping were exposed, however it still seems you should not let a baby get overheated while sleeping, either with too many bedclothes or a high room temperature.

+ **Ensure that your baby's bed and bedding are safe.** Everyone agrees that all soft surfaces should be removed from your baby's bed, including such things as sheepskins, pillows (including adult pillows) and duvets. Some even recommend removing head bumpers, sleep wedges and soft toys. Use a firm mattress in good condition.

+ **Illness and infection can be factors.** It appears that mild illness may be a factor for babies who do not sleep on their backs. However, it is not found to be a factor with babies who do sleep on their backs. Studies indicate that the interaction between illness and sleeping on the stomach is what creates the risk.

+ **Get your baby immunised.** As Mitchell noted in a 2012 article, infants who 'are immunised have half the risk of SIDS and are protected against diphtheria, tetanus, whooping cough, etc'.[17]

+ **Breastfeeding** might help. Although Mitchell states this, he was relying on unproven evidence (see pages 266–269).

+ **Dummies (pacifiers) might help.** Mitchell points out that the Netherlands recommends the use of dummies in bottle-fed babies for several years. Likewise, since 2005, the American Academy of Pediatrics (AAP) has recommended using a dummy for the first year of life. Mitchell says two meta-analyses have shown dummy use lowers the risk of SIDS.

In addition to Mitchell's advice above, there is the issue of swaddling. The AAP says that swaddling becomes a high risk if a baby rolls on to her tummy while swaddled. For this reason, you should stop swaddling your baby as soon as she starts to show any sign of rolling over. The AAP also warns that swaddling should be snug around the chest, but allow ample room at the hips and knees.

The AAP's Task Force on Sudden Infant Death Syndrome regularly releases research-based recommendations, and these are updated regularly. You can find them online at the AAP website (pediatrics.aappublications.org).

THE BED WARS: BED-SHARING AND SIDS

I feel sorry for new mothers. At the same time as being told they should exclusively breastfeed, they also understand that night-time breastfeeding goes hand in hand with bed-sharing (more so than with bottle-feeding) and that bed-sharing is a SIDS risk. I am not going to tell you what to do on any of these fronts, as I believe that you have the right to make your own decisions. However, I also believe you have the right to make informed choices. So, with that in mind, let's take a closer look at the relationship between how you feed your baby, where your baby sleeps and what risks might be associated with those things.

Often, breastfeeding lobby groups tend to also be bed-sharing advocates. This is because breastfed babies tend to cluster feed at times (see page 354), and if a mother has to get out of bed every time she feeds her baby she will soon become exhausted—and might give up breastfeeding altogether. However, in New Zealand in 1992, Mitchell named bed-sharing as a SIDS risk that could be modified. He described the decreased risk of sudden death when infants sleep in the same room as their parents, but the increased risk if they shared their parents' bed. If parents stopped bed-sharing, Mitchell thought it would virtually end what remained of SIDS—his primary concern was reducing SIDS, rather than promoting breastfeeding.[18]

In order to better understand Mitchell's position on bed-sharing, it's important to consider New Zealand's particular demographics. In every country, at least half of sudden infant deaths occur among the bottom 10 per cent in terms of deprivation, and 75 per cent of deaths in the bottom 40 per cent. In New Zealand there is a special problem of high infant deaths among Māori, who have a sudden infant death rate *five* times higher than European New Zealanders.[19] In New Zealand, Māori are disadvantaged on every socioeconomic indicator, from lower rates of school completion to low incomes to living in crowded households.[20] Mitchell was less interested in the possible benefits of breastfeeding in regard to infant deaths than he was in the very visible and very deadly outcomes of bed-sharing in deprived communities.

A few years later in England in 1999, Blair confirmed Mitchell's finding that infant room-sharing with parents was beneficial (up to four months), but disagreed with Mitchell's global sanction against bed-sharing. Although both agreed that falling asleep with a baby on a sofa was very dangerous, Blair felt there was not always a risk with bed-sharing, saying, 'There is no evidence that bed sharing is hazardous for infants of parents who do not smoke.'[21] Then, in 2006, Blair published a major study showing that most cases of SIDS occurred in poor families who were bed-sharing and where mothers were more likely to be single and twice as likely to be smokers. He found that one-third of babies who died of SIDS were pre-term compared with a population average of 5 per cent—and being pre-term is, again, associated with low income.[22] Blair's view was that it was better to simply advise against smoking when bed-sharing. Where Mitchell's view had been focused on eliminating bed-sharing, Blair's focused on allowing for the possible benefits of breastfeeding.

In 2010 Blair and Mitchell were still at loggerheads over this issue. Blair published results of a study looking at sleeping practices and how they impact on breastfeeding, and noted that the parents who were most likely to breastfeed (namely, educated and affluent parents) also bed-shared with little risk. These parents, according to Blair, were the sort of people likely to follow professional advice. As for those who do not tend to breastfeed, Blair believed the most important thing was making it easier for them to do so. He believed that telling these people not to bed-share might put them off breastfeeding, so it would be better to just warn them not to bed-share after drinking, smoking or taking drugs, and not to fall asleep while breastfeeding on a sofa.[23]

In the same year, Mitchell published a review of work in the area and used it as an opportunity to once again express his concerns over bed-sharing. He wrote a heartfelt plea in *Current Pediatric Reviews* to consider the tragic consequences of bed-sharing.[24] Mitchell rejected the claims of those who told mothers that bed-sharing was necessary for attachment and bonding, saying that none of it was supported by evidence. He went on to say, 'One might speculate that improved bonding from bed-sharing should result in less abuse of infants, but the ecological evidence does not support this contention.' He then added:

> Irrespective of one's own personal belief, I would argue that parents have the right to know what risks they are exposing their infants to . . . although it could be debated whether ordinary parents can really weigh up the cost, that is the risk of the loss of

the baby . . . against the comfort of not having to get up and put baby back in the cot. At the minimum, health professionals have the responsibility to provide evidence-based advice.[25]

Notably, in that same paper, Mitchell appeared to approve of a Māori initiative encouraging parents who wanted to bed-share to use wahakura or pēpi pods (see box on page 265).

Soon after, Mitchell's colleagues at the University of Otago undertook a major enterprise, hoping to gather evidence to support his contention that bed-sharing was dangerous even in the absence of smoking. They wanted to show that bed-sharing wasn't safe for anyone, which was already the US position. The public policy message needed to be simple: namely, don't bed share. If the message was 'don't bed-share unless this, that or the other', they feared it would get lost. Their study gathered raw data from four other studies across the UK, Australasia and Europe, and was finally published in 2012—but it had some serious problems.[26] While it did include 1,472 cases of SIDS, joining up the information from various studies proved nearly impossible; furthermore, the authors admitted that almost all variables *except* the age of the baby and which study the data came from had to be guessed at. Bearing in mind these serious limitations, the results indicated that bed-sharing was still a significant risk, even when parents did not smoke or drink, and the baby was breastfed.

At the same time that this study was being conducted, Sally Baddock, a student at the University of Otago, completed her PhD in the same area.[27] Baddock's study actually observed and filmed 40 bed-sharing infants between the ages of two and 27 weeks and compared them with 40 infants sleeping in cots. Baddock did find that bed-sharing was beneficial for breastfeeding, but also noted that the babies tended to sleep on their sides rather than on their backs. In 22 cases, mothers regularly pulled blankets over their baby's mouth and nose, sometimes for up to three hours. This, meanwhile, only occurred in one case of the control babies who slept in cots.

These results would have fuelled the concerns that Mitchell and his colleagues shared about bed-sharing. In their discussion in the 2012 study, they claimed that promoting bed-sharing as a way of encouraging breastfeeding was morally wrong, since bed-sharing nearly triples the risk of cot death. They suggested using the Dutch model from the Copenhagen study (see pages 216–217), which was to take the baby into bed for feeding, then put the baby back in a cot adjacent to the parents' bed.

Blair, for his part, responded to the 2012 study with his own smaller but better study about whether or not bed-sharing could happen safely. Without naming the 2012 study directly, his study described it perfectly—and the comments were not flattering. 'Attempts have been made . . . suffered from lack of data . . . imputing values from whole studies where data are missing has led to major concerns about conclusions drawn.'[28] In his study, Blair considered 400 SIDS cases, and the advantage of his study was that all the cases had the same information and shared the same definitions, so nothing had to be altered or guessed at. Through this study, Blair supported his claim that bed-sharing is safe in the absence of smoking and drinking.[29]

Conversely, following the success of the 'Back to Sleep' campaign, the American Academy of Pediatrics (AAP) decided that almost every infant death was explainable, and the main explanation was bed-sharing with parents. In 2011, science writer Andrea Hsu hosted an episode on National Public Radio's programme 'All Things Considered' called 'Rethinking SIDS: Many deaths no longer a mystery'. (You can listen to the episode and read the transcript online at npr.org/programs/all-things-considered.) In the episode, Hsu speaks to a number of professionals who reiterate the view that very few 'true' SIDS deaths remain—in each professional's experience, most can be explained by the baby being in an 'unsafe' sleep environment. Furthermore, these professionals explain to Hsu that hiding the true cause of a death behind a label of SIDS is not what parents want; many want to know what really happened so that it won't happen again.

Bed-sharing has recently become an unofficial criminal offence in the United States of America and in New Zealand. Even where the charges or the case could have been managed differently, there is a new effort to improve public awareness of the risks of bed-sharing by bringing cases before the Court. However, the following cases seem to support Blair's position that a public policy of no bed-sharing falls on deaf ears where it is most relevant—with those parents who drink, smoke or use drugs.

+ When a Texan mother's three-month-old baby died in 2010 while bed-sharing with her, she was charged and found guilty of 'child endangerment'. The baby was her second baby to die in two years. She was sentenced to two years in prison. Twelve years earlier she had been convicted of assault and had issues with drugs.

+ In 2016 a 25-year-old woman from Florida with a history of drug use was arrested. She had picked her baby up from a bassinet, prepared formula, got back into bed, then fallen asleep. When she woke up, her one-month old baby, Zavier, was dead. This had also happened with a previous child. She was charged with 'felony aggravated manslaughter'.

+ A 32-year-old Michigan mother was charged with 'involuntary manslaughter' after drinking alcohol and bed-sharing, which led to her baby's death. She had previously been warned not to co-sleep, and had previously been treated for drug and alcohol use.

+ In New Zealand, a 27-year-old woman was arrested after being warned repeatedly not to bed-share with her baby. She had been given a pēpi pod to use instead (see opposite). She had put her ten-week-old baby to bed with another child while she and her partner went outside to smoke, but when she found the baby an hour later the older child's arm was over the baby. When she was asked why she hadn't used the pēpi-pod provided, she said it was annoying to lift it up and down.[30]

+ When fathers are on the scene, they are not immune to prosecution either. In September 2018, the Wichita, Kansas, parents of two-month-old twins were both charged with 'involuntary manslaughter' after one of the twins was found dead in bed with the father. Both parents were intoxicated, and the children had previously been removed from the parents for child neglect.[31]

Of course, these were all highly publicised court cases, and involved mothers who had been repeatedly warned of the risks of bed-sharing either because of previous losses or because of their risky behaviours. We know very little about those who have suffered just one loss and have never been given warnings.

We don't know, for example, how many cases do or do not coincide with smoking, alcohol or drug use. Social drinking among middle-class mothers is quite common, however middle-class women also have access to privileges that poorer women don't— including education and resources that would help them to take every precaution possible with a subsequent child.

WAHAKURA: THE SAFE BED-SHARING PROJECT

In 2006, the wahakura was promoted and distributed by the Māori community in response to the disproportionate rates of SUDI among Māori.

The wahakura is a traditional Māori woven, flat-bottomed bassinet, which is portable and can be placed on a bed. A pēpi pod is a plastic version. Wahakura and pēpi pods allow parents and babies to sleep next to each other, while also protecting the baby's face from blankets and keeping parents a safe distance away. Both wahakura and pēpi pods can be used until a baby is five to six months old, when the risk of SUDI lessens.

One study compared a stand-alone bassinet (the gold standard for SIDS prevention) with wahakura in a predominantly Māori sample, and found that there were no significant differences in infant risk behaviours or parental sleep or fatigue levels. Wahakura use was linked with an increase in duration of breastfeeding. The study concluded, 'This suggests wahakura are relatively safe and can be confidently promoted as an alternative to infant–adult bed-sharing. Policies that encourage utilisation are likely to be helpful in this high-risk population.'[32]

Parents living in New Zealand can ask their health provider how to access a wahakura or pēpi pod for free. For those who would like to weave their own wahakura, instructions can be found online.[33] Pēpi pods can be purchased internationally as well as in New Zealand, and the latest version features ventilation slits and windows, includes safety instructions under the mattress, and is made from food-grade plastic. (For more information on pēpi pods, see changeforourchildren.nz.)

Following is a summary of safe sleeping rules when using a wahakura or pēpi-pod.[34]

+ Always sleep your baby on his back.

+ Keep your baby's face clear of blankets.

+ Place your baby to sleep with his feet near the bottom end of the wahakura.

+ Use a firm mattress. There should be no gaps between the mattress and the wahakura. A very thin mattress (20–25 millimetres) is best, with a cotton cover.

+ Don't have any loose blankets, pillows or soft toys in the wahakura.

+ Never let your baby sleep with an adult who is exhausted, drunk or who has been taking drugs.

BREASTFEEDING AND SIDS

Both individual studies and surveys of existing studies have been equally divided about the relationship between breastfeeding and SIDS, which leaves a question mark hanging over whether or not there is a relationship at all. The problem is that the number of cases is just too small for valid results. So, in an attempt to overcome the small numbers, a high-powered team of researchers (including Rachel Moon, chair of the AAP's Task Force on Sudden Infant Death Syndrome) decided to carry out a meta-analysis of the better studies and attempted to combine the results into one big study, which was published in 2011. However, they ran into serious difficulties. It became pretty much impossible to get the studies to line up regarding such factors as the definition of SIDS and the variables such as smoking during pregnancy. If a study doesn't line up with any one of those confounders, researchers have to either guess a value for the missing information or reject the entire study. Either option causes serious biases, making any results unreliable. Nonetheless, the researchers tried to do every single thing right. In terms of the definition of SIDS, they stuck to the restricted sense, and therefore would not include studies which defined SIDS as including deaths which were preventable (as a result of bed-sharing or tummy sleeping).

There are problems with meta-analyses like this that don't exist within individual studies. Individual studies may be small, but at least they are internally consistent. With a meta-analysis, the selection bias increases with every study rejected. Even worse, although in this particular case the researchers might have been very clear in their minds about how SIDS should be defined, it is next to impossible to judge how others separate SIDS (where the deaths are unexplained) from other SUDI deaths. In 2011, in the episode of 'All Things Considered' that I mentioned earlier, Moon told the journalist Andrea Hsu that she did not believe in unexplained baby deaths, and that the acronym SIDS was no longer relevant. When Hsu asked whether she could imagine dropping the term SIDS, Moon said, 'Oh yeah, I can imagine a time when we just talk about safe sleep. And I think we're starting to get there.'[35]

What this means is that a SIDS death in one country might not be called a SIDS death in another country. For example, a baby found with its head covered would not be considered as a SIDS death in the US, but seen to be caused by a parent's neglect regarding bed-coverings. In other countries, by comparison, more recognition might be given to the consideration that a baby's head being covered is not necessarily the cause of death, but the result of frantic movements in the course of an event which would have inevitably led to death anyway.

So, taking all of this into account, what were the results of the meta-analysis?

1. Infants who received any amount of breast milk for up to two months enjoyed a 60 per cent risk reduction in SIDS.

2. After two months or more, the risk rate was much the same. So it appeared there was no significant advantage to breastfeeding for longer than two months.

3. As a bonus, if the mother exclusively breastfed, the advantage would be even bigger.[36] In other words, exclusive breastfeeding confers extra benefits in reducing the chance of SIDS.

4. What's more, the researchers were 95 per cent certain these results were correct.

Six years later, those same lead researchers decided to find out more about the benefits of exclusive breastfeeding.[37] Specifically, how long and how exclusive does it need to be to confer that massive double advantage? The researchers searched worldwide for studies which had collected information which could be helpful, but faced much the same problem as before. So, what did they find with this second meta-analysis?

1. Your baby gets no advantage at all for the first two months of breastfeeding.

2. Any amount of breastfeeding over two months gives a reduced chance of SIDS.

3. Exclusive breastfeeding doesn't confer any extra benefit—
   at all.

Well, those findings are rather different! The results have gone from a 95 per cent certainty that two months of breastfeeding gives massive protection to a 95 per cent certainty that two months of breastfeeding gives no protection at all. What's more, they've also gone from being 95 per cent certain that exclusive breastfeeding gives significant additional protection to a 95 per cent certainty that exclusive breastfeeding offers no additional advantage at all.

It is difficult to see how the results of two studies could be more different—and yet both studies were headed by the same researchers, both times doing their very best. If these two studies have done nothing else, they demonstrate that we will not find a link between SIDS and breastfeeding through statistics. It's just too difficult. It is far more likely that the cause of remaining SIDS deaths will be found in the laboratory—and probably while someone is looking for something else entirely and stumbles upon the next big fix.

THE FINAL WORD ON SAFE SLEEP

It appears that the number of unexplained infant deaths is now so small that any study attempting to link a reduced risk of SIDS with breastfeeding is doomed to fail.

When it comes to bed-sharing, Mitchell's research has shown that the risk is not only related to alcohol or smoking but also to the amount of time spent bed-sharing. If you are exhausted and might fall asleep while feeding your baby, feed him in bed with you rather than on a sofa or stuffed chair, as the latter is riskier. If you do fall asleep, move your baby as soon as you wake up—put him into his own cot or wahakura (pēpi pod). Not bed-sharing should be your goal, but recognise that, like so many mothers, you may have some slip-ups. Don't beat yourself up if you fall asleep with your baby in bed because you are exhausted; the risk increases with the amount of time you are bed-sharing, and occasional lapses cause little risk (as long as you are not smoking or drinking or using drugs).

If you are breastfeeding during the night, but you know that you are exhausted, take a moment to weigh up exclusive breastfeeding with the risks associated with bed-sharing. Use a bottle with expressed milk or formula instead (and remember that using one feed of formula per night won't affect your milk production, despite what some may say). Your baby will feed more quickly with a bottle, so you might consider feeding him while sitting on a kitchen chair instead of a comfortable sofa—once again, remember that a stuffed chair or sofa is the most dangerous place to fall asleep with your baby. Better yet, get someone else to do some of the night feeds so you can get some sleep.

If either you or your partner have been drinking alcohol, do not get into bed with your baby. You will probably want to use expressed milk or formula milk anyway if you have been drinking. The American Academy of Pediatrics recommends no bed-sharing whatsoever until your baby is one year old.

CHAPTER 10: THE MAIN POINTS

+ Sleep isn't just important for your baby; it's also important for you, especially for your mental health and well-being. If you are sleep-deprived, do what you need to in order to get some sleep.

+ Deciding whether or not to sleep train is entirely over to you. It depends on your baby's natural sleep patterns, whatever you have going on in your life, the amount of sleep you need to stay emotionally and physically well, and your values.

+ A few of the sleep-training options available include graduated extinction (controlled crying), bedtime fading, scheduled awakenings, and a more baby-led approach.

+ Safe sleep advice from the experts is to put your baby to sleep on his back, don't smoke, don't bed-share, don't sleep on a sofa, have your baby sleep in your room, ensure your baby doesn't overheat, use safe bedding and get your baby immunised. Using a dummy may also help. It is up to you to weigh up the small risk of bed-sharing in the absence of alcohol, drugs and smoking.

CHAPTER 11
BREASTFEEDING: NICE, BUT NEVER NECESSARY

Mothering myth: You are letting your child down if you do not breastfeed.

Truth: Breastfeeding is unnecessary to provide everything your child needs.

I am all for breastfeeding when it is enjoyable for both mother and baby. I enjoyed breastfeeding all three of my babies, and when breastfeeding goes well it can be great. However, it is not a fairy tale ending for everyone, and it is often difficult for many. Sometimes bottle-feeding (with breast milk or with formula) works out better for both mother and child.

Breastfeeding is a matter of choice for a mother. A new mother might want to make some effort to see if it is for her, including persevering when it can be difficult at the start. Unfortunately the information provided about breastfeeding is not especially balanced and comes with a huge amount of pressure attached; what's more, there is a deep stigma about formula-feeding. If a mother can't breastfeed, or doesn't want to, she often ends up feeling as though she is a failure—a 'bad' mother. The truth of the matter, which many mothers don't know but I believe they have a right to know, is that when the research is examined in depth there is not one long-term benefit from breast milk for children raised in developed countries. Related evidence shows that any advantage of breastfeeding—if it does exist—is a result of the greater amount of time it takes to breastfeed, and the verbalisations that occur between mother and child in the course of breastfeeding.

By looking through the research out there, I want to give women what they are entitled to: a right to be educated in what studies have actually shown about breastfeeding and breast milk versus bottle-feeding and formula. Only once a new mother has all of this information at her disposal can she truly make her own informed, fact-based choices. I strongly believe that this is what all mothers deserve. My hope is that, after reading this chapter, if for some reason you cannot breastfeed or decide not to breastfeed you will know there is no reason to feel guilty or even concerned.

WHAT THE RESEARCH SAYS

The largest, most intensive and most thorough longitudinal study ever carried out in relation to breastfeeding was Dr Michael Kramer's PROBIT trial in Belarus. This trial involved 17,046 mother–child pairs who were observed from three months to sixteen years. The project began in June 1996 and only recently came to an end. There were two aims to the trial: the first was to introduce the WHO/ UNICEF Baby-friendly Initiative (see page 293) to maternity services in randomly selected clinics in Belarus, and find out how effective the initiatives were in getting mothers to breastfeed for longer; the second aim was to investigate the influence of breastfeeding on health outcomes. Effectively, this project compared the outcomes of breastfeeding for less than three months with the outcomes of breastfeeding for at least six months. It canvassed obesity, upper and lower respiratory illnesses, gastro-intestinal illnesses, allergies, eczema, asthma, behaviour and intelligence. A great many studies have been published from this project over the last two decades.

After sixteen years, this major project found only one advantage and one disadvantage associated with exclusive breastfeeding.

+ It found that exclusive breastfeeding for longer than three months was associated with an increased risk of obesity—and this was found at both six years and sixteen years of age.

+ The one medical benefit it found for longer exclusive breastfeeding was a reduced chance of having one low-level (as in, not requiring hospitalisation) case of diarrhoea between the ages of three and six months.

Other major studies support the above findings when comparing breastfeeding for three or more months with not breastfeeding at all.

In addition, Kramer's PROBIT trials found that, at six years of age, the children who were breastfed longer showed improved verbal IQ scores, but—importantly—only for the group of babies from less educated mothers. This led Kramer to speculate that it was the behaviours surrounding breastfeeding rather than the breast milk itself which provided the advantage. He said, 'mothers with higher education may already follow child-rearing practices that stimulate cognitive development of their infants through more frequent verbal interaction and reading'.[1]

Related evidence shows that any breastfeeding advantage that might exist is actually the result of the greater amount of time it takes to breastfeed, and the verbalisations between mother and child during the course of breastfeeding. This is why breastfeeding may be of no benefit to the babies of well-educated women in terms of IQ, because well-educated mothers are more likely to provide that stimulation whether or not they breastfeed.

In PROBIT's follow-up study, no significant difference in IQ was found at sixteen years between the experimental (longer breastfed) and control groups when the two groups were matched for variables such as the mother's educational background.[2] (For more on breastfeeding and IQ, see pages 326–330.)

With regards to the PROBIT studies, it's important to note that, although Kramer considers his studies to be random, there are some good reasons to believe the randomness is compromised. There is ample evidence that the two groups compared were dissimilar, and adjustments were therefore necessary to compare them. As a result, pressure has been put on the researchers to publish the results both as random studies and observational studies. (Observational studies attempt to replicate the advantages of randomness by purposely matching the characteristics in the experimental group with the characteristics in the control group.) It should be noted that the PROBIT studies are observational studies of a high level and that they are prospective; they are good examples of cohort studies. See pages 19–23 for more on the differences between types of studies.

Often, the PROBIT results are the same whether expressed as a random study or an observational study, but where results differ, the observational results are the more reliable. For this reason, wherever both random and observational results have been given in a PROBIT study, I report both of them.

As we saw in Chapter 10, studies into sudden infant death syndrome (SIDS) have never provided the same or even similar results twice. It is generally accepted that the number of infant deaths which are not the result of tummy sleeping or bed-sharing is so small that an association between those few deaths and breastfeeding will never be resolved.

Likewise, studies associating breastfeeding with inflammatory bowel disease (IBD), which includes Crohn's disease and ulcerative colitis, have provided conflicting results—sound studies have shown that breastfeeding reduces the risk and equally sound studies have shown that breastfeeding *increases* the risk. Genetics are what appear to be at the core of IBD. (For more on breastfeeding and IBD see Appendix VI.)

Genetics also appear to be at the core of diabetes. The most intensive study by far into the relationship between breastfeeding and type 1 diabetes was coordinated by the American Diabetes Association, with researchers concluding that the weak association they found in favour of breastfeeding could be the result of recall biases (that is to say, relying on the memory of parents).[3] Meanwhile, a large sibling pair study showed no association between type 1 diabetes and breastfeeding.[4] Taken together, no claim can be made linking breastfeeding with a reduced chance of type 1 diabetes. (For more information on breastfeeding and diabetes, see Appendix IV.)

Despite all this, the message given to new mothers about breastfeeding is that breastfeeding confers a whole raft of benefits that haven't actually been proved. When Kramer was questioned by more astute journalists about the limited benefits of extended breastfeeding that the PROBIT study found, he challenged anyone to show any disadvantage to breastfeeding. In response to this challenge, it can be agreed that breastfeeding is not usually harmful. However, the approach is not always sensible. Too often, it borders on the fanatical. The claims made about the benefits of breastfeeding are not only exaggerated and misleading, but often quite simply absurd. When this kind of misinformation is presented as fact, it often terrifies mothers.

A prime example of this in New Zealand is Hutt Maternity facility's 'Artificial Feeding Policy', which was facilitated by a lactation consultant and approved by the Maternity Quality Committee.[5] This policy requires that mothers who want to formula feed must be informed of the following risks: bacterial meningitis, bacteraemia, diarrhoea, respiratory tract infection, necrotising entercolitis, otitis media, urinary tract infection, late onset sepsis, a 21 per cent increase in infant mortality, type 1 and type 2 diabetes, lymphoma, leukaemia, Hodgkin's disease, obesity, hypercholesterolemia, asthma, and reduced cognitive development. After reading all that, if mothers wish to supplement breastfeeding with formula they are required to sign a 'Formula Consent Form'.

Many workers in the area of maternal care share similarly unproven beliefs to those listed in Hutt Maternity's 'Artificial Feeding Policy'. They then pass these beliefs on to new mothers as facts. Mothers should never be brow-beaten into breastfeeding, but this kind of discourse causes mothers to feel that they will put their children's lives at risk if they do not endure whatever pain or distress is necessary to continue breastfeeding. This kind of discourse, far from being benign, causes harm. It harms an already vulnerable group: new mothers. Namely, it harms the physical and mental well-being of a significant number of mothers, and has the potential to damage the bond and attachment necessary for a baby's healthy development.

MOTHERS HAVE THEIR SAY

A surprising number of mothers I see bring up issues about breastfeeding, and have done so for quite some time. When I first started noticing these issues, I incorporated asking mothers about their breastfeeding memories into my standard questioning, and ultimately perceived a pattern—and possibly an association—between negative breastfeeding experiences and maternal anxiety and depression. I began asking these mothers if I could record their experiences, so that I might possibly use them to help others, and it was extraordinary how eager they were to have their stories told. Many also used the opportunity to ask me what the right thing was to do. 'How much should I endure?' they would ask. 'How important is it, really, to breastfeed?'

I didn't have any answers for them. Since I had been one of the lucky ones able to breastfeed my babies without much difficulty, I'd been looking at the whole process with rose-tinted glasses. I wanted to breastfeed anyway, so I had simply accepted what I was told about the benefits and saw them as icing on the cake.

While I knew that astute journalists had been questioning the benefits of breastfeeding for years, it was obvious to me (and, therefore, no doubt also obvious to many others) that journalists were getting a lot of very fundamental things wrong. Most believed, for example, that Kramer's PROBIT studies were random, and that they compared breastfeeding to not breastfeeding. Neither was true. As we've already discussed, as far as medical benefits were concerned, Kramer's studies were observational—and, although they were particularly good studies, they still needed to take confounding variables into account. Furthermore, no one who participated in these studies failed to breastfeed to some extent. The studies only compared shorter periods of exclusive breastfeeding to longer periods of exclusive breastfeeding; they did not compare breastfeeding with not breastfeeding. More research was needed for that.

Meanwhile, other journalists were also all too ready to jump on any new study as the last word on the subject, and accepted whatever exaggerated claims researchers put in their study's abstract. What many people don't realise is that academia is a 'publish or perish' environment, and abstracts (summaries) are used to 'sell' a study to a journal. Research defects are rarely as transparent as the public might think—and researchers certainly don't trumpet them in their abstracts.

I eventually realised that someone needed to look into the research properly—someone with a background in social science research, someone who understood the games researchers and the media can play with statistics, someone who cared enough to spend a year or more doing it. That someone was looking more and more like *me*.

While I don't expect everyone to thank me for this effort, I do hope every thoughtful person will understand why it was necessary. For many women, persevering with breastfeeding results in a positive and even rich experience—I personally felt content and bonded when I breastfed my babies for the most part. However, it is important to understand that this is not everyone's experience. So, let me share with you just a few of the stories that mothers have told me. Note that these stories come from both women who are clients and women I know from other settings, such as book clubs or from school pick-ups. As you will see from these stories, it's not only emotionally vulnerable women who are having issues with the current breastfeeding regime; it's women everywhere. (In the interests of confidentiality, names have been changed.)

Case study: Alicia

'I had massive trouble breastfeeding Christie from the start. It was hard for her to latch. After three weeks, I still wasn't producing enough milk for her and I knew she was hungry. No one ever told me anything about formula, bottles, sterilisation, or even expressing my own milk. I never considered that running thin on milk could be an issue.

'All I saw were lots of pro-breastfeeding posters everywhere. I internalised all of this—the constant breastfeeding messages and the guilt I felt because I couldn't feed my baby. Christie was losing weight, and I was filled with self-blame. There was no information anywhere about what to do. There was no information about supplemental feeding.

'When Christie was three weeks old, I went to the hospital to talk to a midwife. She was very confrontational and talked to me as though it was my fault there was a problem. "Your baby has lost too much weight," she told me, then gave my baby a bottle of formula.

'After that I supplemented breast milk with formula. Once I got over the guilt, I realised that mixing breastfeeding with formula actually freed both me and my partner. I was able to take time out for work, and my partner was able to help with feeding. It opened the door to my independence and to sharing the responsibility for childcare, which fits in with my ideas about gender roles. No one ever told me how to get the most out of bottle-feeding by eye contact or anything. Luckily, I worked that out naturally.'

Case study: Barbara

'I found breastfeeding easy, but there was a problem: my milk didn't come in for six days. I think Billy should have had something more to eat during that time, but no one talked to me about giving him formula. In hindsight, I wish that I had given him a bottle while I was waiting for my milk to come in, but I trusted the professionals. During that first week, Billy was fussy and cried so much of the time. Later, I expressed breast milk sometimes as well as breastfeeding him.

'When he was older, I remember taking him to a crèche, and the teachers noticed that he didn't look at them when they fed him with a bottle. This upset me, as I wondered if it was because when I bottle-fed him I had turned him around so he was facing away from me. No one ever told me how to bottle-feed.'

After having Billy, Barbara had twins whom she mix-fed. Once again, no one provided her with any information about the correct way to bottle-feed.

Case study: Sonia

Sonia, a maternity nurse, told me she was concerned about the lack of information given to bottle-feeding mothers. She confirmed that some hospital nurses are inflexible, and won't even talk about formula. While Sonia tells mothers that there are cognitive and other advantages to breastfeeding, she is concerned about some of the choices mothers make if they do bottle-feed. For example, she has noticed that some mothers buy goat's milk formula on the assumption that since it is expensive it must be better than cow's milk formula, but it is not a good choice. When she coaches bottle-feeding mothers, Sonia encourages them to look at their baby while they feed them, but she says other nurses don't always do the same. Sonia notes that tongue ties, which can be difficult to diagnose and correct, can interfere with breastfeeding.

Case study: Heather

Heather was a doctor, but that didn't stop her feeling the guilt when she bottle-fed her baby, Greta.

'Breastfeeding was terrible. I didn't have enough milk, so Greta didn't get enough milk. She kept losing weight. I was told to breastfeed, express breast milk and then feed her every three hours—even through the night. I did this for the first two weeks, and became completely exhausted. It was affecting my bonding with Greta, but I was determined to succeed for the sake of her IQ. I kept being told I was doing well, because Greta would gain a tiny bit of weight. I trusted my midwife, and she told me to keep breastfeeding, even though Greta was losing more weight than she should have been.

'When Greta was about three weeks old, my mother noticed that something was wrong. It wasn't just that Greta had stopped gaining weight; she was sleepy and listless. She slept most of the day, and my mother was worried. She phoned my dad, who is a doctor. He got in touch with a paediatrician, who said Greta was so quiet because she was hungry and I needed to top up with formula.

'I felt horrible, and so embarrassed. I couldn't believe I had left my daughter to be hungry. I topped her up with formula, and she started to gain weight. At six weeks, I thought it was important to drop the top-ups, but Greta stopped gaining weight again— even though I was taking medication to help with my breast-milk supply. While I was visiting Plunket, I burst into tears because I was so exhausted. The Plunket nurses were experienced and sensible. They told me to start topping up again.

'This time round I didn't bother trying to stop topping up, but I continued to feel ashamed when I was at mothers' groups. Here I was, a doctor, bottle-feeding my baby.'

No one gave Heather any information about the correct way to bottle-feed Greta. She just had to work it out for herself. A few years later, she gave birth to a little boy, Harry, and things hadn't changed.

'The second time around, I was shocked at how hard breast-feeding was again. After three nights in hospital, Harry hadn't slept nearly enough. However, there was nothing but pressure to continue breastfeeding. After my experience with Greta, I insisted on topping up right away. I was made to sign a consent form that was very negative. I felt both guilty and angry, but Harry was grizzly and unsettled and I knew he needed top-ups. I hate to think how first-time mothers must feel signing that form. When I moved from the hospital to a postnatal-care facility, I had to sign the form yet again.

'Once we went home, Harry continued to struggle to gain weight and he seemed unsettled after a feed, but the midwives kept reassuring me that he was fine and convinced me to drop the top-ups. Eventually, Harry went back on to top-ups, and he became a different baby—much more settled.

'My babies hardly ever got sick compared with a lot of breastfed babies I knew, so I really do question how significant the benefits actually are. I also wonder how many people who say they have a "colicky" baby simply have a baby who isn't getting enough milk, and as a result is very unsettled.'

Case study: Evelyn

'Breastfeeding was so bad. My milk didn't come in until my daughter, Karen, was six weeks old. A midwife at the postnatal-care facility gave Karen formula for the first night because she was screaming and I had been trying unsuccessfully to feed her for six hours. She gave Karen the formula, left us two bottles and some sterilising tablets, then left because she had finished her shift. We didn't know what to do next. No one had ever talked to us about bottle-feeding.

'The next time Karen was hungry, I asked another midwife to help me. I told her that the first midwife had given Karen the formula, and she said there was more formula in the kitchen but she couldn't help us. We looked for other midwives to help, but they all said we were "on our own".'

Here Evelyn starts crying.

'One midwife told me that, since I had "stretched Karen's stomach", I would not be able to breastfeed her again. She said Karen wouldn't want my breast milk. That's when I started feeling depressed. I think that's what started my postnatal depression.

'Other midwives kept making me breastfeed, then express but hardly any breast milk would come out. We then used a syringe to give the breast milk to Karen. My partner and I Googled how to sterilise bottles, how to use formula, and how much to use. We had no idea what we were doing. I felt like such a bad mum. I felt stupid, as though we were a couple of morons doing the wrong thing.

'I was paying about a thousand dollars to stay at this private hospital and, instead of being taken care of, I was left with red puffy eyes from crying. Then I found someone supportive in the community and got back into breastfeeding.

'I think the midwife who gave Karen the formula and the bottle on that first night did the right thing. Karen was hungry and needed to be fed. However, we both also needed advice and support.'

Case study: Francine

'I felt confused after giving birth. Everyone kept giving me different information about how to stop Sarah from crying. One person would give me a schedule for feeding and sleeping, then another would criticise me for following that schedule. I was being questioned about "skin-to-skin" contact which didn't make sense to me, because I didn't really know what that was. I felt terrified, incompetent and desperate to get it right.

'Breastfeeding went well at first, but by the second week Sarah kept coming on and off my breast, and wasn't feeding well. We were both in tears. For those first weeks, she was either on the boob or I was expressing while she slept. I was exhausted. I took her to a specialist, who said she had a tongue tie and snipped it, but that didn't help with Sarah's feeding.

'After four weeks, I was at breaking point. I contacted my local maternal mental health service. They were easy-going about whether or not I breastfed, but I was under so much pressure to breastfeed that I thought, I'm the only one who can keep Sarah alive. I thought I should be able to breastfeed. Finally, I worked my way out of the hellhole of advice and stopped breastfeeding at six weeks.'

Case study: Mary

'When Robert was six days old, I noticed my right nipple was sore and that a layer of skin had come off. Over the next couple of days, my nipple began scabbing up and it felt really bad. I contacted my midwife, who said that she was sorry and should have seen it coming, as Robert had a "bad latch". I started feeling low.

'It was seven days until I saw someone. I had been told to use lanolin on my nipple in the meantime. The lactation consultant advised me to take a "nipple holiday" and to express instead of feeding on the side that hurt. She gave me a pump. I didn't know how to use it properly and turned it on to a strong speed, which really hurt.

'About ten days later—when Robert was three weeks old—I got mastitis and my GP gave me antibiotics and advised me to top up using formula. I did that, but felt really bad about it. My nipple was in an awful condition. There was a blockage and my breast was red and swollen. I went to hospital for a few days and was put on an IV drip. I fed Robert from one breast and expressed manually from the other, with a midwife helping me.

'I was lucky because there wasn't an abscess that needed surgery. Instead, the pus drained out of a pore in my nipple. In hospital, I was told that expressing might have been what caused the mastitis—it seems you're damned if you do, damned if you don't. I felt really bad in hospital.

'When I was discharged, I was given a nipple shield but not shown how to use it. By this time my mood was consistently low and my enjoyment of Robert had deteriorated. I was waking up during the night to express with a breast pump, and also waking Robert for a feed. I had blockages on the feeding side and a sore nipple on the other. When Robert was seven weeks, I got mastitis again, and ended up in hospital for another two nights on antibiotics.

'For the last two weeks I have been feeding on both sides. Some days I am in more pain than others. When feeding goes well, I enjoy mothering. When it hurts, I feel tense, waiting to pull him off when he bites hard, and this spills over into a dark mood. Sometimes I want to run away, to leave my partner and baby and be somewhere else. On a bad day, my partner tells me that I stare into space. Four days ago, I had a bad feeding day and I cried for six hours and didn't feel any pleasure.

'A midwife told me that, since I had topped up, it would now take three weeks for the flora in Robert's stomach to recover. It has been preying on my mind. Another midwife told me I was a "breastfeeding hero" for persevering.'

Of course, some might wonder whether only emotionally vulnerable women are having issues with the pressure to breastfeed. So, bearing this in mind, I asked women I see in settings other than my clinic, such as in my neighbourhood and book club.

Here are some of their stories.

Case study: Grace

'I had a hard birth with Tommie. The obstetrician said we had to stop the induction or his neck would probably break, and advised a C-section. He asked me not to push while he organised things, but when he left the room the midwife kept telling me to push whenever I had a contraction. I had to pretend that I wasn't having contractions.

'After the C-section, I reacted to the anaesthetic and vomited all over myself. Meanwhile, a nurse was shoving Tommie under my top, explaining that he needed "skin to skin" and he had to find my nipple. I was really confused. Lying there covered in my own vomit, my first thoughts were, *I don't want him near me. I want to get cleaned up first. Does this mean I am rejecting him?*

'An hour later, I was cleaned up, but Tommie wouldn't latch. Two nurses milked me—one on each side. My mother-in-law came in and saw me being milked. Tommie wasn't latching and I couldn't move. I felt like a complete failure, like a bad mother. Nurses kept asking me in an accusatory way whether the C-section was elective. A La Leche nurse came in and gave me a lecture about breastfeeding and my baby's future health. I was in pain, my back hurt, the feeding was painful.

'I buzzed for a nurse to help, and she said, "For God's sake" and took my baby away. I was frightened, because another baby had

---

just been stolen from that hospital, so I got my husband to come and get us. I discharged myself.

'It was no better at home. I had cracked nipples and a bit of blood. I had no information about either bottles or pumping. I felt at a complete loss. Since Tommie wouldn't latch, I had to express breast milk in order to feed him. At night, I would cry when it came time to feed him. I felt alone, in pain.

'After six weeks, a La Leche nurse came and gave me a "breast is best" pamphlet and a lecture about diseases. Over the next weeks, I felt constant pressure from friends and professionals alike. I kept being told I was doing something wrong, holding Tommie wrong, eating too much garlic or drinking too much coffee. Feeding hurt so much that I cried the whole time I fed Tommie, and sometimes I thought I hated him when it was time to feed.

'Finally a Plunket nurse came and asked me how I felt. It was the first time any professional had asked me that. She was in her seventies and so kind. She told me that she was "supposed" to tell me to keep breastfeeding, but she wanted me to be happy and bond with my baby. She explained that she was also seeing babies who were malnourished because their mothers were so pressured into breastfeeding. I went straight to the supermarket and bought some formula.

'From then on, I loved being a mother so much. My husband did the night feeds, and he loved them. We were suddenly a unit, a family, the three of us. I was happy. We all were.'

Case study: Maria

'Esther was an easy birth. She was beautiful, and a good sleeper from the start. She didn't latch well, but it wasn't too painful. On the second day that she breastfed, I noticed a bit of blood around my nipple. Then Esther convulsed and threw up blood all over me. It looked as if there was as much blood as milk. I was scared, and wondered if the blood was from inside her as I didn't have cracked nipples. The obstetrician came and checked her out and said she was fine and healthy and he didn't know where the blood was coming from. Even though the bleeding continued, the nurses encouraged me to keep breastfeeding, but I felt uncomfortable about the amount of blood she was drinking. I asked if I could pump my breast milk to see how much blood there was. The nurses refused, saying they were not comfortable with "interventions".

'When I got home, things got worse. Esther started vomiting up blood clots. I had lots of milk, so I would pump four bottles and choose the one that was the least pink to feed Esther. My midwife told me it was normal to feel stressed about breastfeeding, and to keep going. But, after three weeks, I couldn't stand it. I wondered if I was poisoning Esther with blood. There was congealed, vomited blood after some feeds, and no one was giving me a reason. I'd had enough, so I weaned Esther without asking anyone.

'When my midwife came the following week, she was visibly annoyed. She asked me, "What did you do? Why didn't you consult me?" I told her I had been consulting her, but she hadn't given me any answers about the blood. I told her it was my choice and I didn't want to discuss it. After that I was such a happy mum and loved feeding Esther with a bottle.'

Case study: Hazel

'The problems started in hospital. Different midwives kept giving me different advice about how to feed Sam. My colostrum didn't come in, and one of the midwives milked me. Like a cow. I'm a private person, and I really hated that. I did feel a bit of the baby blues, but I knew what they were and that they would pass. The real problem was breastfeeding. I just couldn't do it properly and really felt like I had let my baby down. I would feel confident while a midwife was there, but not on my own. Even worse was the pain—I got shooting pain whenever I fed. My toes would curl with it. I dreaded feeding Sam, but I was told it would get better.

'When I got home, I became really exhausted. The pain of feeding was huge and sharp. After three weeks, I got mastitis, and went to the emergency medical centre. I tried oral antibiotics, but they didn't work, so I was admitted to hospital with Sam. In hospital, they tried to get a line in, but they couldn't, so I was back on antibiotics again. Everyone kept telling me to keep breastfeeding and expressing; no one advised me to stop. I was physically and mentally exhausted. I was the lowest I have ever been in my life—I've never felt that way before or since. When my best friend came to visit me in hospital, I felt so revolting that I asked her to sit on the other side of the curtain and not look at me. I was mentally distraught.

'In hospital, I kept feeding Sam through the shooting pain because I wanted the best start for him. I wanted him to have the antibodies to set him up against colds and diseases in the future. Finally, a nurse said to me, "You don't have to do this, you know." That was all I needed—permission from someone to stop.

'I stopped. I realised my baby would be better off with me being happy. I could get up out of bed and mother him. After I switched to bottle-feeding I was relieved, happy, and felt a huge weight had come off my shoulders. When I had another baby a few years later, I decided not to breastfeed from the start. It had been too traumatic with Sam. I felt a bit of guilt for about a day—and then I just loved mothering my baby. I have an amazing relationship with both my boys.'

THE RISE OF THE 'BREAST IS BEST' MOVEMENT

Here in New Zealand, breastfeeding is unnecessary for health, but women are treated as if they are feeding babies in the Third World. Over the rest of this chapter (and in the Appendices), we'll work through the shibboleths of breastfeeding one at a time—that breast milk is a perfect food for babies, and that formula-fed babies will be less nourished, more obese, more delinquent, more diseased and less intelligent. We have already explored the fallacy of breastfeeding as a protection for SIDS in Chapter 10.

First up, let's delve into the idea of the perfect breast—or, that 'breast is best'. As a slogan, 'breast is best' has a long pedigree. Towards the end of the nineteenth century in New Zealand, it was on the front cover of every booklet handed out to new mothers by nurses working under Truby King (see page 78). During the early nineteenth century, babies were fed non-pasteurised milk and mash from unsterilised containers, but King advocated either breastfeeding or using his own formula. Infant mortality dropped significantly, and King is credited with contributing to this. Under King's guidance, the New Zealand Plunket Society and Karitane Nurses delivered mother and childcare services, which encouraged mothers to breastfeed.

The fifties saw the humble beginnings of what would eventually become a major political force in maternity care worldwide. In Illinois in 1956, a small group of mothers banded together to form the La Leche League. The organisation was named after a shrine in Florida dedicated to Our Lady of Plentiful Milk, and the women were reacting against a culture where breastfeeding was out of fashion and mothers were made to believe that bottle-feeding was better for babies. At the time, babies in postnatal wards were often automatically bottle-fed on a strict four-hourly routine by nurses.

Now a major international organisation present in over 80 countries, La Leche's mission statement is 'to help mothers worldwide to breastfeed'. Their philosophy includes statements such as, 'Human milk is the natural food for babies, uniquely meeting their changing needs,' and, 'For the healthy, full-term baby, breast milk is the only food necessary until the baby shows signs of needing solids, about the middle of the first year after birth.'[6]

La Leche might now be a major international force, but back in 1964 they had only just enough members to hold their first conference in Chicago. Over the next two decades, La Leche extended its reach throughout the world, and in 1981 was granted consultative status with the United Nations Children's Fund (UNICEF).[7] In 2017, the World Health Organization (WHO) and UNICEF joined forces to form the Global Breastfeeding Collective, in which La Leche plays a pivotal role. UNICEF is committed to reducing child poverty, hunger and mortality in underdeveloped nations. However, the Breastfeeding Collective has a different ambition: it wants all mothers on earth to breastfeed. Their vision is 'a world in which all mothers have the technical, financial, emotional, and public support they need to start breastfeeding within an hour of a child's birth, to breastfeed exclusively for six months, and to continue breastfeeding—with complementary foods—for two years or beyond.'[8] At the very heart of the collective lies the idea that it makes no difference whether a mother is in Sub-Saharan Africa or the heart of Manhattan. Mothers *must* breastfeed, as though human survival depends upon it. While the collective's promotional material features women and children in developing countries being encouraged to breastfeed as a lifesaving alternative to life-threatening polluted water, their actual goal is to reach a target of 60 per cent exclusive breastfeeding in *every* member country of the United Nations—that's 193 countries worldwide.[9]

The focus of the collective's activities are reinforced worldwide by the WHO's earlier and continuing 'Baby-friendly Hospitals Initiative'. Founded by the WHO in 1991, the initiative is 'a global effort to implement practices that protect, promote and support breastfeeding'.[10] As a result, in New Zealand the New Zealand Breastfeeding Authority (NZBA) was set up in 1997 and contracted by the Ministry of Health to develop the Baby-friendly Hospitals Initiative in New Zealand. As the NZBA states, 'In New Zealand, all maternity facilities are required to achieve and maintain Baby-friendly Hospital Initiative accreditation.'[11]

The NZBA has a board of eight members, and one is La Leche League New Zealand (LLLNZ).[12] The board determines which maternity services are accredited—and being accredited is now a requirement of the Ministry of Health to access the government funding that goes along with it. Currently there are 71 Baby-friendly accredited facilities in New Zealand.[13] According to Baby-friendly NZ '99.85% of infants born in national maternity services are delivered in BFHI accredited facilities'.[14]

In order for a maternity service to obtain Baby-friendly accreditation, the NZBA board requires them to collect data on every mother. Furthermore, the board requires *all* staff (including medical specialists) to partake in up to eighteen hours of training and to complete a short 'quiz'. This quiz contains loaded short-answer questions, such as 'Why is breastfeeding for six months important?', which essentially force staff to agree at set intervals to a predetermined set of ideologies. If a staff member does not answer these particular questions in the correct, affirmative manner, they may not pass the test.

The quiz also goes well beyond the brief of breastfeeding, with LLLNZ essentially using the authority of the Ministry of Health to elevate a debatable theory of baby-wearing into a mandate for all maternal health professionals. For example, the quiz features the question 'What are the benefits of wearing your baby in a carrier, wrap or sling?', which requires the response that baby-wearing 'plays an important role in creating positive relationship between caregiver and child'. However, there is no research that supports this. Furthermore, the belief that baby-wearing is important for the mother–baby relationship can cause undue stress on the mother. (For more information on forming a positive relationship, see pages 50–75). In fact, the use of baby slings in particular is controversial—between 2003 and 2016, there were seventeen deaths and 67 injuries in the United States from the use of baby slings.[15]

To be accredited, Baby-friendly Hospitals in New Zealand are also required to implement a skin-to-skin policy. Eighty per cent of mothers randomly selected for interview must confirm that 'their babies were in skin-to-skin contact with them immediately or within five minutes after birth and that this contact continued for at least an hour'.[16] Additionally, there is a requirement that 'anaesthetists who regularly work with women during labour and birth [undergo an orientation] to the importance of immediate skin-to-skin contact'.[17] However, the theory behind immediate skin-to-skin contact is based on the unsubstantiated belief that mammals—and therefore humans—have a narrow window of opportunity to form a secure attachment immediately after birth. According to a group of nurse researchers, 'This time may represent a psychophysiologically "sensitive period" for programming future physiology and behaviour.'[18] In an online pamphlet, NZBA claims that 'the best place for your baby to start life is on your chest immediately after birth', and that this supports 'a life-long relationship with you and your baby' and 'develops your baby's brain'.[19] Going one step further, Hutt Maternity adds 'colonisation of baby with maternal bacteria' to the list of supposed benefits.[20]

Research in this area is sparse and largely anecdotal, with researchers surprisingly candid about their bias in favour of the practice. One attempt has been made to carry out a meta-study of other studies in the area, with the objective of seeing if skin-to-skin results in any differences in breastfeeding, infant physiology or mother–infant bonding and attachment. Among healthy full-term babies, the researchers found an increase in the number of mothers breastfeeding for four months or less; however, skin-to-skin was not associated with increasing the duration of breastfeeding. A few hours after birth, skin-to-skin babies had a higher glucose level, which indicated they had their first feed sooner. There were no differences in relation to bonding or attachment.[21]

The problem when it comes to skin-to-skin is simply that a good idea has gone rogue. Babies *do* need cuddling, and they *do* need some skin contact. However, the notion that the need is immediate and that delays can result in cognitive or emotional damage is outrageous, and can in fact lead to bizarre outcomes in the delivery room (see Grace's story on pages 287–288). Even worse, it can cause unwarranted anxieties for women who have been misinformed about the benefits of immediate skin-to-skin contact but have been unable to achieve it, possibly as a result of birth complications.

Baby-friendly accreditation also sets a high bar for a facility allowing a mother to use formula. If a woman in their care is not breastfeeding, staff are required to explain their 'failure'. Reasons deemed 'acceptable' appear to be limited to receiving chemotherapy.[22] In a document available on the NZBA's website (babyfriendly.org.nz) titled 'Implementing the Standards of Care for the Non-Breastfeeding Mother and her Baby', the following advice is given.[23]

Even in situations of tobacco, drug and high alcohol use, breastfeeding remains the feeding method of choice for most infants.

Severe incapacitating illness in the mother may pose challenges to breastfeeding that are difficult or occasionally impossible to overcome . . . When a mother becomes ill, she may need considerable support to establish and maintain a milk supply.

In the case of herpes simplex lesions found on the breast, temporary interruption of breastfeeding from the affected breast is recommended.

For most . . . maternal infections, including tuberculosis, hepatitis, mastitis and breast abscess, breastfeeding can commence and continue providing medical protocols such as the Hepatitis B vaccine is given within twelve hours of birth.

Very few medications are contraindicated in breastfeeding. These include antimetabolite drugs such as those used in chemotherapy, radioactive iodine and some anti-thyroid drugs.

The problem this highlights is that Baby-friendly hospitals are not always very mother-friendly. No matter where a baby is born, whether in Bangladesh or in New Zealand, a mother who is reluctant to breastfeed (for whatever reason) will receive unfriendly and largely unsubstantiated warnings. To get an even greater insight into the rigidity of this ideology, consider the current WHO/UNICEF advice about breastfeeding among women with symptoms of HIV/ AIDS in impoverished countries. Despite the fact that there is up to a 32 per cent chance of passing this deadly disease on to a child through long-term breastfeeding (the risk increases with duration of breastfeeding), the Baby-friendly initiative advises breastfeeding for six months—regardless of the HIV/AIDS status of the mother.[24] This policy has been criticised as it is not for the benefit of the baby, but because the 'danger of promoting replacement feeding is that uninfected women or women with unknown HIV status will adopt the practice'.[25] In other words, if other mothers see a mother with HIV/AIDS feeding her baby formula, they might be encouraged to also feed their babies formula—it would 'set a bad example', and never mind the fact that breastfeeding could be a death sentence for the child whose mother has HIV/AIDS.

As an advocacy movement, La Leche League originally formed to counter a social setting in the fifties where women were made to feel ashamed of breastfeeding and led to believe by formula companies with their own profits in mind that formula was 'healthier' for their babies. The impetus was to support women to feel comfortable and confident breastfeeding, despite what the society of the day had to say about it—and it was a noble intention. However, it seems the pendulum has swung too far the other way. The advocacy aimed at empowering mothers has morphed into a dogma so rigid that it refuses to take the mother into account at all.

This dogma is now so entrenched and inflexible in Baby-friendly hospitals that, even when a mother exhibits extreme pain or distress, there is no relief from the pressure she faces to breastfeed. And this includes the instance in which a mother might want to use formula for the plain and simple reason that she does not want to breastfeed. If you are a 'good girl' and persevere with breastfeeding in spite of your own personal pain or misgivings, then all is well. If you are obstinate enough to refuse, however, you may be forced to sign a waiver declaring you are aware that your actions will lead to a variety of negative outcomes for your child. Some of these forms state that breastfeeding provides lifelong health benefits, including a reduced risk of allergies and asthma.[26] This is not only scare-mongering, but also factually incorrect. Research clearly shows that when family history is taken into account breastfeeding has no effect on either allergies or asthma. (See pages 457–459 for more on breastfeeding and asthma.)

MORE SAFE FEEDING CHOICES IN DEVELOPED COUNTRIES

In impoverished countries, millions of children die every year. Worldwide, the leading cause of preventable death in children under five years is pneumonia, followed by diarrhoea. Between them, pneumonia and diarrhoea kill **two million children** under five each year.[27] Bearing this in mind, any project that separates babies from the contaminated water that causes diseases like diarrhoea must be applauded—and promoting breastfeeding over formula does just that. However, this begs the question: to what extent is the advice given to mothers in a Third World country relevant if you are lucky enough not to live in poverty?

First, let's compare the differences in causes of death under five in underdeveloped (impoverished) nations with the causes in developed (wealthy) ones. In impoverished countries, the leading causes of death are, in order: preterm birth complications, pneumonia, birth asphyxia, diarrhoea and malaria. By contrast, the leading cause of child death in the United States is accidents, followed by developmental and genetic conditions, then conditions due to premature birth. Preventable diseases barely rate a mention.

We'll begin with diarrhoea. In underdeveloped countries, diarrheal diseases are almost entirely attributable to unclean water, and to the absence of medical treatments or immunisations to combat the deadly effects of unclean water. Not only are there numerous diseases in the water children drink that lead to life-threatening diarrhoea, but there is no clean water in which to wash hands, clothes or eating implements. The fact that there are millions of mothers in the world who cannot afford the fuel to boil water or sterilise bottles is unfathomable to those of us who live in wealthy countries. In *Disease Control Priorities in Developing Countries*, the situation of these mothers and their children is described as follows.

> Poverty is associated with poor housing, crowding, dirt floors, lack of access to sufficient clean water or to sanitary disposal of faecal waste . . . and a lack of refrigerated storage for food . . . The impact is exacerbated by the lack of adequate, available, and affordable medical care. Thus, the young suffer from an apparently never-ending sequence of infections.[28]

For children who live in these sorts of conditions, exclusive breastfeeding will protect them from unsafe water—but possibly only while they are exclusively breastfeed, as it sadly may not have the long-term benefits hoped for.[29]

However, the world is not an even playing field, and applying the advantage that breastfeeding confers in a country where there is no clean water to a much wealthier country where water sanitation is not an issue is not comparing apples with apples. While diarrheal diseases kill half a million children in poor countries every year, they kill approximately 80 in the US. Furthermore, two-thirds of those deaths occur in disadvantaged households that are likely to suffer from similar poor hygiene and over-crowding issues found in poorer countries. In the US and other developed countries, sanitation, vaccination and advanced methods of rehydration have almost eliminated child deaths from diarrheal diseases.[30]

Now let's look at pneumonia, the leading killer of children under five in underdeveloped countries. According to WHO figures, pneumonia killed over 920,000 children worldwide in 2015.[31] Some believe that figure is an underestimate because of the lack of death certificates for children in underdeveloped countries, and one researcher has estimated the number of child deaths from pneumonia could be as high as 1.575 million per year.[32] Once upon a time in the US, pneumonia killed 25,000 children a year; accounting for population growth since then, that would be something like 50,000 a year today. However, by the 1990s the annual death toll from pneumonia in children under five in the US was 800. So has breastfeeding played any part in the demise of the disease? Well, no. It doesn't appear that way.

Between 1936 and 1972, breastfeeding rates in the US plummeted from 77 per cent to 22 per cent; at the same time, the rate of pneumonia deaths also plummeted. By 1982, breastfeeding rates had risen again to 61 per cent, but the decline in pneumonia deaths continued. Then, in 1989, breastfeeding once more declined to 52 per cent, and meanwhile pneumonia deaths also continued to decline. The two are completely independent of one another. The rate of breastfeeding has shown no impact whatsoever on pneumonia deaths in the United States. What did have an impact was the use of antibiotics and the continued expansion of welfare programmes that ensured poor children got the medical treatment they needed. In the space of almost 60 years the child death rate from pneumonia in the US decreased by 97 per cent—from 24,637 child deaths in 1939 to 800 in 1996.[33]

Therefore, when it comes to breastfeeding, what applies to a mother living in an underdeveloped country doesn't automatically apply to a mother in a wealthy country. If you are lucky enough to enjoy good sanitation and have a fridge at home, if you are not living in overcrowded conditions, and if you have access to good medical treatment, it puts quite a different weight on the importance of breastfeeding. Whether or not you breastfeed, your child will pick up a bug or two in the early years. Rotavirus diarrhoea seems unavoidable for any child, but in developed countries the disease is simply something to be managed rather than something to fear.

THE IMPERFECT BREAST

If human milk wasn't adequate for a baby's needs, we would not be having this conversation. However, it is a big leap from adequate to perfect. There are limits to what nature can provide. Survival is based on fulfilling a hierarchy of needs. Lesser yet important needs must give way to life-and-death needs. Breast milk has certainly kept our species going, but that doesn't mean it was ever perfect.

For a start, whether you breastfeed or formula-feed, you need to think about making sure your baby gets enough iron and vitamin D. Then there's the fact that breast milk and blood (as a result of cracked nipples, which are common with breastfeeding) can pass on contagious diseases and dangerous contaminants to the baby.

IRON AND VITAMIN D

Breast milk is low in iron, a mineral necessary for healthy blood. If a mother takes iron supplements, however, it will not increase the iron in her breast milk. Fortunately, something quite amazing happens in the last few weeks before a baby is born. As if in preparation for the impending scarcity, a baby is infused with iron through the placenta. This iron boost, in combination with the protein from the mother's milk, will in most cases last up to three or four months—probably about same the time a cave-mother might have started adding pre-chewed meat to her baby's diet.

Nevertheless, that burst of iron still isn't enough for all babies. According to the American Academy of Pediatrics (AAP), between 6 and 20 per cent of exclusively breastfed infants 'remain at risk for reduced iron stores'.[34] Even if the risk is at the lower end of the AAP's range, the impact is high—in this case, it's the risk of anaemia. The AAP recommends that, from four months of age, full-term babies who are breastfed half or more of the time should be given 1 milligram per kilogram of body weight of iron per day until they are eating solid foods that contain iron.

Some people believe it is unnatural to tamper with the proportion of anything in breast milk, and support this position by claiming that additional iron does not always go to the baby, but also feeds bad bacteria—leading to diarrhoea and respiratory illnesses. However, these surmises are not supported by research. One completely random study compared 783 infants who were fed non-fortified milk formula with 872 children who were fed iron-fortified milk formula (containing 15 mg of iron as ferrous sulphate).[35] All of the infants were visited monthly by a nurse who recorded their health from birth to fifteen months of age. The researchers concluded that 'for the infants, the tested form of iron-fortified milk (which is sufficient to lower iron deficiency anaemia) does not result in an increased incidence of diarrhoea or respiratory illness'.

A second study involving partially breastfed babies showed the same results, with the researchers concluding, 'We found no evidence to support the hypotheses that breastfed infants given iron-fortified formula are at greater risk of having diarrhoea. This, in addition to the fact that iron-fortified formula has played a major role in preventing childhood iron deficiency anaemia, supports the current recommendation that any formula given to infants be fortified with iron.'[36]

Two other controlled studies found no differences in 'fussiness, cramping, colic, gastroesophageal reflux, or flatulence' between babies who had iron-fortified formula and babies who didn't.[37]

The AAP would like to see low-iron formulas (which have iron levels matching the amount in breast milk) labelled 'nutritionally incomplete'. If your baby is breastfed, the AAP recommends a liquid iron supplement from four months until iron-containing solid foods are introduced at about six months of age. On the other hand, if your baby is on infant formula, the AAP recommends that you use iron-fortified formula from birth through the entire first year of life.[38]

As for vitamin D, we now know that humans are able to

manufacture it in their own bodies. We need sunshine to produce it. You would think that was the end of the matter, but it isn't. In some places there isn't enough sunlight for long stretches of the year. What's more, often babies are kept inside for the first few months or if they do go outside they are bundled up in a way that doesn't expose their flesh to the sunlight. Parents are warned of the danger of later skin cancers from direct exposure to the sun, and sunscreen is strongly recommended.

Whatever the reason, there are a lot of babies in both the developed and underdeveloped worlds who don't get enough vitamin D. A 2015 study showed that a mother's breast milk provided less than 20 per cent of the recommended daily dose.[39] A lack of vitamin D causes rickets, or bone deformity. Rather than risk exposing infants to unprotected sunlight, the AAP recommends that a breastfed baby gets 400 IU of vitamin D a day from shortly after birth until at least twelve months of age. If you use formula, be sure it is similarly supplemented by at least 400 IU of Vitamin D per litre.[40]

DISEASES

It is not just breast milk that can pass on diseases; they can also be passed on through blood, and cracked and bleeding nipples are common with breastfeeding. Quite nasty diseases can be passed on to a child during breastfeeding through sores or abscesses on the breast. There have been so many studies in this area, and so much agreement, that you can have confidence about what is or isn't a risk.

The difficulty when it comes to breastfeeding, of course, is that what constitutes an acceptable risk for one person may not be acceptable for another. Something may be 'low risk' in the sense that it won't have much impact on a population, but your child is not a population. You have a right to make your own informed decisions, so let's look at the diseases that can be passed on through breastfeeding now.

HIV/AIDS

All types of HIV infections are passed through a mother's milk to her baby. As noted earlier, up to 30 per cent of babies breastfed by infected mothers will contract the disease (the risk increases with duration of breastfeeding). New UNICEF protocols promote breastfeeding regardless of HIV status in underdeveloped countries, and the New Zealand Baby-friendly position is that 'mothers must decide between the risk of transmission versus the risk of infant morbidity/mortality from other causes if breastfeeding is withheld'.[41] All I will say in response is that, in a developed country, feeding your child formula is certainly not going to result in 'infant mortality', but breastfeeding your baby if you have HIV may well do.

Mastitis and breast abscesses

A baby can safely breastfeed, even if her mother is in excruciating pain with mastitis. It doesn't make much difference to the baby. As a result, in New Zealand (as in Baby-friendly hospitals around the world), mothers with mastitis are pressured to carry on breastfeeding with oral antibiotics or intravenous antibiotic treatment.

However, breast abscesses can pass on serious bacterial infection to a baby. The New Zealand baby-friendly advice for breast abscesses is antibiotics, repeated needle aspiration, surgery and, in extreme cases, allowing the affected breast to 'involute' (permanently stop milk production).[42]

Mastitis is a painful condition experienced by up to 20 per cent of mothers at least once.[43] It comes with flu-like symptoms including chills, fever and aches. If caught early, it can in most cases be treated with antibiotics. Sometimes, however, it cannot be successfully treated while breastfeeding, yet mothers in Baby-friendly environments are pressured into suffering prolonged pain and misery. Fairly recently, the case of a Welsh mother gained publicity overseas. After Laura Wright gave birth to her little girl, she suffered one incidence after another of mastitis and abscesses, with pain so severe and unrelenting that she would bite into a towel while breastfeeding. She said, 'Despite speaking to seventeen health workers about breastfeeding over three months, while suffering from six abscesses, I was never told to stop. It took a drug that could potentially harm my baby to make someone intervene.'[44]

Wright underwent eleven courses of antibiotics, but little is known about the effect of various antibiotics babies are exposed to through breast milk. There are possible reasons to be concerned, particularly with premature babies. In a paper titled 'Effect of maternal antibiotics on breastfeeding infants', paediatric researcher J. L. Matthew reviewed the effects of antibiotics on breastfeeding infants and suggested this is a badly neglected area of study.[45] Matthew's review does offer tables of the safest class of drugs for different conditions while breastfeeding.

When it comes to the current prevailing expectation that women should continue to breastfeed even through the extreme pain that can result from mastitis and abscesses, I not only believe that women deserve much better than this but that they *need* much better than this—and so do their babies. It does not take much imagination to consider how a woman's traumatic and painful breastfeeding experience might affect her ability to parent effectively.

Tuberculosis (TB)

New Zealand Baby-friendly protocols recommend a mother continues breastfeeding even if she is actively infected with tuberculosis.[46] It does seem that there is little risk through breast milk, but a significant risk from airborne droplets of a mother's sneeze, for example. There is divided opinion about breastfeeding under these circumstances, but if the mother is the caregiver, the main risk is there regardless of whether a mother is breastfeeding or formula feeding.

Hepatitis B and Hepatitis C

Hepatitis B, which is associated with serious liver disease, is present in breast milk but appears more likely to be transferred through blood if the mother's nipples are cracked or bleeding. In New Zealand Baby-friendly hospitals, mothers with hepatitis B are encouraged to medicate and breastfeed regardless—this recommendation is controversial, and not many doctors outside the public system would recommend it.

Hepatitis C is also associated with liver disease, and there is no preventive medication for mother or child. In Baby-friendly hospitals, mothers with hepatitis C are encouraged to breastfeed unless their nipples are bleeding. If her nipple is bleeding, the mother is encouraged to feed her child from the non-bleeding breast.

Herpes simplex

Otherwise known as cold sores or genital herpes, herpes simplex sores can show up anywhere and are especially common around the mouth. A baby will not get herpes simplex through breast milk, which is very lucky as the disease is common and can cause serious problems in newborns. A baby can, however, get it from any caregiver with an active sore, and sores can appear anywhere on the body, including on the breast. The disease can be passed on if the baby touches the sore or if the caregiver touches the sore and then the baby. On their website, the UK's National Health Service (NHS) advises that it is rare for infants to pick up herpes from cold sores, but it can happen and damage internal organs.

The current Baby-friendly recommendation is not to feed on a breast with a sore until the sore is completely healed, and also to pump and discard milk from the infected breast. In addition, some also advise that it may be necessary to supplement with formula during the process.

There is little research on the effect of breast milk on babies of mothers who are taking medication for herpes, but it is generally thought to be safe. All information sites say the same thing: if you have a sore, wash your hands before touching your baby.

CONTAMINANTS

The main contaminants to be aware of when breastfeeding are nicotine and alcohol. When a breastfeeding mother smokes, nicotine (the main offending ingredient in cigarette smoke) passes into breast milk and on to her baby. The amount of nicotine found in the breast milk is three times greater than that found in the mother's blood. As a 2013 paper on the effects of nicotine on breastfeeding infants pointed out, 'Nicotine is rapidly absorbed by the intestine of the infant and may be accumulated in some tissues causing episodes of apnoea [temporary cessation of breathing, especially during sleep], restlessness and even vomiting.'[47]

Alcohol also passes into breast milk and on to the baby, although it does not concentrate the way nicotine does. The weight-adjusted amount of alcohol the baby receives is only 5 per cent of the mother's dose.[48] There is a useful free app called Feed Safe, which provides information about breastfeeding and alcohol to help mothers to make safe decisions (feedsafe.net).

WHEN BREAST MILK GOES WRONG

Not every baby gets breastfeeding right. Sometimes, when breastfeeding goes wrong and the mother's breasts are not drained, sodium (or salt) builds up in the remaining milk. The baby loses interest in the milk, and loses weight and becomes dehydrated and lethargic. This condition is called hypernatremia, and it can be fatal for the baby. Difficult to diagnose just by looking at a baby, hypernatremia is usually only picked up when a mother is worried her baby isn't feeding enough or is jaundiced, but it could be picked up much sooner.

Back in 1994, *The Wall Street Journal* ran an article titled 'Dying For Milk: Some mothers, trying in vain to breastfeed, starve their infants' that identified an apparently new epidemic concentrated among the babies of affluent professional parents.[49] This epidemic corresponded with the general upward trend in breastfeeding, particularly among the well-off. Hypernatremia is being seen with increasing frequency in developed countries. In Edinburgh over an eighteen-month period ending in 2002, thirteen of 9,000 infants were admitted for hypernatremic dehydration. All had been breastfed.[50] In 2000, the Vancouver Breastfeeding Center did a chart review of their own admissions and found 21 cases between 1991 and 1994. Again, all were breastfed. They described the presenting complaints as weight loss, failure to gain weight, lethargy, poor feeding and infrequent or absent bowel movements. Three babies had passed one or no stools in the preceding seven days, and two had passed none in the preceding two days.[51] In 2005, another study at Children's Hospital of Pittsburgh identified the incidence among healthy newborns over a five-year period as nearly 2 per cent of births (1.9 per cent)—that was 70 out of 3,718 infants.[52] They concluded that 'hypernatremic dehydration requiring hospitalisation is common among breastfed neonates'.

It might not seem it, but 2 per cent is a significant number. In New Zealand on average 60,000 babies are born each year, and 59 per cent of them are exclusively or fully breastfed for up to three months post-birth.[53] Based on this, 2 per cent translates to 708 infants per year at risk of hypernatremia. If you have reason to think your baby is showing any of the symptoms of hypernatremia listed above, it would be prudent to talk to an unbiased health provider immediately.

FEAR-MONGERING ABOUT FORMULA

The New Zealand Breastfeeding Alliance (NZBA) Baby-friendly Community Initiative provides an 'Artificial Feeding Policy' on their website (babyfriendly.org.nz) for health providers that states the following among its aims.

To create an environment where families/whanau who have chosen artificial feeding for their babies are respected and given timely, adequate information and support, to select, prepare, feed and store formulas safely and skilfully.

To guide families/whanau who have chosen artificial feeding, in the use of formula alongside the addition of appropriate, adequate and safe complementary foods.[54]

However, information about formula is specifically excluded from group discussions, and is only made available to 'pregnant women who have a sound clinical indication for which breastfeeding is not recommended'.[55] That means virtually no one is allowed that information.

In order to understand the attitudes towards formula that prevail today, it's useful to cast our eyes back over the history of formula feeding. As I've mentioned, until the fifties and sixties, women were encouraged to use formula by the companies who produced it—companies who had profit at heart more than the well-being of mothers and babies. In order to sell their product, these companies weren't necessarily shy about spreading the idea that breast milk was 'inferior' to formula, and mothers were made to feel ashamed for breastfeeding. It was out of this context that activist groups such as La Leche League arose. By the seventies, breastfeeding support was beginning to gain traction.

In 1974, Nestlé foods promoted the sale of powdered baby

milk in impoverished communities where the water supply was deadly; in response, activist organisation War on Want published a 35-page pamphlet titled *The Baby Killer* which accused Nestlé of using sales girls dressed as nurses to persuade mothers in Third World countries to give up breastfeeding.[56] The pamphlet sparked a worldwide boycott of Nestlé products and the development of the World Health Organization's 'International Code of Marketing of Breast-milk Substitutes', which states that formula products must have plain labelling and cannot show pictures of children.[57] The watchdog group International Baby Food Action Network (IBAN), founded in 1972, continues to monitor international compliance to the code. In a 2011 report on New Zealand, IBFAN recommended that New Zealand legislate the code.[58]

Meanwhile, the Maternity Services Consumer Council (MSCC) is a member of the New Zealand Breastfeeding Alliance (NZBA), which of course spearheads New Zealand's Baby-friendly Hospitals Initiative. In 2017, MSCC's spokesperson Brenda Hinton told *The New Zealand Herald*, 'I do think as a society it would be a good idea if formula was treated like a prescription drug, something that you use if you are unable to breastfeed.'[59] But that just begs the question, if women can't get formula, what might they turn to instead? Doctors report that some of their patients are feeding their newborn babies diluted cow's milk or making up their own formula using ingredients such as condensed milk.[60] This is very dangerous but, given the present context of pervasively negative attitudes to formula, not all that surprising.

Whatever your personal preferences, please know that modern formula is very safe and nutritious. No child has died in a developed country from being fed formula milk—which, I have to point out, is a better safety record than breast milk when things go wrong (see pages 307–308). Scientifically speaking, the complete and authentic description of the qualitative and quantitative composition of breast milk can be written on one side of an A4 sheet of paper. It is not the same as deciphering the human genome. Some 200 substances are found in breast milk, and the main components are water, carbohydrates, proteins, fats, minerals and vitamins.[61]

SCRUTINISING THE 'BENEFITS'

We do not need to drive women back a century to preparing home-made substitutes because they cannot access formula. What we need is to apply a little less pressure and practise a little more compassion.

In the West, we currently live in a culture which is suspicious of anything that isn't 'natural'. The word 'chemical' or 'artificial' strikes fear into the hearts of many. Never mind that in developed countries we live nearly three times longer than our ancestors did thanks to the advances we've made over 'nature'. 'Natural' is still perceived as best. Being aware of this explains why many ordinary people are susceptible to unsubstantiated claims on behalf of breast milk. It doesn't, however, explain why some scientifically trained people—and, in particular, immunologists—are so certain that breast milk has healing powers which cannot be matched by formula.

The reason does not lie with perceived nutritional advantages, but with the fact that breast milk contains substances which are associated with fending off infections. Since almost every known illness can be traced back to one infection or another, the theory goes, surely breast milk must therefore offer some protection against an enormous range of medical problems. There is nothing unscientific about that theory. The difficulty is that the research does not support it. What the research shows is that, in all but a minor way, the protective power of breast milk is overwhelmed by the greater surge of protective antibodies a baby receives through the placenta, clean water, hygiene and immunisations. As a source of protection from illness, breastfeeding is barely relevant in developed countries.

Following are the categories in which consistent claims have been made that breast milk protects against medical conditions. For more information about what the research behind each category shows, please refer to the appendices noted.

+ Diarrheal diseases (refer to Appendix I)

+ All respiratory tract infections, both lower and upper, and colds and middle ear infections (refer to Appendix II)

+ Urinary tract diseases (refer to Appendix III)

+ Type 1 diabetes (refer to Appendix IV)

+ Atopic conditions, including asthma, eczema and hay fever (refer to Appendix V)

+ Inflammatory bowel disease (refer to Appendix VI).

SO WHAT DO IMMUNOLOGISTS SEE IN BREAST MILK?

As we navigate life, we are repeatedly challenged by tiny toxins which have little regard for our survival. They invade our bodies, multiply exponentially, then when we die move on to the next host. Immunologists call these toxins 'pathogens' or 'antigens', and they include bacteria, viruses and fungi. Through the course of evolution, humans have developed various defence systems to destroy or contain these pathogens, and top of the list are 'antibodies'. When pathogens invade, our bodies produce antibodies to fight them off.

Antibodies are very specific to the type of pathogen that they are fending off. Each antibody is perfectly suited chemically and often physically to block the action of a specific antigen. Once our bodies have learned to make a specific antibody, we continue to produce it for many years—and, in some cases, for all of our lives. Antibodies are so specific that laboratory researchers can work out any disease a person has ever been exposed to just by testing for those antibodies. This includes the antibodies produced through vaccination.

There are two basic classes of antibodies:

+ IgG antibodies are suited to looking out for pathogens that migrate to our tissues—which is the main bulk of a human body.

+ IgA antibodies, on the other hand, look out for pathogens which land on our mucosal linings—which is to say, the surfaces or linings of our mouth, nose, eyelids, trachea, lungs, stomach, intestines, ureters, urethra and urinary bladder.

In 1998, Swedish immunologist Lars Hanson wrote a review of evidence he had collected over 40 years of the various advantages of breastfeeding over formula-feeding.[62] In this review, he provided a helpful explanation of why he (incorrectly) thought there were major immunological advantages to breastfeeding. First, he described the journey of a mother's antibodies from her gut to her breast milk—in particular, he discussed the IgA antibody, which is present in breast milk but absent in a newborn. It takes a number of months before a baby produces its own sufficient quantities of IgA antibody.

The IgA antibody should provide protection against pathogens landing on the mucosal lining of the gut and therefore target gut diseases—the diseases which cause diarrhoea. Hanson's theory was that breast milk eliminated pathogens which could migrate to other parts of the body. Migration is not far-fetched, however, the theory that breast milk has any influence whatsoever on migration is simply not borne out by evidence—as I will now explain.

In 1990, Scottish researcher Peter Howie and colleagues

conducted the first methodologically sound, large-scale study of the medical benefits of breastfeeding.[63] After reviewing the then current literature, which showed that 'breastfeeding had, at best, a minimal protective effect in industrialised countries', Howie felt that existing studies were seriously flawed methodologically—they were biased, not adequately adjusted for confounding variables, and neither the outcome events nor the definition of infant feeding were clearly defined. So he and his team decided to see what they would find if they carried out a sound study and compared 672 mother–infant pairs for: gastrointestinal illness; respiratory infections; ear, mouth, eye and skin infections; colic; eczema; and nappy rash.

This study was particularly important as it included mothers who did not breastfeed at all (unlike Kramer's later PROBIT study; see pages 273–274). In Howie's study, 267 mothers chose to formula-feed from birth. As is still the case today, those who breastfed were older, married, wealthier, higher educated, had fewer children and smoked less. Four groups were compared:

+ mothers who did not breastfeed at all

+ mothers who breastfed for less than three months

+ mothers who breastfed for more than three months but also used formula

+ mothers who breastfed exclusively for more than three months.

The study showed no differences between any of the groups for: respiratory infections; ear, mouth, eye and skin infections; colic; eczema; or nappy rash. However, compared with fully formula-fed babies, those babies who had been either fully or partially breastfed for the first three months showed lower rates of gastrointestinal illness. These results are remarkably similar to those found a decade later in Kramer's more ambitious 2001 PROBIT study, which compared mothers breastfeeding less than three months to those breastfeeding for six months or more.[64] To clarify, both studies showed a reduced risk of diarrhoea (with Kramer's study further clarifying that it was restricted to low-level cases—those not requiring hospitalisation—between the third and sixth month of life if the baby was still breastfed).

BREAST MILK AND A NEWBORN'S IMMUNITY

The reality is that while a newborn baby's immune system is not fully developed, it is not quite as defenceless or as vulnerable as some breastfeeding advocates like to claim. Evolutionarily speaking, the antibody and anti-inflammatory constituents of breast milk might once have given some babies a leg up under marginal survival conditions. However, we need to ask ourselves why babies in developed countries don't seem to benefit more from breastfeeding. There are basically four reasons for this.

1. Although an infant's immune system is weak in contrast to an adult's, it is still largely functional.

Unlike most other mammals, a human baby is born with significant defences. All mammals provide milk for their offspring and all mammals have placentas—however, not all placentas are created equal. The placentas of most mammals allow little or no transfer of immunities from the mother to the foetus, so at birth the newborns are completely vulnerable to infections and get every bit of their immunity from their mother's milk.

However, the placentas of humans, apes, monkeys and rodents are quite different. Human placentas allow the free crossing of a mother's IgG antibodies into the foetus. (Remember that IgG antibodies fight off pathogens in our body's tissues.) The passage of a mother's IgG antibodies through the placenta starts slowly at about four months into a pregnancy, and increases progressively until birth. The greatest rate of this antibody transfer happens after 34 weeks of gestation—just a few weeks before birth. The foetus is literally infused with antibodies in preparation for birth. These antibodies are 'passive' or short-lived; they do their job for about three months, while the baby's own immune system builds up, then simply disappear for good.[65]

And that isn't even the whole story. Only a few months after conception, a human foetus starts producing its own wide range of agents to protect against infection. Notably, the system that is critical for preventing inflammation is present at birth, and increases rapidly after birth. Furthermore, since there is a period between the mother's passive IgG immunity diminishing and the child's own permanent IgG taking over, the infant bridges that gap with its own temporary IgM antibodies, which do much the same job.[66]

What a newborn infant *doesn't* have much of is the antibody IgA— the one that protects the mucosal lining of the gut from pathogens. Nonetheless, an infant's immune system is still largely functional.

2. A mother can only offer limited protection by way of her IgA (gut-lining) antibodies.

Although maternal IgA dusts a baby's gut with breast milk on its way through, it is passed out along with other wastes (excrement and urine) after each feed. Furthermore, a mother's IgA can only protect against illnesses she has previously fended off herself. Since there are so many variants of every illness, and new ones appear all the time through mutations, the protection is further limited. Finally, all evidence shows that a mother's IgA antibody cannot protect against more powerful viral infections (such as rotavirus), even when she does have specific antibodies for them.

3. From a few days after birth, no outside antibodies—even from a mother's milk—can make it through to a baby's blood stream.

Aside from a very brief window of opportunity immediately after birth, a mother's immunities can no longer be taken in by a baby. This window is generally thought to last 72 hours after birth, and it is only for these few days that an infant's gut remains porous enough for the mother's IgG immunity to pass through. It is during this brief timeframe that mothers produce colostrum, the first milk that comes in immediately after birth and is rich in IgG antibodies. For pre-term babies in particular, this is a wonderful opportunity to at least partly make up for all the IgG they miss out on by arriving early. For full-term babies, it provides a minor top-up of the surge of IgG antibodies recently received through the placenta.

4. Human intervention has largely overcome a child's immunological vulnerabilities.

In developed countries, things like clean water, good nutrition, refrigeration, improved hygiene and immunisations have all conspired to largely overcome any immunological vulnerabilities a child might once have faced. In the UK, for example, infant mortality dropped from 140 deaths per 1,000 in the year 1900 to 3.8 deaths per 1,000 by the year 2014. The majority of those remaining deaths are due to premature birth, congenital defects and accident—which doesn't leave much room for breastfeeding to prove its case.

A CLOSER LOOK AT OTHER BREASTFEEDING CLAIMS

In the current social context where everything 'natural' is seen to be beneficial, it can be tempting to buy into the idea that breast milk might be our body's natural medicine. However, when you think about it, the notion that a food product passing through the alimentary canal of an infant can have lifelong health benefits anywhere in the body for any known disease is not that far removed from something like 'urotherapy' (see box).

THE BODY'S OWN MEDICINE?

The idea that breast milk is our very own natural medicine is seductive, but it turns out to be more faith-based then science-based—and breast milk isn't the only bodily product for which medical claims have been made.

The belief in the curative powers of urine—or 'urotherapy'—also has a following, with advocates claiming that urine prevents a wide range of illnesses from polio, rabies and AIDS to rashes, arthritis and colds.[67]

Why? Well, apparently because urine contains immunoglobulin, interferon, growth hormone to prevent obesity, and more. Advocates recommend that children be given three small glasses of urine daily. These are the teachings of the Sacred Valley Tribe.

Yes, breast milk contains a variety of substances which appear ready to guard a baby's gut from infection. And, yes, it appears breast milk has a short-term influence on less serious tummy bugs during the first six months of life—that's because breast milk is constantly passing over the tummy. But the evidence that breast milk prevents or cures anything else is simply not there. A great deal of research has attempted to show a connection between breastfeeding and protection against a wide range of diseases—and a lot of public befuddlement has ensued as a result of the way trivial differences are portrayed in abstracts. Minor findings are beefed up. Negative findings are left out, and sometimes outright misrepresented. Fortunately, there is sufficient fear of being found doctoring findings that the truth can be dug out of the body of the papers.

The better studies—those with large numbers of subjects, well-defined parameters and controls for confounding factors—show time and again that breast milk is a feeble adversary against disease. Yet those researchers who find no association between a particular disease and breastfeeding are none the wiser than the general public. They think they are the exception to the rule, and not the rule itself. They apologise for not finding the association expected and advise everyone that advantages must lie elsewhere.

The truth is that breastfeeding advocates are digging a hole for themselves if they rely too heavily on claiming wide-ranging medical benefits that haven't been proved. The truth will out—and it could result in a backlash against breastfeeding, which none of us want. Advocates should instead focus on the actual benefit of breastfeeding, namely that it can be a fast-track to bonding when it is enjoyable. They should concentrate their efforts on women where breastfeeding enhances their connection with their baby, rather than force it upon women who end up distressed or even develop mental health difficulties as a consequence of being forced to breastfeed when they don't want to or don't enjoy it.

But it doesn't stop there. Immunological advantages aren't the only benefits breastfeeding and breast milk are claimed to have. Breastfeeding is often also promoted as being beneficial with regards to reducing obesity, delinquency and mental health difficulties, and increasing IQ—but how reliable are those claims? What does the research have to say? Let's take a closer look.

BREASTFEEDING AND OBESITY

New Zealand ranks high in the English-speaking world for obesity. Being overweight is not just a problem in itself, but it is also associated with numerous related health issues, most notably diabetes and heart disease. It is an issue which deserves serious attention. However, if you have been told that your baby will be more likely to be obese if you do not breastfeed, or that your baby will not be obese if you do, you have been entirely misled. The one and only longitudinal study on the subject tracked babies from birth to sixteen years and pointed in precisely the opposite direction—it showed that babies who are breastfed more than three months are *more* likely to be obese than those who are breastfed less than three months. What's more, the only sibling pair study to look at the relationship between obesity and breastfeeding had the same result. (For more detail on these studies, refer to Appendix VII.)

There is no doubt that genetics play a big part in any person's tendency to gain weight. A study of identical twins raised apart that was reported in the *New England Journal of Medicine* estimated that up to 70 per cent of variation in weight between twins was due to inherited characteristics.[68]

Samoa has one of the most obese populations in the world. In 2016 a genomic analysis of more than 5,000 people in Samoa found a quarter of the population carried a gene variant which causes cells to store more fat and release less energy. Researchers suggested that this would have been beneficial for people who had to endure long voyages between islands, but now leads to obesity in times of nutritional excess. In Samoa today, 80 per cent of men and 91 per cent of women are obese by the study's standards.[69]

One year later researchers found the same gene variant in all other Polynesian populations sampled, including Māori. The second study found the variant gene was significantly associated with growth at four years of age, with a gene-specific increase in weight, height and waist circumference at that age. This variant was not found in non-Polynesians.[70]

A 2007 article in *The New England Journal of Medicine* showed how obesity spreads in much the same way as a disease.[71] A heart study of a densely interconnected social network collected information over a period of 32 years from 1971 to 2003. The body-mass index (BMI) was periodically recorded for all 12,067 people assessed. That Harvard study tracked the spread of obesity through this social network, and its findings were startling. A person's chance of becoming obese increased by 57 per cent if a friend became obese. If one sibling became obese, the chance that the other became obese increased by 40 per cent. If one spouse became obese, the likelihood of the other spouse becoming obese increased by 37 per cent. Finally, people of the same sex had greater influence on a person than the opposite sex did.

The authors suggested that the weight of others alters our perception of ourselves; it changes our norms about the acceptability of being overweight. Obesity becomes the new normal.

A large Scottish study which had a sample size of 32,200 children stated in its abstract (summary) that obesity was *significantly* lower in breastfed children. However, people can be led astray by the word 'significant', especially if it is used in the abstract of a study. Findings can be statistically significant at very low levels with very little consequence. In fact, when you look at the actual conclusion of the study, it states: 'Our findings suggest that breastfeeding is associated with a *modest* [small] reduction in childhood obesity.' In one particular case, an official body was blinded by a study's abstract and concluded it showed a 30 per cent reduction in obesity—which it certainly did not. (For more information, see Appendix VII.) These sorts of misunderstandings are passed on to the public, and contribute to a common misconception that research supports the position that breastfeeding is the key to reducing obesity.[72]

As with most studies attempting to link breastfeeding with certain outcomes, the sum total of observational studies reach conflicting conclusions—and often there's conflict within a study itself. For example, a 2005 Australian longitudinal study of 2,087 children concluded that breastfed children were leaner than non-breastfed children at one year of age; however, the same study also concluded that the difference disappeared by eight years. In other words, it showed no long-term benefit to breastfeeding.[73]

Two sibling pair studies (remember these are high-level studies) also published in 2005 showed no benefit in relation to obesity from breastfeeding. The first study compared 850 sibling pairs and found no benefit from breastfeeding.[74] The second looked at 2,743 sibling pairs from the same source, and concluded that breastfed children were actually more likely to be overweight.[75] Four years later, in 2009, Kramer's Baby-friendly initiative project in Belarus, which followed 17,046 infants from birth to sixteen years of age, reported that at six-and-a-half years of age there was no difference between the longer breastfeeding group and the control group for obesity.[76] Twelve years later, in 2017, Kramer released the follow-up results at age sixteen and concluded that the prevalence of obesity was greater among children who were breastfed longer.

Therefore, the largest study in the area lined up with the largest sibling pair result in the area. Regardless of whether or not these results stand the test of time, one thing can be said for sure: anyone claiming that breastfeeding prevents obesity is doing so without any scientific authority.[77]

These findings should not persuade you one way or the other about how you feed your baby. If there is any pattern to breastfeeding studies, it is that results flutter so closely between there being an effect or not that any additional confounding factor could tip the scale. In the case of obesity, it seems clear that other factors—namely ethnicity and parents' weight—need to be taken into account, but none of these studies include that information. What we do know for sure is that eating habits are important, and parents concerned about obesity can set a positive example for their children to set them up now and later in their lives.

TIPS FOR STARTING HEALTHY EATING EARLY

+ Give babies vegetables like broccoli as soon as they are old enough. If that's the first thing on their tray, they will eat it and learn to like it. Start early.

+ Don't give your baby low-fat milk or artificial sweeteners. Growing kids need full milk, and artificial sweetener will just make them think sweet drinks are the norm.

+ Don't use sweets as a reward. Give praise, stickers or stars instead.

+ If you can, pack your own food when you go on outings.

+ If you can, eat meals as a family to model healthy eating. You can start doing this with your baby as soon as she starts eating solids.

+ Don't lecture your children about these things—just do them. Modelling this behaviour lets your kids know that this is healthy behaviour towards food.

BREASTFEEDING AND DELINQUENCY

On the tail of Bowlby's ground-breaking insights into the relationship between juvenile delinquency and maternal deprivation (see pages 33–35), some breastfeeding advocates have claimed that formula-feeding leads to delinquency. To those who believe this, a failure to breastfeed constitutes a form of maternal deprivation that puts stress on the baby, and therefore causes the production of the hormone cortisol (see pages 228–232). Cortisol in turn switches on aggressive behaviour.

As discussed in Part I of this book, researchers in the area of maternal deprivation do not agree that low levels of normal stress lead to deviant behaviour. Bowlby and current researchers alike have looked to extended periods of maternal separation and extended periods of serious stress (such as ongoing domestic violence) as predictors of deviant behaviour in children. There have been seven studies which have considered an association between breastfeeding and deviant behaviour and none have found consistent results connecting duration of breastfeeding with antisocial behaviour. (For more detail on these studies, refer to Appendix VIII.)

As we've already discussed, stress and cortisol levels have become pet subjects of extreme parenting advocates (see page 79). We can all agree that we want to protect babies from extreme stress, but is *breastfeeding* necessary to reduce stress and its consequences? The answer appears to be a resounding 'no'.

In 2009, researchers tested 166 infants for cortisol levels one hour after feeding (to avoid getting cortisol from the milk itself).[78] Their hypothesis was that, since the lack of mother's comfort is a potent stressor leading to increased production of cortisol, bottle-feeding would result in higher cortisol levels as well. They were surprised by the results—cortisol levels were actually 40 per cent higher among breastfed children.

As interpreting cortisol levels during normal activities can be misleading, it is valuable to have an observational study comparing the temperaments of babies under different feeding conditions. Mothers of 316 infants from the Cambridge Baby Growth cohort were asked to rate their three-month-old baby's temperament on a 191-item 'infant behaviour questionnaire'.[79] In none of the measures were either the exclusively breastfed or mixed breastfed babies ahead of non-breastfed babies. However, in some very important areas, the non-breastfed babies outstripped the breastfed ones. According to the researchers, 'compared to formula-fed infants, breastfed infants were reported to show greater distress, less smiling, laughing and vocalisation, to be slower to calm down following distress or excitement, and more difficult to soothe.'[80]

In conclusion, the association between breastfeeding and delinquency is extremely weak. It does not show itself at all in actual deviant behaviour among young people. To the extent it is rated for children, the result appears to depend on who is doing the rating. The evidence is that mothers who breastfeed longer view their children in a better light than those who do not, and when objective outsiders rate behaviour there is little or no difference. What a number of these studies do agree on is that breastfed children have a more positive view of their parents. This result is part of a pattern of women who are wealthier and better educated choosing to breastfeed, women who also happen to be in a more privileged position to enjoy mothering their children, and in turn their children enjoy being mothered by them. (See Appendix VII for more on breastfeeding and delinquency.)

BREASTFEEDING AND SEVERE MENTAL HEALTH DIFFICULTIES

Severe depression and schizophrenia are the two classes of severe mental health difficulties which have received some interest in relation to breastfeeding. In general, the studies are case-control studies with small numbers and the results are divided. A number of low-level observational studies had no information at all concerning family background. (Out of all mental health difficulties, psychosis has the highest genetic loading so information on family history of psychosis is essential.)

However, there have been four studies which took things a step further. Two of them matched people with a diagnosis of schizophrenia against their siblings, as well as healthy controls. Neither of those studies showed any difference in incidence or duration of breastfeeding between the three groups.[81]

In 2000, an article was published in *The British Journal of Psychiatry* titled 'No Association Between Breastfeeding and Adult Psychosis in Two National Birth Cohorts'.[82] Following 4,447 births from 1946 and a further 18,856 from 1958, the researchers found no difference between formula-fed and breastfed babies in relation to the later incidence of psychosis.

Additional support is provided by the Christchurch Health and Development study, which followed a birth cohort of 1265 New Zealand children.[83] During the first year after birth, information was collected on breastfeeding practices, then between the ages of fifteen and eighteen the children were measured for all mental health issues. No relationship was found between breastfeeding and adolescent mental health.

BREASTFEEDING AND INTELLIGENCE

You may hear people talk about all kinds of intelligence—social intelligence, creative intelligence and cognitive intelligence.

Cognitive intelligence is what helps you do well at standardised tests at school. In general, cognitive intelligence has two main parts: verbal and performance. Verbal includes things you pick up or learn, such as vocabulary and general knowledge. Performance includes your capacity to deal with non-verbal tasks such as object assembly. A relationship exists between the two in the sense that, if you are good at verbal skills, you will probably also be good at non-verbal (performance) skills. However, it is by no means a perfect relationship, and both need to be tested to get an overall picture of a child's cognitive ability. The average score is 100, and most people hover around that mark. This is measured by having a child carry out verbal and performance tests. Their score is then compared to expectations for their age, and a final intelligence quotient (IQ) score is the result.

IQ is thought to be relatively stable over life if tested properly, although it is influenced by environment. People around the world are getting smarter every year in the sense that group IQs are rising steadily; this is because the world is getting increasingly cognitively demanding and people are adjusting to it. That means IQ tests have to be re-standardised every few years, or you won't know where a child stands in relation to other children of the same age. This is now a required practice. This steady rise in IQ is known as the 'Flynn Effect'—and it is named after my father, Jim Flynn.

Since I had gathered figures on breastfeeding rates in the United States since 1936, I asked my father to diagram the trend of US IQs over that same period in order to compare them.[84] As you can see below, there is no relationship between the two.

There have been numerous ideas tested about what makes one child brighter than the other, and in all cases one association stands out: the intelligence of the child's mother. (You may wonder why the father's intelligence is not mentioned. This is because mothers rather than fathers are tested for these studies.) Next in importance is the child's social environment. These and their associated 'confounders'

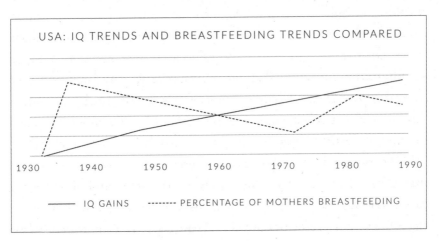

USA: IQ TRENDS AND BREASTFEEDING TRENDS COMPARED

1930   1940   1950   1960   1970   1980   1990

——— IQ GAINS   ------- PERCENTAGE OF MOTHERS BREASTFEEDING

generally swamp the effects of what is being tested—in this case, breastfeeding. Without being able to assign breastfeeding to one large, randomly selected group and comparing the result with another large, randomly selected group, even the best studies fail to agree.

In one example based on the Growing Up in Ireland longitudinal infant cohort, nearly 10,000 children were tested at three and five years of age.[85] The raw scores showed breastfeeding resulted in improved cognitive skills—but when matched for mother's intelligence and social background the effect disappeared. An equally compelling study of 1,312 children from a US birth cohort tested at seven years, also adjusting for maternal intelligence and home environment, said, 'our results support a causal relationship of breastfeeding duration with receptive language and verbal and nonverbal intelligence later in life'.[86] The study showed any kind of breastfeeding resulted in an increase of two IQ points over six months—at the rate of about 0.3 of a point per month. The Ireland study had the advantage of larger numbers, but accounted for maternal intelligence by way of years of education rather than IQ. Meanwhile, the US study had the advantage of an actual intelligence test for the mother (albeit an abbreviated one), but it had only a fraction of subjects compared to the Ireland study.

Observational studies coming down one way or the other have been piling up for years. In 2013, a research team gathered together all the studies meeting the following criteria: 'any prospective or retrospective study, in any language, evaluating the association between breastfeeding and cognitive development using a validated method in healthy term infants, children or adults, was included.'[87] The researchers found 84 studies meeting that criteria, and rated 34 as high quality, 26 as moderate and 24 low quality. They found that, regardless of quality, each category was fairly evenly split as to whether or not there was an effect. This research team hoped sibling pairs where one had been breastfed and the other not might be a way of getting more valid results. They were clearly disappointed that the only two sibling studies already done had also come up with conflicting results about the effect of breastfeeding on IQ. However, the author of one of the two sibling-pair studies is a statistician and claims both can be combined as they draw from the same source. When they are combined the result is that there is no effect on IQ from breastfeeding.

For more information on the history and details of research in the area of breastfeeding and IQ, and on Kramer's PROBIT studies, see Appendix IX. For now, here is a nutshell summary.

+ A 2013 meta study showed even the best studies were evenly divided as to whether or not breastfeeding improved intelligence.[88]

+ Pooled results totalling 3,611 sibling pairs from the only two sibling-pair studies ever done (both taken from the same database) showed no difference between those who had been breastfed and those who had not.[89]

+ 2018 results from Dr Kramer's re-testing of 13,427 children showed that the global IQ gains he reported when the children were six years old were not seen when the same children were retested at the age of sixteen. Dr Kramer concluded that parental educational level is the dominant factor, and therefore genetics.[90]

What research points to is that, if there is any cognitive benefit from breastfeeding, it is small, it is verbal, it is temporary, and any benefit goes to the children of mothers who have less understanding of the need to engage verbally with their child in the first place. The children of high IQ mothers and well-educated mothers are unlikely to benefit from breastfeeding, as these mothers already tend to engage with their baby in a way that enhances cognitive development. Therefore, it cannot be anything in a mother's milk which causes the difference—if that were the case, it should enhance the cognition of *all* children, regardless of their mother's IQ or wealth.

There is also indirect evidence that second and subsequent children, including those of well-educated mothers, might benefit from breastfeeding as it enforces one-on-one time and attention, which tend to grow scarce as a family grows.

When everything is put together, the picture seems fairly clear. Breastfeeding fits in with IQ in that it promotes more quality time with your baby, however any mother who bottle-feeds can easily make up for this by spending more quality time with her baby both during and outside of feeds. To put it simply, it is attention—not breast milk—which makes your baby smarter.

WILL OMEGA OILS MAKE MY CHILD SMARTER?

The widespread belief that breastfeeding increases intelligence has, not surprisingly, generated a few theories. Because breast milk has the essential fatty acid DHA (Omega-3) and because ordinary unfortified formula does not, and because its deficiency in prenatal animals has been associated with cognitive defects—it is commonly thought that adding those fats to baby formula will improve a child's intelligence. Results are conflicting. One research team had some success with one-year-olds, but not later when they were six-year-olds. Another team found no difference in IQ but felt the group which had the supplement were faster 'at processing information'.[91]

Another study of 241 four-year-old children[92] concluded there was no difference between any of the breastfeeding, formula-fed or DHA-enhanced formula-fed groups. So, I thought their comment was very strange: '. . . we found a difference in mean full-scale and verbal IQ between children who had been fed (DHA) fortified [as opposed to] unfortified formula that persisted after adjustment.'

In an aside in one article, another author said—there is no evidence supporting gains, and there is no evidence of bad effects either—so why not?

The bottom line is that studies disagree and disagree differently. The advice given is that you should not take Omega acids while pregnant, but eat fish. If you are breastfeeding, do not take Omega supplements because there needs to be a balance of acids—again, eat fish. If you are formula feeding, do not add drops, always get it with the commercial milk product. The formula producers have been doing this for two decades and they know the right amounts and proportions.

CHAPTER 11: THE MAIN POINTS

+ Breastfeeding is a matter of choice for a mother. If it is enjoyable for both you and your baby, go for it. If it's not, it's perfectly OK to feed your baby formula. You know what is best for you and your baby.

+ Most claims about the benefits of breastfeeding as opposed to formula-feeding have not been backed up by research.

+ Research tells us that longer exclusive breastfeeding in developed countries reduces the chance of having one very low-level tummy bug. (There is no difference in hospitalisation rates).

+ Research does not show that breastfeeding increases global IQ score.

+ A large study of six-year-olds indicated that children of less-educated mothers showed improved verbal skills when breastfed for six months. This suggests that attention to a baby (rather than breast milk) is the cause of the gain. It's possible to bridge the gap with bottle-feeding simply by spending more engaged time with your baby. (See Chapter 12 for more on this.)

+ There is no research to back up claims that breastfeeding improves attachment; attachment styles do not depend on breastfeeding.

+ Current research indicates that breastfeeding increases obesity. However, since the research is inadequate, it's not actually possible to make conclusions either way.

+ Fed is best. It doesn't matter whether your baby gets breast milk or formula; what matters is that your baby is fed enough and that you have a positive relationship with your baby.

CHAPTER 12
THE RIGHT WAY TO FEED—
BREAST OR BOTTLE

Myth: Only mothers who breastfeed can feed in a sensitive and responsive way.

Truth: Both breastfeeding and bottle-feeding can be done in a sensitive and responsive way.

I remember attending a clinical psychology lecture in my younger days about maternal health. At one point, the professor wrote a word on the white board—*feeding*—paused, then said, 'I just want to mention one thing. It doesn't matter whether or not a mother breastfeeds or formula-feeds. The issue is that she should *never* be made to feel guilty.'

Two decades later, I can confirm as a practising psychologist that, so long as parents know what it means to be sensitive and responsive while feeding, their babies can have the same positive bonding experiences no matter whether they are breastfed or bottle-fed. Since evidence does not support any long-term benefits from breast milk itself, there is no reason a father or partner can't also feed their baby, and thereby become part of the bonding and attachment equation from the earliest days. (Just remember that, although attachment security for your baby doesn't depend on just one person carrying out nurturing tasks, the number of different people who regularly feed your baby should be small.)

By one week of age over half of all babies in the UK will have been fed formula, and by six weeks this rises to three-quarters of all babies.[1] By two weeks of age, at least 20 per cent of babies in New Zealand have been fed with formula; by six weeks, at least 40 per cent of them have; and, at six months, at least 70 per cent of babies are receiving formula feeds.[2] Given that by six weeks of age so many babies are at least partially bottle-fed, it is scandalous that it's not standard practice to provide parents with information about how to safely and sensitively bottle-feed. This information shouldn't just be easily available to any parent upon request, but to all mothers after childbirth. Sadly, although on paper there is a requirement for this information to be provided, it does not always happen. Sometimes, women who want to bottle-feed are treated as Enemies of the State, and those who provide them with any information as collaborators. Encouragement is one thing, but bullying is quite another—so is misrepresenting information.

GETTING THE TERMINOLOGY RIGHT

To researchers, clinical psychologists and psychiatrists, terms such as 'secure attachment' and 'bonding' have very specific and researched meanings. As we saw in Part I of this book, these important terms have been co-opted by advocates of extreme parenting and misapplied (see page 37). Much like the misuse of 'secure attachment' and 'bonding', two other crucial words are being misused to frighten resistant mothers into breastfeeding: 'sensitive' and 'responsive'. Sensitivity means recognition of infant cues and needs, and responsiveness is behaviour that meets these needs. Sensitive responsiveness is widely considered to be the most important quality of interactions that build strong relationships and attachment security. Understanding precisely what these terms mean is important.

We briefly touched on the concept of 'maternal sensitive responsiveness' and the woman who first defined it, Mary Ainsworth, in Part I on pages 42–43. It was Ainsworth who first linked maternal sensitive responsiveness with attachment security. She noticed that mothers of securely attached babies tended to feed them promptly on demand or to 'hold them off with gentle coaxing'.[3] These mothers followed their baby's lead when possible, and warmly took charge when appropriate. Ainsworth noticed that the mothers of secure babies who bottle-fed adjusted well to the baby's feeding pace, and didn't attempt to speed up the feed by enlarging the hole in the bottle's teat (which could cause the baby to struggle and gag). She also noticed that sensitive mothers generally responded to their babies with warmth, by smiling, making eye contact, verbalising and so on.

When most health professionals talk about 'responsive feeding', this is what they mean: sensitivity to your baby's cues for hunger and feeding him at his pace. You can feed responsively no matter whether you are using a bottle or a breast.

However, the Baby-friendly Hospital Initiative (which now includes most maternity units in New Zealand and the UK, and 20,000 facilities worldwide) has decided to use the term 'responsive feeding' with quite a different meaning from the generally accepted one I've just described.

On their website (unicef.org.uk/babyfriendly), they define responsive feeding as 'offering the breast on demand and as the first response when a baby signals they are hungry, distressed, lonely, unwell or in an unfamiliar environment'.[4] This definition excludes bottle-feeding from ever being a sensitive response, which is absolutely not true. Furthermore, it adds layers of unnecessary breast activity in order to meet the requirement of appropriate responsiveness. A responsive mother does not need to insert a breast (or indeed a bottle) into her baby in response to every cue in order to be 'sensitive and responsive'. What Baby-friendly is really talking about here is feeding on demand, *not* responsive feeding. Breastfeeding or nursing on demand is not a problem so long as it suits the parent, but there is a problem when a special-interest group misapplies a well-known term with over 50 years of research behind it in this way.

Baby-friendly decided more emphasis needed to be put on promoting what they call 'responsive feeding' as part of a 2014 review. They felt the terms 'demand feeding' or 'baby-led feeding' did not adequately convey the need to offer the breast for reasons outside of hunger, and they provided a four-page information sheet that emphasised the need for hospital staff to better promote nursing (which is to say, offering a breast for reasons other than hunger) as well as feeding on demand.[5] In short, staff needed to be educated to teach new mothers to offer a breast in all manner of circumstances. Baby-friendly said this information should be 'reinforced by community midwives and health visitors as mothers may need to hear messages a number of times in order to help them understand'. The information sheet clarifies in more than one place that their version of 'responsive feeding' excludes bottle-feeding, noting 'it is very important in staff training to emphasise that breastfeeding is the only normal and truly responsive way to feed a baby'[6] and, 'true responsive feeding is not possible with bottle-feeding.'[7]

This terminology is misleading. There is no credible evidence to support these claims, and Baby-friendly's distortion of the term 'responsive' does nothing more than add to the confusion and anxiety new parents already feel. When I told a dear friend of mine who is a psychiatrist specialising in infant attachment that Baby-friendly was using 'responsive feeding' to mean 'breastfeeding and nursing on demand', she almost choked on her coffee. Furthermore, I have spoken to a number of hospital nurses who feel stressed by these demands. They say they are not permitted to mention—much less coach—mothers on how to bottle-feed. Yet they also know that many mothers will be using bottles soon after discharge, and no one is telling them anything about what is the most important ingredient: the joy of your eye contact, smiles and words.

I'd like to set the record straight. To over half of North American mothers who have fed their babies formula by three months, to 40 per cent of New Zealand mothers who have introduced formula by three months post-birth, and to over half of UK mothers formula-feeding by one-week post-birth, let me say this: professionals such as maternal psychiatrists, psychologists and psychotherapists believe that you can easily feed in a sensitive and responsive way via either breast *or* bottle. It's simple. It's not the method by which you feed that matters, but how you do it.

IT'S THE TIME THAT COUNTS

One large-scale study on breastfeeding and cognitive development found that, although breastfeeding provided no cognitive benefit for the children of better-educated mothers, it did increase the verbal scores of children (at age six) among less-educated mothers. Whether this increase persists for that group of children is not known. (For more detail on this study, see Appendix IX.) So what was it that the less-educated women did more when they breastfed than when they fed their baby with a bottle? The answer, as it turns out, was quite simple: they were spending more time cuddling, facing and communicating with their child. Breastfeeding takes more time than bottle-feeding does, and during breastfeeding the mother–child pair look at each other and communicate—to put it another way, being engaged is most often a side-effect of breastfeeding.

At this point, you may well be wondering why less-educated mothers as a group don't appear to spend as much quality time with their babies. Do educated mothers love their babies more? No, they do not! If there is one thing I know from all my years working with mothers it's that income has nothing to do with love. There are two reasons why educated mothers tend to spend more quality time with their babies.

First, poor education is linked to poverty, which is in turn linked to chronic stress from worry about finances, safety and other concerns. This sort of stress makes it hard to focus attention and time on your baby, even if you want to. If you are grappling with how to put food on the table and how to keep your family warm and clothed, you're not exactly going to have a whole lot of time to spend engaging in mutual gaze with your baby, massaging her, or taking a long bath with her. When parents are overwrought or distracted, it becomes more difficult to respond to their baby in a timely, warm and consistent way. Breastfeeding is a time when even women living in a vortex of poverty or stress tend to focus on their baby, no matter what else is happening in their world.

Second, and of particular interest here, women who are less educated often do not have access to valuable resources and information—the kind of information you are getting by being able to afford this book. For example, they might not have sought out information on how to bottle-feed in a 'sensitive and responsive' way; they might not even know such information exists. They might not know things like the fact that it is more beneficial to talk directly to their babies rather than around them. Furthermore, those closest to them might not have access to this information, either.

Here is the thing: *every mother wants the best for her baby, and every mother deserves to be given the right information*. Wouldn't it be great if public resources were targeted to coaching *all* mothers in the importance of how to both breastfeed and formula-feed. Wouldn't it be wonderful if *all* mothers had access to the information that could teach them how to spend time with their babies in a way that promotes bonding and a secure attachment? I have worked with mothers, both privileged and not, who have told me that learning about how to feed their baby in a way that promoted a secure attachment gave them a sense of control, of competence and relieved some stress. All women should have access to this information.

IT IS WORTH THE EFFORT

Feeding your baby—whether by breast or bottle—provides a wonderful opportunity to bond and build your baby's social and emotional development. It's not just about nourishment. Take the time to gaze at him, smile at him and talk to him.

SENSITIVE AND RESPONSIVE FEEDING: THE HOW-TOS

Sensitive and responsive feeding could not be simpler. Here's how to do it.

+ First, be sensitive to your baby's hunger cues. This can take some time to figure out for a new parent. Some cues to look out for are your baby sucking on her hand, fingers or fists, your baby turning her head or mouth towards you, or your baby smacking her lips. Crying is a later sign of hunger.

+ Second, make sure that, at least some of the time, you feed your baby in a quiet place so you can concentrate on her. I realise this is easier said than done with a toddler in the mix! However, even if you have a toddler around, you can still tune in to your baby. (See pages 50–51 for more information on building a positive relationship with your baby.)

+ And an extra note: if you are bottle-feeding, limit the number of primary feeders to yourself plus one or two other people.

Of course, your mental health comes first, so when you need a break to rest or sleep, pass the bottle over to someone else.

These steps are simple, but it's another story to be able to keep motivated or able to do them every single time you feed your baby. Sometimes you will be so tired you just want to watch something on Netflix or scroll through your social media while feeding. Then, of course, there are toddlers who need attention and visitors to entertain. Delightful as your baby is, you will probably have moments where you wonder if you really need to look at him *all* the time he is feeding for *every* feed. My suggestion is to make that your goal—but don't beat yourself up if you fall short every now and then. I watched two whole series of *The Bachelor* during night feeds with one of my babies (not to mention eating my way through a whole case of fundraising chocolate my husband had bought). My goal was simply to stay calm and not fall asleep in a soft chair. Remember, you don't have to be perfect; you just have to be good enough.

For tips and more information on bottle-feeding in a sensitive and responsive way, see Chapter 14.

PUT YOUR PHONE AWAY

You might not like to hear it, but the worst offender when it comes to sensitive and responsive feeding is your phone. I know that connecting with other parents via social media can help you to feel supported and less alone as a new parent. However, the sad reality is that too much time on your phone means not enough time building connections with the people who are right in front of you—and that person, when you are feeding your baby, is your baby!

Notably, your baby finds your lack of expression when you stare at

---

a phone screen extremely upsetting. When people become fixated on a computer or telephone screen, they present a 'still' face to their child. This is not a good thing. (See page 56 for more on still-face studies.)

One of the best things you can do to tune in to your baby while you feed him is to put your phone away. You can check it later. If you absolutely *must* check your phone while feeding, keep it brief.

For more information on technology and your baby, see Chapter 16.

R-E-S-P-O-N-D

Here's some aspirational advice for you to keep in mind and aim for when you are feeding your baby—just remind yourself to R-E-S-P-O-N-D.

+ Remain calm. Feeding is nicer for both of you, if you take some deep breaths and relax any tension in your body.

+ Eye contact. Make sure your baby is in a position where she can make eye contact with you. When you are feeding her, be aware if you are looking at your phone or at the TV. Keep screen time to a minimum. Make sure you are mainly looking at your baby, smiling, and making soft reassuring noises.

+ Skin-to-skin. When possible, have some skin-to-skin contact with your baby. Always make sure you are holding your baby close to you.

+ Pace feeds. Do not take steps to increase the speed at which your baby feeds (unless under medical guidance for special reasons). Notice when she wants to pause feeding. Notice when she has finished—there's no need for her to finish every drop in the bottle, or for you to try to force her to feed from the other breast. (For more information on paced bottle-feeding, see pages 384–386.)

+ One thing at a time. When your mind starts drifting—as it will from time to time—gently bring your focus back to your baby.

+ Notice. What is the experience like for both of you? Do you think your baby is comfortable, relaxed, happy and content? Imagining how your baby feels is truly empathetic. Notice, as well, your own thoughts, feelings and physical sensations. How does your baby's skin feel? What noises is she making?

+ Delight. Let your baby know you like being with her. Talk softly to her about what you are doing and thinking, stroke her head, smile at her. Softly talking to your baby is never a waste of time.

COMMON FEEDING QUESTIONS

Is my baby getting enough milk?
Your baby is getting enough milk if she is gaining weight appropriately, if her nappies are wet, and if she is passing stools with a frequency appropriate for her age (if you're not sure, you can check appropriate frequency with your health provider). It is common for newborn babies to lose weight straight after birth, but a newborn baby should not lose more than 7 to 10 per cent of her body weight before starting to gain weight. If your baby is not back to her birth weight between ten and fourteen days after birth, she may need to be fed more.

If your baby isn't gaining weight and you wish to continue breastfeeding, consult a lactation specialist immediately. If that doesn't result in immediate weight gains, go directly to your doctor. You may need to supplement breastfeeding with formula, at least for a while. Some people may tell you that formula is harmful, but do not pay any attention to them. Formula is *not* harmful. There is not a shred of evidence to support that. Your baby needs to be fed enough milk—that is the bottom line.

Can I be sensitive to my baby's needs if my baby is on a routine?
Yes. Latest editions of routine-based books don't recommend the old-fashioned four-hourly routine. They recognise that newborn infants can't wait this long for food, and that (if you are breasfeeding) four-hour gaps are not good when it comes to building up your milk supply in the early days post-birth. So, nowadays when we talk about 'routine feeding', we are really discussing flexible schedules that don't leave a baby crying, but progressively encourage them to be awake during the day and to sleep at night. (For more information on routines, see pages 76–83.)

As long as you don't leave your baby hungry and you respond to him in an adult and warm way, the choice between whether you feed him on demand or follow a routine is entirely up to you.

Those who advocate for completely baby-led parenting suggest that routines interfere with a breastfeeding mother's milk supply. You do need to be mindful of this in the early days, while your body establishes a good milk supply. However, as time goes on, you will find that your body is pretty amazing and will quickly adapt to producing milk when it is required. Some of these advocates also worry that a routine denies the opportunity for 'breast-soothing' (breastfeeding your baby to soothe her, rather than because she is hungry; also called nursing). Breast-soothing can be lovely for you and your baby—in my experience, I found it so, especially when my babies were sick or after an immunisation. However, while breast-soothing can be very nice, it absolutely is not a requirement for sensitive and responsive mothering. It never has been, and it never will be. There are many ways to soothe a baby.

On the other hand, those who favour routine are sometimes concerned about the adverse effects of sleep loss, both for parents and for the baby with demand feeding. They fear that a baby who feeds on demand may become exhausted if he is having small feeds often. For a breastfeeding mother, cluster-feeding (especially at night; see pages 354–355) is exhausting. Furthermore, those who favour routine are sometimes cautious about breast-soothing, warning that it will interfere with parents looking for alternative reasons for crying, such as their baby needing stimulation or having a wet nappy. Instead, if you want to stretch out the time until the next feed, they might suggest you play with or distract your baby from your breast or the bottle; then, if your baby cannot be distracted, give him a chance to feed. If he is half-hearted about it, you don't need to linger over it. If he remains unsettled, make sure someone is soothing him. (See pages 199–208 for more information on soothing.)

Should I wake my baby to feed her?

Keep in mind that feeding patterns vary from child to child. If you want to wake your baby up during the day in order to encourage her to sleep at night, be gentle about it. Open the curtains quietly, and if she is having trouble waking and the room is warm, remove some of her clothes and lie her down safely near you.

You might want to wake your baby up for an extra feed during the night if you are concerned that she is not gaining enough weight. If this is the case, just as with daytime waking, be gentle about it. Turn on a dim light, and be gentle and quiet. If you are lying down to feed her, be sure you have taken safety into account (see pages 234–235 and 361–362).

How should I burp my baby?

This is an aspect of caregiving which is prone to fashions. It is out of vogue to vigorously pat your baby on the back, and parents nowadays are encouraged to take a gentle approach. It can be enough to simply hold your baby upright and gently rub his back. You might do this periodically during a feed, not just at the end. You can also hold him over your shoulder, softly pat or rub his back or (when he is old enough) bounce him gently on your knee.

Can I breastfeed and formula-feed my baby?

Yes; it's what you are doing while you feed her that counts. There are so many variations in what and how mothers feed their babies. Some mothers breastfeed exclusively, while other parents formula-feed their babies from day one. Many mothers give their baby formula during the first few days while they are getting the hang of breastfeeding, then never use it again. Some mothers mix and match from the start, using both breastfeeding and formula-feeding for months.

Case study: Jane

Jane was tired. Her new baby, Jack, loved to nurse for comfort. He would feed and suckle on and off for over an hour-and-a-half at a time, sometimes taking only short breaks to nap on Jane before wanting to nurse again.

Jane contacted a lactation consultant and followed various advice, but Jack's frequent nursing was taking a toll on her. What's more, she also had her two-year-old toddler, Sam, to care for. She was becoming increasingly exhausted. Jane was tuned in to her baby, and she knew that little Jack just needed to suck and be soothed. She was also tuned in to her toddler, and she saw that he needed more hands-free attention. Then she tuned in to herself and noticed she felt sadness, exhaustion and irritation.

A couple of months after Jack's birth, Jane's parents came to stay. They could immediately see how exhausted she was—so, together, they came up with a plan that allowed Jane to keep breastfeeding but restore her energy. When Jack woke up to feed, then grizzled when Jane tried to gently persuade him off her breast, she whispered to him, 'I love you very much, but I just need to rest now.' Then she handed Jack over to her father, who snuggled him to sleep while he cried. At the same time, her mother built a block house with Sam. Jane slept.

With more sleep, Jane felt noticeably happier and much more in control of her mood. From then on, whenever Jack wanted to keep nursing after he was fed, Jane took charge and made a call: she decided whether she was up to it, or whether Jack could be soothed a different way or by someone else. Jane was being sensitive to her children's needs and responding in a kind and appropriate way.

CHAPTER 12: THE MAIN POINTS

+ If you know what it means to be sensitive and responsive while feeding, your baby can have the same positive bonding experience no matter whether he's breastfed or bottle-fed.

+ Responsive feeding is when you are sensitive to your baby's cues for hunger, you feed her at her pace, and you feed her with warmth. You can feed responsively no matter whether you are using a bottle or a breast.

+ Remember to R-E-S-P-O-N-D: remain calm, eye contact, skin-to-skin, pace feeds, one thing at a time, notice and delight.

CHAPTER 13
BREASTFEEDING: A
PRACTICAL GUIDE

Mothering myth: Breastfeeding comes naturally to all mothers.

Truth: Breastfeeding is a skill that most often takes practice.

Now that you know all about sensitive and responsive feeding, and how to do it, let's take a closer look at the mechanics of feeding itself, starting with breastfeeding. (Turn to Chapter 14 for the nuts and bolts of bottle-feeding.) The information in this chapter comes from the three years I spent breastfeeding, from working with and talking to other maternal health professionals, and from written material.

Before we get into the details, however, there are a few important things to always remember when it comes to breastfeeding.

+   Know that it's your right to breastfeed anywhere you want to.

+   If breastfeeding doesn't come easily to you, know that you are not alone. Breastfeeding is a natural event, but we no longer live in societies where we grow up learning how to breastfeed by watching others. For most mothers, breastfeeding is a new learning experience.

+ Be assertive with any friends and relatives who try to dissuade you from breastfeeding. Tell them that breastfeeding is important to you. Tell them how they can support you to breastfeed.

+ Know that there is a lot of professional support out there, some of it free, such as from your local La Leche League.

+ Know that, despite what some might say, it is in fact possible to have problems with your milk supply. If you suspect that your supply is low, get professional advice as soon as you can. Be in the driver's seat.

+ Know your rights within the health system and advocate for your baby. Insist that medical professionals listen if you are worried that your baby isn't feeding well post-birth. Ask them to help you to come up with a plan. Don't let yourself be pushed into leaving your baby hungry.

GETTING STARTED

I know it can be difficult, especially in the early days, but try to relax and see your breastfeeding journey as a learning process. Your baby doesn't expect to have long feeds as soon as he is born. At the start, you are both learning. Use these early days to experiment with feeding and to get better acquainted with your baby. Hold him to your chest and let him explore.

Don't be shy about asking for help, or of being assertive about what you need. Many of the mothers I have worked with have told me that when they were first learning to breastfeed they felt vulnerable repeatedly asking for assistance, and were worried about irritating the staff they felt dependant on. Feeling tired and vulnerable can get in the way of being assertive. If you find yourself feeling this way, remember that the people caring for you have chosen this line of work. It's their job to be compassionate and to support you to breastfeed. Like any profession, some of them will be amazing, while others will be tired and burnt out. If you aren't getting the help you need and don't feel up to being assertive, ask your partner or a friend or family member to speak up for you. Be clear that you want to breastfeed, but you really need some warm guidance. Also remember that, if you give birth in a hospital or maternity unit, it is likely the facility is (or wants to be) Baby-friendly Accredited (see pages 293–294). So make the most of the opportunity: get frequent support from staff, and speak up if you are feeling unsupported.

When I had my first baby, I might as well have had my finger taped to the buzzer while I was in hospital! I needed all the support I could get. However, by the time our third baby was born, I quickly enjoyed the feeling of breastfeeding my baby, and chatted cheerfully with the nurses and midwives for company as they went by. That being said, it's not always the case that a mother has a smooth run with breastfeeding subsequent babies; if you experience difficulty breastfeeding and it's not your first baby, don't think that you 'should know what you are doing'. It always takes time for a mother and her newborn baby to get to know each other, and to learn together how breastfeeding will work between them.

WHAT'S THE DIFFERENCE BETWEEN 'BREASTFEEDING' AND 'NURSING'?

It depends where you come from.

In North America, 'nursing' and 'breastfeeding' are generally used to mean the same thing—namely, a baby feeding from the breast.

In many other Western countries, however, 'nursing' is used to mean feeding your baby as well as using your breast to soothe her.

> Babies have a biological need to suck and to be close to their caregivers, so nursing can help your baby not only when she is hungry but can also calm her through tiredness or pain.
>
> Your breast isn't the only way to soothe and calm your baby. Alternatives include using a dummy (pacifier), cuddling and rocking. (For more information on soothing your baby, see Chapter 9.)

THE LOW-DOWN ON BREAST MILK

Colostrum is the first milk produced by your breasts, and you start producing it while you're still pregnant. It is thicker and yellower than mature milk, which 'comes in' during the first two weeks post-birth. Colostrum is produced in small amounts, making it a perfect match for your new baby's small stomach. This gentle beginning encourages him to nurse frequently, which in turn increases your milk supply. The amount of milk your baby takes at each feed signals to your body how much milk needs to be produced in the future—when your baby will want to drink more.

If your baby isn't nursing over the first couple of days, you can try expressing to stimulate milk production. It is often easier to express colostrum by hand, rather than with a mechanical pump. Ask your health provider, such as your nurse or midwife, to show you how to do this.

On about the third or fourth day after your baby is born, your milk becomes whiter and increases in volume. When people talk about your mature milk 'coming in', this is what they're talking about (even though the process of your breasts producing milk began while you were still pregnant).

Some people describe mature milk as being composed of 'fore milk' and 'hind milk', but this isn't strictly true. Only one kind of milk is produced, but fat globules move down the ducts as your breasts empty from your baby feeding, so the milk gradually increases in fat as the feed progresses. If you keep your baby on one breast until he is finished feeding, it can give him a chance to get to the creamy milk at the end. However, if you nurse frequently, it's likely the low-fat and high-fat milk stay mixed together anyway. It's all good milk.

THE THREE STAGES OF BREASTFEEDING

Babies tend to move through three stages when breastfeeding.

1. **Quick sucks.** This can last for a couple of minutes, and your baby's lower jaw will move up and down to stimulate the 'let-down' of your milk. The let-down is when the milk releases in response to your baby sucking. During the let-down, some women feel a tingling in their breasts, a feeling of warmth or may even feel a bit tired; other women don't feel the let-down at all.

2. **Active feeding.** When your baby is actively feeding, you will be able to see him swallowing, and you might even hear a 'keh' sound as he swallows. (You are less likely to hear him swallow when he is still drinking colostrum.) Some babies are noisy when they feed; others are quiet. During active feeding, you will see your baby's lower jaw moving up and down in a slow, rhythmic pattern—for example, the pattern might be 'suck, swallow, suck' or 'suck, suck, swallow, suck, suck, swallow'. Your baby might take a break during this phase and he will stop moving his mouth before resuming active feeding.

3. **Flutter-sucking.** This is when your baby's swallows slow down towards the end of the feed, and he has a light, fluttery

suck. Your baby isn't getting much milk when he flutter-sucks. If there is another let-down, he might resume active feeding; otherwise, flutter-sucking can signal either that he wants to move on to your other breast or that he is satisfied and finished his feed. Flutter-sucking is a normal part of the cycle of breastfeeding, and nothing to worry about—unless your baby is spending a large amount of time flutter-sucking rather than active feeding, and is not gaining weight.

In order to tell when your baby is finished feeding, it can help to think of each breast as one serving. If your baby appears satisfied after feeding on one side, you don't need to offer him your other breast. Some women like to know their baby is feeding from both sides equally, and use a bracelet or app to remind them which side their baby fed from last. More seasoned breastfeeders often let the fullness of their breast guide them as to which side to start from.

CLUSTER FEEDING

Cluster feeding is when your baby feeds frequently (or constantly) over a certain period of time, for example for a few hours during the middle of the night. There is nothing abnormal about a newborn baby wanting to cluster feed, and it can happen at any time of the day or night, however it tends to be most common in the late afternoon and evening.

Many mothers worry that their baby is feeding frequently because they are short of milk, but if your baby is gaining weight well this is rarely the case.

When your baby cluster feeds, there are a few options available to you.

+ Go with it. Your young baby is telling your breasts to manufacture a good amount of milk for the future.

+ Be prepared. Gather strength ahead of an afternoon or evening cluster feed by eating a healthy lunch and taking a nap when your baby naps in the afternoon.

+ Take a break. If you or your baby are becoming too tired and someone else is around who can help, pass your baby to them then go and take a shower, have a nap or get yourself something to eat.

+ Offer him more milk. If you are wondering if your baby might be unsettled because he is hungry, you can try offering him a bottle of expressed breast milk or formula. If he drinks it hungrily, that's great. If he doesn't, he's telling you he's had enough.

GETTING A GOOD LATCH

When people talk about the 'latch', they are referring to how your baby latches her mouth on to your breast to feed. A good latch is incredibly important. Not only will your baby feed better with a good latch, but it will also decrease the chances of nipple pain and of your breasts becoming engorged (and therefore of you getting mastitis or abscesses).

Note that many lactation consultants specialise in latching, and can help you with any issues that might arise. As I've mentioned, don't be afraid to ask for help, and be assertive about asking for it early. Each mother and each baby is different, so it's very normal for you both to need some practice to get the latch right.

If your baby continues to have difficulty latching, it might be worth getting a health provider to check that she doesn't have a tongue tie. Since a tongue tie restricts tongue movement, this can mean your baby isn't capable of getting a good, deep latch—and isn't able to feed properly. You need to get a professional to check for a tongue tie, because it can be difficult to see if you don't know what you are looking for.

Below is an illustration showing the three stages of a good latch.

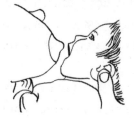

1. Her mouth should be open wide.

2. Your nipple should be pointed slightly towards the roof of her mouth.

3. Some of your breast (approximately 1 cm around the base of your nipple) should be in her mouth. Her lips are flanged.

There are a few things to keep in mind as you and your baby are working out the latch: try to keep things calm, and keep an eye on your baby's jaws, nose and mouth. Let's take a closer look at each of those points in more detail now.

TRY TO KEEP THINGS CALM

Although it's not always possible, it's good to try to calm your baby before he feeds. Yes, I know that your baby's mouth is conveniently wide open while he's crying, and that this can lead to a good latch, but you really want to try to associate breastfeeding with a calm time. Furthermore, your baby is more likely to settle well at your breast when he is calm.

Newborn babies have a better chance of staying calm if you feed them when they show you early cues for hunger. Early hunger cues include your baby sucking on his hand, fingers or fists, turning his head or mouth towards you, or smacking his lips. Crying is a later cue of hunger.

As always, it's much easier to help your baby to be calm if you are also calm. Find any tension in your body and loosen it. Notice your breath. Tune in to your emotions (see Chapter 4 for more on doing this.) Getting a good latch can be tricky while you are both learning, but you will get there. Remind yourself that right now is not forever.

KEEP AN EYE ON YOUR BABY'S JAWS, NOSE AND MOUTH

Your baby's lower jaw needs plenty of room for movement. Their upper jaw stays still when they feed—just like ours does. You don't want your baby to tuck in her chin while latching. Instead, you want her to lift her head slightly, so that her chin is in firm contact with your breast and once latched her lower jaw can move freely. It's fine if you move or shape your breast during latching or feeding, but make sure to keep your fingers well out of the way of your baby's lower jaw so that she can move it freely.

When your baby tilts her head back slightly, this also frees her nose—as much as possible—from your breast. She can still breathe if her nose is lightly touching your breast (and if she can't, she will come off your breast). If you would like to make more space for your baby's nose, you can gently tilt her head back by pulling her back and shoulders in closer to you.

Finally, I probably don't need to say this, but you don't want your baby chewing on your nipples! Not only will your nipples become sore, but your baby won't get a good amount of milk. There is only a little milk in your nipples; most milk comes from the ducts in your breast.

In order to get a good, wide latch, you can use a technique called the 'hamburger hold'. When you buy a hamburger that's bigger than your mouth, you squeeze the burger so you can get your mouth around it, right? Well, in this scenario, your breast is the hamburger—and your baby is the one dining! This technique is particularly useful if you have large breasts or your baby has a small mouth. And have I mentioned that your fingers need to be out of the way of her lower jaw?

BREASTFEEDING POSITIONS

There is no right or wrong position to breastfeed your baby in, as long as your baby is thriving and you are not at risk of falling asleep while feeding. There are a number of well-known positions to choose from—which can be great news if your baby has been cluster feeding and you're keen for a change of position.

First, we'll look at three 'baby-led' feeding positions—one where you are 'laid-back', one where you are sitting up, and one where you lie down. These positions are baby-led in the sense that they take advantage of your baby's instincts. Then, we'll look at three 'mother-led' positions—the cradle hold, the cross-cradle and the football hold. These three positions are mother-led in the sense that you will be more proactive in guiding your baby to latch and feed in a specific position.

I have enjoyed using all of these baby-led and mother-led positions at different times. You can also find descriptions of these positions online, and through apps such as Nancy Mohrbacher's Breastfeeding Solutions (more information available at nancymohrbacher.com).

LAID-BACK BREASTFEEDING

Many mothers and midwives have told me that they love laid-back breastfeeding—and I did too. It felt right and easy, and I felt very bonded with my baby when I fed this way. I didn't have a name for it back then, but laid-back breastfeeding is now routinely taught and can be used right from birth and for as long as you like.

This is a breastfeeding position that humans have used throughout history, but it went out of vogue for a long time. It has made a comeback in recent times with the help of midwife and nurse Suzanne Colson, who calls it 'biological nurturing'. Women who enjoy this position notice (among other things) that it is both relaxing and less likely to be painful. It is also nice to have one arm free. What's more, this position makes a whole lot of sense for your baby. For starters, in this position she drinks with her head straight up (like we do), rather than sideways (as is the case in many other breastfeeding positions).

Following is a description from a midwife friend of how to breastfeed in a laid-back position. For more information, you can also go to the Biological Nurturing website (biologicalnurturing.com).

1. Laid-back does *not* mean lying flat or on your side. Sit back in a semi-reclined position that feels comfortable. Ensure you have good support for your body, head and neck. You can sit back on pillows, but don't fall asleep.

2. Lie your baby on top of your body, so that her front is on your front, with her head near your breast.

3. When your baby's face finds your nipple, she will lift her mouth and latch on. Your baby will most likely move towards

your nipple on her own, but of course you can give her gentle guidance if she doesn't.

4. If your nipple feels uncomfortable, try moving your body or your baby's body around until it feels better.

SITTING UP

Even though you are sitting up, this position is in many ways like the laid-back position. It's a great position to use, especially after your baby is a few weeks old.

1. Lean back a little (not as far as with laid-back breastfeeding).

2. Hold your baby vertically against your chest, skin-to-skin if you like, with his head under your chin.

3. When your baby is hungry, he will most likely work his way down to one of your breasts. When his face finds your nipple, he will lift his mouth and latch. Since this is a baby-led position, he is likely to wriggle or crawl to your nipple on his own and latch on, but of course you can guide him too.

SIDE-LYING

One reason I like the side-lying position is that your baby is drinking with his head straight (just like with the laid-back position). I personally found lying down and feeding nice and relaxing.

1. Lie on your side in a comfortable position with your head supported. Be careful not to fall asleep, and make sure your baby is away from pillows and stuffed toys.

2. Lie your baby on his side, facing you with his eyes or nose level with your nipple. When he latches on, you can bring him in closer to you by pressing the middle of his back (which will tilt his head back, making it easier for him to swallow).

3. If you have bigger breasts it can help to lie a bit more on your back. You can feed him from the bottom breast and then

try feeding from the top breast without rolling over (see illustration).

(By the way, you can try breastfeeding standing up, keeping your baby well supported and with his legs hanging down instead of horizontal. By the time I was nursing my third baby I was walking around while feeding quite a bit—great when you need to answer the door or follow a toddler around the park!)

THE CRADLE HOLD

1. Sit in a chair that has supportive armrests or on a bed with lots of pillows (but make sure not to fall asleep).

2. Make sure your legs aren't dangling, or you will lean towards your baby, which you don't want to do. Use a footrest or other raised surface if your feet don't touch the ground in the chair you are sitting in.

3. Lie your baby across you, on his side, with his stomach and head facing you. If you have chosen your left breast, your baby's head will be resting on the forearm or wrist of your left arm. Make sure to support your baby's head, back and shoulders. His lower hip should be resting on (or close to) your thigh, or pillow if you use one.

4. Line your baby's nose up to your nipple to latch.

5. If your nipple feels uncomfortable, try moving your body or your baby's body around until the latch feels more comfortable.

THE CROSS-CRADLE
This position is particularly good for little babies.

1. Sit in a chair that has supportive armrests or on a bed with lots of pillows (but make sure not to fall asleep).

2. Make sure your legs aren't dangling, or you will lean towards your baby, which you don't want to do. Use a footrest or other raised surface if your feet don't touch the ground in the chair you are sitting in.

3. Lie your baby across you, on his side, with his stomach and head facing you. If you have chosen the left breast, your right arm will be supporting him with your right hand supporting his neck. Make sure to support his neck, back and shoulders. His lower hip should be resting on or close to your thigh, or pillow if you use one.

4. Line your baby's nose up to your nipple to latch.

5. If your nipple feels uncomfortable, try moving your body or your baby's body around until the latch feels more comfortable.

THE FOOTBALL HOLD

This position can be particularly helpful if you have had a Caesarean section, as it keeps your baby away from the incision while you heal.

1. Position your baby next to you, his front against your side, with your hand supporting his shoulders and neck, and his back along your arm beside you.

2. Your baby should be facing you, with his mouth near your nipple to latch.

3. If the latch is uncomfortable, you can try moving him into more of a sitting than a side position.

TROUBLESHOOTING

As I've already mentioned, even though breastfeeding is a natural process, that doesn't necessarily mean it's a straightforward one, or that every new mother innately knows how to breastfeed her baby. Sometimes, it's quite the opposite, and as a learning curve it can come with its own share of challenges. So, let's look at a few of those challenges, and what you can do if you face any of them while you and your baby are working out how to breastfeed.

It's important for mothers to be aware of what can go wrong when breastfeeding in order to get on top of things quickly. However, remember that for most women serious problems either never arise, or are easily resolved—especially if you get on to it quickly.

Hopefully, breastfeeding will go well for you and you will be able to enjoy all the benefits: convenience, perhaps one or two fewer tummy bugs for your baby, and some lovely bonding time.

IT HURTS!

Unfortunately, nipple pain is incredibly common while a new mother is getting used to breastfeeding. If you experience nipple pain, ask a lactation consultant or maternal professional for help. While nipple sensitivity in the beginning is common, actual pain is your body's way of signalling for help.

What makes this a particularly complex issue is that some maternal professionals claim that pain can be avoided entirely, simply by making changes to the way a mother and her baby are feeding. Meanwhile, others disagree, stating that for some women pain is just going to happen for a period of time, no matter what they try.

Neither stance is especially helpful for the new mother who finds herself experiencing pain. It can be very frustrating to be repeatedly told that you shouldn't feel any pain, at the same time as none of the well-meaning advice you are offered is working.

Likewise, it can be upsetting to find yourself being told that the pain you are experiencing is just 'something you have to put up with'. This can lead women to stop asking for help altogether, and to blame themselves for the pain. If you ask for help because you are experiencing pain, statements like, 'He isn't latching properly,' or, 'It looks like it's going well, though,' are not the right answers. The right answer is, 'Let's try something else and see if that relieves your pain,' or, 'I'm sorry you're feeling so much pain. How can I help you to get through it?'

Don't ever be afraid to unlatch your baby if it hurts—but please don't just pull him off your nipple, as this can damage the skin around your nipple. All humans want what is taken from them, and your baby is as human as you are; if you try to pull him straight off, he is likely to suck even harder to try to cling on. Instead, place your (clean) little finger in the corner of his mouth between his gums to break the suction, then gently ease him off and away from your breast.

Giving your baby more breast in his latch by tilting your nipple away from him can sometimes help to relieve nipple pain. You can do this by putting your thumb near the base of your nipple (the side of your nipple nearest your nose and your baby's upper lip), then pressing down so that your baby gets a bigger mouthful of breast. Changing feeding position can also help. For example, if you've been feeding using a cradle hold, try a laid-back position.

Sometimes using a feeding pillow can cause your baby to tug on your nipple if the pillow prevents him from being close enough to your breast.

You might also try the hamburger hold described on page 358. There are also over-the-counter medicines and ointments that you can buy for sore nipples, but be sure to get medical advice as well so it doesn't turn into something more serious like mastitis.

NIPPLE BLEBS

A nipple bleb (also sometimes called a milk blister) is a small white blister that forms on the tip of your nipple. Blebs are harmless, and if you get one you can simply ignore it until it goes away—unless it is painful. Sometimes they can really hurt to touch, and also when you are nursing or expressing.

You can try softening the bleb with a warm bath or cloth. If that doesn't help, you can contact a health provider who can open the bleb with a sterile needle and provide antibiotic ointment to use after the bleb has been cleared.

ENGORGEMENT

Engorgement can occur when your breasts are too full. This feels very uncomfortable, and sometimes your breasts will feel hot and heavy. If you notice these sensations, you need to remove milk from your breasts immediately, either through feeding or by gently expressing milk by hand or using a breast pump. Expressing to relieve engorged breasts won't compromise your milk supply.

You can also try putting a bag of frozen vegetables on your breast as a cold compress—some mothers use chilled green cabbage leaves as a compress and swear by it. Avoid putting heat on your breasts.

Engorgement can lead to blocked ducts, which can in turn lead to mastitis, so be proactive. If engorgement doesn't resolve quickly, contact your heath provider for anti-inflammatories.

THRUSH

Thrush can cause stinging or itching on or around the nipples. Sometimes your breasts will ache with a stabbing or shooting pain. Your nipples might be clear, or they might be red and shiny; less often, a white rash is present.

Your baby might not have any signs of thrush or might have a thick white coating on his tongue or white spots inside his cheeks. You are more likely to get thrush if you have been using antibiotics or have nipple damage. You need to see a medical professional for treatment.

MASTITIS AND BREAST ABSCESSES

Mastitis and breast abscesses are both conditions that you need to take very seriously. Mastitis is essentially an inflammation of the breast, while breast abscesses are painful, puss-filled lumps often associated with mastitis. In New Zealand, the Ministry of Health (MOH) provides detailed information about both conditions on their website (health.govt.nz) on the page 'Mastitis and Breast Abscesses'.[1] They list the following symptoms of mastitis:

+ Tender, hot, swollen wedge-shaped area of breast

+ Temperature of 38.5°C or over

+ Chills

+ Headache

+ Flu-like symptoms

+ Systemic illness (illness that affects the whole body).

Factors that make mastitis more likely include nipple damage, a history of latching problems, stress and exhaustion, missed feedings, milk stasis (obstruction of milk flow, or engorgement), previous mastitis history with other babies, and use of a manual breast pump.

The Ministry of Health also provides thorough guidelines for health practitioners treating and managing both mastitis and breast abscesses, and these can be found on their website as above. With regards to abscesses in particular, the website notes that if a woman has been treated for mastitis but an area of her breast remains hard, reddened and painful, an abscess may have formed and an ultrasound may be needed to identify it.

Case study: Janine

Janine came to see me when her first baby, Michael, was three weeks old. She had been very excited to be pregnant and had an uncomplicated labour, and she really wanted to breastfeed Michael. However, as a new mother she found herself extremely upset, because she wasn't finding breastfeeding easy at all. She didn't find it painful, but Michael kept falling off her breast and seemed to have only short feeds non-stop.

Worried Michael wasn't getting enough milk, Janine was weighing him every day. She couldn't think about anything else, and it was driving a wedge between her and her partner. At the same time, her mother kept telling her to 'get real' and use formula.

I could see that breastfeeding meant a lot to Janine, and health professionals had assured her that Michael was not losing weight. I encouraged her to see a lactation nurse I knew who would really listen and provide support.

When I saw Janine again a couple of weeks later, she was triumphant. She told me that the lactation nurse had guided her to try a number of positions, and one had been promising—so Janine had stuck to it for a few days, and it ultimately did the trick for her and her baby.

Janine described how content and bonded she felt when she breastfed Michael. Getting help quickly had been the right thing to do.

FED IS BEST

If you are breastfeeding, keep an eye on your baby's weight. If your baby is not gaining enough weight, it could be either that your baby isn't feeding in a productive way, or that you have low milk supply.

If it is because your baby isn't feeding in a productive way, you can try feeding your baby more frequently or expressing by hand or pump to build up your supply. You should also consult a health professional to make sure that your baby isn't having trouble as a result of a condition such as tongue tie, or because of an underlying condition that is impeding him getting enough of your milk.

An alternative possibility is that you have low milk supply. This is unusual, but does happen. Check with a health professional that there are not any underlying hormonal or other causes for low milk supply.

Once you and your baby have both been checked, you can try herbal remedies if you like, or take prescription medicine to increase your milk supply.

The most important outcome by far is that your baby is fed, and fed enough. Take control. If your baby is continuing to lose weight two weeks post-birth, you need to feed him more. You can either top up with formula or expressed breast milk, and you should also contact a health professional. If you notice jaundice or signs or hypoglycemia (low blood sugar), such as pale skin or fatigue, you should also contact a health professional.

CHAPTER 13: THE MAIN POINTS

+ Don't be shy about asking for help, or of being assertive about what you need.

+ Babies tend to move through three stages while breast-feeding: quick sucks, active feeding, then flutter-sucking.

+ Your baby will cluster feed at times. You can be prepared by taking an afternoon nap. Alternatively, ask someone else to take your baby if you are too tired to continue nursing.

+ If you are wondering if your baby is still hungry, you can try offering him a bottle of expressed milk or formula. If he drinks hungrily, great; if not, he's had enough.

+ Don't believe anyone who tells you that giving top-ups of formula will 'mess up' your milk supply. That's simply not true.

+ It often takes some practice to get a good latch. Get professional help if you need it.

+ Remember there are lots of different positions you can breastfeed in, both baby-led and mother-led.

+ Be aware of health complications like mastitis so that you can get medical help early if they arise.

+ Enjoy the process! You are doing exactly what a good mother does: feeding your baby.

CHAPTER 14
BOTTLE-FEEDING AND FORMULA: A PRACTICAL GUIDE

Mothering myth: Breast milk is the only perfect food for your baby.

Truth: Formula contains everything your baby needs.

Some mothers have told me encouraging stories of nurses, midwives and lactation consultants who comforted and advised them if they did not want to breastfeed or weren't able to. However, all too often, that doesn't appear to be the case. Many mothers have also told me they felt too intimidated to ask for help with formula and bottles while they were in hospital or during postnatal visits. Some confessed to hiding their formula feeding from community nurses, and even from friends, mother-and-baby groups and relatives. How sad that these mothers felt driven to begin their transition to motherhood by sneaking about.

If you have decided to bottle-feed or formula-feed your baby, you have every right to do so. There are all sorts of reasons a mother might choose to feed her baby formula, including not liking breastfeeding or going back to work. Actually, it doesn't matter why you have chosen formula, and there is no need for you to justify your decision. The important thing is, as always, that your baby is fed. As I've already mentioned, no child has died in a developed country from being fed formula milk (and that's a better safety record than breast milk when things go wrong).

IT'S NOT THE WHY THAT MATTERS

We all need to think a bit carefully before we ask a mother why she isn't breastfeeding. The question itself is a rebuke, and the answer is nobody's business but the mother's. She is doing her baby no harm, and the chances are that she has made her decision based on what is best for her relationship with her baby and for her family.

However, if you are formula-feeding or bottle-feeding and do want to give a reason, it can be helpful to practise what you are going to say—especially when you are asking others for help. For example, you might say, 'I have considered my options carefully and I need to formula-feed my baby. Can you help me do it the best way?' If anyone is abrupt with you, don't be afraid of being direct. It is perfectly polite to ask, 'Are you comfortable with me bottle-feeding?' If they tell you they are not, you can ask them why, then explain how you feel about their response.

By being respectfully assertive in this way, you're not only keeping your own dignity but you are also helping to positively change the feeding culture! Mothers should be encouraged and supported to feed their babies in whatever way works best for them, but in order for that to happen the culture around feeding needs to be pro-choice. Some websites, such as fearlessformulafeeder.com, provide support for mothers who are formula-feeding.

Here are just some of the reasons mothers have given me for choosing to formula-feed their babies.

Breastfeeding hurts so much that I'm not enjoying being a mother. I just can't get it right, no matter how I try.

I had to go back to work earlier than I wanted to, and expressing was really hard for me because not much milk came out.

It was really bringing me down. I'm feeling overwhelmed with all the contradictory advice on how to breastfeed.

My baby just didn't gain enough weight—it was so distressing. I wanted to make sure she got enough to eat.

I keep getting mastitis and abscesses.

I find breastfeeding exhausting. It interferes with my mood.

I have been sexually abused and I'm scared of the memories that breastfeeding brings up for me.

I have had breast operations for cancer and I can't breastfeed.

I have had a breast reduction and I can't breastfeed.

I need to stay on medication that will pass through my milk, but I really wanted to breastfeed.

My baby is adopted.

I hate breastfeeding.

THE BOTTLE-FEEDER'S MANIFESTO

I am a good mother. I am feeding my baby, and I am taking care of the needs of my baby, myself and my family

I do not have to justify why I am bottle-feeding or formula-feeding my baby to anyone.

I am not alone. Over half of North American mothers and 40 per cent of New Zealand mothers feed their babies formula by three months.[1] Over half of UK mothers formula-feed by one-week post-birth.

I can feed my baby formula without risking any proven long-term adverse effects.

Case study: Sally

A year before she became pregnant with her second baby, Sally had moved to New Zealand from California. She missed LA and her parents, but she had quickly made friends at the local playgroup, which she went to a few times a week with her three-year-old, Jay.

Sally loved being a mother. Breastfeeding had gone so well with Jay that she was certain she would breastfeed her next baby. The birth of her daughter, Tilly, went well and was a wonderful experience—but breastfeeding was a different story. Sally felt relaxed, but Tilly just didn't take to latching. After a week, Sally's midwife discovered that Tilly had a tongue tie and it was snipped, but Tilly just wasn't gaining weight so Sally resigned herself to topping up with formula. She soldiered on with breastfeeding and expressing as well. She didn't want to give up.

Unfortunately, Sally soon became exhausted and miserable,

and ended up in hospital for a few nights because of mastitis in both breasts. She finally and reluctantly called it a day on the breastfeeding, but she felt so guilty about it. She couldn't bear the thought of going back to playgroup and having her friends see that she wasn't breastfeeding.

Sally found herself in a dangerous downward spiral of social isolation and low mood—and that's when she came to see me. With time, she understood that she was the same worthwhile friend and mother she had always been, and that breastfeeding didn't define her as a person. She also understood that being child-centred, which was important to her as a parent, meant she needed to socialise for her children's sake, even if she didn't feel like it. Sally went back to playgroup, and guess what? All her friends were completely supportive and very pleased to see her. Sally had chosen her friends well—they just wanted the best for her and Tilly.

EIGHT SIMPLE TIPS FOR SENSITIVE AND RESPONSIVE BOTTLE-FEEDING

1. Bottle-feeding takes less time than breastfeeding, so you need to make up for this time by giving some extra attention to your baby. When a feed is finished, you can keep your baby with you for a while longer, and give her some focused one-on-one time. Spend some extra time engaging in mutual gaze (see pages 53–55), talking to her and stroking her.

2. Know what a baby's hunger cues are (see page 340), and offer the bottle in response by gently offering your baby the teat.

3. Pace the feeds. (See pages 384–386 for more information on paced feeding.)

4. Never, ever prop the bottle up in your baby's mouth. This leads to forced feeding if she can't move the bottle, it is unsafe, and it doesn't allow you to notice when she wants to pause or end the feed.

5. Always have your baby facing you when you feed her, so that you can look into each other's eyes. When feeding, you should engage in eye contact, cuddling, smiling and talking. You can communicate to your baby directly using words, soft sounds or just gentle face movements.

6. Give your baby skin contact when practical. You can unbutton your top and rest your baby on your exposed skin.

7. After feeding, check whether your baby needs more sucking time. Sucking is a powerful reflex in babies, but bottle-feeding provides less sucking time than breastfeeding does, so it's important to give bottle-fed babies additional opportunities to suck. Once you are sure your baby is no longer hungry, you can offer her a dummy or a clean finger.

8. Try to limit the number of people who primarily feed your baby to yourself and one or two others. A baby's parents should give most of the feeds, particularly in the early weeks post-birth.

THE LOW-DOWN ON FORMULA

Formula is basically cow's milk adjusted to match human milk, with some supplements added. It is generally accepted that human breast milk does not have enough iron for a baby in the first year, so formula milk is fortified with iron and a few other supplements.

On the other hand, human breast milk has more Omega-3 (sometimes referred to as 'fish oils') than standard baby formula does, so you can buy 'premium' formula, which is fortified with

Omega-3. There isn't actually any convincing evidence that formula fortified with Omega-3 makes any difference, however there is no harm done by it either. If you are considering giving your baby supplements, it is much safer when the supplements are already included in the formula you buy.

Generations of babies raised in developed countries with safe water supplies have thrived on formula, growing tall, strong and bright with long life expectancies—just like breastfed babies. When it comes to choosing a brand, there is not much difference between them in quality. Well-known formula brands have been around for a long time, their quality is monitored, and they get the supplement proportions correct. All infant formula sold in shops must comply with composition requirements monitored by the Food Code, which is the joint food standards programme established by the United Nations' Food and Agriculture Organization (FAO) and the World Health Organization (WHO).[2] Formula contains everything your baby needs for healthy development. However, it might be reassuring to buy a brand that has been around for a long time. There is no problem switching brands if you don't think a certain formula agrees with your baby.

Formula is extremely user-friendly. It is graded according to your baby's age, and comes with very clear instructions (and a measuring scoop) for month-by-month proportions. It is important to remember, though, that once it is mixed into liquid milk, formula goes off and must be used within an hour of preparation or else refrigerated.

EXERCISE CAUTION WITH COW'S MILK ALTERNATIVES

Some people think that goat's milk is superior to cow's milk. It is certainly more expensive. However, there is no evidence that goat's

---

milk is better, and it often has fewer of the added nutrients which might be beneficial. Think twice before you go down the goat's milk track, and only buy it if it agrees better with your baby—not just because it is more expensive.

Be even more cautious before going dairy free with soy milk. I'd advise you to only make that decision under a doctor's supervision.

A few people put their own formula together with canned milk— but I would beg you not to consider this. It's terribly unsafe, and also unnecessary.

KEEP IT STERILE

In the first year of life, formula-feeding can lead to one or two more minor tummy bugs when compared to breastfeeding. The good news is that these tummy bugs can be reduced by practising good hygiene and sterilisation of bottles and equipment for the first six months.

Replace your bottles and teats regularly. If bottles are not made of glass, they will scratch, and those scratches can grow and hold bacteria. (NUK makes glass bottles.) The same goes with tears or cracks in the teats; as soon as they show any sign of wear and tear, replace them. Do not keep bottles or teats to use with later children.

There are a variety of teats to choose from, and different babies have different preferences. Rather than buying a whole lot of one type of bottle and teat right away, you might consider getting a few different types of each and trying them out, before you commit to one.

Finally, for good hygiene, bottles are for feeding time only—not for your baby to crawl or toddle around with, and certainly not to have in their cot.

Here are some step-by-step instructions for keeping everything clean and sterile when you're bottle-feeding.

Before sterilising:

1. First, wash your hands and clean all kitchen surfaces.

2. Next, wash all the feeding equipment either in the dishwasher or in the sink with hot, soapy water. Remember to include tongs if you plan to sterilise the equipment with boiling water. Clean the bottle and teat thoroughly, inside and out, remembering to unscrew all the bottle parts. Remove all traces of milk (it's a good idea to rinse your bottles as soon as your baby finishes a feed).

3. Rinse everything in hot water.

Now you can sterilise the feeding equipment. There are four options for sterilising bottles and other feeding equipment: a steam steriliser, a microwave steam steriliser, boiling water and store-bought sterilising tablets or solution. You cannot sterilise equipment in the dishwasher or on its own in the microwave—the heat is not enough in either to ensure sterilisation.

To sterilise equipment using store-bought sterilising tablets or solution, follow the manufacturer's instructions carefully. This takes longer than steam sterilisers or microwave steam sterilisers but it's a good option if you are travelling.

A steam steriliser makes things very easy. You do still need to wash bottles and teats first, but after that the steriliser takes over, including keeping the bottles sterile until they are used. They're not a cheap option, however, and do take up quite a bit of space in the kitchen. A slightly cheaper (and smaller) alternative is a microwave steam steriliser.

You can also sterilise feeding equipment using boiling water. Here are step-by-step instructions.

1. Once you have washed all the feeding equipment as above, put it in a pot with a lid.

2. Fill the pot with water. Make sure that no big air bubbles are trapped inside any of the equipment, and that everything is completely covered with water.

3. Put the lid on the pot and heat the water to a rolling boil. Boil rapidly for at least five minutes.

4. Remove the pot from the heat, but keep the lid on. Leave to cool.

5. Before you remove the equipment for use, make sure you wash your hands. Use the sterilised tongs to remove the equipment.

6. Keep the sterilised equipment in a clean place, such as a clean part of the kitchen bench or a special pot.

HOW TO MAKE UP A BOTTLE OF FORMULA

You can buy ready-to-feed formula or powdered formula. Powdered formula comes with instructions on the packaging for how much to use and how to mix it up. The quantities given for each age are a guide; if your baby is thriving but doesn't want to finish feeds, you can make smaller bottles for her. Always wash your hands before touching the formula scoop and bottles. The basic instructions for mixing formula are usually something like this.

1. Fill a kettle with fresh tap water. (Pour out any old water, and refill the kettle.)

2. Boil the water, then leave to cool.

3. Wash your hands and clean all kitchen surfaces. Don't let the teat touch any bench surfaces.

4. Pour the cooled boiled water into your baby's bottle.

5. Scoop out the correct measurement of formula for your baby. (Refer to the quantities given on the packaging.) Don't compact down the formula in the scoop.

6. Screw the teat onto the bottle, put the lid over the teat, then shake until the formula powder has dissolved.

7. Test the temperature of the milk by squeezing some out onto your wrist. It should be at room temperature or at body temperature. If necessary, cool the milk by putting the bottle in a bowl of cold water or holding it under cold, running water. Shake the bottle, then test the temperature again. You will know the milk is at body temperature if you can barely feel it.

8. Feed your baby!

For convenience, you can make up a whole bottle and keep it in the back of the fridge for up to 24 hours, heating it up under the hot tap or with a bottle warmer (never put an unfinished feed back in the fridge though). Alternatively, keep airtight bottles containing fresh boiled water in the fridge for up to 24 hours, take out as needed and warm to room temperature, then add formula. This is a great method for night feeds, and you don't waste formula as you only add it to the bottle when needed.

PACED BOTTLE-FEEDING

Paced bottle-feeding is a way to ensure that you are feeding your baby at her speed, and not going too fast, which can be uncomfortable for your baby. Essentially, when you pace a feed, you periodically remove the bottle from your baby's mouth, or tip the bottle down until the milk runs away from the teat. Doing this gives your baby a chance to decide whether she wants to keep feeding, or whether she's done. If she isn't interested when you offer the bottle again, that means she's done.

Note that paced bottle-feeding might not be appropriate if your baby is not gaining weight. If that's the case, she might require supplemental bottles and you should seek professional guidance.

Here are step-by-step instructions for paced bottle-feeding.

1. First, choose a teat that is age-appropriate. Buy a few sizes at the same time, in case the flow is too fast or too slow for your baby. Never cut a teat to make the hole bigger.

2. Watch out for your baby's early hunger cues. If she is hungry, she might suck on her fingers, hand or fist, move her head around in a groping way, and smack her lips. Crying is a late hunger cue.

3. Hold your baby fairly upright for feeds, with her head supported so that she can breathe and swallow comfortably. Make sure you are comfortable too, and always hold your baby close while you feed her. Look into her eyes to make her feel loved and secure.

4. Brush the teat or nipple of the bottle to your baby's lips. When your baby opens her mouth wide, allow her to draw the teat into her mouth.

5. Hold the bottle horizontally to slow down the feed.

6. Allow your baby short breaks during the feed. After 20 to 30 seconds, gently remove the bottle from her mouth or tip it down. This slows the feed, and gives her a chance to decide if she is still hungry or if she's done. Keep an eye out for cues that she wants a break or to finish, for example pulling away from the teat, crying, closing her lips together and spitting out milk.

In paced bottle-feeding, the baby is fairly upright and the bottle is horizontal.

Does she need a break? Gently remove the bottle (picture 2) or tip the bottle down (picture 3).

7. After a break, see if she wants to resume.

8. When she has finished her feed, hold her upright and gently rub her back to bring up any wind. You might also need to do this periodically during the feed.

TIPS FOR AVOIDING WIND

All babies swallow air while feeding, and this can cause wind. Here are some tips to reduce swallowing air.

+ Slow the feed, as rapid gulping can trap air. You can do this by sitting your baby up and holding the bottle more horizontally.

+ Tip the bottle so that the teat is full of milk.

+ Try to avoid lying your baby down too soon after a big feed, as this can trap air in her stomach.

+ Some people suggest swirling the bottle of formula to mix it, instead of shaking it, to avoid air bubbles.

CHAPTER 14: THE MAIN POINTS

+ It is your right to bottle-feed or formula-feed your baby, and you don't have to justify yourself. However, if you do want to give a reason, it helps to practise what you're going to say.

+ Remember you are not alone. Many, many mothers all over the world bottle-feed and formula-feed their babies.

+ You can feed your baby formula without risking any proven long-term adverse effects.

+ Be aware that bottle-feeding takes less time than breastfeeding does, and ensure you make up that extra time with your baby.

+ Focus on feeding your baby sensitively and responsively.

+ Enjoy the process! You are doing exactly what a good mother does: feeding your baby.

CHAPTER 15

IMMUNISATION

Mothering myth: You don't need to immunise your baby because most diseases aren't around any more.

Truth: Nearly all babies and children should be immunised, or those diseases will come back.

Immunisation is the process of making a person immune to infection, typically by vaccinating them with a milder form of a dangerous disease in order to encourage their body to build an immunity to the disease. Throughout the Western world, immunising babies against once-lethal diseases such as measles, mumps, rubella, whooping cough and rotavirus is standard practice, and immunisations start as early as six weeks old.

A baby's immune system is an awesome thing. At birth, a newborn is only protected by maternal antibodies for three months. Right from the day he is born, a baby's immune system has a lot of work to do to create antibodies against a world of antigens before it is left entirely to its own devices. Nowadays, we can help a baby's immune system with the most dangerous of these antigens through early immunisation.

However, there's a lot of fear and misinformation surrounding the process of immunisation, especially when it comes to immunising babies and children. Sometimes, the scaremongering obscures the very significant advantages, and can lead to even more dangerous practices, such as 'chickenpox parties'. So let's take a closer look at first the history of immunisation, then at the safety and associated risks. As elsewhere in this book, I want to provide you with the information you need to make informed choices as a parent—and to help you sift through all the theories.

A BRIEF HISTORY OF IMMUNISATION

It was smallpox that first taught humankind that a milder version of a disease can protect against the stronger version. Once the greatest killer known to humankind, smallpox has now been entirely wiped off the face of the earth thanks to immunisation with a vaccine. It was officially declared eradicated in 1979.

Before then, however, the highly contagious disease spread through any kind of contact, and during the twentieth century alone smallpox was responsible for up to half a billion deaths. In the early fifties, it struck down 50 million people a year; it had a mortality rate as high as 60 per cent for adults and 80 per cent for children, and left those it didn't kill blinded or with deep, disfiguring pockmarks. According to researcher Jonathan Tucker, the origins of smallpox lie in the wild rodents of Africa.[1] The disease has been seen in Egyptian mummies who died 3,000 years ago, but it is thought smallpox originally jumped to humans some 10,000 years ago.

The combination of the high prevalence and the high mortality rate of smallpox made it a good candidate for what might otherwise have been considered risky treatments. The first reference to inoculations against smallpox appears in 1549 in China. According to the late historian and researcher Joseph Needham, the Chinese banned the use of smallpox material (scabs) from those who had the full-blown disease; instead, they used material from someone already 'inoculated', or who had few scabs.[2] An account written in 1741 suggested that scabs should be left to dry naturally on the body, then stored for use. The scabs were powdered and blown (most likely by a physician) up the nostril of a person being inoculated, a method claimed to be effective in nine out of ten people. The East India Company, which was stationed in China, reported this method to the Royal Society of London around 1700.

The French writer Voltaire, the voice of eighteenth-century Enlightenment, described in 1742 how the Turks successfully used a method of controlling smallpox that was borrowed from the women of Circassia. These women, Voltaire wrote, had 'from time immemorial' given a mild case of smallpox to their children before the age of six months. They did so by making a small incision in the child's arm, then placing in it a 'pustule' from another child who had been inoculated. Voltaire went to pains to point out that this was a winning strategy, writing, 'From these natural observations, they concluded that in [the] case an infant of six months or a year old should have a milder sort of small-pox, he would not die of it, would not be marred, nor be ever afflicted with it again.'[3] This method, so similar to that used in China, had been reported to the Royal Society in London in 1714.

English aristocrat and poet Lady Mary Wortley Montagu was also a product of the Enlightenment, and had first-hand experience of smallpox: she'd lost a brother to the disease, and bore the scars of it herself. Furthermore, her husband was ambassador to the Ottoman Empire so she had witnessed the Turkish practice of inoculation. In 1721, she very publicly had her daughter inoculated against smallpox in the Turkish style. A year later, the daughters of the Prince of Wales were likewise inoculated. Voltaire heartily praised these actions, saluting the English for their wisdom and condemning the French—and, in particular, the French clergy and the Sorbonne—for their religious arguments against inoculation.[4]

Not to be outdone as an Enlightened royal, Queen Catherine of

Russia called on an English doctor to inoculate both herself and her son against smallpox after she ascended the throne in about 1768. Smallpox was not a major disease in Russia at the time; it appears Queen Catherine's highly publicised inoculations were as much an act of support for Voltaire and the Enlightenment, as to protect her family and nation from the scourge of smallpox. And, indeed, her actions may have assisted—at almost the same time, the Sorbonne's outdated and rigid views on medicine were dramatically replaced by those developed during the Enlightenment.

An even safer approach than the Turkish method of inoculation was not far off. While not the first to notice that many people who had direct contact with cattle came down with a mild, smallpox-like illness that protected them against the more serious smallpox, English physician Edward Jenner was the person who gave the name 'vaccine' to artificially weakened diseases. In May 1796, Jenner (who himself had been inoculated 'Turkish style') vaccinated eight-year-old James Phipps with a lesion taken from a milkmaid suffering from cow-pox. After a mild fever, the boy recovered. Two months later, Jenner inoculated the boy with smallpox—and, remarkably, the boy showed no reaction at all to the smallpox vaccination.

French chemist and bacteriologist Louis Pasteur took Jenner's principle of vaccinating against a disease by using a mild form to protect against the severe form many steps further. Pasteur admired Jenner immensely, and hoped that, if a vaccine could tame smallpox, then there could be vaccines for all diseases. Pasteur's work involved 'attenuating' (weakening) a disease before inoculation. In 1879, he cultured the bacteria that caused chicken cholera, then reduced the disease's potency by aging the culture. He then injected this weakened culture into chickens, and found they remained healthy yet became resistant to chicken cholera. Pasteur's work led directly to the development of vaccines against diphtheria, plague, tuberculosis, yellow fever, measles, mumps and rubella.

HERD IMMUNITY

It is not only possible to attenuate (weaken) a disease until it is safe to use as a vaccine. In many cases, a completely dead vaccine can also provide protection. The disease-causing microorganisms are killed off by heat, and examples of inactivated (killed) vaccines include polio, cholera and typhoid fever. Many other vaccines are available in either live or killed forms. The presence of a dead virus is usually enough for a person's immune system to create antibodies to fight off the real thing.

While weakened or inactivated vaccines have the significant advantage of great safety, they may also have the disadvantage of being less effective than a stronger vaccine. This loss of effectiveness could mean that a percentage of those treated with an inactivated vaccine will not be protected, or will be only partly protected, or the protection will be only short-lived. As a result, children require repeated immunisations, or 'booster shots', to gain or retain full protection from diseases. Once a vaccine has been around for a long time, it's possible to know how long it is effective for and therefore to plan booster shots well before any effectiveness runs out.

The bottom line is this: in order for our children to enjoy the benefits of being protected through safe and gentle vaccines like this, the entire community needs to cooperate. This is referred to as 'herd immunity', because when almost all children are immunised it creates a safety blanket for those who may lose immunity over time. In this scenario, children are simply unlikely to come into contact with the disease. Significantly, herd immunity helps to protect children who cannot be immunised because they have compromised immune systems, for example as a result of autoimmune disease or chemotherapy.

In order to be effective, herd immunity requires parents who have children who can be safely immunised to get their children immunised. Doing so helps to protect *everyone's* children. The World

Health Organization suggests that a 95 per cent compliance rate is necessary with immunisation in order to maintain herd immunity. Very few objectors can be tolerated before the herd immunity breaks—but, as soon as the number is too high, everyone is at risk. Those who haven't been immunised are most at risk, but so are many of those who have been.

MEASLES AT DISNEYLAND

When talking about herd immunity, a case in point is the measles outbreak that occurred at the end of 2014 at two adjacent Disney theme parks in California. This outbreak received a great deal of publicity and ultimately resulted in law changes in the state so that immunisation before entering a public kindergarten is no longer a matter of parental choice.[5] Only a medical certificate asserting an incompatible condition will result in an exception.

The virus was believed to have been brought to one of the parks by an overseas visitor, and 39 people at the same park that day contracted measles. It quickly spread so that, within one month, 140 cases were reported in eight states. Twenty per cent were hospitalised.[6] Most of them were children who had not been immunised. Although a few of the children who contracted measles *had* been immunised, hundreds of the immunised children who were exposed to the disease did not get it. For those who did, it seems that their immunisation may have reduced the severity of their illness, although it did not prevent it entirely.[7]

This incident showed that, when it comes to being in contact with a contagious disease like measles, not only is an unimmunised child in personal danger—but that child also presents a danger to immunised children.

HOW SAFE ARE VACCINES?

Vaccines have a high degree of safety.

Since a very small number of children can have an allergic reaction, doctors ask parents to wait at the clinic for a specified amount of time before leaving; this is so that, if their child has a reaction, a doctor is nearby. Allergic reactions can be handled easily by a doctor. A study published in 2003 found that after 7.6 million vaccine doses were given to children in the United States there were only five cases of allergic reaction, and none resulted in death.[8]

Another risk with vaccines arises when a child is immunocompromised, or has a weakened or impaired immune system. It is recommended that immunocompromised children should be screened before receiving any vaccination. There have been six confirmed deaths among immunocompromised children following vaccination: one child had been in remission following chemotherapy, another had HIV, and the others had a history of hospitalisation for immune-system problems.[9]

Historically, there has been one notable instance of human error with a vaccine resulting in deaths. This occurred in 1955, and is referred to as the 'Cutter Incident'. It was the worst pharmaceutical disaster in US history—the polio vaccine administered was still live, and was therefore delivered incorrectly, resulting in 51 cases of paralysis and five deaths. As a consequence, the US Government installed regulations that make such a disaster next to impossible, and it has a safety record lasting well over half a century.

When investigated, claims of death or illness following vaccination almost inevitably turn out to be coincidental or unrelated to the vaccine itself. In 2018, two toddlers in Samoa died after being given the measles, mumps and rubella (MMR) vaccine. Following autopsies, two nurses were charged with manslaughter over the deaths; it appears there was nothing wrong with the vaccine. University of Auckland's Helen Petousis-Harris told media,

'Looking at how quickly the deaths occurred really leaves only one real possibility and that is that something other than water was used in the vaccine.'[10] New Zealand Ministry of Health's Dr Stewart Jessamine said, 'The same batch of vaccine has been used safely across the Pacific, the Caribbean and South America.'[11]

As I have discussed in previous chapters, newborn babies are not out of the woods in terms of threats to their survival, and death rates are still relatively high in the first six months of life. This period corresponds with the time babies are given their first vaccinations, and parents can quite naturally fear that it was vaccinations that caused the problem. Investigations do not confirm that. In fact, the health benefits of vaccination can be detected almost immediately. A 2013 database study of 13 million vaccinated children found their death rate was lower one to two months after vaccination than that of the general population.[12]

There is a relatively new vaccine for rotavirus, which is the main cause of serious diarrheal disease—and a leading cause of death in underdeveloped countries. While death is unlikely in developed counties, where rotavirus disease can be managed, one serious complication can be intussusception, or a folding of the bowel causing blockage. Treatment may require sending a tube (similar to a colonoscopy) through the intestine to sort out the fold. In a very few cases, intussusception has occurred following immunisation. However, one study has shown that if a US birth cohort of 4.3 million babies were all immunised with the latest version of the rotavirus vaccine, it would prevent fourteen deaths, 53,000 hospitalisations and 169,000 emergency-room visits.[13]

Rotavirus is a nasty illness and almost inevitable without immunisation. Whether your child gets the illness itself or is immunised, keep an eye out afterwards for blood and mucus in the stools, or a lump in the abdomen. If you see any of those symptoms, have your child checked by your doctor.

DELAY IS A RISK

The guiding hand behind scheduling immunisations in the US is the Centers for Disease Control and Prevention (CDC). The main concern of the CDC is that children should be immunised before they are exposed to potentially life-threatening diseases, and their views both inform and are approved by the American Academy of Family Physicians (AAFP) and the American Academy of Pediatrics (AAP).

If the CDC's immunisation schedule is followed, by two years of age a child will have immunity to fourteen deadly diseases, including polio, diphtheria, tetanus, whooping cough, measles, mumps, rubella, pneumonia and chickenpox. The CDC position is that spreading out grouped immunisations, such as measles, mumps and rubella (MMR), will take more time and put children at risk longer; they are therefore adamant that grouped vaccines should be delivered together.

Parents sometimes worry that the increasing number of vaccines, and in particular grouped vaccines, might stress a baby's system. However, as the CDC points out, the amount of antigens given to babies is a drop in the ocean compared with what children are naturally exposed to everyday. What's more, even though babies nowadays are given protection against more diseases than they were 20 years ago, today's vaccines are more gentle and involve fewer antigens than used to be the case.

In 2013, in response to family doctors facing pressure from parents to spread out grouped vaccines, the National Academy of Medicine called for research into the safety of the entire immunisation schedule.[14] While at that time individual vaccines had been studied, the impact of all vaccines together had not. The academy's specific concern was establishing whether high levels of vaccine resulted in increased risks for illnesses which had not been targeted by the vaccines—or, in other words, did many immunisations stress the immune system generally?

In 2018, the findings of a study of 1,000 children under the age of four years were published. A group admitted to hospital because of infections unrelated to their vaccinations were compared to controls and showed no difference in terms of having been given vaccines. This showed there was no additional stress on the immune system from vaccinations.[15] Another study of a cohort of Danish children under five years old similarly showed no increased risk for non-targeted infectious diseases among those with multiple vaccine exposure.[16]

THE AUTISM LIE

Although there is no scientific evidence whatsoever that group vaccines (and, in particular, the MMR vaccine) place additional stress on a child's immunity, fear around these vaccines persists as a result of a terrible fraud. In 1998, now-discredited British medical practitioner Andrew Wakefield claimed in an article in medical journal *The Lancet* (since retracted) to have found a link between the live measles vaccine and autism. He falsified evidence and lied to support his 'theory' that the live measles vaccine in combination with other vaccines was dangerous, and his 'finding' panicked parents around the world. There was a sudden decline in measles immunisations, and a corresponding rise in the rate of measles, resulting in hospitalisations, injury and deaths. It took years to uncover Wakefield's fraud, but the fears aroused by his bogus study linger even to this day.

Wakefield's research had already come under scrutiny from his professional peers long before that *Lancet* article. Some years earlier, he had published findings claiming that measles in conjunction with other viruses produced a persistent infection in the gut, which could lead to Crohn's disease. This prompted no less than six research studies by other researchers attempting to replicate his findings— but not one of them was able to do so. One of the fundamentals of proving a fact scientifically is being able to reproduce results.

This did not, however, diminish Wakefield's conviction that a combined measles vaccine was dangerous. He theorised that the persistent gut infection (the one that no one else was able to find) released toxins which went to the brain and caused behavioural disorders, including autism. His views were picked up by groups of parents of children with autism, who had been searching for a reason why autism appeared to be increasing. Wakefield's triple-vaccine theory made sense to them—after all, the vaccine was given about the same time that children were first diagnosed with autism.

THE 'RISE' OF AUTISM

In 2017, an article in *Scientific American* explored the increase in the number of diagnoses of autism since Leo Kanner had first described a condition he called 'infantile autism' in 1943.[17] Kanner identified six criteria, including repetitive movements and an inability to make eye contact or communicate verbally, which a child had to meet in order to be diagnosed with autism. In 1966, the prevalence was one in 2,500 children. However, in 1987 the *Diagnostic and Statistical Manual of Mental Disorders, Third Edition Revised* (DSM-III R) expanded the diagnosis to sixteen criteria, with a child needing to meet only half to be diagnosed with autism. The significance of this change is that suddenly a child no longer needed the more debilitating symptoms that the general population associates with autism. This took the prevalence of autism in children to one in 1,400.

In 1991, the United States Department of Education ruled that a child diagnosed with autism qualified for special education. This resulted in families and practitioners actively seeking a diagnosis of autism. In 1994, the *Diagnostic and Statistical Manual of Mental*

Disorders, Fourth Edition (DSM-IV) broadened the definition of autism to include Asperger's syndrome. Finally, in 2006, a screening programme was recommended in the US for routine paediatric visits at eighteen and 24 months of age.[18] In the latest version of the *Diagnostic and Statistical Manual of Mental Disorders, Fifth Edition* (DSM 5), which was published in 2013, Asperger's syndrome and autism were combined to form a diagnosis of autism spectrum disorder (ASD), and those diagnosed with the condition include people who hold down important jobs, have loving relationships, marry and raise families.

In actual fact, autism was not increasing. The broadened definition was resulting in increased publicity surrounding the condition. Combined with proactive screening, this made almost everyone believe autism was on the rise. Therefore, a community of parents existed who were actively looking for the cause of a situation which did not exist. Wakefield went beyond offering an explanation to these parents; he offered them a false hope that, through treatment of the gut, their children's autism would improve.

The parents of twelve children suffering from both digestive and behavioural issues sent their children to see Wakefield; nine of those children had been diagnosed with autism. Wakefield saw this as an opportunity to get funding to test his hypothesis that measles in the gut had behavioural repercussions—however, he knew he wouldn't get very far if he revealed that the children were highly selected. So, in his grant application, he claimed that the children had randomly appeared in his surgery. It was the first of many deceptions.

When British journalist Brian Deer investigated (and ultimately exposed the falsity of) Wakefield's claims, he discovered that Wakefield had actually had access to the medical records of those twelve children from the outset—records that revealed in each and every case that the child had been diagnosed either well before being immunised with MMR or long afterwards. However, instead of using that evidence, Wakefield interviewed the parents, who had by this time convinced themselves that their children's conditions were related to immunisation. Wakefield used their biased recall rather than written medical records to claim that in each case symptoms arose only after the MMR vaccination, and within a very short time. In some cases, he just made it up.

Wakefield needed proof, namely to find the footprint of measles in the gut tissue of those twelve children. The final—and possibly most outrageous—claim he made was that he had found it. He then called a news conference to proclaim that he had found the link between the MMR vaccine and autism. When later questioned, he said that an independent laboratory had carried out the tissue analysis, but in 2002 one of Wakefield's assistants testified that Wakefield had instructed him to carry out the analysis. He also testified that the results were 100 per cent negative.

When judging the morality of Wakefield's actions, most particularly calling the press conference to spread the word that the MMR vaccine was dangerous, keep in mind the following facts. In 1963, before the measles vaccine was widely used, there were 500,000 cases of the disease and 500 deaths a year in the United States alone. By 1978, those figures had been reduced by 95 per cent.[19] You can learn more about Wakefield's fraud by watching Brian Deer's 2004 film *MMR: What They Didn't Tell You* on his website (briandeer.com).[20]

The impact of Wakefield's falsified 'research' was immediate. The rate of measles rose in England, Wales and some European countries. In 2013, CBS News reported that the United Kingdom, which once recorded only a few dozen cases of measles a year, had recorded 2,000 cases in 2012. British doctor David Elliman, on behalf of the

Royal College of Paediatrics and Child Health has been quoted as saying, 'This is the legacy of the Wakefield scare.'[21]

Perhaps the biggest impact was felt in Italy. The rate of immunisation tumbled so dramatically following the Wakefield scare that measles cases *tripled* in just one year. At its height, there were 18,000 registered cases and fifteen deaths. The decline in immunisations passed a critical point, dropping below 86 per cent, so that in 2017 the Italian Premier Paolo Genitoni announced that twelve vaccines, including measles, would become mandatory from 2018 for all children attending preschool through to high school. This follows the North American model, where vaccinations are required before a child can attend a public school. All US states require vaccinations for diphtheria, tetanus, whooping cough, polio, measles and rubella before a child can step foot into a public school; plus, various states have additional requirements.

The hope in other countries is that enough people will recognise that providing their children with protection against debilitating and fatal diseases is one of the great gifts they can give their babies. In a world where polio, for example, is 'only a plane ride away', most parents are able to see that the benefits far outweigh any fear of something unlikely occurring.

Case study: Chloe

Chloe came to see me when she was 32 weeks pregnant with her first baby. I assessed her as having mild to moderate perinatal anxiety and low mood. Part of her difficulty was that she was feeling overwhelmed with the responsibility of making decisions for her baby. At every turn, she worried about whether she was making the right choice—from deciding about amniocentesis to a birth plan.

One pressing issue on her mind was immunisation. She knew the link between immunisation and autism was a hoax, but she had been told by her neighbours that immunisations 'didn't work' and were just promoted by drug companies for profit. Her neighbours had shown her a compelling film that convinced her drug companies couldn't be trusted.

I didn't tell Chloe what she should do, but I did give her some alternative literature to read—namely *Bad Science* by Ben Goldacre. After looking at alternative statistical evidence, Chloe decided to immunise her baby. Once she had made up her mind, she no longer worried about it.

When I saw Chloe again three months later, she told me she had taken her baby, April, to the hospital with her first fever. When the doctor asked whether April was up to date with her immunisations, Chloe had been glad to look the doctor in the eye and say, 'Yes.'

SAY NO TO CHICKENPOX PARTIES

Any normal person who received an invitation to attend a gathering where the purpose was to transmit full-blown, full-strength smallpox to their child might go a step further than declining. They might call the police. And yet, there is a group of parents who think it is a clever idea to have 'chickenpox parties' in order to expose their children to the 'natural' disease. They believe that this is a safer option than getting their children immunised, but they couldn't be more misguided.

This makes no sense. There is a perfectly safe vaccine available to prevent your child from getting chickenpox at all. At the same time, the vaccine will massively reduce your child's chances of getting painful shingles later in life. Why would any parent deprive their child of these benefits? Not to mention at the same time risking their child contracting:

+ bacterial infections of the skin and soft tissues, including streptococcal infections

+ pneumonia

+ infection or inflammation of the brain

+ bleeding problems

+ blood-stream infections (sepsis)

+ death (including among any adults exposed to the disease from their children).

According to the Centers for Disease Control and Prevention (CDC), these complications are not common but do all occur.[22]

If you get invited to one of these parties, run! And I mean in the opposite direction.

CHAPTER 15: THE MAIN POINTS

+   In order for our children to enjoy the benefits of being protected through safe and gentle vaccines, the entire community needs to cooperate. This is referred to as 'herd immunity'.

+   In order to be effective, herd immunity requires parents who have children who can be safely immunised to get their children immunised. Doing so helps to protect everyone's children.

+   Vaccines have a high degree of safety and a long history. Thanks to vaccines, once devastating diseases such as smallpox no longer exist or are incredibly rare.

+   There is no evidence that group vaccines lead to autism, or that they stress a child's immune system. The autism theory is the product of one doctor's entirely fabricated 'findings', and the shadow still unfortunately lingers.

+   If you get invited to a chickenpox party (or anything like it), don't go!

CHAPTER 16

TECHNOLOGY AND THE

DEVELOPING BRAIN

Mothering myth: Your baby doesn't notice when you are on your phone.

Truth: Babies learn to disengage from us when they don't get a response—for example, because we are staring at a screen instead.

Children today are born into a very different world from the one their parents and grandparents grew up in. Now, screens proliferate, all the way to the tiny computers we carry around in our pockets. Technology is everywhere, and pretty much unavoidable, but the long-term effects on a baby's developing brain and on the parent–child relationship aren't fully understood. So, in this screen-obsessed era, what should new parents do? Do you shelter your baby entirely from the evils of technology and the internet? Or do you embrace the digital and give them access to your phone from the get-go? Is there some kind of middle ground—and, if there is, what does it look like?

And all of this doesn't even touch on your own relationship with technology. What's the best way to behave, and how do you maintain it when you're exhausted and brain dead and don't feel capable of much more than zoning out in front of the telly or your social media feeds?

PARENTS AS ROLE MODELS

For many years now, we've been hearing stories about high-tech parents in Silicon Valley sending their children to low-tech schools. We're informed that both Bill Gates and Steve Jobs strictly limited their kids' use of the internet and other technology. The irony in this, of course, is that many Silicon Valley businesses have one interest at heart: to make your phone (or computer) screen more appealing to you than anything else, including your children. App developers and technology companies invest a huge amount of time and resources trying to get you to spend as much time as possible staring at your phone. Bearing this in mind, it's understandable that many of us have a hard time breaking a damaging habit.

'But I don't spend *that* much time on my phone!' you might already be saying defensively. 'And sometimes I need some time out. I'm exhausted. Give me a break!'

Please know that I'm not trying to pick on you; I'm just trying to introduce the idea that screen time is something you need to be aware of. You aren't a bad parent because you want to have an adult conversation, or because you need a distraction from mothering. However, look at yourself through your child's eyes—because your baby is watching you very closely, even when you think he's not. Long before your baby can focus sensibly on your phone screen, he is already focusing on you with your phone screen. While he's sitting there innocently in your lap, he's absorbing everything. He's busy learning communication etiquette from you.

While your baby might understand that you can check in on him while you are busy cleaning or caring for other children, he doesn't get it at all when you are staring at a screen instead of at him. All he understands is that you don't see him, and you're not showing any expression on your face. It's very upsetting and confusing for him. On the flip side, if he sees you exercising self-control over your own use of fun technology, this will put you in good stead for the future when it comes to enforcing how he uses gadgets as he gets older. Children learn from what they see their parents doing; if your child has seen you utterly mesmerised by your phone and disengaged with everything and everyone around you, you'll have a hard time convincing your school-age child to limit his screen time.

In 2014, a Boston University study observed 55 mothers and fathers with their children while they ate a meal together in town.[1] Of those adults (or adult pairs), sixteen used their phone continuously throughout the meal. Nine of the adults only used their phone to receive calls, and kept the device out of view otherwise. There was no gender difference in the use of phones. The most continuous use came from those who typed or swiped, rather than those who only talked on the phone; this group also answered their children's questions briefly and without taking their eyes off their phone. Meanwhile, the parents who only used their phones for calls did it quickly and while their children were otherwise engaged with drawing or talking to another child.

The children of the parents who were continuously on their device showed two types of response.

+ Some clearly had no expectation of parental engagement, and did not seek any communication.

+ Others showed provocative behaviour. This behaviour was not noticed by the parent until it escalated, at which point the parent would react with a scolding tone of voice. One woman kicked her child's foot under the table, and another pushed her little boy's hands away when he was trying to lift her face up from looking at her screen.

A blank face—and especially a parent's blank face—is a hard thing for a child to deal with. Back in the 1970s, developmental psychologist Edward Tronick experimented with what happened when a mother kept her face blank, or held a 'still face'. In his experiment, a mother was asked to turn away from her baby, then turn back but not react to her baby in any way. She was to keep her features still. All of the babies, including those as young as three months old, reacted the same way: they first tried to engage with their mother, often by smiling. Then they stopped smiling, looked away, and tried once more. Most finished looking sad and helpless. (For more on still-face studies, see page 56.)

Children depend on their parents to respond to them. The response doesn't need to be perfect. In fact, Tronick thought that moving in and out of sync is part of the learning experience. However, no response at all is frightening and confusing. This situation is often seen when a parent is seriously depressed. After a while, the behaviour of a baby with an emotionally absent parent can show symptoms of insecure attachment.

Recently a group of researchers wanted to find out if babies react to a mother's use of her phone in the same way that was found in the Tronick's still-face studies.[2] The researchers observed babies between six months and two years of age, and noted that the 'patterns of child behaviour . . . mirrored those of the traditional [still-face study], with infants showing the most distress when mothers were disengaged'. Furthermore, the children of the mothers who reported the greatest phone usage took longer to recover from being upset.

Don't worry, I'm not telling you about these studies to try to convince you to throw away your phone. Rather, I simply want you to be aware that how you look and behave when you use your phone is having an impact on your child—even if you don't realise it. Your baby is busy learning everything from you, and that includes interpreting you when you are staring at your phone or any other screen. The more we look at our screens, the more likely it is that our children will model our behaviour when they have access to screens themselves. So, I know this is really hard, but here's what you need to try to do: be as discreet as you can when you use your phone or other screens, especially when your children are babies or pre-schoolers. If you possibly can, try to hold off until your baby is napping or sleeping. You can even check your phone when you are in the bathroom and they can't see you, if you must! Importantly, train yourself not to continually check your phone. In the Boston study, it was the checking and scanning which resulted in the least attentive parenting—and the most distressed or distanced children.

BREAKING THE PHONE HABIT

When it comes to training yourself not to check your phone all the time, there are a couple of strategies you can consider.

First up, an app called Moment tracks your screen time—many of us like to believe we spend less time on our phones than we actually do! Then, if you find you are using your phone more than you would like to, you can set daily limits on your screen time, get periodic updates about how long you have been looking at your phone, and even force yourself off your device if you go over your limit. I know another app doesn't sound like the solution to using your phone too much, but the advantage of Moment is that it will only give you notifications when you are actually already looking at your phone. (For more information, visit inthemoment.io.)

Here are a few other strategies than can be helpful.

+ Turn off all non-essential notifications. By this I mean turn off every kind of notification, except for the ones you truly need to get, such as incoming phone calls or messages.

+ Save it for later. If you use your phone to read news and articles, you can use apps like Instapaper to save things to read later.

+ Keep your phone out of the bedroom. Don't charge your phone overnight on your bedside table. Instead, plug it in and leave it on the lounge or on the kitchen bench.

+ Give yourself some space. When you're not using it, put your phone somewhere out of your reach. That way, if you get the urge to check it, you'll have to get up to do so. Often, you'll realise the effort isn't really worth it.

+ No phones at the table. When you're eating dinner, don't look at your phone. If you are eating with someone else, such as your baby or your partner, focus on spending time with them. If you are on your own, read a book or a magazine, or listen to some music or a podcast instead.

THE OFFICIAL PAEDIATRIC POSITION

The only public agency providing research-based guidance on screen use is the American Academy of Pediatrics (AAP), which public-health services in Britain, Australia and New Zealand either discuss or rely on. Until a few years ago, the AAP provided a simple formula for very young children: no screen time at all until the age of two.

However, confronted with information such as that 75 per cent of zero- to four-year-olds from low-income families in the US have their own mobile device,[3] and that children begin interacting with digital media from four months of age, the AAP modified its recommendation in 2016.[4] The AAP still recommends no screens until eighteen months of age, but now makes an exception for video-calling grandparents and relatives, so long as a parent is present.

The AAP points to evidence that children younger than two-and-a-half have difficulty learning from a two-dimensional screen.[5] However, the AAP now concedes that recent research shows children between the ages of fifteen and 24 months can learn from 'repeated viewing of video demonstrations without adult help'.[6] They refer specifically to a study teaching sign language, but are also quick to point out that the comparison group who were taught sign language from a book and a parent retained the information longer.

For children between the ages of eighteen months and five years, the AAP recommends less than one hour a day of screen time, noting that the best programmes can help with 'literacy and numeracy, and prosocial behaviour'. The AAP's approved site for choosing appropriate video and film content is called Common Sense Media (commonsensemedia.org), an independent non-profit organisation dedicated to helping kids thrive in a world of media and technology. They cite a 2013 study of over 500 children aged three to five who were randomly divided between watching normal TV, and watching TV which modelled less aggression than is usually found in children's programming. The researchers found a significant improvement in behaviour scores among the group that watched high-quality 'prosocial' and educational programming.[7] Of course, the flip side of this is that children learn poor behaviour from aggression-laden programming.

The AAP also provides a unique Family Media Plan tool, which gives advice according to your children's ages on such things as where, what and how much they should watch. As well as providing a Media Time Calculator, the site also allows you to create your own, personalised Family Media Plan. You can do this at: healthychildren. org/MediaUsePlan.

SCREEN TIME AND
COGNITIVE FUNCTION

A number of small studies have suggested there is a link between excessive television viewing and school readiness and performance. An important study in 2014 involving 107 preschoolers (averaging four years old) considered whether screen time damaged the most important cognitive feature: executive function.[8]

Executive function stems from the front of the brain and it is essentially the control centre for mental activities, including planning, problem-solving, and regulating and controlling behaviour. It is necessary for both social and cognitive functioning. The children in this 2014 study were tested individually on four executive function tasks, on vocabulary and on several other fronts. Parents were asked to provide information about background television, viewed television, age of first television viewing, and programmes viewed. The programme categories included action cartoons, classic cartoons, live-action children's programmes, fast-paced cartoons, situation comedies for children and educational cartoons.

Children who watched the most television overall had poorer executive function scores than those who watched less television. Children who began watching television earlier had poorer scores than those who began watching later. Infants who had been exposed to rapid pace and 'atypical sequencing' were associated with poorer scores. Educational cartoons were associated with poorer scores. Programmes such as *Dora the Explorer* were not considered quality programmes, and cartoons of all kinds were associated with poorer scores. Only high-quality programming (meaning storytelling without commercials) was associated with better scores.

The researchers concluded by noting that their findings were associations, and the cause of poorer or better scores may have been the result of other factors of family life; they pointed out that parents who allow a greater amount of screen time may also have a lower level of parent–child communication quality.

These findings were supported by another very important study. New Zealand is a pioneer of intensive longitudinal studies of children from birth, and the first of its kind began in Dunedin in 1972.[9] The children of the Dunedin Study (who are now adults) are still flown back from all over the world at regular intervals, and this study has provided a rich source of information that researchers all over the world rely on.

In 2007, lead researchers on the project looked back over data to answer the question *'Does childhood television viewing lead to attention problems in adolescence?'*[10] Data had been collected on the cohort's television-viewing times at the ages five, seven, nine and eleven, and thanks to the depth of information collected on each child this study was (uniquely) able to control for early-childhood attention problems. Attention measures were also collected from parents and teachers at thirteen and fifteen years of age. The researchers found the following.

+ Between the ages of five and eleven, the cohort watched on average two hours of television on weekdays.

+ Between the ages of thirteen and fifteen, they watched on average just over three hours each weekday.

+ The results showed that screen time predicted adolescent attention problems, even when adjusted for gender, early attention problems, early cognitive ability, and childhood socio-economic status.

+ What's more, an increase in attention problems could be seen for every additional hour of screen watching.

The study then asked whether the impact of early screen watching could be reversed by reduced screen watching in adolescence. The result was that early screen watching and adolescent screen watching time are independent predictors of attention problems. In other words, the effects of childhood screen time persisted even when screen time was reduced in adolescence. Screen-time exposure in adolescence was an additional factor.

SCREEN TIME AND PSYCHOLOGICAL WELL-BEING

Since there is a strong link between the type and amount of screen time children are exposed to and socio-economic status, some assumptions about the harmful effects of screen time are being questioned. Some researchers are asking whether apparent negative associations may have more to do with surrounding environmental conditions than time spent on a digital device or watching television.

In 2017, researchers Andrew Przybylski and Netta Weinstein put the AAP's position on a one hour per day screen-time limit for children between the ages of two and five to the test.[11] Their goal was to answer the following questions related to psychological well-being.

+ Do children who follow the 2016 AAP advice of one hour per day demonstrate higher levels of psychological well-being compared with those who watch more?

+ Do children who watch two hours per day demonstrate higher levels of well-being compared with those who watch more?

+ Were there positive benefits from low to moderate viewing?

Data was collected through nearly 20,000 telephone interviews representing approximately 5,000 each of two-, three-, four- and five-year olds. Caregivers were asked questions reflecting attachment, resilience, curiosity, and positive affect (for example, being affectionate and happy) in the preceding month.

What the researchers found was that screen use was higher in non-Caucasian, less affluent and less educated households. Males used screens more than females. Before correcting for those variables, children who limited screen time in accordance with AAP guidelines showed slightly greater resilience and slightly lower positive affect (mood). However, once background factors were taken into account, those differences disappeared. Surprisingly, the study found small gains in mood for children who watched up to seven hours a day (for both television and computer-based media).

The researchers concluded that their findings suggested 'there is little or no support for harmful links between digital screen use and young children's psychological well-being'. However, they went on to note that their results needed to be seen as part of the wider picture, which suggests there may be costs to physical health (in particular, obesity) and executive function (see page 412 for more on executive function). Although screen time may have no impact on the psychological well-being of children under five, they said, it might nevertheless have other undesirable cognitive and physical outcomes.

ADDICTION

Clinicians and academics alike are becoming increasingly concerned about a subgroup of children—sometimes as young as three years old—who are addicted to technology. These children exhibit the same types of behaviours as people with substance addictions, namely a constant urge to use technology, irritability when it is removed, and use of technology to the exclusion of other activities.

There is also a growing concern about structural brain differences found among adolescents who are addicted to technology.[12] It is hard to know whether these brain differences are the cause or effect of screen addiction. But why wouldn't we be cautious and limit modelling and providing excessive screen time for our babies?

TWO BOOKS, TWO VIEWS

There are two very recent parenting books specifically focused on screen use, both written by seasoned journalists who write for major publications.

Be the Parent, Please: Stop banning seesaws and start banning Snapchat by Naomi Schaefer Riley takes the more conservative position of the two.[13] The title gives a bit of a clue to Riley's position: in the book, she offers 'tough mommy tips' to help parents take back control.

Meanwhile, in *The Art of Screen Time: How your family can balance digital media and real life*, Anya Kamenetz takes a more relaxed view about technology.[14] Kamenetz has won many awards for her writing on education and technology, and in this book takes the position that there is no inherent evil in technology, but lost opportunities can result from overuse. Her advice is to make sure your children are getting the exercise, sleep and other stimulation they need, then don't worry about screen use in the leftover time.

Both books claim to be science-based, but the research is limited. The difference between the two has more to do with attitude than science. If you are looking for tips which fit in with your own view, these are two well-regarded books to choose from.

Case study: Briar

Like most mothers, Briar found that some days at home with her baby dragged on and on. Increasingly, she used her phone to distract herself from clock-watching, but she was having second thoughts about her phone use. In fact, she was worried about it.

When she came to see me, she explained that she'd thought following other mothers on Instagram would give her 'inspiration' and cheer her up—but instead she had begun to notice that, rather than feeling better, she felt worse after looking at her phone. Seeing other mothers posting photos of themselves with their hair all shiny, going to the gym with a three-month-old baby in tow, or making homemade baby food for smiling twins in matching, sparkling-clean onesies was getting her down. Even though she knew that what she saw wasn't real life, she couldn't help feeling she wasn't measuring up.

Briar would initially check her phone to read the news and keep up with what was going on in the world, but before long would find herself scrolling through Instagram, watching trivial videos and reading celebrity gossip. To begin with her baby, Camilla, had grizzled whenever Briar was on her phone, but soon she began to simply look away and seemed less responsive. Briar was worried about this; she knew her phone time was a problem, but she found it hard to stop herself.

We talked about 'seemingly innocent choices', and discussed how Briar could identify them. Whenever she caught herself thinking *I need to check my phone because* . . . she questioned the thought, and asked herself whether she really *did* need to. If the answer was an honest yes, she would go ahead and check her phone—but she set a timer on her phone to let her know when she had been on it for longer than ten minutes. Before long, Briar had greatly reduced the amount of time she spent on her phone when Camilla was awake. She also joined a mothers' group which met once a week, and found interacting with 'real' mothers in person achieved what she had thought Instagram would: she felt less bored and much happier.

CAN WE PUT THE GENIE BACK IN THE BOTTLE?

The short answer is probably not. Children are—just like adults—beguiled by technology, and it is a hard ask for parents to determine what safe limits are. It's nigh on impossible to turn back the clock entirely. We might need more governmental control over the ways producers of technology seduce young people into overuse, but it is really up to parents to put on the brakes. Parents who are concerned about their children's technology use might be surprised by how many other parents have exactly the same concerns.

If the idea of taking control appeals to you, it's so much easier if you start from birth. I have seen a number of parents of teenagers struggling with screen addictions, and it is heartbreaking. The way to avoid this is to never lose control of screen use in the first place. When you have a baby, you still have control—and you can keep that control. I would love to say that early exposure to technology can't harm your baby or your child, but the evidence is building in the other direction. It might be an inconvenient truth for all of us as mothers, but I hope the word spreads, as forewarned is forearmed.

CHAPTER 16: THE MAIN POINTS

+ Model the sort of behaviour around technology that you want your children to have as they grow older. Your baby is learning by watching you, so your technology habits matter.

+ Your blank expression (or 'still face') when you stare at your phone screen is extremely upsetting and confusing for your baby. Try not to use your phone where your baby can see you, unless you absolutely must.

+ It doesn't look as though technology and the use of it is benign. The evidence so far points towards early exposure to technology having more negative than positive effects on babies, so bear this in mind.

CHAPTER 17
NANNIES, DAYCARE AND
WORKING MOTHERS

Mothering myth: Mothers who work care less about their children.

Truth: There are many reasons why mothers choose to work, and working mothers love their babies just as much as stay-at-home mothers do.

For mothers, most decisions about returning to work are largely driven by economics and maternity-leave provisions. The reality is that most working mothers do not have a real choice about when or if they return to work. They must weigh up the financial impact and the effect on their career progression against the advantages of staying at home, then make decisions based on that. Only a privileged minority enjoy the luxury of choice.

The US stands out among developed countries for having the least generous statutory maternity-leave provisions imaginable. By law, women are entitled to a meagre two weeks of unpaid leave. Figures from Pew Research Center show that 34 per cent of mothers who do not work are living in poverty; that is compared with 12 per cent of working mothers who live in poverty.[1] Anything beyond the legal leave requirement depends on the generosity of a woman's workplace. Many middle-class occupations provide fully paid leave for up to three months, plus the right to unpaid time off for up to one year. (Pew Research Center defines middle-class income as being between 67 per cent and 200 per cent of the median income.) As a result, the lowest-paid mothers return to the workforce almost immediately, while middle-class mothers stay home for longer. However, even middle-class mothers in the US are typically back at work after three months, when their maternity pay stops, even if their positions would have been held for much longer. Only 5 per cent of middle-class mothers choose not to go back to paid work indefinitely, and their partners have a median income of US$132,000. They are predominantly white or Asian.[2]

Meanwhile, in France, 80 per cent of women who worked before having a baby return to work before the baby's first birthday. To protect the job security of mothers and allow for a woman's recovery post-birth, France provides paid maternity leave of 16 weeks for the first two children, and 26 weeks for subsequent children. A 2013 study demonstrated that the time a mother stayed at home after birth matched the time she was on paid maternity leave.[3]

Another study compared the very different economic incentives between Denmark and Sweden, and found that they too predicted the amount of time before a mother returned to work. Incentives went beyond the obligations of an employer to hold a job, or the actual income received, but also included the cost and availability of childcare.[4]

Research indicates very few long-term negative effects from mothers returning to the workforce and placing their children in alternative care—and, what long-term adverse effects have been found, appear to be the result of children in less-than-optimal care facilities, particularly if they start attending during their first year of life. Those adverse effects are not seen in all children, and some are no longer detected by age seven; in particular, social deficits all but disappear, while a slight cognitive disadvantage seems to persist.

These studies are of great importance to policymakers as well as to mothers. Back in 1986 a young scholar named Jay Belsky tentatively suggested that childcare might result in bad outcomes for children, and there has been considerable controversy around the topic ever since.

THE EMOTIONAL LOAD

When both parents work it seems there is a hidden, unequal burden on mothers. Sociologist Shira Offer has written two papers comparing the load of being a worker and a father to the load of being a worker and a mother.[5] On the face of it, based on data from the US 500 Family Study in which parents kept diaries, there are apparently more similarities than differences in workload. Neither parent spends much time thinking about family while they are at work, and both parents appear to spend about the same time on domestic chores.

However, there are some big differences.

+ Mothers spend ten more hours every week multitasking— usually between housework and childcare. What's more, mothers find multitasking stressful and report feeling rushed.

+ When they are at home, men generally leave their work behind. Women do not. That is partly because mothers are generally the ones to leave work early for school pick-ups, or to stay home with sick children. Mothers are more likely to have to play catch-up at home, while also tending to household management.

> + Offer highlights the hidden emotional load mothers carry. Mothers are expected to run their households smoothly, to be intensely involved with their children, and to contribute financially in order for their family to enjoy middle-class privileges.
>
> Although these things don't make a quantitative difference in terms of workload (as in, the hours are the same), they do make a serious qualitative difference in terms of the level of stress on the mother.

THE IMPACT OF DAYCARE

It is fair to say that, of all the emotionally charged issues surrounding childcare, the question of when a mother should return to work is possibly the most political. At the state level, it is important for women to be in the workforce: Western governments believe that unemployed women reduce productivity and are a drain on public finances. Both in the United States and in Britain, public funds are sunk into daycare facilities to encourage mothers back into work.

At the level of gender politics, many feminists protest the suggestion that women should give up their careers and their financial security so that men can continue to be paid for their work and to progress in their careers. Researchers who come up with findings that suggest children are better off in the first year if their mothers stay at home are at risk of being labelled misogynists if their evidence isn't rock solid.

Back in 1986, North American researcher Jay Belsky was among the first to raise the possibility that more than 20 hours of daycare per week in the first year of life resulted in worse outcomes for children in an article titled 'Infant Daycare: A cause for concern?'[6] In it, Belsky noted, 'There is an emerging pattern in supplementary daycare, especially that initiated in the first year, sometimes associated with the tendency of the infant to avoid or maintain a distance from the mother following a series of brief separations.' Belsky was referring to the recognised method for assessing attachment between a mother and child known as the 'Strange Situation Procedure' (see page 42), and to anyone with a background in psychology it was a profoundly worrying comment. An infant with a secure attachment will show pleasure and seek comfort when her mother returns after a short absence; a child who is insecurely attached, on the other hand, may ignore her mother's return, cling, or refuse to be comforted despite showing distress. A lack of secure attachment is associated with greater anxiety and poorer behavioural outcomes than for children who are securely attached. (For more on attachment theory, see Chapter 2.)

Belsky's article was not received well. No one wanted to hear that early daycare might have adverse effects. Two years later, in 1988, he published a follow-up article titled 'The "Effects" of Infant Daycare Reconsidered' in which he acknowledged that several studies showed evidence that the insecure attachment and heightened aggressive behaviour associated with early childcare dissipates over time.[7] Furthermore, other studies pointed to different learned behaviour between children in daycare and those at home when interacting with their mothers, rather than a failure of secure attachment. However, Belsky continued to question whether these findings applied to all children who experienced daycare.

In a nearly unprecedented step, the prestigious journal which published Belsky's second study decided to devote the entire issue to infant daycare. Greta Fein and Nathan Fox were appointed as guest editors, and contributors questioned every aspect of Belsky's concerns. Some argued that it wasn't the separation from the mother but rather unresponsive caregiving which was the problem. Others argued different outcomes on the Strange Situation Procedure were to be expected, as children in daycare would no longer find the new situation as 'strange'. Yet another article provided evidence that the outcome of the Strange Situation Procedure at twelve months did not reliably predict the outcome at ages three, four and five. Editors Fein and Fox also discussed the work of another researcher, which explained the more aggressive behaviour of daycare children as showing assertiveness, confidence and expectations of control.[8]

In 1999, Belsky took up a university position in London, and in 2001 returned to the United States to deliver a lecture titled 'Developmental Risks (Still) Associated with Early Child Care'. It was something of an 'I told you so' lecture, in the sense that the most recent research at that time tended to support his concerns— which, by the way, have always been modest. Belsky's 1986 research never predicted disaster; he always said the impact was that a small number of children were at an increased risk of insecure attachment with their caregiver, but that this should be considered. He always said there was no difference at all when women worked 20 hours a week or less in the first year. In the 2001 lecture, Belsky focused on the need to look separately at different aspects of early childcare to see where there are or are not effects. For example, does the amount of time at work matter? Does the quality of childcare matter? Does the family background matter?

Despite the critique and discussion surrounding Belsky's research, no serious study fails to reference him. What's more, in the past decade researchers have attempted to do exactly what he has asked: they are considering the various aspects of early childcare separately to sort out what does or does not make a difference.

CHILDCARE IN BABY'S FIRST YEAR

For mothers who want or need to work in the first year of their baby's life, there's a dual outcome. Ordinary full-time daycare in those early months is something of a leveller: it appears to lift the social and cognitive skills of babies from deprived families, but seems to have some minor yet lasting negative cognitive effects on children from more advantaged families.

This dual outcome is consistently reported in research. A 2014 North American study of 10,000 children entering kindergarten at age five concluded 'as non-maternal household income decreased, maternal employment begun prior to nine months was linked with higher cognitive skills [and] lower conduct problems'.[9] Another review of studies concluded that early maternal employment was associated with 'decreases in formal measures of achievement for middle-class and upper middle-class families'.[10]

Before we address some common questions and see what the research says, bear in mind that a number of prominent researchers are at pains to point out the following.

+ Despite being *statistically* significant', any long-term differences in real life are actually very small. Even those researchers who are most concerned by the negative impact of early childcare concede that children are mainly the product of their home environment and their genes.

+ The financial benefits of work continuity could be more positively significant in your child's life than any disadvantage from working in the child's first year.

+ Whether a mother works or doesn't work can affect her mental health, and therefore have an impact on how sensitively she responds to her child's needs. Sensitivity is associated with better long-term outcomes for a child. So, in the context of work, if returning to work avoids a mother feeling resentment and contributes to a better mood, the positive effects of this could balance out any reduction in time spent with her children. For a child, being at home with a mother who is depressed is generally less positive than being in a good-quality daycare. Conversely, if working causes depression, that is an increased negative impact.

+ A number of researchers comment that, while they did not specifically study fathers as caregivers, they suggested that a father could be the equal of a mother as a primary caregiver. After all, we know that babies can be securely attached to their father or same-gender other parent, irrespective of whether they are securely attached to their birth mother. Next best caregiver (while you work) would be a warm and loving relative, such as a grandparent, followed by a sensitive and responsive nanny, followed by a high-quality childcare centre with a high staff-to-child ratio and trained and warm caregivers.

DOES THE QUALITY OF THE CHILDCARE FACILITY MATTER IN THE FIRST YEAR?

There are no studies of babies who have only experienced childcare in the first year. However, studies of children one or two years older show there is a relationship between quality of childcare and cognitive outcomes, so by implication that should also be true in the first year (see pages 431–432).

DOES THE STYLE OF CHILDCARE MAKE A DIFFERENCE?

Overall it is the quality, not the style, which matters. A high-quality childcare centre could be better than an average nanny. Various reviews of work related to first-year childcare express frustration at the lack of research into care style during the first year.[11] However, parents who are in a position to arrange a mother substitute—

someone who not only is sensitive and responsive to their baby's cues, but who will initiate interaction—will be very reassured by a study which showed no difference in infant behaviour or cortisol (stress hormone) levels than when a baby is with its own mother.[12]

ARE NEGATIVE EFFECTS LONG-TERM?

Most studies are not able to fully address this question as, at best, they stop at age five, when children are just starting school; they therefore do not get to assess whether differences are ironed out once children are in school. Teachers (who are 'blind' or unaware which children had early childcare) report that five-year-old children who were in daycare during their first year more often display aggression and do worse in school than those children who started daycare later. However, most studies have focused on disadvantaged children from poor-quality childcare centres.

One large-scale and detailed study in 2010 used data which followed 1,013 children from birth to seven years.[13] Extensive information was gathered at frequent intervals on work hours, cognitive and socio-emotional skills, attachment, home environment, and other matters related to childcare. Unusually, the children in this study were predominantly middle-class—or, in other words, children who were likely to show a disadvantage from early childcare. When socio-emotional behaviour was measured, there was no difference overall between the children whose mothers worked full-time in the first year and those who stayed at home—but, when the children were fully matched for similar family background, there were significant differences. Namely, the children who had attended early childcare were reported by both mothers and teachers as being more difficult and displaying aggressive behaviour. These differences persisted until school entry, but had disappeared by age seven. Therefore, the socio-emotional differences arising from early childcare appear to be the result of learned behaviour, which can be unlearned.

The cognitive outcomes showed a different pattern. Even when matched for family, the differences between the children in early daycare and those at home were very small, and required careful testing to be found at all. However, unlike the socio-emotional differences, these small differences seem to persist even at age seven. It is interesting to note how this small cognitive loss lines up with research in other areas: time spent feeding, birth order and time spent verbalising with an infant before speech even emerges (see pages 488–489) have similar outcomes.

This study showed that middle-class mothers who worked full-time in the first year tend to be professional and highly paid. The researchers were clearly supportive of this decision, pointing out that for these women a failure to work in the first year is likely to have an enduring impact on family income. They consider that the wider picture of overall benefits to a child could be more significant than a barely measurable cognitive loss—benefits such as living in a higher decile zone with better schools. Furthermore, the study found that mothers who worked in jobs they valued in their baby's first year were less likely to be depressed and were seen to be more appropriately responsive to their child when the child was four-and-a-half years old than mothers who started full-time work later.

DOES THE TIME OF STARTING WITHIN THE FIRST YEAR MATTER?

Researchers have attempted to test whether starting work at different points during a baby's first year make a difference, however there is not enough data to reach a conclusion.

DO THE NUMBER OF WORK HOURS MAKE A DIFFERENCE?

Research since 1985 generally agrees that part-time work up to 20 hours a week in a baby's first year has no ill-effect on children.

Although all working mothers spend less time with their baby, the difference is not as large as you might think. They tend to 'sacrifice' household tasks and leisure activities in order to spend more time with their baby. They spend more time with their baby on weekends than stay-at-home mothers do, and the time they spend with their baby is social rather than functional. When a mother works 33 hours a week, there is about 45 minutes' a day difference in direct interaction with her child throughout the week compared with a stay-at-home mother.[14]

It is at about 30 hours a week in the first year that some larger studies start to find small adverse effects.[15] When various studies of the effect of part-time work in the first year are compared, something of a sliding scale emerges. Working between ten and 20 hours a week can actually show benefits; however, by the time to you get to 30 hours, negative impacts are being seen, and they are even more evident when a mother is working full-time. In all likelihood, it boils down to this: the more hours a parent works, the more difficult it is to make up for lost time on weekends or through reducing housework and other activities.

CHILDCARE AFTER BABY'S FIRST YEAR

Mothers who return to work full-time after their baby turns one have less to worry about regarding socio-emotional or long-term cognitive effects. The 2010 study mentioned above showed the small cognitive effects seen in children who started care during their first year were not seen when childcare started in the second, third or fourth years.[16]

Although, as discussed earlier, researchers have not been able to reach strong conclusions about the effect of quality care during the first year due to lack of data, it is possible make inferences from data on older children in daycare. However, after the first year, research has demonstrated that quality of care has a palpable impact on outcomes. For cognitive skills, one 2014 study of a cohort of 8,350 two-year-olds measured quality as 'the extent to which adults provide frequent stimulating and sensitive interactions, children have the opportunity to interact with a variety of age-appropriate objects and activities (e.g. water, sand, dress-up clothes), and the child's health and safety is maintained within that environment'.[17] According to the study's lead researcher, Erik Ruzek, a survey of numerous other studies points to the significant factor being the quality of care rather than the type of care (for example, home-based, centre-based or nanny-based). In Ruzek's study, only 13 per cent of children were considered to be in high-quality settings, and when the children were assessed for cognitive skills at nine months and at two years, the results showed a very strong positive effect from being in high-quality care. This effect was far greater in degree than the negative effect of being in low-quality care. Ruzek pointed out, due to the high cost of high-quality care, the social impact of this difference perpetuates inequalities between rich and poor.

An even more ambitious project came to the same conclusion. In 1991 the US National Institutes of Health (NIH) began the longitudinal Study of Early Child Care and Youth Development (SECCYD) with the express purpose of examining how childcare quantity, quality and type are linked to a child's cognitive and socio-emotional development. The study drew from a cohort of nearly 9,000 children, half of which were born into poverty or near poverty, while the other half extended well into the middle-classes. At four-and-a-half years, the study found the following.[18]

+ Almost all cognitive and social differences between children were attributable to family and genetic factors.

+ A small cognitive gain from childcare was seen for children from low-income families (because even a low-quality facility was an improvement on home environment), while a small loss was seen in other groups. However, children in higher-quality childcare did not suffer that loss.

+ The same pattern as above was seen with socio-emotional behaviour (and attachment). Overall, there was a slight increase in 'externalising' (difficult) behaviour. However, this was not seen with higher-quality care. What's more, within the group in high-quality care, the higher the quality, the more positive the outcome.

The same cohort was assessed again at age fifteen, and differences in socio-emotional traits had all but disappeared.[19] These traits were not evident at all among those who had attended high-quality care, but were seen among those who had received lower-quality care, as exhibited in higher risk-taking. No gender differences were found. Jay Belsky—who first raised the possibility that early childcare could have risks—was one of the authors of this study, and discussed a different pattern of cortisol among youths who attended low-quality care-centres. However, he did not consider—as perhaps he should have—whether that might have been the result of the poverty and related social issues among children in that category.

At age fifteen, the same pattern was present as seen at age four-and-a-half regarding cognitive skills. Those who suffered a loss through low-quality childcare continued to show that loss. However, those non-disadvantaged children who received high-quality care in the early years showed a significant gain. Their childcare was positively associated with higher academic achievement. Once again, the higher the care, the better. Another study in 2014, which considered mainly middle and higher socio-economic status children, measured cognitive skills and found they were higher with better-quality childcare.[20]

What this shows is that, alongside family background and genes, quality of childcare may well be one of the most important factors in your child's life. Given this, it is worth having a look at what the NIH's Child Development Group believes to be the *minimum* standard of a care centre.[21] Note that, sadly, only a quarter of care centres in the United States met that minimum standard, which is as follows.

+ Up to one-and-a-half years of age: One staff member to three children, a maximum of six children (in the same age group) in a setting, formal training of staff.

+ One-and-a-half to two years: One staff member to four children, a maximum of eight children (in the same age group) in a setting, formal training of staff.

+ Two to three years: one staff member to seven children, a maximum of fourteen children (in the same age group) in a setting, formal training of staff.

In New Zealand, daycare centres have a minimum standard for child-teacher ratios.[22] There needs to be at least one teacher to five children for full-day sessions when children are under two years of age. Notice that this does not meet the NIH recommendations for children under two years. For children over two years, and in full-day sessions, the New Zealand standard is a minimum of one teacher to six children. This does meet the NIH recommendations of a one-to-seven ratio for children between two and three years old. However, once there are more than six children over two years old in a daycare centre, the New Zealand minimum ratio changes to one teacher to ten children. So, whether the New Zealand daycare ratio standards meet the NIH standards depends on the age of the children and the size of the centre.

DOES GENDER MATTER?

A much-cited 2004 study by Marc Bornstein tracked 113 children who used regular non-maternal care from birth to four-and-a-half years. He found that the total hours of care did not predict cognitive or social development, but the child-to-caregiver ratio did. This impact was not the same for all children.

+ For cognitive and language scores, children from the higher socio-economic status families benefitted most from a lower child-to-teacher ratio.

+ For socio-emotional scores, there was a difference between boys and girls. Boys needed a lower child-to-teacher ratio. Girls, on the other hand, seemed to thrive socially when there was a higher child-to-teacher ratio.[23]

These gender results appear quite robust, but some caution should be taken when considering the general conclusion. First, the sample size is small, and second, the control group is 'all American children'. As most American children are in childcare, there is not much room for contrast between this study group and the general population.

QUESTIONS TO ASK WHEN CHOOSING CHILDCARE
The NIH's Child Development Group has a booklet that includes a form which parents can use when choosing a childcare facility.[24] This form addresses interactions between the caregiver and your child, and parents are to ask themselves the following questions.

+ Is the caregiver generally happy and encouraging in manner?

+ Does the caregiver smile at your child?

+ Does the caregiver hug or comfort your child?

+ Does the caregiver repeat your child's words, comment on what your child says, and answer your child's questions?

A further six questions are provided, which focus on discovering the cognitive and social learning that will take place in the centre.

CHILDCARE AND CORTISOL

There has been a great deal made of the fact that children in childcare have higher cortisol levels than children who stay at home. (For more information on cortisol, see pages 228–232.) It has been found that delinquent children have a different pattern of cortisol levels throughout a 24-hour period when compared to non-delinquent children. The link was then made between cortisol levels and delinquency, or any social or emotional deficit.

Cortisol is a response to stress. As a consequence, almost no study of children seems complete without an obligatory cortisol test—and occasionally that leads to some unexpected findings. For example, those who most avidly watch for cortisol changes when a mother disappears around the corner also tend to be those who most avidly promote breastfeeding. However, in 2009, a group of researchers found that breastfeeding actually resulted in a 40 per cent *rise* in cortisol levels, but the same was not true for bottle-fed babies.[25] Interestingly, the researchers concluded that breastfeeding might therefore result in more resilient babies!

Quite a few researchers are taking that view seriously. A University of Chicago study in 2008 found there was an 'inverted-

U-shaped relationship' between cortisol and learning in baby ground squirrels.[26] The squirrels were observed learning signals and learning how to exit a complex maze, and their cortisol levels were manipulated through food. If the level was too high or too low, learning was impeded. However, if it was raised a bit, learning was enhanced. The same has been observed in both rats and monkeys, and has been referred to as 'the Goldilocks zone'—not too much cortisol, and not too little.

In a randomised study of baby monkeys, some were stressed by being separated from their mothers for one hour, and this was repeated weekly; the baby monkeys could see but not make physical contact with other monkeys, and the separation evoked increased levels of cortisol.[27] At nine months of age, the monkeys and their mothers were put in a new environment. At first, all of the monkeys exhibited anxiety; however, the monkeys who had been exposed to separation earlier were the first to become less anxious. This was shown by decreased clinging to their mothers and increased exploration. At one-and-a-half years, the monkeys were given a task that required them to self-regulate their behaviour and use their executive function (high-level problem-solving) in order to obtain food. All of the previously stressed monkeys (the ones who had been separated) completed all their tasks, compared with only half of the monkeys who had not been stressed earlier.

Pointing to these and other animal studies, childcare researcher Megan Gunnar recommends exercising caution when it comes to interpreting cortisol measurements in human children in daycare.[28] In one study, Gunnar found that, contrary to expectations, it was not the shy or fearful child showing heightened cortisol when starting a new school, but the more extroverted and better socialised children.[29]

Case study: Leila

Leila came to see me when her baby, Fred, was six months old. She was facing a dilemma that was causing her to lose sleep and to ruminate: she was enjoying being a stay-at-home mother, but she also loved her career in film—and she had recently been approached to work on a documentary part-time for six months. The documentary had themes that interested Leila, and the job would be a step up the ladder in her career. She was worried about agreeing to the contract, but she was also distressed at the thought of missing out.

Leila liked to be organised, and had a pattern with Fred's naps and feeding that she didn't want to disrupt with childcare. What's more, she worried that her relationship with Fred might be interrupted by someone else looking after him.

First, we discussed her relationship with Fred. It was secure, and didn't need to be compromised so long as Leila planned carefully. Her first task was to find childcare she was happy with, and luckily she managed to find a facility within her budget that also had a very small child-to-teacher ratio.

Next, Leila and I explored her values. Although she loved to have the house organised, there were some things that she could let go of—for example, folding the laundry and home-cooking every night—in favour of nurturing her values. (For more information on exploring your values, see pages 190–193.)

We also looked at catastrophising thoughts that were distressing Leila, such as *I am being selfish if I work*, and balanced them so that she could see that wanting a career was not selfish; in fact, it was part of her self-care, and therefore in the long run was good for Fred as well as for her.

> We then explored and practised mindfulness, so that when Leila was with Fred after work she could focus fully on him, and leave thoughts about work for later. This meant that she could be even more sensitive and responsive to his needs than she already was. (For more information on mindfulness, see pages 89–91.)
>
> Finally, Leila and I role-played her asking her partner to take over more of the household chores.
>
> In the end, Leila took the job, loved it and remains a caring and happy mother.

IT'S A BALANCING ACT

Belsky has spent his professional life arguing in favour of improved childcare facilities. His research is convincing, and shows that whether or not a mother going to work has a negative impact on a child is largely dependent on the quality of childcare. Quality is quite separate from type—there are good and bad childcare centres, just like there are good and bad nannies. As Belsky notes a 'child needs stable, enduring and sensitive relationships' with caregivers, whether they are at home with a nanny or in a group setting. According to Belsky, parents need not worry about a mother working if her child is receiving high-quality care, but his concern was that in the US high-quality non-parental care is the exception rather than the rule.[29]

Coming in second to the quality of care is the number of hours a mother works in a week multiplied by the number of preschool years she works—in other words, the cumulative amount of time a child might have experienced less-than-optimal care over their first five years. For example, if a child is in an average, fairly low-quality childcare centre in the US for the first year of his life then has little exposure to childcare afterwards, there are no lasting negative consequences. However, if that same child stays in that same low-quality childcare centre until he goes to school, there will be lasting negative consequences. Studies indicate that children will be fine even with average care if mothers work around 20 hours a week.

So, it is something of a balancing act. The better the quality of childcare, the more hours a parent can work without worrying. The problem, of course, is that as quality increases so does the price; meanwhile, the women who must work full-time because their family depends on their income are also the women who can least afford good-quality care. Then, even if you can afford high-quality care, you might not be able to find it.

There is really no simple answer that a modern woman wants to hear, and I am not here to lie to you. If you must work full-time to avoid the trap of poverty, that is your top priority. Being poor trumps attending poor-quality childcare for negative outcomes. However, if you are lucky enough to have options and you can't find quality care, perhaps consider reducing your working hours or working from home part of the time. If only the whole world could be Norway, where preschool caregivers have three years of training and the level of interaction and stimulation is remarkable. Fees are paid according to family income. How great would that be for women (and their children) everywhere?

CHAPTER 15: THE MAIN POINTS

+ Research generally agrees that a mother working part-time up to 20 hours a week in her baby's first year has no ill-effect. At about 30 hours of work per week, some studies start to find small adverse effects.

+ Your mental health and well-being matter. It is no good to your or your baby if you stay at home all of the time but resent it; being at home with a mother who is depressed is generally less positive than being in good-quality daycare.

+ The quality of the childcare your baby receives is more important than the type of care.

+ Unfortunately, as quality of childcare increases, so too does the price. Mothers don't always have the choice about whether or not they go back to work, and they don't always have the luxury of being able to afford the childcare they would ultimately like—or of being able to stay at home if that's what they'd prefer.

+ The good news is that even those researchers who are most concerned about any negative impacts of early childcare concede that a child is mainly the product of their home environment and their genes.

APPENDICES

APPENDIX I

DIARRHEAL DISEASES AND BREASTFEEDING

In developed countries, it is extremely rare for a baby to die from diarrheal diseases. There are only two adequate longitudinal studies that consider the relationship between breastfeeding and diarrheal diseases in developed countries, and both were undertaken in direct response to all the methodologically weak studies showing conflicting results.

One of these studies came from Kramer's PROBIT project in Belarus. This large-scale longitudinal study was the most intensive in terms of variables considered and children being followed by paediatricians. It involved 17,000 mother–infant pairs where the babies were full-term and of normal birth weight, and found that babies who were breastfed for more than six months had a significantly reduced chance of having one or more episodes of gastrointestinal tract infection compared to babies who were breastfed for three months or less. The longer breastfeeding group had a 9 per cent rate of gastro infection in the first year, while the shorter breastfeeding group had a 13 per cent incidence of gastro infection in the first year. That difference held true whether the study was viewed as a random study or as an observational study.[1]

However, there was little difference between the groups for more serious infections where hospitalisation was required. The longer breastfed babies had a 3.2 per cent rate of hospitalisation, while the shorter breastfed babies had a 3.6 per cent rate of hospitalisation. In this study, some of the longer-feeding mothers breastfed well beyond six months, but the benefit of breastfeeding in relation to gastro illness was only seen between the ages of three and six months.

There are limitations with the PROBIT study in that it sheds little light on the first three months, and it fails to tell us whether it is the breast milk which is protective or formula which is causing harm. Fortunately, there's another study to fill in the gaps: Howie's Scottish longitudinal study of 672 mother–infant pairs.[2] This study found that both the exclusively breastfed babies and the partially breastfed babies had less diarrheal illness. This points to breast milk's IgA antibody being protective rather than formula being harmful. (The IgA antibody protects the mucosal lining of the gut from pathogens; see page 316.) Babies who were exclusively formula-fed from birth had higher rates of diarrheal illnesses compared with those who were either exclusively or mixed breastfed.

So, if we put the results of those studies together, the evidence shows that a mother's IgA offers a baby some limited protection up to six months of age, whether the IgA is provided through exclusive breastfeeding or mixed feeding. However, the IgA appears too weak to fend off anything more serious than a low-level tummy bug; the equal rates of hospitalisation between formula-fed babies and breastfed babies suggest that a mother's breast milk offers little or no protection against more serious diarrheal disease such as rotavirus. The most common and serious diarrheal disease for children, rotavirus accounts for 72 per cent of gastro illnesses in babies.

There are only two studies that consider the relationship between rotavirus and breastfeeding in developed countries, and neither show a benefit from breastfeeding. In the first, researcher R. J. Weinberg matched 50 infants under one year of age who had rotavirus with controls for breastfeeding. The study found no difference in terms of average age of infection, duration of diarrhoea, number of bowel movements in 24 hours, or fever and irritability. According to Weinberg, the results of the study 'suggest that breastfeeding offers little protection against rotavirus gastroenteritis'.[3]

The second study followed 100 families in Winnipeg, Canada and confirmed that rotavirus was by far the most common gastro illness in children, occurring in 72 per cent of all cases associated with gastrointestinal problems. This study also checked the blood serum of children for the presence of antibodies, and found that a mother's antibodies offered no protection. The study concluded, 'Neither breastfeeding nor the presence of antibody to rotavirus in cord blood appeared to be effective.'[4]

DOES BREASTFEEDING HELP?

There is no doubt that exclusive breastfeeding in underdeveloped countries is a life-saver. However, in developed countries the benefits of breastfeeding appear to be limited to protection against less acute diarrheal illnesses. It offers no protection against more serious diarrheal illnesses (such as rotavirus) which result in hospitalisation.

APPENDIX II
RESPIRATORY ILLNESSES
AND BREASTFEEDING

Lower respiratory illnesses include bronchitis and pneumonia. Upper respiratory illnesses include tonsillitis, colds and middle ear infections (otitis media).

The confounding variables for respiratory illnesses are far more extensive than for intestinal illnesses, and all of the following (and more) must be taken into account.

+ What a child breathes in, including exposure to second-hand cigarette smoke

+ The number of other children or adults a child comes into contact with, for example at childcare

+ The child being in any situation where someone nearby coughs or sneezes

+ Dampness in the home

+ Lack of home heating.

The most important of these confounding variables is exposure to parental smoking, so at the very least researchers would need to control for that in a sound experiment—yet, it is glaringly absent in most studies.

In 1986, a group of researchers reviewed 20 studies, and found that four showed breastfeeding was not protective against respiratory infections, while two showed that it was.[1] When the studies claiming a benefit to breastfeeding were adjusted for maternal smoking, however, the effect disappeared. The researchers concluded that studies which met important methodological standards and controlled for confounding variables 'suggest that breastfeeding has at most a minimal protective effect in industrialised countries'.

Importantly, to clarify what is meant by 'exposure to smoking', a more recent study in 2012 indicates it is exposure to smoke *after* birth which matters for respiratory illnesses—not exposure before birth.[2] It is not just the mother's smoke, either, but also the father's or anyone else in the home who smokes. (Of course, there are nonetheless many very good reasons not to smoke during pregnancy.)

Since that 1986 review, it has become common for researchers to believe they have made an adjustment for smoking as a confounding variable when, in actual fact, they have not done so at all. When investigated, most of those studies in the 1986 review only had information about smoking during pregnancy. For example, an Australian birth cohort study that has been much cited for showing a strong relationship between breastfeeding and respiratory illnesses makes this very mistake—it includes information about smoking during pregnancy, but none at all about parental smoking after birth.[3]

In 2017, one study claimed that breastfeeding duration for six months or longer was significantly associated with lower and upper respiratory tract infections.[4] However, what the results also showed were exactly the same outcomes for breastfeeding less than three months, and for three to six months. The associations found were all weak, with each outcome range including a possible value of no association at all. Furthermore, any information about exposure to parental smoking after birth was completely missing.

While smoking during pregnancy may be a good predictor of smoking after pregnancy, it includes only a small portion of mothers who will take up smoking again after pregnancy. Not only do most mothers stop smoking during pregnancy for the protection of the foetus, but others stop smoking during pregnancy as they find the taste and smell unpleasant during that time.[5]

Studies have been so consistent about the impact of passive smoking on the respiratory health of babies that even back in 1999 a couple of English researchers suggested the time had come to stop doing studies to prove it, and instead to look at ways changes to exposure could improve outcomes.[6] In 2003, an Australian study did just that: it followed a cohort of 4,486 infants in Tasmania from birth to twelve months, and looked at the difference if parents made a real effort to smoke in a different room from their infant.[7] The study found the risk of hospitalisation was 56 per cent greater if parents smoked in the same room as their infant than if they consistently smoked in a different room. This suggests the outcome could be even more improved if parents smoked outside the home.

On the website for UNICEF UK's Baby-friendly Initiative (unicef. org.uk), the breastfeeding promotion group has posted a review of research ongoing called 'Respiratory Illness' that claims to provide 'robust evidence for the increased incidence of respiratory infections amongst . . . babies who are not breastfed'.[8] Among the studies cited is the 2017 Australian study mentioned above, which did not control for exposure to parental smoking. The review cites one 2003 meta-analysis, but when I looked more closely at that review of studies, I found that nearly all 33 of the studies selected for inclusion had already found a relationship between breastfeeding and reduced respiratory illness.[9] In other words, the meta-analysis was biased towards studies which already supported the researchers' position.

The Baby-friendly UK review cited a third study which claimed to be adjusted for confounding variables, but only used a home address instead of socio-economic information. Again, exposure to parental smoking was not a factor considered.

Interestingly, Baby-friendly ignored the findings of Kramer's massive PROBIT study, which had among its aims introducing the Baby-friendly Initiative to maternity services in randomly selected clinics in Belarus. Kramer's study found no association between breastfeeding and any respiratory disease (including ear infections) at any time, including the months one group was breastfeeding and the other was not.[10] What his study did find, however, was a strong association between exposure to smoking and respiratory illness.

As well, Howie's Scottish longitudinal study (discussed on pages 314–315) found no association between any level of breastfeeding and respiratory illness, including ear infections.

DOES BREASTFEEDING HELP?

Longitudinal studies show no benefit for respiratory illnesses from breastfeeding. The 1986 review of 20 studies showed there were no benefits from breastfeeding once all studies were adjusted for smoking; those studies which *do* show a relationship between breastfeeding and respiratory illnesses have not been adjusted for exposure to smoking. As smoking has been proven to have such a powerful impact both in the frequency and severity of respiratory illnesses, it places studies which have not taken exposure to parental smoking into account on the back foot. Studies show little or no protection for respiratory illnesses from breastfeeding once exposure to passive smoke is taken into account.

APPENDIX III
URINARY TRACT DISEASES
AND BREASTFEEDING

The urinary tract includes the kidneys and the bladder. It also includes the tubes which connect the bladder to the kidneys (ureters) and the tube which empties the bladder (urethra). This system prevents the build-up of wastes and surplus fluid in the body. Urinary tract infection (UTI) is a relatively common illness, which can almost always be treated with antibiotics prescribed by a doctor. More serious cases of UTI usually show themselves from birth, and are often related to structural abnormalities or a type of reflux that draws the urine back up the urethra. The first may require surgery, and the latter ongoing antibiotics until the issue is resolved.

UTI is pretty much an equal-opportunity illness. Aside from family history, there appears to be no difference in incidence related to income, education, position in a family, number of children in a family, age of mother, and so on.[1] In their first year, uncircumcised male babies have a 4 per cent chance of having a UTI compared with a 0.2 per cent chance for circumcised male babies. That means uncircumcised male babies are 20 times more likely to get a UTI than a circumcised male baby. A boy's risk is highest in the first few months of life. After that, females have twice the chance of contracting a UTI; this is thought to be because of a girl's shorter urethra.[2]

Shortly after birth, protective bacteria from a baby's own intestine colonise the urethral area. This combats any disease-causing bacteria that is in the baby's nappy and comes in to contact with the urethral area. 'Good' bacteria and forceful urination work together to keep 'bad' bacteria from entering the urethra. However, sometimes pathogenic bacteria and *Escherichia coli* (E. coli) get in anyway. A common reason for this is the use of broad-spectrum antibiotics that destroy the protective bacteria.[3]

However, it is not only broad-spectrum antibiotics given to a baby which could have this effect. If you are breastfeeding *and* using broad-spectrum antibiotics yourself (for example, to treat mastitis), some of the antibiotic will pass to your baby through your breast milk. If you do need antibiotics, you should talk to your doctor about avoiding broad-spectrum antibiotics either during pregnancy or lactation; more specific antibiotics might be better.

The main symptom of a UTI to look out for is a high fever. Next, about 20 per cent of confirmed cases of UTI are also associated with 'malodorous' (smelly) urine. However, 30 per cent of babies with malodorous urine did not have a UTI. A baby may also be irritable, have feeding problems, have diarrhoea or vomit. Another possible symptom is weak urination.[4] The presence of a UTI needs to be confirmed with laboratory tests, as up to 80 per cent of suspected cases will turn out not to be a UTI after all.

Despite UTIs being common, and despite recurring assertions that breastfeeding is protective against UTIs, actual research is almost entirely lacking. Immunologist Lars Hanson is something of a lone voice in this regard.[5] In a 2004 commentary, Hanson pointed out that lactoferrin in breast milk ends up in the urine of breastfed babies. Lactoferrin is antimicrobial, and Hanson concluded that breastfeeding should reduce the incidence of UTIs.

However, Hanson's commentary and one other piece of research are the only two studies cited in articles that claim breastfeeding is protective against UTI. In 2004, Swedish researchers looked at 200 cases of children aged between birth and six years of age.[6] Girls who had a UTI had been exclusively breastfed for an average of sixteen weeks, while their matched controls had been breastfed exclusively for eighteen weeks. Boys with a UTI had been exclusively breastfed for on average eleven weeks, while their matched controls had been exclusively breast fed for twelve weeks. Based on two extra weeks of breastfeeding for girls but only one extra week of breastfeeding for boys, the study concluded that breastfeeding was protective for boys but not for girls.

There's one more study that doesn't get cited, which showed no evidence that breastfeeding protects against UTI. This study was carried out in the US in 2009, and looked at 64 cases of infants from zero to three months at a clinic in New Orleans.[7] The 64 cases were taken from a larger sample of suspected cases of UTI, but the 64 were the ones with cultures confirming the illness. (As an interesting aside, only 20 per cent of those children investigated for a UTI actually had the illness.) The study compared three groups: exclusively breastfed, mixed breastfed, and exclusively formula-fed babies. This study found no evidence that breastfeeding protects against UTIs.

DOES BREASTFEEDING HELP?

All that can be said is that for the one study showing a benefit there was little difference in the amount of breastfeeding received between children with UTIs and the general population. It probably isn't through oversight that researchers have ignored investigating a link between breastfeeding and UTIs. Since a case of UTI must be established through laboratory cultures, and because of complex confounding variables (such as structural and functional abnormalities, family history, circumcision, gender differences, exposure to broad-spectrum antibiotics), researchers may recognise it's somewhat of a futile exercise.

APPENDIX IV
TYPE 1 DIABETES AND BREASTFEEDING

Type 1 diabetes is an autoimmune disease which can appear in childhood, so it merits a close look. We need insulin to break down sugar, and if sugar isn't broken down the results can be fatal. Our bodies produce insulin in the pancreas and, in particular, in the beta cells in the pancreas. In some people, the immune system makes a mistake; it confuses the beta cells with dangerous invaders and destroys them. When your own immune defences hurt you in this way, it is called an autoimmune disease.

Susceptibility to type 1 diabetes is genetic, and a number of the genes have been located on human chromosomes. However, 'susceptibility' means an environmental factor may also be needed to trigger the disease. For instance, evidence that genetic factors alone may not be enough lies in the fact that an identical twin has less than a 50 per cent chance of having type 1 diabetes if the other twin has it. The disease often arises before the age of five, and this has led some to consider early childhood exposure to illness or a feeding practice as possible triggers.[1]

Rates of type 1 diabetes vary according to geography. China has the lowest rate. New Zealand, on the other hand, is in the highest category with over 20 cases per 100,000.[2] (It is interesting to note that China has the lowest rate of type 1 diabetes *and* one of the lowest breastfeeding rates in the world at 20 per cent.[3] By comparison, New Zealand's rate of exclusive or full breastfeeding at three months, according to Plunket figures, is 59 per cent.[4]) In the US and in other countries, the incidence of type 1 diabetes is rising, and it does not seem that lifestyle plays a great role in that. Some epidemiological research shows the increase is most likely the result of improved treatment and survival rates. In former generations, many people with type 1 diabetes would not have survived long enough to have children, but they have done so for a number of generations now, and their susceptibility is spreading out to an increasing number of offspring.[5]

Symptoms of type 1 diabetes tend to come on very quickly, and the most striking are being thirsty, drinking a lot and urinating a lot. Following that is being hungry, tired, having blurry vision, or cuts and sores that don't heal quickly. The failure to break down sugars also often gives rise to ketones, which have a distinctive smell on the breath.

DOES BREASTFEEDING HELP?

The American Diabetes Association was concerned about conflicting results associating breastfeeding and diabetes. For example, a meta-analysis of studies published in 1994 concluded breastfeeding for a short period reduced the risk of type 1 diabetes by 40 per cent. Another meta-analysis on nearly the exact same studies was published two years later which concluded there was a weak reduction in diabetes risk after breastfeeding—and suggested that even the remaining small advantage could be the result of methodological defects.

Consequently, funding was gained by the American Diabetes Association from independent sources, including the National Institutes of Health and China's Department of Health, and a grant from the German Research Foundation, to carry out a major investigation of all previous studies.[6] No less than 34 high-level researchers collaborated on this study, which unpicked research carried out in any language that had considered an association between breastfeeding and type 1 diabetes. Between them, the team of researchers identified 43 studies with all the information necessary for analysis—most crucially, maternal type 1 diabetes. Combined, those studies provided individual information on 9,874 patients with type 1 diabetes. When analysed, the overall conclusion was as follows:

> The pooled analysis suggests weak protective associations between exclusive breastfeeding and type 1 diabetes risk. However, these findings are difficult to interpret because of the marked variation in effect and possible biases (particularly recall biases) inherent in the included studies.

The only sibling-pair study (of 2,734 sibling pairs) considering an association between diabetes and breastfeeding found no association between breastfeeding and diabetes.[7] Thus, the strongest studies do not support an association between breastfeeding and type 1 diabetes.

APPENDIX V
ATOPIC CONDITIONS (ASTHMA, ECZEMA AND HAY FEVER) AND BREASTFEEDING

Although atopy includes conditions with very different symptoms—asthma, eczema and hay fever—the mechanism for all of them is similar. The body sees harmless intruding particles as dangerous, and as part of the body's attack strategy many IgE antibodies are produced, along with other mechanisms intended to destroy or remove the unwanted antigen (sneezing, coughing and so on). Even when everything is calm, a large amount of IgE remaining in the blood can indicate a tendency for an atopic illness. Curiously, some people can have high levels of IgE antibodies without having any symptoms.

Asthma is very hard to diagnose before five or six years of age, as many of the symptoms, such as wheezing, are also commonly associated with viral infections. However, a precursor, such as eczema or hay fever, may point in that direction earlier. Eczema itself usually clears up by adolescence.

As is so often the case in this type of research, two studies considering infant feeding and eczema gave different results. In one, a vegetable-based alternative to milk (hydrolysed whey) showed a reduced incidence of eczema compared with a cow's milk-based formula. In contrast, another study compared soy milk with cow's milk, human milk and hydrolysed whey and found no difference in outcome between any of them.[1]

Atopy is strongly genetic, and the main risk factor is having a close family member with any kind of atopic illness. Higher socio-economic status is also a strongly relevant risk factor.[2] Some have speculated about a link between hyper-cleanliness and atopy, but that has not been proven. That theory proposes that fighting off infections early in life has a beneficial effect. One meta-analysis indicated exposure to passive smoking does not cause atopic diseases, while another study showed smoking can increase the severity of asthma.[3]

The prevalence of atopy is high in children. Hay fever is the most common, with 32 per cent of fourteen-year olds experiencing it in Denmark in 2016. In adolescence, 12 per cent suffer from asthma and 8 per cent eczema.[4]

In 1988, Kramer (of the cluster-randomised PROBIT study) wrote a special article for the *Journal of Pediatrics* about studies connecting breastfeeding with atopic diseases.[5] He said it had been 50 years since two researchers reported that breastfeeding protects against 'infantile eczema', and studies since then had gone no further than that original study. Various studies showed a strong effect, no effect at all, or even negative effect. Kramer chided researchers for producing work of such low quality that results differed wildly from one study to the next. In order to prevent a further 50 years passing without any progress, Kramer provided a list of twelve standards to keep when carrying out research into breastfeeding and atopic diseases. The list included strict diagnosis, blind ascertainment of the disorder, amount of time of exclusive breastfeeding, separate analysis for at-risk children, and control for confounding factors. (Confounding factors included the infant's age, racial-ethnic origin, socio-economic factors, family history of atopic disease and family smoking.) Kramer then went on to rubbish the 22 existing studies, regardless of their results.

ASTHMA: DOES BREASTFEEDING HELP?

The short answer is no. The research shows that breastfeeding does not protect against asthma. Let's take a closer look at the research.

Determined to follow Kramer's twelve standards, in 2001 Israeli researcher Michael Gdalevich and colleagues located 2,041 studies, letters and reviews related to breastfeeding and asthma; of these, 41 studies were assessed as fulfilling Kramer's criteria.[6] In the end, twelve studies including a total of 8,183 subjects were selected, and these were all from developed countries. The results were that breastfeeding had no protective effect for children without close relatives with atopic diseases. However, there appeared to be a protective effect for those children who were at risk because of family history of asthma.

In 2011, a group of researchers responded to Gdalevich's meta-analysis.[7] They commented that two-thirds of the studies Gdalevich relied on for an association with asthma included children between the ages two and five, and pointed out that this was an age at which virus-associated wheeze predominates and it is not possible to diagnose asthma. In the ten years since Gdalevich had published his studies on atopic disease and breastfeeding, large prospective studies had become available to consider—so, using Kramer's criteria, this group of researchers carried out a meta-analysis from 31 international studies, which included 417,880 participants between the ages of five and eighteen. Overall, this study found no association between breastfeeding and asthma, with the researchers concluding, 'we believe that prevention of asthma in childhood should not be used as a reason to encourage mothers to breastfeed.'

The Copenhagen Prospective Study on Asthma in Childhood (COPSAC) is a longitudinal project following a cohort of children born to mothers with asthma.[8] In one 2015 study, 335 children from that cohort were followed from birth to twelve months to collect information about breastfeeding. These children were individually followed up at six months, one-and-a-half years, four years and seven years. Thus, when last tested, these children were old enough for an asthma diagnosis. There were no cut-off points for breastfeeding; instead, the researchers used statistics which could test for differences attributable to all different durations of breastfeeding (from zero to any amount). This study showed no difference in outcome for any duration of breastfeeding in relation to eczema, wheeze, asthma or allergic rhinitis at seven years of age.[9]

So, everyone has been trying to abide by Kramer's twelve standards since 1988, but what did his study show about the relationship between the duration of breastfeeding and asthma? Kramer's 2007 results on the effects of longer duration breastfeeding were based on 13,889 children who had been followed by doctors since birth. In 2007 and 2017, Kramer published results of findings from those children when they had turned six, and ten years later when they turned sixteen.[10] Whether considered as a random study or as an observational study, there was no protective effect for asthma from longer breastfeeding.

In 2005, US researchers Eirik Evenhouse and Siobhan Reilly considered 2,734 sibling pairs where one had been breastfed and the other had not, and found no association between breastfeeding and asthma.[11] In Hong Kong, a 2016 study considered 8,327 children from three months to twelve years of age.[12] The children were divided into four groups: those who were never breastfed, those who were partially breastfed, those who were breastfed for less than three months, and those who were breastfed for more than three months. Adjustments were made for, according to the researchers, 'parental characteristics and socioeconomic position'. This study found no association between any type of feeding and asthma although the raw scores tended to show a very slight increased risk from breastfeeding.

ECZEMA: DOES BREASTFEEDING HELP?

The short answer is that, when adjusted for family history of atopic disease, breastfeeding is shown to offer no protection against eczema.

In 1990, Scottish researcher Peter Howie, following Kramer's guidelines, found no association between breastfeeding and eczema based on 672 mother–infant pairs.[13] In 2001, Gdalevich followed the same process noted above in order to select studies for a meta-analysis; in this case, eighteen studies were accepted and there were 4,158 participants. However, in a study where family history of atopic disease was critical, only half the subjects had information about family history. As a result this study was less than ideal, and showed that breastfeeding was mildly protective for those at risk but appeared to increase the chance of having eczema among children who were not at risk.[14]

Once again, the 2015 COPSAC contradicted Gdalevich's results.[15] Their population of children at high risk as the result of having a mother with atopic disease showed that there was no relation between any duration of breastfeeding and eczema at seven years of age. Kramer's study similarly found no reduction in eczema from longer breastfeeding when 13,889 children turned six and a half. At age thirteen, when his study is considered as a random study, breastfeeding shows significant protection against eczema. However, when considered as an observational study (readjusted for family history of atopic disease) there is no protective value from any duration of breastfeeding.[16]

HAY FEVER: DOES BREASTFEEDING HELP?

When children are old enough for asthma to be diagnosed, breastfeeding does not show any protective effect either for children generally or for those children at risk because of family history of atopic disease. There is general agreement that breastfeeding makes no difference for hay fever either.

Gdalevich and his team recovered relevant papers and studies from a database covering the years 1966 to 2000. Combing through 2,346 studies, letters and reviews, they first located 36 promising studies; after careful review, only six were found which matched Kramer's criteria. The six studies included 3,303 subjects. In contrast to what they imply in the abstract, the authors noted in the discussion section of their article that:

> A non-significant association was found between exclusive breastfeeding and prevention of childhood AR [allergic rhinitis or hay fever]. The analysis did not show a significant protective effect in the subgroup of children with a positive family history of atopy, as previously suggested.[17]

This time, Gdalevich's study corresponded with the COPSAC, which showed no protection from breastfeeding for seven-year-olds at risk of hay fever due to a family history of atopic disease.[18]

Dr Kramer's study of 13,889 children showed longer breastfeeding was associated with an increase in allergic response to pinprick tests at six-and-a-half years.[19]

Finally, Evenhouse and Reilly's sibling pair study found no association between breastfeeding and allergies.[20]

APPENDIX VI
INFLAMMATORY BOWEL
DISEASE (IBD) AND
BREASTFEEDING

Irritable bowel syndrome (IBS) is the umbrella term for all types of bowel complaints, including temporary ones. In contrast, inflammatory bowel disease (IBD) is limited to two main diseases: ulcerative colitis, and Crohn's disease. Both are chronic recurring conditions, which involve inflammation of the gastrointestinal tract and usually make their first appearance in late childhood or early adulthood. With Crohn's disease (and possibly with ulcerative colitis), the condition is caused by the immune system mistakenly attacking healthy bacteria in the intestine. The chronic inflammation which follows is what triggers symptoms.

Ulcerative colitis can be more extensive, affecting the entire colon, but it affects the surface layers of bowel linings. Crohn's disease, on the other hand, occurs in patches, but affects deeper layers. Especially in the early stages, it is hard to diagnose which condition is occuring. To confuse things even further, there is a list of bacterial diseases which mimic the symptoms of IBD, which means a clear diagnosis could take a few years.

IBD diseases can be debilitating. During episodes, IBD can cause symptoms such as nausea, vomiting, diarrhoea, considerable pain, discomfort and bloating. (One particularly cruel aspect of IBD is that, until recently, it was believed that women who complained of these symptoms had psychological disorders.)

The rate for Crohn's disease, in particular, is rising steadily in countries like India, the Philippines, the United States, Europe and in Australasia. Studies of immigrants from less-developed countries to more developed countries show the original immigrants retain their lower rate of IBDs, but their children share the same incidence of the host country.[1] Thus, picking up 'Western habits' is thought to be a risk factor. Once a person has IBD, it follows much the same disease pattern, no matter what country they are from originally.

At present, in developed countries such as England, the proportion of the population affected is about five people in 1,000. Almost everywhere, ulcerative colitis is about twice as common as Crohn's disease.

Since IBD has in the past been associated with wealthy countries, for a while it was thought to be linked with high socio-economic status. It was thought that children from high-income families were kept too sanitised, leaving them vulnerable to later infections. However, in 1987, a large cooperative study of 500 patients from nine countries found that families with IBD were in fact less well educated with lower incomes—a finding that has been confirmed repeatedly in studies.[2]

On the other hand, there is no doubt that genetics play a big role in IBD, and particularly with Crohn's disease. About one in ten people with IBD have at least one close relative with either ulcerative colitis or Crohn's disease. A further group will have cousins with IBD, and further out again IBD patients will belong to higher-risk ethnicities. Markers have been found for Crohn's disease on chromosomes for some years, and only recently have they been found for ulcerative colitis as well. People of Ashkenazi Jewish decent have a clear genetic predisposition for both Crohn's disease and ulcerative colitis. While the overall rate of IBD in England is five out of 1,000, for Ashkenazi the rate is 20 out of 1,000—four times the average rate.

Germany has a national IBD twin registry, and as a result, an extremely rare and valuable study was made possible.[3] In 2012, Spehlmann and colleagues selected monozygotic twins (who have identical genetic material) from the registry and questioned them as adults about environmental factors which could have triggered IBD for them. The first thing the study was able to determine was the specific genetic component for IBD. For Crohn's disease, in 35 per cent of cases where one twin had IBD the other twin did as well—putting the genetic component at 35 per cent. The component was 16 per cent for ulcerative colitis. So, even for the highest risk people possible (where both parents have IBD, for example) about 70 per cent and 85 per cent respectively of the cause is determined by environmental factors.

Compared to a group of non-identical twin-pairs from the same IBD registry, identical twin-pairs were eight times more likely to both have Crohn's disease, and eight times more likely to both have ulcerative colitis. Thus, genetics rather than pre-birth environmental differences dominate. (To clarify, unlike identical twins who share both pre-birth environment *and* all genetic material, non-identical twins share the same pre-birth environment, but do not share all genetic material.)

Compared to healthy controls, there was no difference between people with IBD and controls for living environment including exposure to animals (farms), being in kindergartens, physical activity, living near a nuclear plant, or swimming in community pools. This points away from the 'overcleanliness' theory that IBD results from overprotection against environmental antigens.

A significant finding was that, within the cohort of twins, twin-pairs where both had Crohn's disease had more frequently lived for more than three months in an undeveloped country. This points to the importance of infection as a precursor to IBD. Finally, where one identical twin had IBD and the other did not, the environmental differences found were as follows.

+ Greater consumption of sausages, processed meat, red meat, nuts, and soft drink for the twin with IBD. (Sausages and ground beef combine the meat of several animals, thereby increasing the risk of infection with E. coli, which is thought to be a precursor of IBD.)

+ Increased antibiotic use by the twin with IBD. (One other study has found an association between antibiotic use and later IBD.[4] However, caution has been suggested as it may be only certain types of antibiotic. Furthermore, the need for antibiotics could simply indicate an existing issue with IBD. Everyone is saying there is a need for research about antibiotic use and IBD, but not much is being done.)

The study was clear that one factor stood out head and shoulders above all the rest: a prior bacterial infection. According to the researchers, 'The most remarkable results from our German twin study were found in the area of gastrointestinal infections prior to diagnosis of IBD. All diseased twins had significantly more bacterial infections of the gastrointestinal tract.'

Common gastro diseases associated with later IBD include: E. coli, campylobacter, salmonella and Yersinia enterocolitica. Evidence has been found that traces of E. coli infection are more common in biopsies of tissue from individuals with Crohn's disease.[5] E. coli is found in vegetables, fruit, undercooked ground beef and contaminated water from tanks and bores. It can also be found on uncooked vegetables and the outside of fruit. (Tap water in cities is tested for E. coli regularly, and use of tap water is a standard question for IBD studies, which all show there is no risk from the use of regulated tap water.)

Two studies have made a connection between campylobacter and IBD. One was based on biopsies of 28 patients.[6] The other was a population-based study in Denmark where these diseases are recorded in a registry.[7] Campylobacter is found in meat (especially chicken) that is undercooked or left out of the refrigerator, and it can contaminate other foods.

The same study showed a similarly increased risk from salmonella. Salmonella is associated with poultry and ground beef, and is additionally associated with eggs and unpasteurised dairy products. (It's also associated with the handling of amphibians, such as frogs and turtles.)

Yersinia enterocolitis is found in raw pork, including pork intestine and therefore some sausages. Dogs are susceptible to it, and can pass it back to humans who come in to contact with diarrheic dog faeces.[8]

TIPS FOR AVOIDING THE ONSET OF IBD

The 'overcleanliness' theory has generally been dismissed in all countries where it has been assessed.

Instead, the association of a gastrointestinal infection preceding IBD is favoured as a potential cause. Many are pinning their hopes on vaccines that target specific infections linked with IBD. A number of trials are underway, including one which began at Oxford University in 2017. However, it will be years before this line of research bears any results.

What is more certain is that hygiene—and, in particular, food hygiene—is a significant factor in avoiding IBD-linked infections.

Parents showing higher risk of IBD through family history may consider taking extra precautions about food handling and replacing teats on dropped bottles or dummies.

If a mother has diarrhoea, bacteria will not transfer into her milk, but it could be transferred to the breast skin—so, if you have diarrhoea, clean your breasts with soap and water before feeding.

TIPS FOR AVOIDING E. COLI, CAMPYLOBACTER AND SALMONELLA

+ People often believe that washing fruit is all about removing the spray, but it is also about getting rid of the E. coli. Wash fruit even if you are going to peel it, as E. coli can be moved to the peeled portions.

+ Be sure to buy pasteurised fruit juices.

+ Keep meat—especially raw meat—separate from other foods.

+ Refer to the Crafty Baking website for tips on how to pasteurise eggs for use in things like meringues and dressings (craftybaking.com/learn/ingredients/eggs).

DOES BREASTFEEDING HELP?

Research is conclusive that breast milk is ineffective against rotavirus, the most common gastro infection, even during the time a child is breastfed.[9] Antibodies in breast milk do not seem to have the power to combat the more serious gastrointestinal illnesses which land a child in hospital. It is these more violent infections which are associated with the onset of Crohn's disease and ulcerative colitis. Studies associating IBD and breastfeeding are so evenly divided that it is very hard to form an opinion about any possible benefit or risk of IBD from breastfeeding. It would be wrong to claim either that it is beneficial or that it is harmful. When results go one way and then the other again and again like this, the more important question is really: How important can the effect of breastfeeding be?

In 1987, a major international study showed that there was no difference in the rate of hospitalisation during the breastfeeding period in relation to later IBD conditions.[10] This international study is possibly the largest *actual* study of IBD (as opposed to meta-study reviews). There were 497 cases in fourteen centres in nine countries. All participants with IBD were under the age of 25 at the time, and all had mothers still alive to answer questions about breastfeeding. The countries involved included the USA, Canada, the UK, Sweden, Denmark, Holland, France, Italy and Israel. The study was controlled for socio-economic status, and other confounders which are often not included (such as controls coming from the same locations as their matched case). The study concluded:

> Neither the frequency nor the duration of breastfeeding, measured in months, showed any differences between patients and controls. In our study there was also no difference in milk consumption during childhood between patients and controls.

In 2004, a meta-analysis considered that, out of all the research available, only four studies for Crohn's disease and four for ulcerative colitis were worthy of consideration.[11] Among those studies was the 1987 study mentioned above. The researchers concluded:

> The results of this meta-analysis support the hypothesis that breastfeeding is associated with lower risks of Crohn's disease and ulcerative colitis. However, because only a few studies were graded to be of high quality, we suggest that further research, conducted with good methodology and large sample sizes, should be carried out to strengthen the validity of these observations.

A year later, in 2005, French researcher Sabine Baron claimed her methodology met up to the standards called for by the 2004 meta-analysis. Baron's study of 282 cases of IBD disease in Northern France showed breastfeeding was not at all protective—in fact, it was claimed to be a highly significant risk factor.[12] Eyal Klement, one of the researchers involved in the 2004 meta-analysis, agreed Baron's was a particularly careful study and wondered if there were geographical differences in the way breast milk influenced IBD. Unlike in many other developed countries today, breastfeeding is not very popular in France. Only one hospital in all of France is Baby-friendly accredited, and baby formula is advertised inside maternity units. In any case, Baron's study was really only comparing mothers of children with IBD breastfeeding for nine weeks with control mothers who breastfed for seven weeks—a difference of two weeks.

In 2009, Barclay singled out studies which gave information about early onset IBD in those under the age of sixteen.[13] However, Barclay's study had a few hitches. While he restricted his search to studies giving separate information about children under the age of sixteen, he eventually included a substantial number of results from young adults up to age 22 as well. Thus, the search and the outcome of participants were not in line, and relevant studies were left out, creating bias. One of the studies included was not really a study so much as another meta-analysis, and important information was guessed at for almost a third of the cases. Overall, Barclay's analysis showed there was no significant benefit from breastfeeding for either Crohn's disease or ulcerative colitis separately, but when combined there was a benefit for IBD generally. It was, in other words, a rather confusing and inconclusive result.

The 2012 German twins study mentioned in Appendix V did not find any statistical benefit from breastfeeding, but it pays to be careful not to read too much into that. It is a study of twins, rather than a twin study—in a twin study one of each pair has to be breastfed while the other is not. In the end, it is just one more study not finding a benefit.

APPENDIX VII
OBESITY AND
BREASTFEEDING

In November 2012, the New Zealand Breastfeeding Alliance (NZBA) sent a submission to the Government Administration Committee in support of a Bill to increase parental leave for breastfeeding mothers to six months.[1] In the submission, they claimed that there is a dose dependent association between longer duration of breastfeeding and a decreased risk of becoming overweight—in other words, they claim the evidence shows that the longer children are breastfed, the less likely they are to become obese.

They also noted that an Australian study comparing breastfed children of different breastfeeding durations[2] supported this dose dependent relationship, but this was misleading. What that study actually showed was exactly the opposite—that any advantage observable at one year among the longer breastfeeding group was completely lost by the time the child was eight years old.

The NZBA then called upon another study to support their position that breastfed children in general were less likely to be obese, saying, 'Researchers from the University of Glasgow and the Child Health Information Team in Edinburgh studied 32,000 Scottish children and found obesity to be less common in breastfed children with a 30 per cent reduction in risk of the condition.' However, where their claim that the study showed a 30 per cent reduction in the risk of obesity came from is anyone's guess. The study in question is 'Breastfeeding and lowering the risk of childhood obesity'[3] and after adjusting for social factors, such as social environment, mother's IQ and marital status, the difference in the risk of obesity between differently breastfed children all but disappeared. All the researchers could say at the end was the findings 'suggest that breastfeeding is associated with a modest reduction in childhood obesity risk . . . Breastfeeding may confer protection against obesity later in life, but the evidence is inconclusive'.

By comparison, a study that the NZBA should have factored in was Professor Michael S. Kramer's PROBIT study, which followed 14,000 children in Belarus from birth. In this study, correct measurement techniques were strictly monitored and there was minimal shrinkage of the original sample. Kramer has an impressive background combining both medical knowledge and statistical sophistication, and as part of the PROBIT study has helped the WHO/UNICEF Baby-friendly Hospital Initiative study measure effective ways to encourage women to breastfeed—something terribly important in undeveloped nations. He did an impressive job of increasing the numbers of mothers in the Belarus study who breastfed exclusively for more than six months. At the same time, he collected an enormous amount of detailed information related to greater or lesser breastfeeding—making good use of the medical expertise on hand in the hospitals.

At any rate, Kramer's highly regarded PROBIT study showed there was no evidence linking extended breastfeeding with a lowered risk of obesity at six-and-a-half years of age, either when viewed as an observational study or as a random study. In fact, Kramer's study showed the opposite: longer breastfeeding was associated with increased risk of obesity.

'Wait a minute!' I hear you say. 'How did NZBA, the umbrella organisation for New Zealand's Baby-friendly Hospitals Initiative, not know about it?' That's a very good question. It was practically their own study—and, in fact, the results regarding obesity had already been published twice in leading journals, including in the *Journal of Nutrition* under the heading, 'A randomized breast-feeding promotion intervention did not reduce child obesity in Belarus'.[4] It is, indeed, odd that there's no mention of it in the NZBA's submission on breastfeeding and obesity.

A follow-up to the Belarus study showed that at sixteen years of age the same association persisted.[5] Teenagers who had been breastfed longer continued to be at greater risk of obesity.

What's more, these findings are corroborated by sibling pair studies. There have been two sibling pair studies showing either no association between breastfeeding and obesity, or an increased risk from breastfeeding. In sibling pair studies, much is the same except one child in a family is breastfed and the other is not. That keeps unknown (and unknowable) factors constant—similar to how it would be if they had been twins growing up in the same family.

The first sibling pair study came out of the US and was titled 'Are Adolescents Who Were Breastfed Less Likely to Be Overweight? Analyses of sibling pairs to reduce confounding'.[6] This study drew data from the National Longitudinal Study of Adolescence, and the authors found that unmatched (for background) samples showed breastfeeding was associated with a lower risk of obesity. However, that was no longer the case when 850 sibling pairs were compared—as the researchers said, 'Our results illustrate the utility of sibling analysis in understanding the true effect of early-life exposures independent of confounding factors that may not be satisfactorily controlled.' This study won an award from the Society for Epidemiology research.

The second sibling pair study was titled 'Improved Estimates of the Benefits of Breastfeeding Using Sibling Comparisons to Reduce

Selection Bias', and looked at a much larger sample from the same source: 2,743 sibling pairs.[7] It showed the same effect, but this time sibling pairs showed that breastfeeding actually increased the chance of obesity.

DOES BREASTFEEDING HELP?

These powerful near-twin studies having the same result as the Belarus longitudinal trial is a tough act to follow. When you get one top-level study verifying results from another top-level study, that is extremely strong evidence. The bottom line is that the most reliable three studies that have ever been done on the subject came up with the same result: formula-feeding is not the culprit when it comes to obesity.

An unanswered question remains. Why *should* breastfeeding lead to a greater risk of obesity? Those who claim breastfeeding cures obesity point to the hormone leptin, which is one of nature's appetite regulators. Breastfeeding advocates claim that additional leptin from a mother's milk helps keep a baby's appetite in check.

But the human body is like a maze—you can work backwards from any outcome and point a finger at some association. Thinking that breastfeeding may increase the risk of obesity can give rise to the speculation that babies who have to fight harder for calories in infancy continue to feel deprived in later years. If we work backwards we can always come up with a theory. What we do know is, ethnicity and parental weight are important factors in predicting childhood obesity.

APPENDIX VIII
ANTISOCIAL BEHAVIOUR
AND BREASTFEEDING

Few studies have considered an association between breastfeeding and deviant behaviour. It appears the very first was a New Zealand study published in 1987. In that study the researchers claimed it was 'the first prospective study of a large representative population of children which has examined the association between infant feeding practices and subsequent social adjustment'.[1] This study came from data collected during the first eight years of the Christchurch Health and Development Study, which began in 1977 and follows a cohort of 1,265 children from birth. The duration of breastfeeding was obtained in terms of months. At six, seven and eight years of age, child behaviour was evaluated, with dimensions including conduct disorder, timidity/withdrawal, hyperactivity and social isolation. Confounding variables accounted for included maternal education, ethnicity and socio-economic status, as well as ratings of family living standards, family income and family stability. An early finding of the study was that maternal ratings of disorders were higher than teacher ratings, which suggested 'that the method of measuring conduct disorder influences the strength of the association'. While teacher ratings showed no advantage for breastfeeding, maternal ratings did. However, the researchers considered that the 'women who elect to breastfeed see their children in a more positive light and this tendency is reflected in their ratings of child behaviour'.

The second study we will look at is the follow-up on those same children as teenagers, conducted by two of the researchers from the 1987 study and published in 1999.[2] This study found that children who were breastfed longer 'reported higher levels of positive parental attachment and tended to perceive their mothers as being more caring and less overprotective towards them compared to bottle-fed children'. However, no association was found between the extent of breastfeeding and subsequent rates of juvenile offending, substance use or mental-health outcomes. The researchers concluded that 'these findings suggest an absence of association between mothers' breast-feeding practices and children's later psychosocial adjustment.'

The next study, which was published in 2008, came from Kramer's PROBIT study in Belarus.[3] In Kramer's opinion, the study remained semi-randomised even at the secondary level, where mothers interfered with that randomness by choosing whether or not to breastfeed. This study evaluated data from questionnaires given to parents and teachers independently. When Kramer analysed the behaviour data on 13,889 children without taking into account confounding variables (as though the study was truly random), he found no differences at six-and-a-half years of age on the measures of emotional symptoms, conduct problems, hyperactivity, peer problems or prosocial behaviour, and concluded, 'On the basis of the largest randomized trial ever conducted in the area of human lactation, we found no evidence of risks or benefits of prolonged and exclusive breastfeeding for child and maternal behaviour.'

Two years later, in 2010, an Australian study led by Wendy Oddy was published that examined data from 2,366 participants in the Western Australian Pregnancy Cohort (Raine) Study when the children were fourteen years old.[4] This study focused on a child-behaviour checklist completed by parents, which covered much the same measures as Kramer's PROBIT study. The results showed increased behavioural problems with shorter breastfeeding durations.

As a consequence of this study, in 2011 Kramer reconsidered his data as an observational study, adjusting for confounding variables such as maternal and paternal education.[5] This time, he did find an association between breastfeeding and antisocial behaviour, but commented that the difference he found was much smaller than that found by Oddy. He suggested that the associations were the result of variables not taken into account, such as different mother–child interactions between mothers who breastfeed and those who do not.

Interestingly, Oddy had raised similar possibilities in her discussion. One important factor was that Oddy's study only used mothers' ratings, whereas the other two mentioned above (Kramer's PROBIT study and the 1987 New Zealand study) used external ratings from teachers. The New Zealand study had earlier pointed out that breastfeeding mothers are likely to have a more positive attitude towards their children, and this will affect the results.

One study investigated an association between breastfeeding and violent delinquency covering an age group where results can be measured in the real world—25 years. This 2010 study used data from a Brazilian birth cohort of 5,228 children, and a total of 106 males and females from that group had at least one conviction.[6] Neither unadjusted nor adjusted analyses showed any association between breastfeeding and convictions for violent delinquency. The single most important factor was family income, followed by mother's education.

Finally, a recent 2017 study by a group of researchers attempted to circumvent the issues of confounding variables through random selection from a birth cohort, and used 8,000 families randomly selected from the Growing Up in Ireland longitudinal infant cohort.[7] Parent assessments were used at three years of age, then both parent and teacher assessments at five years of age. The attributes measured were similar to those in the previous studies mentioned. The results were that, of the thirteen attributes measured, the only difference was that at three years of age parent-rated scores of hyperactivity were lower for those children who had been fully breastfed for at least six months. At five years of age, however, that single advantage was lost, when parent and teacher results were available.

DOES BREASTFEEDING HELP?

These studies show that the association between breastfeeding and delinquency is extremely weak. It isn't exhibited in actual deviant behaviour among young people, and whether or not it's present in young children appears to depend on who is doing the rating.

Of the studies above which considered characteristics of young children such as hyperactivity which may be associated with later offending, only Oddy's showed a significant link between formula-feeding and 'pre-delinquent characteristics'.

The New Zealand studies, which found a weak association between breastfeeding and delinquency at ages six to eight, no longer found an association when those children were reassessed as teenagers. Meanwhile, the two studies which were able to assess the effect of breastfeeding on actual delinquent behaviour showed no association at all; instead, delinquency was found to be associated primarily with family income and those attributes connected with income (namely, teenage mothers, family violence, lower maternal education, the number of younger siblings and smoking during pregnancy).

APPENDIX IX
INTELLIGENCE AND
BREASTFEEDING

For many years, observational studies considering the beneficial effect of breastfeeding on cognition piled up evenly on either side of the debate.[1] Then, in 2005, the first non-observational study took place: a sibling pair study conducted by Eirik Evenhouse and Siobhan Reilly in 2005. This study surveyed 2,734 sibling pairs from the 1994 US National Longitudinal Study of Adolescent to Adult Health on fourteen measures.[2] They found a small increase in intelligence among breastfed children (based on results from an abbreviated Peabody Picture Vocabulary Test).

The following year, a high-powered research team including Geoff Der, David Batty and Ian Deary (a world expert in the field of intelligence), used Evenhouse and Reilly's sibling technique as a way to test the validity of their own study.[3] They realised that the difficulty in finding out whether or not there is a causal relationship between breast milk and intelligence lies in the fact it is so hard to get rid of confounding variables; consequently, they took rigorous steps to control for variables—more than is ever seen in the usual studies. These researchers used data on 5,475 children and their mothers, and they also had the mothers' full cognitive scores from the Armed Forces Qualifying Test. (The importance of this cannot be overstated. A mother's intelligence is universally agreed to be by far the most important predictor of a child's intelligence.) The children in this study were assessed every other year on the Peabody Individual Achievement Test, and there were also independent teacher scores on mathematics, reading comprehension and reading recognition. The research team found that all of the variance between the breastfeeding and non-breastfeeding groups was accounted for by the mother's IQ.

Next, the researchers took 332 sibling pairs where one child had been breastfed and the other had not (discordant), and a further 545 sibling pairs discordant for the duration of breastfeeding. The advantage of comparing sibling pairs is that it keeps not only the social setting the same, but more importantly in the case of intelligence the mother as well. Remember, it is the mother's IQ which in observational studies accounts for most of the difference between two groups. The results confirmed the researcher's original finding that there was no significant effect from breastfeeding.

Since their sibling pairs were taken from exactly the same database as Evenhouse and Riley had used, the second research team (which included the statistician Der) were entitled to carry out a weighted average of their study and Evenhouse and Reilly's study—the only other sibling pair study on the topic of breastfeeding. They found that, when the two studies were joined, the results did not support any advantage for breastfeeding, and concluded, 'Thus, the evidence from the only two sibling pair studies to date, when taken together, offer no support for an advantage of breast feeding.'

At much the same time as the first sibling pair studies were taking place, Kramer's PROBIT study in Belarus was underway. In many ways, Belarus was a good choice for the study as it is relatively uniform in terms of social and economic status, with initial breastfeeding rates of 95 per cent. Mothers are paid to stay home for three years after a child's birth, which eliminates having to work as an impediment to breastfeeding. However, what made this study hit the public eye was that it claimed randomness along with a massive number of participants. A total of 16,492 mother–infant pairs were studied from birth to one year, and 13,889 from one to six-and-a-half years of age. The randomness came from randomly selecting approximately 30 experimental hospitals in which the WHO/UNICEF Baby-friendly Initiative (see page 293) would be tested and 30 control hospitals in Belarus.

Those interested in a possible link between IQ and breastfeeding waited a long time to see published results regarding cognitive function from this 'cluster-randomised' PROBIT study. The IQ tests given to the children were the very best, and comprehensive—everyone was curious. But then bizarre results for IQ started rolling in from PROBIT's 60 hospitals. They were a mess. As Kramer later commented, 'It is not credible . . . that true average verbal IQ scores [between hospitals] would vary by nearly 50 points'.[4] Although when the study was published these and other flaws were admitted in the discussion section, the distorted results were nevertheless noted in the abstract (summary). The abstract claimed a near six-point global IQ advantage from breastfeeding and, a 7.5 verbal IQ gain for children in the experimental group (the group which was breastfed for longer).[5] To justify this surprising result, Kramer claimed that teacher classroom marks supported the verbal IQ difference. Teachers, who were blind as to which child was in the experimental or control group, provided individual classroom marks on learned skills. The table opposite shows how the teachers assessed the children from each group. Note that a score of 3.0 is average, and that the results are virtually identical—it's pretty difficult to see how the minute differences between them could support such massive IQ gains.

So, what went so wrong for Kramer's intelligence-test results, then? The primary problem was that, in this instance, he failed to

	LONGER BREASTFEEDING GROUP	SHORTER BREASTFEEDING GROUP
Reading	3.26	3.19
Writing	3.19	3.13
Mathematics	3.23	3.20
Other subjects	3.30	3.27

take his own advice. Whenever he has criticised the studies of other researchers, the first thing he almost always looks for is whether or not the study has been carried out 'blind' (in the sense that a tester doesn't know whether a subject is in the experimental or control group). However, in the case of this study, the paediatricians who carried out the oral IQ test were the same paediatricians who had been helping with the breastfeeding project; they therefore had prior knowledge of the children, and suffered from an experimenter bias. If there is an experimenter bias as well as interaction with a research participant, the participant will pick up on subtle cues and behave as expected—children are particularly prone to doing this. Then, in turn, the experimenter measures according to their own expectations. It is a double whammy, and is precisely what happened here. Other researchers were quick to jump on this wreckage and challenge the findings of such large IQ gains.[6] It was not until Kramer's follow-up of these children at sixteen years of age, however, that the challengers were proved correct: at sixteen years there was no IQ advantage from breastfeeding.

Not all of the available information on children's IQ at six years of age was revealed in Kramer's initial article. Some information was published under unexpected titles—for example, it wasn't until a 2014 article on socioeconomic inequalities that the gains of six-year-olds were clarified as being restricted to children of mothers with less education.[7] While Kramer provided adjusted observational results for other aspects of his project (for example, eczema and obesity), he did not do so in any accessible way for his study on the intelligence of six-year-olds. The only adjusted information he provided is scattered in various publications. In one, Kramer reveals that the study of six-year-olds showed no cognitive benefit for the children of higher-educated women, saying, 'maternal education is a stronger determinant of child IQ than breastfeeding. Mothers with higher education may already follow child-rearing practices that stimulate cognitive development of their infants through more frequent verbal interactions and reading. Genetic factors may also play a role in determining child cognitive ability.'[8]

Conversely, breastfeeding provided a marked advantage for the children of less-educated mothers. Kramer said, 'Mean verbal IQ scores of children in the lowest maternal-education category in the intervention were substantially higher than those of their counterparts in the control group.'[9]

Despite all the difficulties with the PROBIT data for IQ, the news that was broadcast was of the supposed global IQ six-point advantage for breastfed babies—a claim that only added to the fears and anxieties of parents regarding breastfeeding. It has been a long wait for more valid and reliable results on those same children, but the follow-up results when those six-year-olds turned sixteen was finally published in mid 2018.[10] These results paint a very different picture to the one that was presented when the children were six. At sixteen, no matter how the results were analysed, exclusive breastfeeding for at least six months did not result in any gain in IQ compared with babies breastfed for three months or less.

In order to avoid a repeat of the human failures which dogged the earlier PROBIT study at age six years, the IQ tests given at age sixteen were carried out on computers, with a minimum of human intervention. Overall intelligence of the sixteen-year-olds was assessed, and the data was analysed both as a random study and an observational study.

+ As a random study, the randomly selected group encouraged to exclusively breastfeed (the experimental group) was compared with the randomly selected group which was not encouraged to breastfeed (the control group). However, adjustments were made so that characteristics relevant to intelligence were matched—in particular, parental income, education and birth order.

+ As an observational study, the study ignored the existence of groups, but compared all the children from both groups who were exclusively breastfed for less than three months to all those who were exclusively breastfed for more than three months, while controlling for confounding variables known to impact on intelligence (such as parental income, education and birth order).

Either way, there was no difference between groups in overall (global) IQ. However, the seven domains that made up the global IQ score (memory, executive function, visual-spatial, verbal function, attention, information processing and fine motor skills) were looked at individually. Verbal function scores in particular were assessed in three ways: as a random study, as an observational study and after applying a statistical technique referred to as an 'IV' (instrumental variable) approach.

When viewed as a random study comparing hospitals, there was a small (1.4-point) gain in 'verbal function' for those exclusively breastfed for longer. (Keep in mind the randomness of this study is debatable.) When assessed as an observational study (after adjusting for confounding variables such as mothers' education, etc.) that verbal advantage disappeared. The researchers said the observational study indicated that: 'exclusive breastfeeding yielded little beneficial effect on neurocognitive function, including verbal function, at age 16 years.'[11]

Only by applying the instrumental variable approach could the researchers pull out a significant verbal benefit for extended exclusive breastfeeding. Using this analysis, they found a 3.5-point 'verbal function' advantage. It is this result which made it to the abstract, rather than the observational result showing no advantage. Yet, some caution is required before accepting results from an IV approach. It requires estimating unobserved confounders and can therefore potentially introduce errors rather than remove them.

Nevertheless, let's take a closer look at those IV results. What are we to make of them? To start with, 3.5 'verbal function' points have little, if any, real-life importance. While on standardised IQ tests, verbal IQ typically makes up one half of the test (global IQ is split into verbal and non-verbal IQ), the 'verbal function' domain that this study used is one of seven domains, so is only one-seventh of the overall IQ score. To put it crudely, you would need to divide 3.5 by 7 to get an idea of its impact on global intelligence. (I've done the math for you, it is half an IQ point.)

And then you need to look at the surprising results in all seven of the domains using this technique. The body of the study includes a table, 'IV estimates of breastfeeding effects', which reports that the memory and verbal domains show a small increase in score from extended breastfeeding. However, executive function, visual-spatial and motor skills show a decreased score from extended breastfeeding. Therefore, anyone advocating for extended breastfeeding on the basis that it *might* have a positive effect on verbal skills should also consider the opposite effect it *might* have on executive function.

Having failed to find any significant IQ advantage from breastfeeding, the PROBIT researchers instead discuss how these new results—which show no long-term advantage for intelligence at sixteen years of age—are in line with other research, namely:

+ one study showing that genetic differences in intelligence become more apparent with age[12]

+ another randomised study that showed no cognitive differences between pre-term children who had been fed breast milk from birth and those fed formula from birth[13]

+ and their own findings regarding the impact of a child's social and physical environment on cognitive development.

I would add that the finding of no long-term advantage for intelligence at sixteen is also in line with statistician Der's analysis of sibling pair studies (see page 479), and Flynn's contrast of IQ gains over time with breastfeeding trends (see page 327).

The PROBIT study at sixteen years of age concludes 'our randomized intervention to promote prolonged and exclusive breastfeeding showed little evidence of beneficial effect of breastfeeding on overall neurocognitive function at age sixteen years'.[14] Even so, the researchers made a plea for verbal gains based on a 'pattern'—specifically, verbal gains appearing in some shadowy form or another at both six years and sixteen years. However, even if we accept that, it is very important to keep in mind the proviso on that gain found in the study of six-year-olds. The benefit there was restricted to the children of less-educated women. Such a finding makes it fairly conclusive that it is not breast milk which makes the difference—otherwise, the effect would impact on the children of all women, whether they are well educated or not. Remember that, as a result of that finding, Kramer himself suggested it was not the breast milk which made the difference, but some maternal behaviour surrounding breastfeeding.

While Kramer does not speculate as to what those behaviours might be, as a clinical psychologist, I would like to step in and suggest that the reason the children of less-educated women benefitted is because breastfeeding enforces focused attention and verbal interactions with babies. This is the sort of behaviour an educated woman is more likely to engage in automatically, given the privileges of her own learned knowledge, the knowledge of people she associates with, and the way she herself was raised.

There is good evidence that focused attention—in particular, focused verbal attention—improves cognition. And, there is good evidence that breastfed babies receive more attention. This strongly supports the view that any verbal gains from breastfeeding are the result of the additional time and attention required when breastfeeding (as compared with bottle-feeding).

So, if it's not breast milk which makes a child smarter, but time and care, what does the research have to say about the effect of parental attention on IQ? Let's start back in 1939, when American psychologist Harold Skeels wrote of the positive effect that resulted from transferring orphans with a low IQ to an environment where they received one-on-one attention and affection.[15] After attempting to educate orphan children with low IQs in order to improve their intelligence (so that they might be adopted), but seeing little effect, Skeels devised an experiment. Thirteen babies with low intelligence scores were transferred from an orphanage to a nearby residence for 'feeble-minded' women called Glenwood State School. At the same time, twelve children of average or low intelligence were left behind at the orphanage.

At Glenwood, the babies were showered with affection, and each enjoyed a one-on-one relationship with a woman resident at the school; the 'feeble-minded' women, for their part, were encouraged to talk to the babies and taught how to elicit language from them. As a result, these babies were talked to a lot. Two-and-a-half years later, their average IQ had gained 28 points—and all but two of them were adopted. (The two who were not adopted went back to the orphanage, and subsequently lost the IQ gain.) Meanwhile, the twelve children who had remained behind at the orphanage had very little adult contact. Two-and-a-half years later, these children had lost on average 27 IQ points.

From this, in the special case of children with a low IQ, it appears that the love, attention and speaking provided by a mother (or mother figure) may matter as much for the child's outcome as the mother's IQ.

Moving a bit closer to the present day, in 1998 researchers Manuela Lavelli and Marco Poli filmed 32 first-time mothers feeding their babies.[16] Of those mothers, 20 were breastfeeding and 12 bottle-feeding. They were filmed during feeding when the babies were three and ten days old, and later at one and three months. Lavelli and Poli found the following.

+ Most of the mother–infant interaction during breastfeeding was based on mutual contact, but was very scarce during bottle-feeding.

+ During breastfeeding, bouts of mutual gaze (see pages 53–55) were significantly longer than during bottle-feeding.

+ Consistent with the two findings above, the breastfeeding mothers gazed at their infants and caressed them significantly more than the bottle-feeding ones.

Then, in 2011, researchers Julie Smith and Mark Ellwood asked 188 mothers to record the time spent with their babies using an electric tracking device.[17] Specifically, each mother was to record, in the following order:

1. the time spent feeding her baby

2. the time spent soothing, comforting or holding her baby

3. the time spent engaging in any other kind of interaction with her baby.

By three months, there was already a large weekly difference in time spent with babies when comparing breastfeeding mothers with formula-feeding mothers. In particular, breastfeeding mothers spent significantly more time feeding and comforting. By six months, the gap was even larger—a total of 54 hours a week for breastfeeding mothers versus 30 hours for formula-feeding mothers. That's 50 per cent more time for the breastfeeding mothers at six months.

Finally, a 2013 study by Anne Fernald and Adriana Weisleder from Stanford University analysed all-day recordings of infant–caregiver (usually mother) language environments. They took measures from birth to two years of age, and found it was 'only speech addressed directly to the infant, and not speech in adult conversations overheard by the child, [which] facilitated vocabulary learning at this age.'[18]

It's clear from these studies that one of the side-effects of breastfeeding is more time during which a mother is focused on her baby, through mutual touch and gaze, and through verbal interactions. This brings us to the question of birth order, and whether a child's position in a family has an effect on their intelligence. The follow-up study of the children in Kramer's PROBIT study at the age of sixteen showed a significant IQ difference between first and third children.[19] Compared with firstborns, second-born children had a global IQ score 1.5 points lower, and third or subsequent children had a global IQ score 5.1 points lower. For quite some time, researchers have pondered whether it is the extra attention firstborns receive (which makes them smarter) or a deteriorating foetal environment (which causes later children to be less intelligent). Luckily for us, the question has been resolved.

In 2007, a Norwegian study contradicted the theory that gestational deterioration determined birth-order intelligence.[20] The researchers showed that it was the first-*raised* child rather than the firstborn who got the IQ advantage. They did this by comparing first-raised children where an older sibling had died and found no difference in IQ advantage for those children than for first-raised children who had not lost earlier siblings.

Then in 2015, a Swedish study showed that if there is more than a six-year gap between a first and second child, the effect of the second child having a lower IQ disappears.[21] This study went on to question why many other studies have not shown similar results about birth order and IQ, with the researcher pointing out differences between the US and Norway and Sweden that affect the time a parent spends with their child. As the researcher noted, most of the other studies are from the US, where maternity leave is only a matter of weeks and usually unpaid; meanwhile, both Norway and Sweden effectively provide an entire year's paid parental leave (shared between parents). What this means is that a first-born (or first-raised) baby in the US does not get the family resources a first baby gets in Norway or Sweden.

DOES BREASTFEEDING HELP?

What all of these studies point to is that it's not breast milk but attention that will make your baby smarter. In particular, parental attention in the form of quality time and baby-focused language are especially important, while birth order can have an effect on the amount of attention a child receives.

The good news is that you don't need to be Madam Curie playing Baby Einstein games to help improve your baby's IQ. The bad news is that, if you are bottle-feeding, you will need to make a special effort to ensure you are giving your baby more individual, focused attention in order to make up for the time lost compared with breastfeeding. And you can do this! Just remember that there will be a ceiling to this effect. You won't necessarily get a rise in IQ where children are not adversely affected—but you could get some.

When you consider the fact that it's attention that matters here— not whether you're feeding your baby via a breast or a bottle—it highlights the sad irony that the very group of babies who might benefit the most from the extra time that breastfeeding demands is also the very group least likely to be breastfed. Meanwhile, middle-class mothers desperate to squeeze the last IQ point out of a breast will go to extremes in order to do so, when their babies would probably receive the maximum benefit from caregiver attention whether they were breastfed or not. It's hard not to feel that the energy that goes into pushing mothers into breastfeeding (and ultimately ends up causing a lot of women harm) would be better placed simply encouraging mothers to spend more time talking to and enjoying their babies.

NOTES

CHAPTER 1: BOMBARDMENT STRESS: SORTING FACT FROM FICTION

1   S. S. Iyengar and M. R. Lepper, 'When choice is demotivating: Can one desire too much of a good thing?', *Journal of Personality and Social Psychology*, 2000, vol. 79, no. 6, pp. 995–1006.

CHAPTER 2: THE CHANGING FACE OF THE PARENTING RELATIONSHIP

1   'Blame him for brats: Spock swallows his words', *Beaver County Times*, 23 January 1974, p. A16.

2   D. Baumrind, 'Effects of authoritative parental control on child behaviour', *Child Development*, 1966, vol. 37, no. 4, pp. 887–907.

3   K. Lorenz, 'Der Kumpan in der Umwelt des Vogels: Der Artgenosse als auslösendes Moment sozialer Verhaltensweisen', *Journal fur Ornithologie*, 1935, vol. 83, pp. 137–215, 289–413 (and popularly, in English, in his book *King Solomon's Ring*).

4   H. F. Harlow and R. R. Zimmerman, 'The development of affective responsiveness in infant monkeys', *Proceedings of the American Philosophical Society*, 1958, vol. 102, pp. 501–509.

5   J. Bowlby, 'The nature of a child's tie to his mother', *The International Journal of Psychoanalysis*, 1958, vol. 39, pp. 350–373.

6   J. Bowlby, 'Forty-four juvenile thieves: their characters and home-life', *The International Journal of Psychoanalysis*, 1944, vol. 25, pp. 19–53.

7   J. Bowlby, *Maternal Care and Mental Health*, Geneva: World Health Organization, 1951.

8   The Leidloff Continuum Network, 'Understanding the Continuum Concept', <www.continuum-concept.org/cc_defined.html>. Article extracted from Jean Leidloff, *The Continuum Concept, Revised Edition*, Reading, MA: Addison-Wesley, 1985.

9   M. Mendizza, 'Allowing human nature to work successfully: A very candid conversation with Jean Liedloff', *Touch the Future*, 1988, Fall issue.

10 J. Bowlby, *Can I leave my baby?*, London: The National Association for Mental Health, 1958.

11 Interview with Bowlby, 23 July 1977, as quoted in Robert Karen, *Becoming Attached: First relationships and how they shape our capacity to love*, New York: Oxford University Press, 1998, p. 89.

12 Annalisa Barber, 'Jean Liedloff obituary', *The Guardian*, 11 April 2011.

13 William Sears and Martha Sears, *The Attachment Parenting Book: A commonsense guide to understanding and nurturing your child*, New York: Little, Brown & Company, 2001.

14 Jeffrey Kluger, 'The science behind Dr. Sears: Does it stand up?', *Time*, 10 May 2012.

15 L. Ahnert et al., 'Transition to child care: Associations with infant-mother attachment, infant negative emotion, and cortisol elevations', *Child Development*, 2004, vol. 75, no. 3, pp. 639–650.

16 A. F. Lieberman and C. H. Zeanah, 'Disorders of attachment in infancy', *Child and Adolescent Psychiatric Clinics of North America*, 1995, vol. 4, no. 3, pp. 571–587.

17 Kate Pickert, 'The man who remade motherhood', *TIME Health*, 22 May 2012, <http://time.com/606/the-man-who-remade-motherhood/>.

18 M. Main and J. Solomon, 'Procedures for identifying infants as disorganized/disoriented during the Ainsworth Strange Situation', 1990, cited in Mark T. Greenberg et al. (Eds), *Attachment in the Preschool Years: Theory, research, and intervention*, Chicago, IL: University of Chicago Press, 1990, pp. 121–160.

19 Mary D. Salter Ainsworth, *Infancy in Uganda: Infant care and the growth of love*, Baltimore: John Hopkins University Press, 1967, ch. 20; and Robert Karen, *Becoming Attached: First relationships and how they shape our capacity to love*, New York: Oxford University Press, 1998, ch. 11.

20 Jerome Kagan, *The Human Spark: The science of human development*, New York: Basic Books, 2013.

21 Mark Carey, 'Building resilience in children and young people', article based on a talk given at The School of Total Education, Queensland, Australia, 29 July 2010, <www.sote.qld.edu.au/articles/building-resilience.html>.

22 A. Dettmer et al., 'Neonatal face-to-face interactions promote later social behaviour in infant rhesus monkeys', *Nature Communications*, 2016, vol. 7.

23 T. Field et al., 'Infants of depressed mothers show "depressed" behavior even with nondepressed adults', *Child Development*, 1988, vol. 59, no. 6, pp. 1569–1579; and

T. Field, 'Infants of depressed mothers', *Infant Behavior and Development*, 1995, vol. 18, no. 1, pp. 1–13.

24 Martin Seligman, *Flourish: A visionary new understanding of happiness and well-being*, Sydney: Random House Australia, 2011, p. 14.

25 J. Milgrom et al., 'The mediating role of maternal responsiveness in some longer term effects of postnatal depression on infant development', *Infant Behavior & Development*, 2004, vol. 27, no. 4, pp. 443–454.

26 J. Milgrom and P. McCloud, 'Parenting stress and postnatal depression', *Stress & Health*, 1996, vol. 12, no. 3, pp. 177–186.

27 J. Milgrom and C. Holt, 'Early intervention to protect the mother-infant relationship following postnatal depression: Study protocol for a randomised controlled trial', *Trials*, 2014, vol. 15, no. 485, <www.ncbi.nlm.nih.gov/pubmed/25277158>.

28 H. Dejon et al., 'Rumination and postnatal depression: A systematic review and a cognitive model', *Behaviour Research and Therapy*, 2016, vol. 82, pp. 38–49.

29 Cited in I. G. Wickes, 'A history of infant feeding, Parts I–IV', *Archives of Disease in Childhood*, 1953, vol. 28, p. 154.

30 Ibid., p. 501.

31 Ibid., p. 333.

32 Ibid, p. 338.

33 I. G. Wickes, 'Overfeeding in Early Infancy', *British Medical Journal*, 1952, vol. 2, no. 4795, p. 1178.

34 'The great Gina Ford debate', *The Independent*, 12 January 2010, <independent.co.uk/life-style/health-and-families/features/the-great-gina-ford-debate-1864825.html>.

35 M. Iacovou and A. Sevilla, 'Infant feeding: The effects of scheduled vs. on-demand feeding on mother's well-being and children's cognitive development', *European Journal of Public Health*, 2013, vol. 23, no. 1, pp. 13–19.

36 Lucy Rock, 'Babies fed on demand "do better at school"', *The Observer*, 17 March 2012, <www.theguardian.com/society/2012/mar/17/babies-fed-demand-better-school>.

37 J. Golding, 'Children of the nineties: A longitudinal study of pregnancy and childhood based on the population of Avon', *West of England Medical Journal*, 1990, vol. 105, no. 3, pp. 80–82.

38 K. Sainani, 'Propensity scores: Uses and limitations', *American Academy of Physical Medicine and Rehabilitation*, 2012, vol. 4, no. 9, pp. 693–697.

CHAPTER 3: HAPPINESS AND WELL-BEING

1   Martin Seligman, *Authentic Happiness: Using the new positive psychology to realize your potential for lasting fulfillment*, New York: Free Press, 2002.

2   Martin Seligman, *Flourish: A visionary new understanding of happiness and well-being*, Sydney: Random House Australia, 2011.

3   Association of Salaried Medical Specialists (ASMS), 'Dr Tony Fernando—The science of happiness' (presentation to the 26th annual ASMS conference in Wellington, 2014), YouTube, published 11 December 2014, <www.youtube.com/watch?v=-71koNsCEds>.

4   Jon Kabat-Zinn, cited on the Medivate Quote Database at <http://medivate.com/quote/122/> and credited to his book *Wherever You Go, There You Are: Mindfulness meditation in everyday life*, New York: Hyperion Books, 1994.

5   S. L. Shapiro and L. E. Carlson, *The Art and Science of Mindfulness: Integrating mindfulness into psychology and the helping professions*, Washington, DC: American Psychological Association, 2009.

6   Paul Gilbert and Choden, *Mindful Compassion: Using the power of mindfulness and compassion to transform our lives*, London, UK: Robinson, 2013.

7   J. J. Froh et al., 'Counting blessings in early adolescents: An experimental study of gratitude and subjective well-being', *Journal of School Psychology*, 2008, vol. 46, pp. 213–233.

8   J. C. Huffman et al., 'Feasibility and utility of positive psychology exercises for suicidal patients', *General Hospital Psychiatry*, 2014, vol. 36, pp. 88–94.

9   S. T. Cheng et al., 'Improving mental health in health care practitioners: Randomized controlled trial of a gratitude intervention', *Journal of Consulting and Clinical Psychology*, 2015, vol. 83, no. 1, pp. 177–186.

10 Dr Kristin Neff, 'Does self-compassion mean letting yourself off the hook?', <http://self-compassion.org/does-self-compassion-mean-letting-yourself-off-the-hook/>.

11 Dr Kristin Neff, 'Definition of self-compassion' and 'The three elements of self-compassion', <https://self-compassion.org/the-three-elements-of-self-compassion-2/#3elements>.

CHAPTER 4: TUNING IN AND KEEPING CALM

1   Matthew McKay et al., *Mind and Emotions: A universal treatment for emotional disorders*, Oakland, CA: New Harbinger Publications, 2011.

CHAPTER 5: REFLECTING ON YOUR BIRTH EXPERIENCE

1   Shaili Jain, 'Perinatal psychiatry, birth trauma and perinatal PTSD: An interview with Dr. Rebecca Moore', 24 August 2016, *PLOS Blogs Network*, <https://blogs.plos.org/blog/2016/08/24/perinatal-psychiatry-birth-trauma-and-perinatal-ptsd-an-interview-with-dr-rebecca-moore/>.

2   Ministry of Health, 'Report on Maternity 2015', Wellington: Ministry of Health, published August 2017, <www.health.govt.nz/publication/report-maternity-2015>.

3   NHS Digital, 'NHS Maternity Statistics—England, 2013–14', <www.hscic.gov.uk/catalogue/PUB16725>.

4   CDC (Centers for Disease Control and Prevention), 'Cesarean Delivery Rate by State', 2016 figures published 2018, <www.cdc.gov/nchs/pressroom/sosmap/cesarean_births/cesareans.htm>.

5   M. G. Dominguez-Bello et al., 'Partial restoration of the microbiota of Cesarean-born infants via vaginal microbial transfer', *Nature Medicine*, 2016, vol. 22, no. 3, pp. 250–253.

6   L. F. Stinson et al., 'A critical review of the bacterial baptism hypothesis and the impact of Caesarean delivery on the infant microbiome', 2018, *Frontiers of Medicine*, vol. 5, no. 135.

7   Ibid.

8   S. Y. Huh et al., 'Delivery by caesarean section and risk of obesity in preschool age children: A prospective cohort study', *Archives of Disease in Childhood*, 2012, vol. 97, no. 7, pp. 610–616.

9   Montgomery (Appellant) v Lanarkshire Health Board (Respondent), 2015, UKSC 11, Justices Neuberger, Hale, Kerr, Clarke, Wilson, Reed and Hodge.

10 'Nadine Montgomery wins £5m from NHS Lanarkshire over brain damage to son', *BBC News*, 11 March 2015, <www.bbc.com/news/uk-scotland-glasgow-west-31831591>.

11 K. Wang et al., 'The effects of epidural/spinal opioids in labour analgesia on neonatal outcomes: A meta-analysis of randomized controlled trials', *Canadian Journal of Anesthesia*, 2014, vol. 61, no. 8, pp. 695–709.

CHAPTER 6: BABY BLUES AND BEYOND

1   N. I. Gavin et.al., 'Perinatal depression: A systematic review of prevalence and incidence', *Obstetrics & Gynecology*, 2005, vol. 106, no. 5, part 1, pp. 1071–1083.

2   M. W. O'Hara and K. L. Wisner, 'Perinatal mental illness: definition, description and

aetiology', *Best Practice & Research: Clinical Obstetrics & Gynaecology*, 2014, vol. 28, no. 1, pp. 3–12.

3   C. R. Reynolds and R. W. Kamphaus, 'BASC3: Major Depressive Disorder', <https://images.pearsonclinical.com/images/assets/basc-3/basc3resources/DSM5_ DiagnosticCriteria_MajorDepressiveDisorder.pdf>, details reprinted from American Psychiatric Association, *Diagnostic and Statistical Manual of Mental Disorders, Fifth Edition*, Arlington, VA: American Psychiatric Publishing, 2013.

4   J. L. Cox et al., Department of Psychiatry, University of Edinburgh, 'Detection of Postnatal Depression: Development of the 10-item Edinburgh Postnatal Depression Scale', *The British Journal of Psychiatry*, 1987, vol. 150, pp. 782–786.

5   S. K. Crowley and S. D. Youngstedt, 'Efficacy of light therapy for perinatal depression: A review', *Journal of Physiological Anthropology*, 2012, vol. 31, no. 1.

6   M. Carlberg et al., 'Paternal perinatal depression assessed by the Edinburgh Postnatal Depression Scale and the Gotland Male Depression Scale: Prevalence and possible risk factors', *American Journal of Men's Health*, 2018, vol. 12, no. 4, pp. 720–729.

7   S. L. Mott et al., 'Depression and anxiety among postpartum and adoptive mothers', *Archives of Women's Mental Health*, 2011, vol. 14, no. 4, pp. 335–343.

8   L. E. Ross et.al., 'Perinatal depressive symptomatology among lesbian and bisexual women', *Archives of Women's Mental Health*, 2007, vol. 10, no. 2, pp. 53–59.

9   H. B. Simpson et al., 'Obsessive-compulsive disorder in adults: Epidemiology, pathogenesis, clinical manifestations, course, and diagnosis', last updated 17 October 2017, <www.uptodate.com/contents/obsessive-compulsive-disorder-in-adults-epidemiology-pathogenesis-clinical-manifestations-course-and-diagnosis>.

CHAPTER 7: RELATIONSHIPS AND SEX

1   M. A. Scheppingen et al., 'Self-esteem and relationship satisfaction during the transition to motherhood', *Journal of Personality and Social Psychology*, 2018, vol. 114, no. 6, pp. 973–991.

2   Ibid.

3   Dr Martien Snellen, *Rekindling: Your relationship after childbirth, Revised Edition*, Melbourne, Australia: Text Publishing Co, 2013.

CHAPTER 8: MOTHERHOOD AND IDENTITY

1   S. Kanji and E. Cahusac, 'Who am I? Mothers' shifting identities, loss and sensemaking after workplace exit', *Human Relations*, 2015, vol. 68, no. 9, pp. 1415–1436.

CHAPTER 9: CRYING

1   B. Taubman, 'Clinical trial of the treatment of colic by modification of parent–infant interaction', *Pediatrics*, 1984, vol. 74, no. 6, pp. 998–1003.

2   Gina Ford, *The One Week Baby Sleep Solution: Your 7 day plan for a good night's sleep—for baby and you!*, London: Ebury Publishing, 2018.

3   R. Butler et al., 'Pacifier use, finger sucking, and infant sleep', *Behavioral Sleep Medicine*, 2016, vol. 14, no. 6, pp. 615–623.

4   R. Campos, 'Rocking and pacifiers: Two comforting interventions for heelstick pain', *Research in Nursing & Health*, 1994, vol. 17, no. 5, pp. 321–331.

5   American Academy of Pediatrics, 'The changing concept of sudden infant death syndrome', *Pediatrics*, 2005, vol. 116, no. 5, pp. 1245–1255.

6   L. Bayer et al., 'Rocking synchronizes brain waves during short sleep nap', *Current Biology*, 2011, vol. 21, no. 12, pp. 461–462.

7   R. Campos, 'Rocking and pacifiers: Two comforting interventions for heelstick pain', *Research in Nursing & Health*, 1994, vol. 17, no. 5, pp. 321–331.

8   G. Yilmaz and D. Arikan, 'The effect of two different swinging methods upon colic and crying durations among infants', *Indian Journal of Pain*, 2015, vol. 29, no. 3, pp. 172–180.

9   E. Sezici and D. Yigit, 'Comparison between swinging and playing white noise among colicky babies: A paired randomised controlled trial', *Journal of Clinical Nursing*, 2018, vol. 27, no. 3–4, pp. 593–600.

10 J. A. Spencer et al., 'White noise and sleep induction', *Archives of Disease in Childhood*, 1990, vol. 65, no. 1, pp. 135–137.

11 G. Yilmaz and D. Arikan, 'The effect of two different swinging methods upon colic and crying durations among infants', *Indian Journal of Pain*, 2015, vol. 29, no. 3, pp. 172–180.

12 S. C. Hugh et al., 'Infant sleep machines and hazardous sound pressure levels', *Pediatrics*, 2014, vol. 133, no. 4, pp. 677–681.

13 Ibid.

14 Harvey Karp, *The Happiest Baby on the Block: The new way to calm crying and help your newborn baby sleep longer*, New York: Random House, 2002.

15 B. E. Van Sleuwen et al., 'Comparison of behavior modification with and without swaddling as interventions for excessive crying', *The Journal of Pediatrics*, 2006, vol. 149, no. 4, pp. 512–517.

16 H. L. Richardson et al., 'Influence of swaddling experience on spontaneous arousal patterns and autonomic control in sleeping infants', *The Journal of Pediatrics*, 2010, vol. 157, no. 1, pp. 85–91.

17 L. E. Meyer and T. Erler, 'Swaddling: A traditional care method rediscovered', *World Journal of Pediatrics*, 2011, vol. 7, no. 2, pp. 155–160.

18 R. H. Horwich, 'Regressive periods in primate behavioural development with reference to other mammals', *Primates*, 1974, vol. 15, no. 2–3, pp. 141–149.

19 H. H. C. van de Rijt-Plooij and F. X. Plooij, 'Infantile regressions: Disorganization and the onset of transition periods', *Journal of Reproductive and Infant Psychology*, 1992, vol. 10, no. 3, pp. 129–149.

20 C. de Weerth and P. van Geert, 'Emotional instability as an indicator of strictly timed infantile developmental transitions', *British Journal of Developmental Psychology*, 1998, vol. 16, no. 1, pp. 15–44.

21 M. Sadurni and C. Rostan, 'Regression periods in infancy: A case study from Catalonia', *The Spanish Journal of Psychology*, 2002, vol. 5, no. 1, pp. 36–44.

22 I. St James-Roberts and P. Gillham, 'Use of a behavioural programme in the first 3 months to prevent infant crying and sleeping problems', *Journal of Paediatrics and Child Health*, 2001, vol. 37, no. 3, pp. 289–297.

23 D. Wolke et al., 'Systematic review and meta-analysis: Fussing and crying durations and prevalence of colic in infants', *The Journal of Pediatrics*, 2017, vol. 185, 55–61, e4.

24 R. G. Barr et al., 'Crying in !Kung San infants: A test of the cultural specificity hypothesis', *Developmental Medicine & Child Neurology*, 1991, vol. 33, no. 7, pp. 601–610.

25 I. St James-Roberts et al., 'Infant crying patterns in Manali and London', *Child: Care, Health and Development*, 1994, vol. 20, no. 5, pp. 323–337.

26 B. Taubman, 'Clinical trial of the treatment of colic by modification of parent–infant interaction', *Pediatrics*, 1984, vol. 74, no. 6, pp. 998–1003.

27 Ian St James-Roberts, *The Origins, Prevention and Treatment of Infant Crying and Sleeping Problems*, London: Taylor & Francis Ltd, 2012.

28 D. Wolke et al., 'Systematic review and meta-analysis: Fussing and crying durations and prevalence of colic in infants', *The Journal of Pediatrics*, 2017, vol. 185, 55–61, e4.

29 A. Lucas et al., 'Crying, fussing and colic behaviour in breast and bottle-fed infants', *Early Human Development*, 1998, vol. 53, no. 1, pp. 9–18.

30 I. St James-Roberts et al., 'Infant crying and sleeping in London, Copenhagen and when parents adopt a "proximal" form of care', *Pediatrics*, 2006, vol. 117, no. 6, e1146–1155.

31 I. St James-Roberts and P. Gillham, 'Use of a behavioural programme in the first 3 months to prevent infant crying and sleeping problems', *Journal of Paediatrics and Child Health*, 2001, vol. 37, no. 3, pp. 289–297.

32 B. P. White et al, 'Behavioural and physiological responsivity, sleep, and patterns of daily cortisol production in infants with and without colic', *Child Development*, 2000, vol. 71, no. 4, pp. 862–877.

33 C. Stifter and P. Backer, 'Crying behaviour and its impact on psychosocial child development', *Encyclopedia on Early Childhood Development*, March 2017, revised edition, <www.child-encyclopedia.com/crying-behaviour/according-experts/crying-behaviour-and-its-impact-psychosocial-child-development>.

34 Ruth Margalit, 'How Harvey Karp turned baby sleep into big business', *The New York Times Magazine*, 18 April 2018.

35 H. N. Karp, [Letter to the Editor] 'Re: A randomized, controlled trial of a behavioral intervention to reduce crying among infants', *Journal of the American Board of Family Medicine*, 2010, vol. 23, no. 5, pp. 689–90.

36 J. M. McRury and A. J. Zolotor, 'A randomized, controlled trial of a behavioral intervention to reduce crying among infants', *Journal of the American Board of Family Medicine*, 2010, vol. 23, no. 3, pp. 315–322.

37 H. N. Karp, [Letter to the Editor] 'Re: A randomized, controlled trial of a behavioral intervention to reduce crying among infants', *Journal of the American Board of Family Medicine*, 2010, vol. 23, no. 5, pp. 689–90.

38 Harvey Karp, *The Happiest Baby on the Block: The new way to calm crying and help your newborn baby sleep longer*, New York: Random House, 2002, pp. 186–187.

39 Ronald. G. Barr, 'Common features and principles of soothing', undated, *The Period of PURPLE Crying*, <www.purplecrying.info/sub-pages/soothing/common-features-and-principles-of-soothing.php>.

40 Sandra Blakeslee, 'Colicky baby? Read this before calling an exorcist', *The New York Times Magazine*, 8 March 2005.

41 Marilyn Barr, 'What is the Period of PURPLE Crying?', undated, *The Period of PURPLE Crying*, <www.purplecrying.info/what-is-the-period-of-purple-crying.php>.

42 Magda Gerber and Allison Johnson, *Your Self-Confident Baby: How to encourage your child's natural abilities—from the very start*, New York: John Wiley & Sons, Inc., 1998.

43 'The Nobel Prize in Physiology or Medicine 1950', undated, *The Nobel Prize*, <www.nobelprize.org/prizes/medicine/1950/summary/>.

44 L. M. Glynn et al., 'When stress happens matters: The effects of earthquake timing on stress responsivity in pregnancy', *American Journal of Obstetrics and Gynaecology*, 2001, vol. 184, no. 4, pp. 637–642.

45   S. King et al., 'Using natural disasters to study the effects of prenatal maternal stress on child health and development', *Birth Defects Research: Embryo Today*, 2012, vol. 96, no. 4, pp. 273–288.

46   E. P. Davis and C. A. Sandman, 'The timing of prenatal exposure to maternal cortisol and psychosocial stress is associated with human infant cognitive development', *Child Development*, 2010, vol. 81, no. 1, pp. 131–148.

47   H. M. Schreier, 'Lifetime exposure to traumatic and other stressful life events and hair cortisol in a multi-racial/ethnic sample of pregnant women', *Stress*, 2016, vol. 19, no. 1, pp. 45–52.

48   M. Kruk, 'Fast positive feedback between the adrenocortical stress response and a brain mechanism involved in aggressive behaviour', *Behavioural Neuroscience*, 2004, vol. 118, no. 5, pp. 1062–1070.

49   A. S. Fleming and C. M. Corter, 'Factors influencing maternal responsiveness in humans: Usefulness of an animal model', *Psychoneuroendocrinology*, 1988, vol. 13, nos 1–2, pp. 189–212.

50   Moshe Szyf, 'How early life experience is written into DNA', TED Talk at TEDxBratislava, July 2016, <www.ted.com/talks/moshe_szyf_how_early_life_experience_is_written_into_dna>.

51   R. Stremler et al., 'Effect of behavioural-educational intervention on sleep for primiparous women and their infants in early postpartum: Multisite randomised controlled trial', *The BMJ*, 2013, vol. 346, f1164.

52   Gina Ford, *The One Week Baby Sleep Solution: Your 7 day plan for a good night's sleep—for baby and you!*, London: Ebury Publishing, 2018, p. 11; and Gina Ford, *The New Contented Little Baby Book: The secret to calm and confident parenting*, London: Random House, 2002, p. 126.

CHAPTER 10: SLEEPING

1   M. Gradisar et al., 'Behavioural interventions for infant sleep problems: A randomized controlled trial', *Pediatrics*, 2016, vol. 137, no. 6, e20151486.

2   H. Hiscock et al., 'Improving infant sleep and maternal mental health: A cluster randomised trial', *Archives of Disease in Childhood*, 2007, vol. 92, no. 11, pp. 952–958.

3   A. M. H. Price et al., 'Five-year follow-up of harms and benefits of behavioral infant sleep intervention: Randomized trial', *Pediatrics*, 2012, vol. 130, no. 4, pp. 643–651.

4   W. Middlemiss et al., 'Response-based sleep intervention: Helping infants sleep without making them cry', *Early Human Development*, 2017, vol. 108, pp. 49–57.

5   Statistics drawn from three sources: Ministry of Health New Zealand, 'Fetal and Infant

Deaths 2008 and 2009', published online 18 December 2012, *Ministry of Health*, <www.health.govt.nz/publication/fetal-and-infant-deaths-2008-and-2009>; Ministry of Health New Zealand, 'Fetal and Infant Deaths 2014', published online 31 October 2017, *Ministry of Health*, <www.health.govt.nz/publication/fetal-and-infant-deaths-2014>; and US Department of Health and Human Services, 'U.S. Rates of SIDS and Other Sleep-Related Causes of Infant Death (1990–2013)', in 'Fast Facts About SIDS', undated, *Safe to Sleep*, <https://safetosleep.nichd.nih.gov/safesleepbasics/SIDS/fastfacts>.

6 E. A. Mitchell et al., 'Results from the first year of the New Zealand cot death study', *New Zealand Medical Journal*, 1991, vol. 104, no. 906, pp. 71–76.

7 E. A. Mitchell and P. S. Blair, 'SIDS prevention: 3000 lives saved but we can do better', *New Zealand Medical Journal*, 2012, vol. 125, no. 1359, pp. 50–57.

8 H. C. Kinney and B. T. Thach, 'The sudden infant death syndrome', *The New England Journal of Medicine*, 2009, vol. 361, no. 8, pp. 795–805.

9 A. Perkins, 'Back to sleep: The doctor who helped stem a cot death epidemic', *The Guardian*, 26 August 2016.

10 Ibid.

11 E. A. Mitchell et al., 'Results from the first year of the New Zealand cot death study', *New Zealand Medical Journal*, 1991, vol. 104, no. 906, pp. 71–76.

12 Ibid.

13 P. S. Blair et al., 'Major epidemiological changes in sudden infant death syndrome: A 20-year population-based study in the UK', *The Lancet*, 2006, vol. 376, no. 9507, pp. 314–319.

14 Ministry of Health New Zealand, 'Fetal and Infant Deaths 2014', published online 31 October 2017, *Ministry of Health*, <www.health.govt.nz/publication/fetal-and-infant-deaths-2014>.

15 E. A. Mitchell, 'Recommendations for sudden infant death syndrome prevention: A discussion document', *Archives of Disease in Childhood*, 2007, vol. 92, no. 2, pp. 155–159.

16 P. S. Blair et al., 'Bed-sharing in the absence of hazardous circumstances: Is there a risk of sudden infant death syndrome? An analysis from two case-control studies conducted in the UK', *PLoS ONE*, 2014, vol. 9, no. 9, e107799.

17 E. A. Mitchell and P. S. Blair, 'SIDS prevention: 3000 lives saved but we can do better', *New Zealand Medical Journal*, 2012, vol. 125, no. 1359, pp. 50–57.

18 E. A. Mitchell, 'Four modifiable and other major risk factors for cot death: The New Zealand study', *Journal of Paediatrics and Child Health*, 1992, vol. 28, no. s1, pp. S3–S8.

19 South Island Alliance, 'Infant mortality and sudden unexpected death in infancy', in 'Determinants of health for children and young people in the South Island 2012', *South Island Alliance*, <www.sialliance.health.nz/our-priorities/child-health/health-reports>.

20 Ministry of Health New Zealand, 'Table 5: Socioeconomic indicators, by gender, Maori and non-Maori, 2013', data sourced from Statistics New Zealand, *Ministry of Health*, <www.health.govt.nz/our-work/populations/maori-health/tatau-kahukura-maori-health-statistics/nga-awe-o-te-hauora-socioeconomic-determinants-health/socioeconomic-indicators>.

21 P. S. Blair et al., 'Babies sleeping with parents: Case-control study of factors influencing the risk of the sudden infant death syndrome', *British Medical Journal*, 1999, vol. 319, no. 7223, pp. 1457–1462.

22 P. S. Blair et al., 'Major epidemiological changes in sudden infant death syndrome: A 20-year population-based study in the UK', *The Lancet*, 2006, vol. 376, no. 9507, pp. 314–319.

23 P. S. Blair et al., 'Relationship between bed-sharing and breastfeeding: Longitudinal population-based analysis', *Pediatrics*, 2010, vol. 126, no. 5, e1119–e1126.

24 E. A. Mitchell, 'Bed sharing and the risk of sudden infant death: Parents need clear instructions', *Current Pediatric Reviews*, 2010, vol. 6, no. 1.

25 Ibid.

26 R. Carpenter et al., 'Bed sharing when parents do not smoke: Is there a risk of SIDS? An individual level analysis of five major studies', *BMJ Open*, 2012, vol. 3, no. 5, e002299.

27 S. A. Baddock et al., 'Differences in infant and parent behaviors during routine bed sharing compared with cot sleeping in the home setting', *Pediatrics*, 2006, vol. 117, no. 5.

28 P. S. Blair et al., 'Bed-sharing in the absence of hazardous circumstances: Is there a risk of sudden infant death syndrome? An analysis from two case-control studies conducted in the UK', *PLoS ONE*, 2014, vol. 9, no. 9, e107799.

29 Ibid.

30 Kaysha Brownlie, 'Mother ignored repeated warnings', *Hawke's Bay Today*, 5 December 2015.

31 Tim Potter, 'Wichita parents charged with involuntary manslaughter in death of baby at motel', *The Wichita Eagle*, 4 September 2018, <www.kansas.com/news/local/crime/article217801430.html>.

32 S. A. Baddock et al., 'Wahakura versus bassinet for safe infant sleep: A randomized trial', *Pediatrics*, 2017, vol. 139, no. 2, e20160162.

33 David Tipene-Leach, 'The wahakura: The safe bed-sharing project', 5 March 2007,

Manageme, <www.manageme.org.nz/assets/Uploads/W-Wahakura-book-Sudden-Infant-Death-Syndrome-instructions.pdf>.

34 'Wahakura/Pepi-Pods', undated, *Whanganui District Health Board*, <www.wdhb.org.nz/content/page/wahakura-pepi-pods/m/0/pre/3555>.

35 Andrea Hsu, 'Rethinking SIDS: Many deaths no longer a mystery', *National Public Radio* (NPR), 15 July 2011, <www.npr.org/2011/07/15/137859024>.

36 F. R. Hauck et al., 'Breastfeeding and reduced risk of sudden infant death syndrome: A meta-analysis', *Pediatrics*, 2011, vol. 128, no. 1, pp. 103–110.

37 J. M. D. Thompson et al., 'Duration of breastfeeding and risk of SIDS: An individual participant data meta-analysis', *Pediatrics*, 2017, vol. 140, no. 5, e20171324.

CHAPTER 11: BREASTFEEDING: NICE, BUT NEVER NECESSARY

1 S. Yang et al., 'Do population-based interventions widen or narrow socio-economic inequalities? The case of breastfeeding promotion', *International Journal of Epidemiology*, 2014, vol. 43, no. 4, pp. 1284–1294.

2 S. Yang et al., 'Breastfeeding during infancy and neurocognitive function in adolescence: 16-year follow-up of the PROBIT cluster-randomised trial', *PLOS Medicine*, 20 April 2018, <www.doi.org/10.1371/journal.pmed.1002554>.

3 C. R. Cardwell et al., 'Breast-feeding and childhood-onset type 1 diabetes', *Diabetes Care*, 2012, vol. 35, no. 11, pp. 2215–2225.

4 E. Evenhouse and S. Reilly, 'Improved estimates of the benefits of breastfeeding using sibling comparisons to reduce selection bias', *Health Services Research*, 2005, vol. 40, no. 6, pt 1, pp. 1781–1802.

5 Hutt Valley Maternity Care, 'Artificial Feeding Policy', document ID MATY009, undated, *Hutt Maternity*, available under Health Professionals > Policies & Guidelines > Breastfeeding—Maternity Policies and Guidelines or <www.huttmaternity.org.nz/content/548c2302-db48-44e0-b67c-fe3dbd00a4b5.cmr>.

6 La Leche League International, 'Philosophy', undated, *La Leche League International*, <www.llli.org/about/philosophy>.

7 R. J. Saadheh, 'The role of mother support groups', WHO, 1993, p. 66.

8 Global Breastfeeding Collective, 'Global Breastfeeding Collective', undated, *World Health Organization*, <www.who.int/nutrition/topics/global-breastfeeding-collective>.

9 *WHO Bulletin of the World Health Organization*, 2017, vol. 95, pp. 621–623.

10 World Health Organization and UNICEF, 'Baby-friendly Hospital Initiative', undated, *World Health Organization*, <www.who.int/nutrition/topics/bfhi>.

11 NZBA Baby Friendly Aotearoa New Zealand, 'Baby Friendly Hospital Initiative (BFHI)', undated, *NZBA*, <www.babyfriendly.org.nz/going-baby-friendly/baby-friendly-hospital-initiative-bfhi>.

12 NZBA Baby Friendly Aotearoa New Zealand, 'Submission to the Government Administration Committee on the Parental Leave and Employment Protection (Six Months' Paid Leave) Amendment Bill', October 2012, *New Zealand Parliament*, <www.parliament.nz/en/pb/sc/submissions-and-advice/document/50SCGA_EVI_00DBHOH_BILL11276_1_A280885/new-zealand-breastfeeding-authority-incorporated>.

13 NZBA Baby Friendly Aotearoa New Zealand, 'BFHI Accredited Facilities', accreditation dates listed to August 2018, *NZBA*, <www.babyfriendly.org.nz/going-baby-friendly/baby-friendly-hospital-initiative-bfhi/bfhi-accredited-facilities>.

14 NZBA Baby Friendly Aotearoa New Zealand, 'Baby Friendly Hospital Initiative (BFHI)', undated, *NZBA*, <www.babyfriendly.org.nz/going-baby-friendly/baby-friendly-hospital-initiative-bfhi>.

15 'New federal standard to improve safety of infant slings take effect', 1 February 2018, *United States Consumer Product Safety Commission*, <www.cpsc.gov/content/new-federal-standard-to-improve-safety-of-infant-slings-takes-effect>.

16 UNICEF and WHO, 'Baby Friendly Hospital Initiative Part Two: The New Zealand Criteria', July 2017, *NZBA*, available at <www.babyfriendly.org.nz/going-baby-friendly/baby-friendly-hospital-initiative-bfhi/bfhi-documents>, p. 16.

17 Ibid., p. 8.

18 E. R. Moore et al., 'Early skin-to-skin contact for mothers and their healthy newborn infants', *Cochrane Database of Systematic Reviews*, May 2012, <www.ncbi.nlm.nih.gov/pubmed/22592691>, (not peer reviewed).

19 NZBA Baby Friendly Aotearoa New Zealand, 'Skin to Skin Contact—Kiri ki te kiri', updated 6 March 2018, *NZBA*, available at <www.babyfriendly.org.nz/education/resources>.

20 Hutt Valley Maternity Care, 'Skin to Skin Care Following Birth Policy', document ID MATY067, November 2009, *Hutt Maternity*, available under Health Professionals > Policies & Guidelines > Postnatal—Maternity Policies and Guidelines or <www.huttmaternity.org.nz/content/4e616a6e-88b9-48dc-8033-5dfaa418534a.cmr>.

21 E. R. Moore et al., 'Early skin-to-skin contact for mothers and their healthy newborn infants', *Cochrane Database of Systematic Reviews*, May 2012, <www.ncbi.nlm.nih.gov/pubmed/22592691>, (not peer reviewed).

22 NZBA Baby Friendly Aotearoa New Zealand, 'WHO/UNICEF Baby Friendly Hospital Initiative', p. 2.

23 BFCI (Baby Friendly Community Initiative), 'Implementing the standards of care for the non-breastfeeding mother and her baby', undated, *NZBA*, available at <www.

babyfriendly.org.nz/going-baby-friendly/baby-friendly-community-initiative-bfci/ standards-of-care-for-the-non-breastfeeding-mother-and-her-baby>.

24 G. John-Stewart et al, 'Breast-feeding and transmission of HIV-1', *Journal of Acquired Immune Deficiency Syndromes*, 2004, vol. 35, no. 2, pp. 196–202.

25 Gerald Keusch et al., 'Diarrheal Diseases' (ch. 19) in *Disease Control Priorities in Developing Countries*, 2nd edition, New York: Oxford University Press, 2006.

26 Danielle Clent, 'Parents forced to sign hospital consent forms to feed their babies formula', *Stuff*, 28 November 2017.

27 World Health Organization, 'Pneumonia' (fact sheet), 7 November 2016, *World Health Organization*, <www.who.int/news-room/fact-sheets/detail/pneumonia>; and 'Diarrhoeal disease' (fact sheet), 2 May 2017, *World Health Organization*, <www.who.int/news-room/fact-sheets/detail/diarrhoeal-disease>.

28 Gerald Keusch et al., 'Diarrheal Diseases' (ch. 19) in *Disease Control Priorities in Developing Countries*, 2nd edition, New York: Oxford University Press, 2006, p. 373.

29 J. Clemens et al., 'Breastfeeding and the risk of life-threatening rotavirus diarrhoea: Prevention or postponement?', *Paediatrics*, 1993, vol. 92, no. 5, pp. 680–685.

30 T. Fischer et al., 'Hospitalizations and deaths from diarrhea and rotavirus among children <5 years of age in the United States, 1993–2003', *The Journal of Infectious Diseases*, 2007, vol. 195, no. 8, pp. 1117–1125.

31 World Health Organization, 'Pneumonia' (fact sheet), 7 November 2016, *World Health Organization*, <www.who.int/news-room/fact-sheets/detail/pneumonia>.

32 R. E. Black et al., 'Global, regional and national causes of child mortality in 2008: A systematic analysis', *The Lancet*, 2010, vol. 375, no. 9730, pp. 1969–1987.

33 S. F. Dowell et al., 'Mortality from pneumonia in children in the United States, 1939 through 1996', *The New England Journal of Medicine*, 2000, vol. 342, no. 19, pp. 1399–1407; and 'Ross Laboratories Mothers Survey (RLMS)', data available through: Ross Products Division of Abbott Laboratories, Columbus, OH 43215, attention: Alan Ryan.

34 AAP (American Academy of Pediatrics) Committee on Nutrition, 'Iron fortification of infant formulas', *Pediatrics*, 1999, vol. 104, no. 1, pp. 119–123.

35 G. Heresi et al., 'Effect of supplementation with an iron-fortified milk on incidence of diarrhoea and respiratory infection in urban-resident infants', *Scandinavian Journal of Infectious Diseases*, 1995, vol. 27, no. 4, pp. 385–389.

36 P. D. Scariati et al., 'Risk of diarrhea related to iron content of infant formula: Lack of evidence to support the use of low-iron formula as a supplement for breastfed infants', *Pediatrics*, 1997, vol. 99, no. 3, E2, p. 1.

37 AAP (American Academy of Pediatrics) Committee on Nutrition, 'Iron fortification of infant formulas', *Pediatrics*, 1999, vol. 104, no. 1, pp. 119–123.

38 Based on an AAP clinical report; see R. D. Baker et al., 'Diagnosis and prevention of iron deficiency and iron-deficiency anemia in infants and young children (0–3 years of age)', *Pediatrics*, 2010, vol. 126, no. 5, pp. 1040–1050.

39 S. við Streym et al., 'Vitamin D content in human breast milk: A 9-mo[nth] follow-up study', *The American Journal of Clinical Nutrition*, vol. 103, no. 1, pp. 107–114.

40 American Academy of Pediatrics, 'Vitamin D & iron supplements for babies: AAP recommendations', last updated 27 May 2016, *Healthychildren.org*, <www.healthychildren.org/English/ages-stages/baby/feeding-nutrition/Pages/Vitamin-Iron-Supplements.aspx>.

41 BFCI, 'Implementing the standards of care for the non-breastfeeding mother and her baby', undated, *NZBA*, available at <www.babyfriendly.org.nz/going-baby-friendly/baby-friendly-community-initiative-bfci/standards-of-care-for-the-non-breastfeeding-mother-and-her-baby>, p. 3.

42 Ministry of Health New Zealand, 'Mastitis and breast abscesses', last reviewed 7 February 2014, *Ministry of Health*, <www.health.govt.nz/our-work/life-stages/breastfeeding/health-practitioners/mastitis-and-breast-abscesses>.

43 V. Khanal et al., 'Incidence of mastitis in the neonatal period in a traditional breastfeeding society: Results of a cohort study', *Breastfeeding Medicine*, 2015, vol. 10, no. 10, pp. 481–487.

44 Laura Wright, 'Breast is best fanatics left me weeping with pain: One woman's story of the pressure she felt to breastfeed her infant daughter', *Daily Mail Australia*, 5 March 2015.

45 J. L. Matthew, 'Effect of maternal antibiotics on breastfeeding infants', *Postgrad Medical Journal*, 2004, vol. 80, no. 942, pp. 196–200.

46 BFCI, 'Implementing the standards of care for the non-breastfeeding mother and her baby', undated, *NZBA*, available at <www.babyfriendly.org.nz/going-baby-friendly/baby-friendly-community-initiative-bfci/standards-of-care-for-the-non-breastfeeding-mother-and-her-baby>, p. 4.

47 C. Caniçali Primo et al., 'Effects of maternal nicotine on breastfeeding infants', 2013, *Pediatria*, vol. 31, no. 3, pp. 392–397.

48 M. B. Haastrup et al., 'Alcohol and breastfeeding', *Basic & Clinical Pharmacology & Toxicology*, 2014, vol. 114, no. 2, pp. 168–173.

49 Kevin Helliker, 'Dying for milk: Some mothers, trying in vain to breastfeed, starve their infants'. *Wall Street Journal*, 22 July 1994, cited in I. Laing and C. Wong, 'Hypernatraemia in the first few days: Is the incidence rising?', *Archives of Disease in Childhood Fetal & Neonatal Edition*, 2002, vol. 87, no. 3, pp. F158–F162.

50 I. Laing and C. Wong, 'Hypernatraemia in the first few days: Is the incidence rising?', *Archives of Disease in Childhood Fetal & Neonatal Edition*, 2002, vol. 87, no. 3, pp. F158–F162.

51 V. H. Livingstone et al., 'Neonatal hypernatremic dehydration associated with breast-feeding malnutrition: A retrospective survey, *Canadian Medical Association Journal*, 2000, vol. 162, no. 5, pp. 647–652.

52 M. L. Moritz et al., 'Breastfeeding-associated hypernatremia: Are we missing the diagnosis?', *Pediatrics*, 2005, vol. 116, no. 3, e343–347.

53 Plunket, 'Annual breastfeeding statistics', 2008–2017, *Plunket*, <www.plunket.org.nz/news-and-research/research-from-plunket/plunket-breastfeeding-data-analysis/annual-breastfeeding-statistics>.

54 NZBA Baby Friendly Aotearoa New Zealand, 'Artificial Feeding Policy', undated, *NZBA*, <www.babyfriendly.org.nz/fileadmin/user_upload/Artificial_Feeding__Policy.pdf>.

55 BFCI, 'Implementing the standards of care for the non-breastfeeding mother and her baby', undated, *NZBA*, available at <www.babyfriendly.org.nz/going-baby-friendly/baby-friendly-community-initiative-bfci/standards-of-care-for-the-non-breastfeeding-mother-and-her-baby>, p. 2.

56 Mike Muller, *The Baby Killer: A War on Want investigation into the promotion and sale of powdered baby milks in the Third World*, London: War on Want, 1974, available at <www.waronwant.org/resources/baby-killer>.

57 World Health Organization, *International Code of Marketing of Breast-Milk Substitutes*, Geneva: World Health Organization, 1981, available at <www.who.int/nutrition/publications/code_english.pdf>.

58 IBFAN (International Baby Food Action Network), 'The convention on the rights of the child: Report on the situation of breastfeeding in New Zealand', 2011, *IBFAN*, <www.ibfan.org/art/IBFAN-56_NewZealand2011.pdf>.

59 M. Johnston, 'Infant formula should be prescription only—maternity group', *The New Zealand Herald*, 28 November 2017.

60 Jania Matthews, 'Good intentions that may lead to bad outcomes: Home-made infant formula', 22 October 2013, last updated 16 October 2017, *Food Insight*, <www.foodinsight.org/Good_Intentions_that_May_Lead_to_Bad_Outcomes_Home_Made_Infant_Formula>.

61 R. Jenness, 'The composition of human milk', *Seminars in Perinatology*, 1979, vol. 3, no. 3, pp. 225–239.

62 L. A. Hanson, 'Breastfeeding provides passive and likely long-lasting active immunity', *Annals of Allergy, Asthma & Immunology*, 1998, vol. 81, no. 6, pp. 523–533.

63 P. W. Howie, 'Protective effect of breastfeeding against infection', *Obstetrical and Gynaecological Survey*, 1990, vol. 45, no. 9, pp. 615–616.

64 M. S. Kramer et al., 'Promotion of breastfeeding intervention trial (PROBIT): A randomized trial in the Republic of Belarus', *JAMA* (The Journal of the American Medical Association), 2001, vol. 285, no. 4, pp. 413–420.

65 T. M. Chucri et al., 'A review of immune transfer by the placenta', *Journal of Reproductive Immunology*, 2010, vol. 87, no. 1–2, pp. 14–20.

66 A. K. Simon et al., 'Evolution of the immune system in humans from infancy to old age', *Proceedings of the Royal Society B: Biological Sciences*, 2015, vol. 282, no. 1821, e20143085.

67 Diego Palma, 'Urine therapy', undated, *Sacred Valley Tribe*, <www.sacredvalleytribe.com/articles-and-teachings/urine-therapy>.

68 A. J. Stunkard et al., 'The body-mass index of twins who have been reared apart', *New England Journal of Medicine*, 1990, vol. 322, no. 21, pp. 1483–1487.

69 R. L. Minster et al., 'A thrifty variant in CREBRF strongly influences body mass index in Samoans', *Nature Genetics*, 2016, vol. 48, no. 9, pp. 1049–1054.

70 S. D. Berry et al., 'Widespread prevalence of a CREBRF variant amongst Maori and Pacific children is associated with weight and height in early childhood', 20 September 2017, published in *International Journal of Obesity*, 2018, vol. 42, pp. 603–607.

71 N. A. Christakis and J. H. Fowler, 'The spread of obesity in a large social network over 32 years', *The New England Journal of Medicine*, 2007, vol. 357, no. 4, pp. 370–379.

72 J. Armstrong and J. J. Reilly, 'Breastfeeding and lowering the risk of childhood obesity', *The Lancet*, 8 June 2002, vol. 359, no. 9322, pp. 2003–2004.

73 V. Burke et al., 'Breastfeeding and overweight: Longitudinal analysis in an Australian birth cohort', *The Journal of Pediatrics*, 2005, vol. 147, no. 1, pp. 56–61.

74 M. C. Nelson et al., 'Are adolescents who were breast-fed less likely to be overweight? Analyses of sibling pairs to reduce confounding', *Epidemiology*, 2005, vol. 16, no. 2, pp. 247–253.

75 E. Evenhouse and S. Reilly, 'Improved estimates of the benefits of breastfeeding using sibling comparisons to reduce selection bias', *Health Services Research*, 2005, vol. 40, no. 6, pt 1, pp. 1781–1802.

76 M. S. Kramer et al., 'A randomized breast-feeding promotion intervention did not reduce child obesity in Belarus', *The Journal of Nutrition*, 2009, vol. 139, no. 2, pp. 417S–421S.

77 R. M. Martin et al., 'Effects of promoting long-term, exclusive breastfeeding on adolescent adiposity, blood pressure, and growth trajectories: A secondary analysis of a randomized clinical trial', *JAMA Pediatrics*, 2017, vol. 171, no. 7, e170698.

78 Y. Cao et al., 'Are breastfed infants more resilient? Feeding method and cortisol in infants', *The Journal of Pediatrics*, 2009, vol. 154, no. 3, pp. 452–454.

79 B. de Lauzon-Guillain et al., 'Breastfeeding and infant temperament at age three months', *PLoS One*, 2012, vol. 7, no. 1, e29326.

80 Press Association, 'Breastfed babies show more challenging temperaments, study finds', *The Guardian*, 10 January 2012.

81 T. Sasaka et al., 'Type of feeding during infancy and later development of schizophrenia', *Schizophrenia Research*, 2000, vol. 42, no. 1, pp. 79–82; and M. Amore et al., 'Can breastfeeding protect against schizophrenia? Case-control study', *Biology of the Neonate*, 2003, vol. 83, no. 2, pp. 97–101.

82 S. J. Leask et al., 'No association between breastfeeding and adult psychosis in two national birth cohorts', *The British Journal of Psychiatry*, 2000, vol. 177, no. 3, pp. 218–221.

83 See D. M. Fergusson and L. J. Woodward, 'Breastfeeding and later psychosocial adjustment', *Paediatric and Perinatal Epidemiology*, 1999, vol. 13, no. 2, pp. 144–157.

84 'Ross Laboratories Mothers Survey (RLMS)', data available through: Ross Products Division of Abbott Laboratories, Columbus, OH 43215, USA, attention: Alan Ryan. Various additional sources used for graph data, but in particular A. S. Ryan et al., 'Breastfeeding continues to increase into the new millennium', *Pediatrics*, 2002, vol. 110, no. 6, pp. 1103–1109.

85 L. Girard et al., 'Breastfeeding, cognitive and noncognitive development in early childhood: A population study', *Pediatrics*, 2017, vol. 139, no. 4, e20161848.

86 M. B. Belfort, 'Infant feeding and childhood cognition at ages 3 and 7 years: Effects of breastfeeding duration and exclusivity', *JAMA Pediatrics*, 2013, vol. 167, no. 9, pp. 836–844.

87 A. Walfisch et al., 'Breast milk and cognitive development—the role of confounders: A systematic review', *BMJ Open*, vol. 3, no. 8, e003259.

88 Ibid.

89 G. Der et al., 'Effect of breast feeding on intelligence in children: Prospective study, sibling pairs analysis, and meta-analysis', *The BMJ*, 2006, vol. 333, 945.

90 S. Yang et al., 'Breastfeeding during infancy and neurocognitive function in adolescence: 16-year follow-up of the PROBIT cluster-randomised trial', *PLOS Medicine*, 20 April 2018, <www.doi.org/10.1371/journal.pmed.1002554>.

91   P. Willatts et al., 'Effects of long-chain PUFA supplementation in infant formula on cognitive function in later childhood', *American Journal of Clinical Nutrition*, 2013, vol. 98, no 2, pp. 5365–5425.

92   C. R. Gale et al., 'Breastfeeding, the use of docosahexaenoic acid-fortified formulas in infancy and neuropsychological function in childhood', *Archives of Disease in Childhood Fetal and Neonatal Edition*, 2009, vol. 95, no. 3, pp. 174–179.

CHAPTER 12: THE RIGHT WAY TO FEED—BREAST OR BOTTLE

1   UNICEF UK Baby Friendly Initiative, 'Responsive feeding: Supporting close and loving relationships', October 2016, *UNICEF UK*, <www.unicef.org.uk/babyfriendly/baby-friendly-resources/relationship-building-resources/responsive-feeding-infosheet>.

2   Ministry of Health New Zealand, *Report on Maternity 2015*, Wellington: Ministry of Health, 2017; and Plunket, 'Annual breastfeeding statistics', 2008–2017, *Plunket*, <www.plunket.org.nz/news-and-research/research-from-plunket/plunket-breastfeeding-data-analysis/annual-breastfeeding-statistics>.

3   Robert Karen, *Becoming Attached: First relationships and how they shape our capacity to love*, New York: Oxford University Press, 1988, p. 157.

4   UNICEF UK Baby Friendly Initiative, 'Responsive feeding: Supporting close and loving relationships', October 2016, *UNICEF UK*, <www.unicef.org.uk/babyfriendly/baby-friendly-resources/relationship-building-resources/responsive-feeding-infosheet>.

5   Ibid., p. 4.

6   Ibid., p. 3.

7   Ibid., p. 2.

CHAPTER 13: BREASTFEEDING: A PRACTICAL GUIDE

1   Ministry of Health New Zealand, 'Mastitis and breast abscesses', last reviewed 7 February 2014, *Ministry of Health*, <www.health.govt.nz/our-work/life-stages/breastfeeding/health-practitioners/mastitis-and-breast-abscesses>.

CHAPTER 14: BOTTLE-FEEDING AND FORMULA: A PRACTICAL GUIDE

1   CDC (Centers for Disease Control and Prevention), 'Breastfeeding Report Card: United States, 2018', last reviewed 20 August 2018, *CDC*, <www.cdc.gov/breastfeeding/data/reportcard.htm>.

2   Clare Naden, 'New standards for testing infant formula just published', 10 July 2018, *ISO* (International Organization for Standardization), <www.iso.org/news/ref2308.html>.

CHAPTER 15: IMMUNISATION

1   Jonathan B. Tucker, *Scourge: The once and future threat of smallpox*, New York: Atlantic Monthly Press, 2001.

2   Joseph Needham, *Science and Civilization in China: Volume VI Biology and Biological Technology, Part 6 Medicine*, Cambridge: Cambridge University Press, 2000, p. 134.

3   François Marie Arouet de Voltaire, 'Letter XI—On Inoculation' in *Letters on the English*, The Harvard Classics, vol. 34, pt 2, New York: P. F. Collier & Son, 1909–14, available at <www.bartleby.com/34/2/11.html>.

4   Ibid.

5   Emily Oster and Geoffrey Kocks, 'After a debacle, how California became a role model on measles', *The New York Times*, 16 January 2018.

6   CDC (Centers for Disease Control and Prevention), 'Measles Outbreak—California, December 2014–February 2015', *Morbidity and Mortality Weekly Report*, 20 February 2015, vol. 64, no. 6, pp. 153–154.

7   Katie Palmer, 'Why did vaccinated people get measles at Disneyland? Blame the unvaccinated', *Wired*, 26 January 2015, <www.wired.com/2015/01/vaccinated-people-get-measles-disneyland-blame-unvaccinated>.

8   K. Bohlke et al., 'Risk of anaphylaxis after vaccination of children and adolescents', *Pediatrics*, 2003, vol. 112, no. 4, pp. 815–820.

9   E. R. Miller et al., 'Deaths following vaccination: What does the evidence show?', *Vaccine*, 2015, vol. 33, no. 29, pp. 3288–3292.

10 Dominic Godfrey, 'Medical error likely cause of Samoa baby deaths—vaccinologist', *RNZ* (Radio New Zealand), 26 July 2018, <www.radionz.co.nz/international/pacific-news/362706/medical-error-likely-cause-of-samoa-baby-deaths-vaccinologist>.

11 Ibid.

12 N. L. McCarthy et al., 'Mortality rates and cause-of-death patterns in a vaccinated population', *American Journal of Preventive Medicine*, 2013, vol. 45, no. 1, pp. 91–97.

13 R. Desai et al., 'Trends in intussusception-associated deaths among US infants given an oral rotavirus vaccine from 1979–2007', *Pediatrics*, 2012, vol. 160, no. 3, pp. 456–460.

14 Committee on the Assessment of Studies of Health Outcomes Related to the Recommended Childhood Immunization Schedule, *The Childhood Immunization Schedule and Safety: Stakeholder concerns, scientific evidence, and future studies*, Washington DC: National Academic Press, 2013, available at <https://www.ncbi.nlm.nih.gov/pubmed/24901198>.

15 J. M. Glanz et al., 'Association between estimated cumulative vaccine antigen exposure

through the first 23 months of life and non-vaccine-targeted infections from 24 through 47 months of age', *JAMA*, 2018, vol. 319, no. 9, pp. 906–913.

16   A. Hvid et al., 'Childhood vaccination and nontargeted infectious disease hospitalization', *JAMA*, 2005, vol. 294, no. 6, pp. 699–705.

17   Jessica Wright, 'The real reasons autism rates are up in the US', *Scientific American*, 3 March 2017, <www.scientificamerican.com/article/the-real-reasons-autism-rates-are-up-in-the-u-s>.

18   Ibid.

19   J. S. Gindler et al., 'Update—The United States measles epidemic, 1989–1990', *Epidemiologic Reviews*, 1992, vol. 14, no. 1, pp. 270–276.

20   Brian Deer, 'Dispatches: MMR—What they didn't tell you' (Brian Deer's 2004 film on Andrew Wakefield), broadcast in the UK on 18 November 2004, *Brian Deer Award-winning Investigations*, <www.briandeer.com/wakefield/mmr-what-they-didnt-tell-you. htm>.

21   The Associated Press, 'Measles uptick in Britain: Blame Andrew Wakefield's autism-vaccine study?', *CBS News*, 20 May 2013.

22   CDC (Centers for Disease Control and Prevention), '[Chickenpox] Complications', last reviewed 1 July 2016, *CDC*, <www.cdc.gov/chickenpox/about/complications.html>.

CHAPTER 16: TECHNOLOGY AND THE DEVELOPING BRAIN

1   J. S. Radesky et al., 'Patterns of mobile device use by caregivers and children during meals in fast food restaurants', *Pediatrics*, 2014, vol. 133, no. 4, e843–e849.

2   S. Myruski et al., 'Digital disruption? Maternal mobile device use is related to infant social-emotional functioning', *Developmental Science*, 2018, vol. 21, no. 4, e12610.

3   H. K. Kabali et al., 'Exposure and use of mobile media devices by young children', *Pediatrics*, 2015, vol. 136, no. 6, pp. 1044–1050.

4   Y. R. Chassiakos et al., 'Children and adolescents and digital media', *Pediatrics*, 2016, vol. 138, issue 5, e20162593.

5   A. Brown, 'Media use by children younger than 2 years', *Pediatrics*, 2011, vol. 128, no. 5, pp. 1040–1045.

6   S. Dayanim and L. Namy, 'Infants learn baby signs from video', *Child Development*, 2015, vol. 86, no. 3, pp. 800–811.

7   A. Christakis et al., 'Modifying media content for preschool children: A randomized controlled trial', *Pediatrics*, 2013, vol. 131, issue 3, pp. 431–438.

8   A. I. Nathanson et al., 'The relation between television exposure and executive function among pre-schoolers', *Developmental Psychology*, 2014, vol. 50, pp. 1497–1506.

9   The Dunedin Multidisciplinary Health and Development Unit, 'The Dunedin Multidisciplinary Health and Development Study', undated, *The Dunedin Study*, <https://dunedinstudy.otago.ac.nz/studies>.

10 C. E. Landhuis et al., 'Does childhood television viewing lead to attention problems in adolescence? Results from a prospective longitudinal study', *Pediatrics*, 2007, vol. 120, issue 3, pp. 532–537.

11 A. Przybylski and N. Weinstein, 'Digital screen time limits and young children's psychological well-being: Evidence from a population-based study', *Child Development*, 2017, ePub ahead of print, available at <www.doi.org/10.1111/cdev.13007>.

12 A. M. Weinstein, 'An update overview on brain imaging studies of internet gaming disorder', *Frontiers in Psychiatry*, 2017, vol. 8, no. 185, <www.doi.org/10.3389/fpsyt.2017.00185>.

13 Naomi Schaefer Riley, *Be the Parent, Please: Stop banning seesaws and start banning Snapchat—Strategies for solving the real parenting problems*, Pennsylvania: Templeton Press: 2018.

14 Anya Kamenetz, *The Art of Screen Time: How your family can balance digital media and real life*, New York: Ingram Publisher Services, 2018.

CHAPTER 17: NANNIES, DAYCARE AND WORKING MOTHERS

1   D. Cohn et al., 'After decades of decline, a rise in stay-at-home mothers', *Pew Research Center, Social and Demographic Trends*, 8 April 2014, <www.pewsocialtrends.org/2014/04/08/after-decades-of-decline-a-rise-in-stay-at-home-mothers>.

2   Ibid.

3   M. Wallace et al., 'Returning to work one year after childbirth: Data from the mother-child cohort EDEN', *Maternal Child Health Journal*, 2013, vol. 17, no. 8, pp. 1432–1440.

4   E. Pylkkänen and N. Smith, 'Career interruptions due to parental leave—A comparative study of Denmark and Sweden', OECD Social, Employment and Migration Working Papers 1, 2003, *OECD*, <www.oecd.org/sweden/2502336.pdf>.

5   S. Offer and B. Schneider, 'Revisiting the gender gap in time-use patterns: Multitasking and well-being among mothers and fathers in dual-earner families', *American Sociological Review*, 2011, vol. 76, no. 6, pp. 809–833; and S. Offer, 'The costs of thinking about work and family: Mental labor, work–family spillover, and gender inequality among parents in dual-earner families', 2014, *Sociological Forum*, vol. 29, no. 4, pp. 916–936.

6   J. Belsky, 'Infant daycare: A cause for concern?', *Zero to Three*, 1986, vol. 7, no. 1, pp. 1–7.

7   J. Belsky, 'The "Effects" of infant daycare reconsidered', *Early Childhood Research Quarterly*, 1988, vol. 3, no. 3, pp. 235–272.

8   G. Fein and N. Fox, 'Infant daycare: A special issue', *Early Childhood Research Quarterly*, 1988, vol. 3, no. 3, pp. 227–234.

9   M. Bornstein et al., 'Long-term cumulative effects of childcare on children's mental development and socioemotional adjustment in a non-risk sample: The moderating effects of gender', *Early Child Development and Care*, 2006, vol. 176, no. 2, pp. 129–156.

10 R. Lucas-Thompson et al., 'Maternal work early in the lives of children and its distal associations with achievement and behaviour problems: A meta-analysis', *Psychological Bulletin*, 2010, vol. 136, no. 6, pp. 915–942.

11 C. M. Lombardi and R. L. Coley, 'Early maternal employment and children's school readiness in contemporary families', *Developmental Psychology*, 2014, vol. 50, no. 8, pp. 2071–2084.

12 M. Gunnar et al., 'The stressfulness of separation among nine-month-old infants: Effects of social context variables and infant temperament', *Child Development*, 1992, vol. 63, no. 2, pp. 290–303.

13 J. Brooks-Gunn et al., 'First-year maternal employment and child development in the first seven years', *Monographs of the Society for Research in Child Development*, 2010, vol. 75, no. 2

14 A. Huston and S. R. Aronson, 'Mothers' time with infant and time in employment as predictors of mother–child relationship and children's early development', *Child Development*, 2005, vol. 76, no. 2, pp. 467–482

15 J. Brooks-Gunn, 'First-year maternal employment and child development in the first seven years', *Monographs of the Society for Research in Child Development*, 2010, vol. 75, no. 2, pp. 7–9.

16 Ibid.

17 E. A. Ruzek et al., 'The quality of toddler child care and cognitive skills at 24 months: Propensity score analysis results from the ECLS-B', *Early Childhood Research Quarterly*, 2014, vol. 28, no. 1, pp. 12–21.

18 NICHD (National Institute of Child Health and Human Development, US), 'The NICHD study of early child care and youth development: Findings for children up to age 4½ years', 2006, *NICHD*, <www.nichd.nih.gov/publications/pubs/documents/seccyd_06.pdf>, (includes a parent's checklist for assessing a child-care facility).

19 J. Belsky et al., 'Do effects of early child care extend to age 15 years? Results from the NICHD study of early child care and youth development', *Child Development*, 2010, vol. 81, no. 3, pp. 737–756.

20 E. A. Ruzek et al., 'The quality of toddler child care and cognitive skills at 24 months: Propensity score analysis results from the ECLS-B', *Early Childhood Research Quarterly*, 2014, vol. 28, no. 1, pp. 12–21.

21 NICHD, 'The NICHD study of early child care and youth development: Findings for children up to age 4½ years', 2006, *NICHD*, <www.nichd.nih.gov/publications/pubs/documents/seccyd_06.pdf>.

22 'Education (Early Childhood Services) Regulations 2008', Order in Council made by Anand Satyanand, Governor-General, 7 July 2008, reprinted 29 September 2018, pp. 43–45, available at <www.legislation.govt.nz/regulation/public/2008/0204/42.0/DLM1412501.html>.

23 M. Bornstein et al., 'Long-term cumulative effects of childcare on children's mental development and socioemotional adjustment in a non-risk sample: The moderating effects of gender', *Early Child Development and Care*, 2006, vol. 176, no. 2, pp. 129–156.

24 NICHD, 'The NICHD study of early child care and youth development: Findings for children up to age 4½ years', 2006, *NICHD*, <www.nichd.nih.gov/publications/pubs/documents/seccyd_06.pdf>, p. 37.

25 Y. Cao et al., 'Are breastfed infants more resilient? Feeding method and cortisol in infants', *The Journal of Pediatrics*, 2009, vol. 154, no. 3, pp. 452–454.

26 J. M. Mateo, 'Inverted-U shape relationship between cortisol and learning in ground squirrels', *Neurobiology of Learning and Memory*, 2007, vol. 89, no. 4, pp. 582–590.

27 D. M. Lyons and K. J. Parker, 'Stress inoculation-induced indications of resilience in monkeys', *Journal of Traumatic Stress*, 2007, vol. 20, no. 4, pp. 423–433.

28 M. Gunnar et al., 'The stressfulness of separation among nine-month-old infants: Effects of social context variables and infant temperament', *Child Development*, 1992, vol. 63, no. 2, pp. 290–303.

29 E. P. Davis et al., 'The start of a new school year: Individual differences in salivary cortisol response in relation to child temperament', *Developmental Psychobiology*, 1999, vol. 35, no. 3, pp. 188–196.

30 Interview with Belsky in Robert Karen, *Becoming Attached: First relationships and how they shape our capacity to love*, New York: Oxford University Press, 1988, p. 336.

APPENDIX I: DIARRHEAL DISEASES AND BREASTFEEDING

1   M. S. Kramer et al., 'Promotion of breastfeeding intervention trial (PROBIT): A randomized trial in the Republic of Belarus', *JAMA* (The Journal of the American Medical Association), 2001, vol. 285, no. 4, pp. 413–420.

2   P. W. Howie et al., 'Protective effect of breast feeding against infection', *The BMJ*, 1990, vol. 300, no. 6716, pp. 11–16.

3   R. J. Weinberg, 'Effect of breast-feeding on morbidity in rotavirus gastroenteritis', *Pediatrics*, 1984, vol. 74, no. 2, pp. 250–253.

4   M. Gurwith, 'A prospective study of rotavirus infection', *The Journal of Infectious Diseases*, 1981, vol. 1444, no. 3, pp. 218–224.

APPENDIX II: RESPIRATORY ILLNESSES AND BREASTFEEDING

1   H. Bauchner et al., 'Studies of breast-feeding and infections: How good is the evidence?', *JAMA*, 1986, vol. 256, no. 7, pp. 887–892.

2   L. L. Jones et al., 'Parental smoking and the risk of middle ear disease in children: A systematic review and meta-analysis', *Archives of Pediatrics and Adolescent Medicine*, 2012, vol. 166, no. 1, pp. 18–27.

3   W. H. Oddy et al., 'Breast feeding and respiratory morbidity in infancy: A birth cohort study', *Archives of Disease in Childhood*, 2002, vol. 2003, no. 88, pp. 224–228.

4   I. Tromp et al., 'Breastfeeding and the risk of respiratory tract infections after infancy: The generation R study', *PLOS One*, 2017, vol. 12, no. 2, e0172763

5   P. K. Pletch and A. T. Kratz, 'Why do women stop smoking during pregnancy? Cigarettes taste and smell bad', *Health Care for Women International*, 2004, vol. 25, no. 7, pp. 671–679.

6   D. G. Cook and D. P. Strachan, 'Summary of effects of parental smoking on the respiratory health of children and implications for research', *Thorax*, 1999, vol. 54, no. 4, pp. 357–366.

7   L. Blizzard et al., 'Parental smoking and infant respiratory infection: How important is not smoking in the same room with the baby?', *American Journal of Public Health*, 2003, vol. 93, no. 3, pp. 482–488.

8   UNICEF UK Baby Friendly Initiative, 'Respiratory Illness', undated, *UNICEF UK*, <www.unicef.org.uk/babyfriendly/news-and-research/baby-friendly-research/infant-health-research/infant-health-research-respiratory-illness>.

9   V. R. Bachrach et al., 'Breastfeeding and the risk of hospitalization for respiratory disease in infancy: A meta-analysis', *Archives of Pediatrics & Adolescent Medicine*, 2003, vol. 157, no. 3, pp. 237–243.

10 M. S. Kramer et al., 'Promotion of breastfeeding intervention trial (PROBIT): A randomized trial in the Republic of Belarus', *JAMA*, 2001, vol. 285, no. 4, pp. 413–420 (reference to smoking p. 418).

APPENDIX III: URINARY TRACT DISEASES AND BREASTFEEDING

1   J. M. Stansfeld, 'Clinical observations relating to incidence and aetiology of urinary-tract infections in children', *British Medical Journal*, 1966, vol. 1, no. 5488, pp. 631–635.

2   S. Hellerstein, 'Urinary tract infections in children: Why they occur and how to prevent them', *American Family Physician*, 1998, vol. 57, no. 10, pp. 2440–2446.

3   M. Katouli, 'Population structure of gut Escherichia coli and its role in development of extra-intestinal infections', *Iran Journal of Microbiology*, 2010, vol. 2, no. 2, pp. 59–72.

4   J. M. Stansfeld, 'Clinical observations relating to incidence and aetiology of urinary-tract infections in children', *British Medical Journal*, 1966, vol. 1, no. 5488, pp. 631–635.

5   L. A. Hanson, 'Protective effects of breastfeeding against urinary tract infection', *Acta Paediatrica*, 2004, vol. 93, no. 2, pp. 154–156.

6   S. Marild et al., 'Protective effect of breastfeeding against urinary tract infection', *Acta Paediatrica*, 2004, vol. 93, no. 2, pp. 164–168.

7   R. Katikaneni, 'Breastfeeding does not protect against urinary tract infection in the first 3 months of life, but vitamin D supplementation increases the risk by 76 per cent', *Clinical Pediatrics*, 2009, vol. 48, no. 7, pp. 750–755.

APPENDIX IV: TYPE 1 DIABETES AND BREASTFEEDING

1   C. R. Cardwell et al., 'Breast-feeding and childhood-onset type 1 diabetes', *Diabetes Care*, 2012, vol. 35, no. 11, pp. 2215–2225.

2   D. M. Maahs et al., 'Epidemiology of type 1 diabetes', *Endocrinology Metabolism Clinics of North America*, 2010, vol. 39, no. 3, pp. 481–497.

3   Li Hongyang and Chinadaily.com.cn, 'Breast-feeding rate remains low in China', *China-daily.com.cn*, 2 August 2017, < www.chinadaily.com.cn/china/2017-08/02/content_30330467.htm>.

4   Plunket, 'Annual breastfeeding statistics', 2008–2017, *Plunket*, <www.plunket.org.nz/

news-and-research/research-from-plunket/plunket-breastfeeding-data-analysis/annual-breastfeeding-statistics>.

5   W. P. You and M. Henneberg, 'Type 1 diabetes prevalence increasing globally and regionally: The role of natural selection and life expectancy at birth', *BMJ Open Diabetes Research & Care*, 2016, vol. 4, no. 1, e000161.

6   C. R. Cardwell et al., 'Breast-feeding and childhood-onset type 1 diabetes', *Diabetes Care*, 2012, vol. 35, no. 11, pp. 2215–2225.

7   E. Evenhouse and S. Reilly, 'Improved estimates of the benefits of breastfeeding using sibling comparisons to reduce selection bias', *Health Services Research*, 2005, vol. 40, no. 6, pt 1, pp. 1781–1802.

APPENDIX V: ATOPIC CONDITIONS AND BREASTFEEDING

1   T. Y. Lien and R. D. Goldman, 'Breastfeeding and maternal diet in atopic dermatitis', *Canadian Family Physician*, 2011, vol. 57, no. 12, pp. 1403–1405.

2   D. V. Wallace et al., 'The diagnosis and management of rhinitis: An updated practice parameter', *The Journal of Allergy and Clinical Immunology*, 2008, vol. 122, no. 2 suppl., pp. S1–84.

3   D. P. Strachan and D. G. Cook, 'Parental smoking and childhood asthma: Longitudinal and case-control studies', *BMJ Thorax*, 1998, vol. 53, no. 3, pp. 204–212.

4   E. Christiansen et al., 'The prevalence of atopic diseases and the patterns of sensitization in adolescence', *Pediatric Allergy and Immunology*, 2016, vol. 27, no. 8, pp. 847–853.

5   M. S. Kramer, 'Does breast feeding help protect against atopic diseases? Biology, methodology, and a golden jubilee of controversy', *Journal of Pediatrics*, 1988, vol. 112, no. 2, pp. 181–190.

6   M. Gdalevich et al., 'Breast-feeding and the risk of bronchial asthma in childhood: A systematic review with meta-analysis of prospective studies', *The Journal of Pediatrics*, 2001, vol. 139, no. 2, pp. 261–266.

7   B. K. Brew et al., 'Systematic review and meta-analysis investigating breast feeding and childhood wheezing illness', *Paediatric and Perinatal Epidemiology*, 2011, vol. 25, no. 6, pp. 507–518.

8   Copenhagen Prospective Study on Asthma in Childhood, 'About COPSAC', undated, *COPSAC*, <www.copsac.com/home/about>.

9   E. Jelding-Dannemand et al., 'Breast-feeding does not protect against allergic sensitization in early childhood and allergy-associated disease at age 7 years', *The Journal of Allergy and Clinical Immunology*, 2015, vol. 136, no. 5, pp. 1302–1308.

10 M. S. Kramer et al., 'Effect of prolonged and exclusive breast feeding on risk of allergy and asthma: Cluster randomised trial', *The BMJ*, 2007, vol. 335, 815.

11 E. Evenhouse and S. Reilly, 'Improved estimates of the benefits of breastfeeding using sibling comparisons to reduce selection bias', *Health Services Research*, 2005, vol. 40, no. 6, pt 1, pp. 1781–1802.

12 J. Y. Y. Leung et al., 'Breastfeeding and childhood hospitalizations for asthma and other wheezing disorders', *Annals of Epidemiology*, 2016, vol. 26, no. 1, pp. 21–27.

13 P. W. Howie, 'Breastfeeding provides passive and likely long-lasting active immunity', *Annals of Allergy, Asthma & Immunology*, 1998, vol. 81, no. 6, pp. 523–533.

14 M. Gdalevich et al., 'Breast-feeding and the onset of atopic dermatitis in childhood: A systematic review and meta-analysis of prospective studies', *Journal of the American Academy of Dermatology*, 2001, vol. 45, no. 4, pp. 520–527.

15 E. Jelding-Dannemand et al., 'Breast-feeding does not protect against allergic sensitization in early childhood and allergy-associated disease at age 7 years', *The Journal of Allergy and Clinical Immunology*, 2015, vol. 136, no. 5, pp. 1302–1308.

16 M. S. Kramer et al., 'Effect of an intervention to promote breastfeeding on asthma, lung function and atopic eczema at age 16 years: Follow-up of the PROBIT randomized trial', *JAMA Pediatrics*, 2017, vol. 172, no. 1, e174064.

17 M. Gdalevich et al., 'Does breastfeeding protect against allergic rhinitis during childhood? A meta-analysis of prospective studies', *Acta Paediatrica*, 2002, vol. 91, no. 3, pp. 275–279.

18 E. Jelding-Dannemand et al., 'Breast-feeding does not protect against allergic sensitization in early childhood and allergy-associated disease at age 7 years', *The Journal of Allergy and Clinical Immunology*, 2015, vol. 136, no. 5, pp. 1302–1308.

19 M. S. Kramer et al., 'Effect of an intervention to promote breastfeeding on asthma, lung function and atopic eczema at age 16 years: Follow-up of the PROBIT randomized trial', *JAMA Pediatrics*, 2017, vol. 172, no. 1, e174064.

20 E. Evenhouse and S. Reilly, 'Improved estimates of the benefits of breastfeeding using sibling comparisons to reduce selection bias', *Health Services Research*, 2005, vol. 40, no. 6, pt 1, pp. 1781–1802.

APPENDIX VI: INFLAMMATORY BOWEL DISEASE (IBD) AND BREASTFEEDING

1 Y. Ko et al., 'Inflammatory bowel disease environmental risk factors: A population-based case-control study of Middle Eastern migration to Australia', *Clinical Gastroenterology and Hepatology*, 2015, vol. 13, no. 8, pp. 1453–1463.

2   T. Gilat et al., 'Childhood factors in ulcerative colitis and Crohn's disease: An international cooperative study', *Scandinavian Journal of Gastroenterology*, 1987, vol. 22, no. 8, pp. 1009–1024.

3   M. E. Spehlmann et al., 'Risk factors in German twins with inflammatory bowel disease: Results of a questionnaire-based survey', *Journal of Crohn's and Colitis*, 2012, vol. 6, no. 1, pp. 29–42.

4   V. Tieng et al., 'Binding of Escherichia coli adhesin AfaE to 55 triggers cell-surface expression of the MHC class 1-related molecule MICA', *Proceedings of the National Academy of Sciences*, 2002, vol. 99, no. 5, pp. 2977–2982.

5   Ibid.

6   V. Mahendran et al., 'Prevalence of campylobacter species in adult Crohn's disease and the preferential colonization sites of Campylobacter species in the human intestine', *PLOS One*, 2011, vol. 6, no. 9, e25417.

7   K. O. Gradel et al., 'Increased short- and long-term risk of inflammatory bowel disease after salmonella or campylobacter gastroenteritis', *Gastroenterology*, 2009, vol. 137, no. 2, pp. 495–501.

8   G. de Hertogh and K. Geboes, 'Crohn's disease and infections: A complex relationship', *Medscape General Medicine*, 2004, vol. 6, no. 3, p. 14.

9   R. I. Glass et al., 'Observations questioning a protective role for breast-feeding in severe rotavirus diarrhoea', *Acta Paediatrica Scandinavica*, 1986, vol. 75, no. 5, pp. 713–718.

10   T. Gilat et al., 'Childhood factors in ulcerative colitis and Crohn's disease: An international cooperative study', *Scandinavian Journal of Gastroenterology*, 1987, vol. 22, no. 8, pp. 1009–1024.

11   E. Klement, 'Breastfeeding and risk of inflammatory bowel disease: A systematic review with meta-analysis', *The American Journal of Clinical Nutrition*, 2004, vol. 80, no. 5, pp. 1342–1352.

12   S. Baron et al., 'Environmental risk factors in paediatric inflammatory bowel diseases: A population-based case control study', *Gut*, 2005, vol. 54, no. 3, pp. 357–363.

13   A. R. Barclay, 'Systematic review: The role of breastfeeding in the development of pediatric inflammatory bowel disease', *Journal of Pediatrics*, 2009, vol. 155, no. 3, pp. 421–426.

APPENDIX VII: OBESITY AND BREASTFEEDING

1   NZBA Baby Friendly Aotearoa New Zealand, 'Submission to the Government Administration Committee on the Parental Leave and Employment Protection (Six Months' Paid Leave) Amendment Bill', October 2012, *New Zealand Parliament*,

<www.parliament.nz/en/pb/sc/submissions-and-advice/document/50SCGA_
EVI_00DBHOH_BILL11276_1_A280885/new-zealand-breastfeeding-authority-
incorporated>.

2   V. Burke et al., 'Breastfeeding and overweight: Longitudinal analysis in an
     Australian birth cohort', *The Journal of Pediatrics*, 2005, vol. 147, no. 1,
     pp. 56–61.

3   J. Armstrong et al., 'Breastfeeding and lowering the risk of childhood obesity',
     The Lancet, 8 June 2002, vol. 359, no. 9322, pp. 2003–2004.

4   M. S. Kramer et al., 'A randomized breast-feeding promotion intervention did
     not reduce child obesity in Belarus', *Journal of Nutrition*, 2009, vol. 139, no. 2,
     pp. 417S–421S.

5   R. M. Martin and M. S. Kramer, 'Effects of promoting long-term, exclusive
     breastfeeding on adolescent adiposity, blood pressure, and growth trajectories:
     A secondary analysis of a randomized clinical trial', *JAMA Pediatrics*, 2017, vol. 171,
     no. 7, e170698.

6   M. C. Nelson et al., 'Are adolescents who were breast-fed less likely to be overweight?
     Analyses of sibling pairs to reduce confounding', *Epidemiology*, 2005, vol. 16, no. 2,
     pp. 247–253.

7   E. Evenhouse and S. Reilly, 'Improved estimates of the benefits of breastfeeding using
     sibling comparisons to reduce selection bias', *Health Services Research*, 2005, vol. 40,
     no. 6, pt 1, pp. 1781–1802.

APPENDIX VIII: ANTISOCIAL BEHAVIOUR AND BREASTFEEDING

1   D. M. Fergusson et al., 'Breastfeeding and subsequent social adjustment in six- to eight-
     year-old children', *Journal of Child Psychology and Psychiatry*, 1987, vol. 28, no. 3,
     pp. 378–386.

2   D. M. Fergusson and L. J. Woodward, 'Breast feeding and later psychosocial
     adjustment', *Paediatric and Perinatal Epidemiology*, 1999, vol. 13, no. 2, pp. 144–157.

3   M. S. Kramer, et al., 'Effects of prolonged and exclusive breastfeeding on child
     behaviour and maternal adjustment: Evidence from a large randomized trial', *Pediatrics*,
     2008, vol. 121, no. 3, e435–e440.

4   W. H. Oddy, et al., 'The long-term effects of breastfeeding on child and adolescent
     mental health: A pregnancy cohort study followed for 14 years', *Journal of Pediatrics*,
     2010, vol. 156, no. 4, pp. 568–574.

5   M. S. Kramer, et al., 'Long-term behavioural consequences of infant feeding', *Paediatric
     and Perinatal Epidemiology*, 2011, vol. 25, no. 6, pp. 500–506.

6   B. Caicedo et al., 'Violent delinquency in a Brazilian birth cohort: The roles of breast feeding, early poverty and demographic factors', *Paediatric and Perinatal Epidemiology*, 2010, vol. 24, no. 1, pp. 12–23.

7   L. Girard et al., 'Breastfeeding, cognitive and noncognitive development in early childhood: A population study', *Pediatrics*, 2017, vol. 139, no. 4, e20161848.

APPENDIX IX: INTELLIGENCE AND BREASTFEEDING

1   A. Walfisch et al., 'Breast milk and cognitive development—the role of confounders: A systematic review', *BMJ Open*, 2013, vol. 3, no. 8, e003259.

2   E. Evenhouse and S. Reilly, 'Improved estimates of the benefits of breastfeeding using sibling comparisons to reduce selection bias', *Health Services Research*, 2005, vol. 40, no. 6, pt 1, pp. 1781–1802.

3   G. Der et al., 'Effect of breast feeding on intelligence in children: Prospective study, sibling pairs analysis, and meta-analysis', *The BMJ*, 2006, vol. 333, 945.

4   M. S. Kramer et al., 'The double jeopardy of clustered measurement and cluster randomisation', *The BMJ*, 2009, vol. 339, b2900.

5   M. S. Kramer et al., 'Breastfeeding and child cognitive development: New evidence from a large randomized trial', *Archives of General Psychiatry*, 2008, vol. 65, no. 5, pp. 578–584.

6   G. Der et al., 'Results from the PROBIT breastfeeding trial may have been overinterpreted', *Archives of General Psychiatry*, 2008, vol. 65, no. 12, pp. 1456–1457.

7   M. S. Kramer et al., 'Do population-based interventions widen or narrow socioeconomic inequalities?: The case of breastfeeding promotion', *International Journal of Epidemiology*, 2014, vol. 43, no. 4, pp. 1284–1292.

8   Ibid.

9   Ibid.

10   S. Yang et al., 'Breastfeeding during infancy and neurocognitive function in adolescence: 16-year follow-up of the PROBIT cluster-randomized trial', *PloS Medicine*, 2018, vol. 15, no. 4, e1002554.

11   Ibid.

12   R. E. Nisbett et al., 'Intelligence: New findings and theoretical developments', *American Psychologist*, 2012, vol. 67, no. 2, pp. 130–159.

13   A. Lucas et al., 'Randomised trial of early diet in preterm babies and later intelligence quotient', *The BMJ*, 1998, vol. 317, no. 7171, pp. 1481–1487.

14   S. Yang et al., 'Breastfeeding during infancy and neurocognitive function in adolescence:

16-year follow-up of the PROBIT cluster-randomized trial', *PloS Medicine*, 2018, vol. 15, no. 4, e1002554, p. 7.

15 H. M. Skeels and H. B. C. Dye, 'A study of the effects of differential stimulation on mentally retarded children', *Proceedings and Addresses of the American Association on Mental Deficiency*, 1939, vol. 44, no. 1, pp. 114–136; and H. M. Skeels, 'A Study of the effects of differential stimulation on mentally retarded children: A follow-up report', *American Journal of Mental Deficiency*, 1942, vol. 46, pp. 340–350.

16 M. Lavelli and M. Poli, 'Early mother–infant interaction during breast- and bottle-feeding', *Infant Behaviour & Development*, 1998, vol. 21, no. 4, pp. 667–684.

17 J. P. Smith and M. Ellwood, 'Feeding patterns and emotional care in breastfed infants', *Social Indicators Research*, 2011, vol. 101, no. 2, pp. 227–231.

18 A. Weisleder and A. Fernald, 'Talking to children matters: Early language experience strengthens processing and builds vocabulary', *Psychological Science*, 2013, vol. 24, no. 11, pp. 2143–2152.

19 S. Yang et al., 'Breastfeeding during infancy and neurocognitive function in adolescence: 16-year follow-up of the PROBIT cluster-randomized trial', *PloS Medicine*, 2018, vol. 15, no. 4, e1002554, p. 6.

20 P. Kristensen and T. Bjerkedal, 'Explaining the relation between birth order and intelligence', *Science New Series*, 2007, vol. 316, no. 5832, p. 1717.

21 K. Barclay, 'A within-family analysis of birth order and intelligence using population conscription data on Swedish men', *Intelligence*, 2015, vol. 49, pp. 134–143.

INDEX